LINCOLN, MASTER OF MEN

Abraham Lincoln

LINCOLN

MASTER OF MEN

A Study in Character

BY

ALONZO ROTHSCHILD

WITH PORTRAITS

BOSTON AND NEW YORK
HOUGHTON MIFFLIN COMPANY
The Riverside Press Cambridge

Published March, 1906

FOURTEENTH IMPRESSION

TO THE MEMORY OF

MY FATHER

JOHN ROTHSCHILD

ONE OF THE PLAIN PEOPLE

WHO BELIEVED IN LINCOLN

THIS BOOK

IS AFFECTIONATELY

DEDICATED

CONTENTS

ILLUSTRATIONS

LINCOLN, MASTER OF MEN

CHAPTER I

A SAMSON OF THE BACKWOODS

THE spirit of mastery moved Abraham Lincoln at an early age — how early, history and tradition are not agreed. Scantily supported stories of boyish control over his schoolmates, supplemented by more fully authenticated narratives of his youthful prowess, leave no doubt, however, that his power came to him before the period at which some of his biographers are pleased to take up the detailed account of his life. Trivial as the records of these callow triumphs may seem, they are essential to an understanding of the successive steps by which this man mounted from obscurity to the government of a great people.

If, as has been asserted by an eminent educator, the experiences and instructions of the first seven years of a person's life do more to mold and determine his character than all subsequent training, the history of Lincoln's development, like that of most great men, lacks an important chapter; for the scraps about this period of his childhood that have been preserved yield but a meagre story. A ne'er-do-well father, destined to drift from one badly tilled patch of land to another, a gentle mother, who is said to have known refinements foreign to the cheerless Kentucky cabin,[1] a sparsely settled community of "poor whites," two brief snatches of A B C schooling under itinerant masters, stinted living, a few chores, still fewer pastimes, and all is said. Not quite all, for the playmates of that childhood have, in their old age, recalled a few incidents that are not without interest.

One of these anecdotes belongs here. It reveals "a mere spindle of a boy," as one old gentleman[2] describes the little Abraham, giving a good account of himself in possibly his first impact with opposing strength. The lads of the neighborhood, so runs the story, were sent after school hours to the mill with corn to be ground. While awaiting their turn, they passed the time, as at the noon recesses, with frolics and fights. In these Lincoln did not participate.

"He was," says Major Alexander Sympson, who tells the tale, "the shyest, most reticent, most uncouth and awkward-appearing, homeliest and worse dressed of any in the entire crowd." So superlatively wretched a butt could not hope to look on long unmolested. He was attacked one day, as he stood near a tree, by a larger boy with others at his back. "But," said the major, "the very acme of astonishment was experienced by the eagerly expectant crowd. For Lincoln soundly thrashed the first, second, and third boy, in succession; and then, placed his back against the tree, defied the whole crowd, and taunted them with cowardice." We may fancy this juvenile Fitz-James shouting: —

> "Come one, come all! this tree shall fly
> From its firm base as soon as I."

Yet who shall say whether in the other little boys' discolored eyes

> "Respect was mingled with surprise,
> And the stern joy which warriors feel
> In foemen worthy of their steel"?

The veracious historian has nothing to offer under this head; but he assures us, which is perhaps more to the point, that the hero of the scene "was disturbed no more, then or thereafter."[3]

Abraham was in his eighth year when the Lincoln family migrated from its rude surroundings on Knob

Creek to a still ruder frontier settlement in southern Indiana.[4] Here the boy grew to manhood under the crass conditions at that time peculiar to the New West. Frontier life with its toil, its hardships, and its ever recurring physical problems furnished, no doubt, certain of the elements which were some day to be combined in his much-extolled strength of character. What is not so easily accounted for, is the eagerness of easy-going Tom Lincoln's son to lead his fellows, in school and out, on that uninspiring dead level called Pigeon Creek. The settlers were, in the main, coarse-grained and illiterate; for education was an exotic that, naturally enough, did not thrive in the lower fringe of the Indiana wilderness. "There were some schools so called," wrote Mr. Lincoln many years later, "but no qualification was ever required of a teacher beyond 'readin', writin', and cipherin'' to the Rule of Three. If a straggler, supposed to understand Latin, happened to sojourn in the neighborhood, he was looked upon as a wizard. There was absolutely nothing to excite ambition for education."[5] Nothing, indeed, unless we accept Mr. Emerson's theory of life as a search after power, an element with which the world is so saturated to the remotest chink or crevice, that no honest seeking for it goes unrewarded. How honestly Abraham at this time pursued the search, and with what success, may be learned from the early companions upon whom his strenuous efforts to learn "by littles," as he himself once quaintly expressed it,[6] left a lasting impression. They supply glimpses of him snatching a few minutes for reading while the plow-horses rested at the end of a row, trying his hand at odd hours on the composition of "pieces" like those in the newspapers, poring at night over his books in the uncertain light of the logs, and covering the blade of the wooden fire-shovel, in lieu of a slate, with examples, which were laboriously scraped off by means of a drawing-knife after they had been transferred to his carefully economized exercise-book.[7]

Such industry could not, even in a backwoods "chink or crevice," fail of its reward. The twelve months of sporadic schooling [8] that stretched between Abraham's seventh and seventeenth years yielded many small triumphs. "He was always at the head of his class," writes Nathaniel Grigsby, "and passed us rapidly in his studies." [9] As spelling was the most popular branch, he made himself so proficient in it as to become the acknowledged leader of the school. In fact, the whole country is said to have gone down before him in spelling-matches, the side upon which he happened to stand holding a guaranty of victory. Hence he was not infrequently, like the old medal winners at the art exhibitions, ruled out of the contest. Becoming by dint of practice, moreover, the best penman in the place, he was often called upon to write the letters of his untutored neighbors; and his younger schoolfellows, in their admiration of his penmanship, also paid tribute to his skill by asking him to set them copies.[10] One man recalled, many years later, this text, which, among others, Lincoln had written for him:—

> "Good boys who to their books apply
> Will all be great men by and by."

The writer of the couplet, it may be added, applied himself so eagerly to his own books, and to those that he managed to borrow, as to increase betimes his modicum of importance.[11] "He was the learned boy among us unlearned folks," says a lady whose girlish ignorance he, on more than one occasion, sought to enlighten.[12] Nor was she the only schoolmate upon whom he impressed this superiority. "Abe beat all his masters," says another, "and it was no use for him to try to learn any more from them." [13] While still another testifies: "When he appeared in company, the boys would gather and cluster around him to hear him talk. . . . Mr. Lincoln was figurative in his speeches, talks, and conversations. He argued much from analogy, and explained things hard for us to understand, by stories, maxims, tales, and figures. He would almost always point his lesson or idea by some story that was plain and near to us, that we might instantly see the force and bearing of what he said." [14] Reference is here made, no doubt, to some of the accomplishments that Abraham owed to no school; but which he employed, none the less, in these youthful attempts at scholastic leadership.

The taste for stump speeches that prevailed in the Pigeon Creek region, as in other western communities, offered an early incentive to Lincoln's ambition. As a boy, he gathered his playmates about him and repeated with droll mimicry what he could remember of some sermon that he had recently heard; or improvised his own discourse, if some transgression on the part of one of his auditors happened to suggest a subject. The topics to which he devoted his eloquence, as he grew older, were naturally based upon the political controversies of the day. So clever did he become at these "speeches" that he lost no opportunity for winning applause with them when an appreciative audience was at hand. Then, not even the ordinary considerations of time and place restrained his enthusiasm. "When it was announced that Abe had taken the stump in the harvest-field, there was an end of work," records Mr. Lamon. "The hands flocked around him, and listened to his curious speeches with infinite delight. 'The sight of such a thing amused us all,' says Mrs. Lincoln, though she admits that her husband was compelled to break it up with the strong hand; and poor Abe was many times dragged from the platform, and hustled off to his work in no gentle manner." [15] But after working-hours, he met with no such check in the nearby village store at Gentryville, where he entertained the admiring loungers until midnight with arguments, stories, jokes, and coarse rhymes.[16] The qualities, moreover, that made him the oracle of the grocery won for him undisputed preëminence at the primitive social gatherings of the neighborhood. His arrival was the signal for the festivities to begin, and his lead, as the chronicles indicate, was maintained with a sure hand, to the end.

It is not to be assumed that Abraham was generally considered a prodigy by the people among whom he grew to manhood, or that he himself was at all times conscious of his steady trend toward leadership in these small affairs of his daily life. The few incidents strung together here have a significance to the student of history that they could not have had for the rude settlers who saw them in unrelated parts, and unillumined by the search-light which the halo of the great man's later career casts back over his humble beginnings. Yet there can be no doubt that the superiority of "the learned boy" was recognized by many of his associates. His second-mother — for why apply to this sterling woman a title that would ill describe her? — had a confidence in his powers which she influenced her husband, not without difficulty, to share.[17] Thomas Lincoln, like some of his relatives and neighbors, was inclined to regard as lazy this son who preferred a book to a spade. And speaking of Abraham many years later, cousin Dennis Hanks, one of the companions of his boyhood, said: —

"Lincoln was lazy, a very lazy man. He was always reading, scribbling, writing, ciphering, writing poetry and the like." [18]

To which neighbor John Romine, whose recollections had also somehow escaped becoming steeped in the incense of hero-worship, adds: —

"He worked for me, but was always reading and thinking. I used to get mad at him for it. I say he was awfully lazy. He would laugh and talk — crack his jokes and tell stories all the time; did n't love work half as much as his pay. He said to me one day that his father taught him to work, but he never taught him to love it." [19]

None of these persons understood the boy, but it is not at all clear that the boy understood himself. With Abraham's desires to excel his schoolfellows were mingled vague dreams of larger competitions, that carried him, in fancy, far beyond the narrow horizon of his chinks and crevices, into the broad world beyond. There, like his favorite hero, Parson Weems's impossible Washington, he hoped to achieve greatness.[20] Indeed, when Mrs. Josiah Crawford, who took a motherly interest in the lad, reproved him for teasing the girls in her kitchen, and asked him what he supposed would become of him, he promptly answered, "I'll be President." This prediction, so common in the mouths of American boys, whose eyes are fixed early upon the first place in the nation, is said to have been repeated by him, from time to time, whether seriously, some of his biographers are inclined to doubt.[21] There can be no question, however, as to the more important fact — this particular boy had taken his first halting steps up the steep which leads to that eminence.

The mental superiority which gave Lincoln a certain distinction in the eyes of some of the settlers among whom he spent his youth would have been regarded, even by them, with scant respect, had it not been accompanied by what appealed to the admiration of all his neighbors alike — physical preëminence. Strength of body was rated high by these frontiersmen, whose very existence depended upon the iron in their frames. Overcoming, with rugged self-reliance, the obstacles which uncompromising nature opposed to them on every side, they had hewn their homes out of the wilderness by sheer force of muscle. Somewhat of that same vigor was required, after the clearings had been made and the rude shelters had been thrown up, to win day by day a semblance of human comfort. What wonder that these men were concerned with facts, not theories; with the hardening of the sinews, not the cultivation of the brain! No mere bookman, however witty or wise, could long have held their esteem. Their standard of excellence, though rough, had the merit of being simple — so simple that the very children might grasp its full meaning. One of them certainly did. For Abraham's singular ambition to know was not allowed to diminish his part in the more common ambition to do. On the contrary, the two aspirations appear to have kept pace so evenly in him as to reënforce each other. What of ascendancy his alert mind alone failed to gain was easily established when the intellect called into play his powerful physique.

The sturdy constitution that Lincoln inherited from five generations of pioneers was hardened by the toil and exposure to which, even more than most backwoods boys, he was subjected from early childhood.[22] "Abraham, though very young, was large of his age, and had an ax put into his hands at once," wrote he, referring, in that all too brief autobiography, to the time of the settlement near Little Pigeon Creek, "and from that till within his twenty-third year he was almost constantly handling that most useful instrument — less, of course, in plowing and harvesting seasons."[23] The fifteen years of labor thus summarily disposed of constituted, for the most part, the physical discipline of Lincoln's life. How severe this was may be inferred from the mere mention of what was required of him. As he became strong enough, he cleared openings in the forest, cut timber, split rails, chopped wood, guided the cumbrous shovel-plow, hoed corn, and pulled fodder. When the grain was ripe, he harvested it with a sickle, threshed it with a flail, cleaned it with a sheet, and took it to the mill, where it was laboriously ground into unbolted flour with equally primitive contrivances. Together with these tasks of seed-time and harvest, he fetched and carried, carpentered and tinkered, in short, earned his supper of corn-dodgers and his shake-down of leaves in the loft, many times over. Nevertheless, when the home work was done, Thomas Lincoln, who, whatever may have been his faults, cannot justly be accused of erring on the side of indulgence, hired him out as a day laborer among the neighbors.[24] They, of course, did not spare the boy any more than did his father. No chore was deemed too mean, no job too great, for this good-natured young fellow. So that, all in all, heavy drafts must have been made upon him.[25] He met them — despite his dislike for manual labor — on demand, checking out freely of his strength, while unconsciously acquiring, by way of exchange, more than the equivalent in virile self-reliance; and the perfect command over his resources, in any emergency, that later became characteristic of him, should in large measure be credited to this pioneer accounting. In fact, of Lincoln may be said what Fuller quaintly said of Drake, the "pains and patience in his youth knit the joints of his soul."

For the more palpable returns in kind from his outlay of brawn, Abraham did not have to wait long. As early as his eleventh year began the remarkable development in physique which culminated before he had reached his seventeenth birthday. At that time, having attained his full height, — within a fraction of six feet and four inches, — he was, according to accepted descriptions of him, lean, large-boned, and muscular, thin through the chest, narrow across the slightly stooping shoulders, long of limb, large of hand and foot, sure of reach, and powerful of grip, — the very type of the North Mississippi valley pioneer at his best.[26] The strength of the young giant, as well as his skill in applying it, easily won for him the lead among the vigorous men of this class on Pigeon Creek. They have handed down tales of his achievements that call to mind the legends with which have been adorned the histories of Samson and of Milo. Like these heroes, Lincoln is said to have performed prodigies of muscle; and still further like them, despite the skepticism aroused, naturally enough, by extraordinary details, he may be looked upon as having been endowed with the attributes upon which the stories essentially rest. Whether or not he performed this or that particular feat exactly as it is described, he did, beyond question, impress himself upon the settlers as "the longest and strongest" of them all.

Lincoln's employment throughout the neighborhood as a hired man afforded him abundant opportunity for the display of his powers. A certain good-humored sense of duty, no less than a never flagging ambition to excel, stimulated him to make "a clean sweep," as he once phrased it, of whatever he did. These jobs, it should be remembered, were not entirely to his taste, and he "was no hand," says one old lady, "to pitch into his work like killing snakes";[27] yet, when he did take hold — and his services were always in request — he was bound to outwork his employers. One of them, who became his fast friend, asserted: —

"He could strike with a maul a heavier blow — could sink an ax deeper into wood than any man I ever saw."[28]

And cousin Dennis, a not too consistent Boswell, forgot, in a moment of enthusiasm, his published opinion that Abraham was "lazy, very lazy," long enough to exclaim:

"My, how he would chop! His ax would flash and bite into a sugar-tree or sycamore, and down it would come. If you heard him fellin' trees in a clearin', you would say there were three men at work by the way the trees fell."[29]

A stripling who handled, in that fashion, the backwoodsmen's favorite implement could not fail to command their respect; but it was when Lincoln threw the ax aside and put forth his strength unhampered, that he compelled the homage so grateful to his pride. "Some of his feats" — Mr. Lamon is our authority — "almost surpass belief. . . . Richardson, a neighbor, declares that he could carry a load to which the strength of 'three ordinary men' would scarcely be equal. He saw him quietly pick up and walk away with 'a chicken-house, made of poles pinned together and covered, that weighed at least six hundred, if not much more.' At another time the Richardsons were building a corn-crib. Abe was there, and, seeing three or four men preparing 'sticks' upon which to carry some huge posts, he relieved them of all further trouble by shouldering the posts, single-handed, and walking away with them to the place where they were wanted."[30] The Richardson chicken-house and the posts of the corn-crib should obviously go down in story, side by side with those doors and posts of Gaza that were carried, with similar ease, on the shoulders of the Hebrew Hercules.

More remarkable even than the feats that, on occasion, distinguished Lincoln at work, were the exploits in sport, to which the applause of the crowd quickened his sinews.[31] Not content with a mastery easily maintained over his comrades in the rough games and contests popular on the frontier, he gave exhibitions of strength that established his reputation as an athlete without a peer. This preëminence he held against all comers during his youth on Pigeon Creek and his early manhood in New Salem.[32] At the latter place he seems to have reached the acme of his physical powers; and some of his recent biographers, the limit of their credulity. Messrs. Lamon and Herndon, however, whose records of this period are the most complete, sustain each other in the story that Lincoln one day astonished the village by lifting a box of stones which weighed about a thousand pounds.[33] This, they explain, was done by means of a gearing of ropes and straps, with which he was harnessed to the box — a method somewhat like that employed at the present time by the "strong men" who, for the entertainment of dime-museum spectators, raise even heavier weights.

Another of Lincoln's notable performances, for the authenticity of which Mr. Herndon also vouches, grew out of the admiration with which the young giant was regarded by his companions. One of them, William G. Greene by name, was once lauding him, so the story goes, as the strongest man in Illinois, when a stranger, who happened to be present, claimed that honor for another. The dispute led to a wager in which Greene bet that his champion could lift a cask holding forty gallons of whiskey, high enough to take a drink out of the bung-hole. In the test that ensued, Lincoln with "apparent ease" and "to the astonishment of the incredulous stranger," did as had been stipulated. "He did not," the narrator is careful to add, "stand erect and elevate the barrel, but squatted down and lifted it to his knees, rolling it over until his mouth came opposite the bung."

"The bet is mine," said Greene, as the cask was replaced upon the floor; "but that is the first dram of whiskey I ever saw you swallow, Abe."

"And I have n't swallowed that, you see," replied Lincoln, as he spurted out the liquor.[34]

In this final episode of the little story is to be found a clue, if not to the source of his extraordinary vigor, at least to its continued preservation, unimpaired by the vices that have shorn so many Samsons of their strength.[35]

Physique was not the only criterion of leadership among the rough-and-ready settlers of the West. Neither the strong man nor the tall man was necessarily "the best man." That title was reserved for him who, when there were no Indians to cope with, made good his claim to it against his neighbors, in the friendly wrestling-matches of common occurrence, as well as in the more serious, though happily less frequent, fights by which the backwoodsmen, remote from courts and constables, were wont to settle their disputes. Under such conditions, the most peaceable of men learn — as the phrase goes — to give a good account of themselves. This was probably the case with our five generations of Lincoln pathfinders; for the strain of Quaker blood, that flowed at some distant point into their veins, had lost much, if not all, of its non-resistant quality before reaching Abraham.[36] His father, although a man of quiet disposition, had allowed no scruples to get between him and the adversary who aroused his slow anger. A sinewy, well-knit frame, handled with courage and agility, had marked Thomas Lincoln, in his prime, as a dangerous antagonist. "He thrashed," says the chronicle, "the monstrous bully of Breckinridge County, in three minutes, and came off without a scratch."

Several other border Hectors, according to tradition, found him to be invulnerable; and one, with whom he had a bitter quarrel, came out of a rough-and-tumble combat of teeth, as well as of fists, without his nose.[37] Moreover, it should be borne in mind that Abraham's uncle Mordecai, "fond," as we are told, in his younger days, "of playing a game of fisticuffs," had been an inveterate Indian hunter;[38] and that the father of Mordecai and Thomas, he for whom Abraham was named, had, in the days of Daniel Boone, been killed by the savages, while taking part in the struggle for Kentucky. The scion of such stock could not, under favorable circumstances, lack the qualities that, in personal encounters, make a man formidable. In fact, these traits, when combined with the intelligence and strength that so early distinguished Abraham, rendered him, as was to be expected, almost invincible.

Lincoln's advantage during this pioneer period is to be ascribed largely, but not altogether, to preponderance of size and muscle. Those abnormally long arms and legs, impelled by sinews of iron, counted, it is true, for much. On the other hand, there was little that suggested the wrestler in his lank, loosely jointed form with its thin neck, contracted chest, and insufficient weight. These defects must therefore have been offset, as indeed they were, by alertness, skill, and — most important of all — those inherited attributes of mastery which were summed up by the ancients in the single word, stomach. The spirit with which, as a schoolboy, Abraham was observed, in the opening scene, to defend himself against heavy odds, carried him successfully through many subsequent encounters. Whether these were in sport or in earnest, they usually left him, as one old friend expressed it, "cock of the walk."[39] Another, who presumably made frequent trials in boyhood of Abraham's powers, said: "I was ten years older, but I could n't rassle him down. His legs was too long for me to throw him. He would fling one foot upon my shoulder and make me swing corners swift."[40] Still others bore witness to his pugilistic triumphs; and Mr. Lincoln himself found pleasure in recalling his chaplet of wild olives many years later — even after the ballots of a nation had been woven into his ripest laurels. "All I had to do," said he, "was to extend one arm to a man's shoulder, and, with weight of body and strength of arms, give him a trip that generally sent him sprawling on the ground, which would so astonish him as to give him a quietus."[41] Such victories had carried his fame, by the time he had reached his nineteenth year, throughout the Pigeon Creek clearings and beyond, so that none of the Hoosiers who knew him or who knew of him were willing — if the record may be trusted — to hazard at once their bones and their reputations, in unequal combat against so redoubtable a champion.

Debarred from the wrestling-ring as he had been excluded from the spelling-match, and for the same flattering reason, our Crichton of the backwoods wore his honors as soberly as could be expected. He appears, notwithstanding the coarse, unrestrained manners of the people about him, to have misapplied his superiority in comparatively few instances. These cases, such as they are, should, nevertheless, not be overlooked, however much the mention of them may offend the sensitive piety of the hero-worshipers. They need a reminder, now and then, do these worthy people, that their idol, when in the flesh, stood, like other human creatures, on the earth. If their image of him, therefore, is to be faithful, its head may be reared to the clouds in all the glory of fine gold, so they see to it that the feet are of clay. What of sludge lies hidden at the bottom of the character usually rises, when agitated by passion, to the surface. As this is observed in the case of ripened manhood, how much more is it to be looked for during those hobbledehoy days that, lying between youth and maturity, partake at times of the nature of both — the mischievousness of the boy together with the pride of the man. It was at such a period that Abraham's resentment toward those against whom he had grievances, real or fancied, sometimes found vent. His weapons, in this respect at least, like those of the versatile young Scot, might have been physical or intellectual, at will; for, among other accomplishments, he had attained a certain facility at the scribbling, in prose and in doggerel verse, of the coarsest of satires. These, thanks to their wit no less than to their audacity, are said to have left deeper and more enduring hurts than even his fists could have inflicted. Hence the few persons who were so unfortunate as to incur the satirist's anger were impaled on the nib of his goose-quill, amidst laughter which started with the grocery store loungers and did not cease until it had echoed and reëchoed through the neighborhood for many a day. That some of these lampoons were indelicate, even indecent, need not be dwelt upon here. It is sufficient to notice that they were well adapted to their purpose, and that the author employed them as a means of laying low those whom he might not otherwise have overcome.

The victims of these attacks did not, for obvious reasons, retaliate in kind. Nor might they hope, on any field, to humiliate this masterful "fellow, who could both write and fight and in both was equally skilful." One quarrel, however, waxed so hot that, by common consent, nothing would cool the fevered situation but bloodletting. And this is how it happened. Abraham's only sister had died shortly after her marriage to Aaron Grigsby. Thereupon arose between the Grigsbys and the Lincolns a feeling of ill-will, the cause of which is not clear, nor is it material now. It was important enough then to result in the exclusion of the tall young brother-in-law from the joint wedding celebration of Aaron's two brothers — a memorable entertainment, full to overflowing with feasting, dancing, and merry-making. Such a frolic was not to be had every day, and Abraham's regret that he was not present to lead the fun, as was his wont, must have been keen. The slight vexed him even more than did the disappointment, for the Grigsbys constituted "the leading family" in the community. To punish them, he forthwith wrote The First Chronicles of Reuben, a narration in mock-scriptural phrase, of an indelicate prank that is said to have been played upon the young wedded couples, at his instigation.[42] The public ridicule which this brought down upon the family failed to appease the satirist's wounded self-love; and he followed it, in rhyme, with an onslaught even more stinging. The outraged honor of the Grigsbys demanded satisfaction according to the Pigeon Creek code; so the eldest son, William, throwing discretion to the winds, issued a challenge for a fight, which their tormentor readily accepted.

When the combatants were about to enter the ring, Abraham chivalrously announced that as his antagonist was confessedly his inferior in every respect, he would forego the pleasure of thrashing him, and would let his step-brother, John, do battle in his stead. This offer, having, together with other magnanimous declarations, been applauded by the spectators, was accepted by Grigsby. The fight then began; but alas! for Abraham's good resolutions. They were not proof against his champion's defeat. By a singular coincidence, moreover, Lincoln's biographers, as well as he, deviate just a trifle, at this point, from the straight course; that is to say, all of them save Mr. Lamon, who sticks to his text, and, in the face of popular disapproval, describes the unworthy scene which ensued. "John started out with fine pluck and spirit," says he, "but in a little while Billy got in some clever hits, and Abe began to exhibit symptoms of great uneasiness. Another pass or two, and John flagged quite decidedly, and it became evident that Abe was anxiously casting about for some pretext to break the ring. At length, when John was fairly down and Billy on top, and all the spectators cheering, swearing, and pressing up to the very edge of the ring, Abe cried out that Bill Boland showed foul play, and, bursting out of the crowd, seized Grigsby by the heels, and flung him off. Having righted John and cleared the battle-ground of all opponents, he swung a whiskey bottle over his head, and swore that he was 'the big buck of the lick.' It seems that nobody of the Grigsby faction, not one in that large assembly of bullies, cared to encounter the sweep of Abe's tremendously long and muscular arms, and so he remained master of 'the lick.' He was not content, however, with a naked triumph, but vaunted himself in the most offensive manner. He singled out the victorious but cheated Billy and, making sundry hostile demonstrations, declared that he could whip him then and there. Billy meekly said he did not doubt that, but that if Abe would make things even between them by fighting with pistols, he would not be slow to grant him a meeting. But Abe replied that he was not going to fool away his life on a single shot; and so Billy was fain to put up with the poor satisfaction he had already received."[43] The question naturally suggested, as to whether Abraham was justified in his behavior, may be disregarded here. Not so, the account of the incident itself, which, irrespective of ethics or good taste, is essential to an understanding of what may be termed the aggressive side of his character, during these formative days.

Equally significant, though not so discreditable as the Grigsby broil, was an encounter in which young Lincoln figured not long after this. It brings us to his river life, with the novel responsibilities and dangers that must have entered — how much or how little no one can say — into the making of the master. Like so many native Kentuckians, he evinced, while still a boy, an aptitude for the management of a boat among the uncertain currents of the Ohio. This made him particularly useful to James Taylor, the ferry-keeper at the mouth of Anderson's Creek, to whom he was hired in his seventeenth year; but, what was of greater importance, it secured to him, three years later, his first voyage down the Mississippi.[44] A trading expedition to the towns on the banks of the river as far as New Orleans was projected, after the manner of the times, by James Gentry, the storekeeper in Gentryville, near by. His son, Allen, was placed in charge of a flat-boat, with a cargo of produce, and Lincoln was hired to accompany him as bow-hand.[45]

The trip was, so far as is known, prosperous and uneventful, until the voyagers tied up, one night, at the plantation of Madame Duchesne, a few miles below Baton Rouge. A gang of her slaves, seven in number, thinking, no doubt, that to rob and perhaps to murder the two boys while they slept would be a simple affair, boarded the boat. Their shuffling footsteps aroused Allen, who, to frighten them off, shouted, "Bring the guns, Lincoln! Shoot them!" The big bow-hand responded promptly, but, for reasons that we need not stop to explain, he brought no guns. He did bring what must have been very like a grievous crab-tree cudgel, with which, after the fashion of the giant in the allegory, he laid about him so impartially that those of the negroes who were not tumbled overboard took to their heels. As they fled, he carried the war into Africa, pursuing them, with Gentry, in the darkness for some distance. Then, bleeding but triumphant, the boys hastened back, and to avoid a return of the enemy in force, they speedily, as Mr. Lincoln himself once, in nautical phraseology, expressed it, "cut cable, weighed anchor, and left." This was the first occasion on which the negro question brought itself to his attention forcibly. It may be said to have left its impression in more ways than one. For, many years afterward, he showed his friends the scar on his forehead from a wound received in the fracas; and still later, when he briefly put before a nation the important incidents of his life, a place was found for that midnight victory over brute strength and superior numbers.[46]

During the ensuing few years, the young boatman must have kept his laurels green. At least, he did not, even in the first absorbing struggles of life on his own account, suffer them to wither. His reputation as a wrestler appears to have preceded him to Thomas Lincoln's last home, in Coles County, Illinois, when Abraham, after his second flat-boat voyage down the Mississippi in the summer of 1831, came there on a brief visit. The arrival of so noted a wrestler called for action on the part of Daniel Needham, the local champion. This worthy lost no time in issuing a challenge, which the newcomer as promptly accepted. In the public contest that ensued, the boatman grassed his opponent twice with such ease as to arouse the latter's anger and the delight of the spectators.

"Lincoln," he shouted, "you have thrown me twice, but you can't whip me!"

"Needham," was the answer, "are you satisfied that I can throw you? If you are not, and must be convinced through a thrashing, I will do that too, for your sake."

Upon second thought, the defeated bully, who had no doubt expected to overawe his antagonist with the threat of a fight, concluded that he was "satisfied," and his honors reverted to Lincoln.[47]

Several weeks later, the young man, then in his twenty-third year, entered upon his duties as clerk of Denton Offutt's country store, which had just been opened at New Salem, in western Illinois. The village was infested by a lawless, rollicking set of rowdies from a neighboring settlement, known as "the Clary's Grove boys." Easy-going in everything save mischief, and always ready on the shortest possible notice for sport or riot, they dominated the place at an expenditure of energy that would have worked wonders had it not been misapplied. As it was, they lived up to certain crude notions of chivalry that led them, at times, into acts of generosity toward the village folk; but kindness to the stranger within their gates had no place, be it understood, in their code. On the contrary, the desire to test a newcomer's mettle appears to have prompted conduct the reverse of kind. When their impertinent challenges to contests of various sorts were not acceptable to a stranger, he was asked to say what he would do in case another gentleman should pull his nose or otherwise make free with him. "If," says the sympathetic historian, "he did not seem entirely decided in his views as to what should properly be done in such a contingency, perhaps he would be nailed in a hogshead and rolled down New Salem hill; perhaps his ideas would be brightened by a brief ducking in the Sangamon; or perhaps he would be scoffed, kicked, and cuffed by a great number of persons in concert until he reached the confines of the village, and then turned adrift as being unfit company for the people of that settlement. If, however, the stranger consented to engage in a tussle with one of his persecutors, it was usually arranged that there should be foul play, with nameless impositions and insults, which would inevitably change the affair into a fight." These gentle ruffians had either taken the measure of Offutt's tall clerk, or had accepted the standing with which rumor invested him. At all events, they made no attempt "to naturalize" him, as they termed it; and Lincoln might have enjoyed entire immunity had it not been for the boastful tongue of his employer.

Denton Offutt, a good-hearted, talkative, reckless speculator, of the Colonel Sellers type, regarded Lincoln as the most promising of his many investments. His admiration for the young fellow, whom he had previously employed as a boatman, was, unlike most of his fads, based upon experience. Indeed, he had sounded the depths of Lincoln's talents, mental as well as physical, with remarkable precision. From repeated predictions of his protégé's destined greatness, Offutt usually turned to the more timely declaration that Abe could whip or throw any man in Sangamon County. Such a boast could of course not go long unchallenged in the hearing of "the

Clary's Grove boys." Presently Bill Clary himself laid a wager of ten dollars with Offutt, matching against Lincoln the biggest bruiser of the gang, Jack Armstrong by name, a sort of local Brom Bones, who is described as "a powerful twister, square built and strong as an ox." The proposed contest, in view, perhaps, of "the boys'" reputed disregard of fair play, had no charms for the new clerk. He would gladly have kept clear of it, but Offutt had committed him so far that he could not refuse without incurring the charge of cowardice. Moreover, as the gang had looted several stores of the village, they would in all probability not have spared Offutt's for any length of time after they had ceased to respect the clerk in charge. Lincoln accordingly consented, stipulating, however, that the match was to be a friendly one and fairly conducted.

All New Salem, with money, drinks, and portable property of various kinds staked on the result, gathered at the ring. The contestants were well matched. They struggled and strained, for some time, with seemingly equal strength and equal skill. They appear to have resembled the mighty two who wrestled before Achilles, as

> "with vigorous arms
> They clasped each other, locked like rafters framed
> By some wise builder for the lofty roof
> Of a great mansion proof against the winds.
> Then their backs creaked beneath the powerful strain
> Of their strong hands ; the sweat ran down their limbs;
> Large whelks upon their sides and shoulders rose,
> Crimson with blood. Still eagerly they strove
> For victory and the tripod. Yet in vain
> Ulysses labored to supplant his foe,
> And throw him to the ground, and equally
> Did Ajax strive in vain, for with sheer strength
> Ulysses foiled his efforts."

But here, we grieve to say, the parallel, such as it was, ceased. When the Homer of the prairies sings the story of the later combat, he will not, if truth as well as beauty has a claim upon him, picture his champions leaving the field, as did the Greek heroes, with gallantly divided honors. Such a conclusion, indeed, appeared fitting to Lincoln; for, when neither he nor the man from the Grove seemed able to prevail he said: —

"Now, Jack, let's quit. You can't throw me, and I can't throw you."

Armstrong, rendered desperate by his failure and urged on by the clamor of his friends, instead of answering, hurled himself upon Lincoln to get a foul hold. The latter, enraged at the trick, seized the fellow by the throat and, putting forth all his strength, "shook him," as the chronicler tells us, "like a rag." Some of "the boys" hurried to their leader's assistance, while others rushed to Offutt and demanded the stakes. Above the tumult could be heard Lincoln's voice ordering Offutt not to pay, and declaring his willingness to fight all Clary's Grove, if necessary. He had, in fact, backed against the store to meet the gang's attack. At that moment, it might have gone hard with him against such odds, had not the leading citizen of the place interfered. Then Armstrong, having recovered breath, expressed his admiration of so much pluck and muscle, in this outburst: —

"Boys, Abe Lincoln is the best fellow that ever broke into this settlement! He shall be one of us."

And one of them, in a sense at least, Lincoln became. His quondam opponent, like most men of his class, knew no middle ground between enmity and affection. Ever afterward, Armstrong, together with all that he had, was at Lincoln's command, and the rest of "the Clary's Grove boys" passed with their chief under the yoke.[48]

How Lincoln exercised his influence over these rough fellows is illustrated by an incident that occurred not long after the fight. A stranger to the village was attacked one day, in a spirit of frolic, by the gang, under Armstrong's leadership. Jack applied to him a string of epithets, among which "coward" and "damned liar" were the least objectionable. The victim of this onslaught, finding himself at a disadvantage, backed up to a woodpile, seized a stick, and struck Armstrong a blow that felled him. Regaining his feet, Jack rushed forward to punish the stranger, when Lincoln, who happened upon the scene, persuaded "the boys" to make him arbitrator of the difficulty.

"Well, Jack," he asked, proceeding in Socratic fashion, "what did you say to the man?" Armstrong repeated his language.

"Well, Jack," was the next question, "if you were a stranger in a strange place, as this man is, and you were called a damned liar, and so forth, what would you do?"

"Whip him, by God!" was the ready answer.

"Then this man," said the arbitrator, "has done no more to you than you would have done to him."

Even Armstrong felt the force of the golden rule when so lucidly applied by the only man whose interference he would not resent.

"Well, Abe," said he, taking the stranger by the hand, "it's all right." Then, in accordance with the time-honored custom, for such occasions established, he treated.[49]

The pastimes of these wild young fellows, no less than their quarrels, suffered a change under the pressure of Lincoln's authority. He vetoed one of the gang's favorite diversions, that of rolling persons who had incurred their displeasure down a perilously steep hill in a hogshead. A form of amusement so rich in possibilities, Jack and his playful savages were disinclined to relinquish. If they were not to have their little fun, now and then, with an unwilling victim, said they, what harm could there be in rolling one that was willing? Accordingly, an elderly toper was hired by Armstrong to make the descent, for a gallon of whiskey. Even this unprecedented concession to decorum did not, strangely enough, satisfy the censor. He insisted that the sport — brutal under any conditions — must be stopped, and stopped it was.[50] On another occasion, when the spirit of deviltry animated an election celebration, "the boys" enticed a fellow, endowed with more pluck than sense, into a bet that he could ride through their bonfire, on his pony. The animal trotted nimbly enough up to the edge of the blaze, where he balked and tossed his rider headforemost into the flames. The affair had been observed by Lincoln, who, laughing in spite of himself, ran to the fellow's assistance. "You have carried this thing far enough," he said angrily to Armstrong. The big rowdy, upon the arrival of his "conscience," became so contrite that, not content with leading the sufferer to a doctor to have the burns dressed, he took him to his own cabin for the night, and sent him home the next morning, after giving him a breakfast and a sealskin cap.[51]

The encounters of Offutt's brawny clerk with the exuberant young men of New Salem, in behalf of law and order, were not always, even ostensibly, of a friendly character. One day, while waiting upon some women in the store, he was annoyed at the loud profanity of a fellow who made a practice of lounging about the place. Lincoln, leaning over the counter, asked him, as ladies were present, not to use offensive language. The other retorted that he would talk as he pleased, and intimated that the clerk was not man enough to check him. His abuse continued until the women had left the store. Then Lincoln, stepping forward, said: —

"Well, if you must be whipped, I suppose I may as well whip you as any other man."

The offender, nothing loath, followed his critic out of doors, where ensued a contest, brief but decisive. Throwing the fellow to the ground, Lincoln held him down with one hand, while with the other he rubbed a bunch of the smart-weed, which grew within reach, into the upturned face and eyes. The man of oaths bellowed with pain, while he of the protests, having administered plenary discipline, hastened for water and tenderly bathed the aching parts. These ministrations were accompanied, it is surmised, by "quaint admonition," from which the sufferer may be assumed to have profited. For he became, as we are told, the life-long friend of the man who tutored him thus violently in gentle manners.[52]

During these early days of "wooling and pulling," to use one of Lincoln's phrases, his conquests over the hearts of his antagonists were, in most cases, as complete as his triumphs over their bodies. To defeat a man in such a manner as to compel his lasting friendship, no less than his respect, was apparently easy for this manly young fellow. A singularly fine character had already, undeveloped though it was, manifested itself, here and there, in traits which shone through his commonplace life like veins of gold in a lump of quartz. To inquire how these qualities came to enter into the make-up of a lad reared in the fringe of the western wilderness, is as foreign to the purpose of this study as would be an effort to account, in an essay on the currency, for the presence of the precious metal in a dirty clod. The social no less than the physical marvel might draw us fruitlessly far afield. Suffice it to say that Lincoln did, even at this time, have moral as well as muscular strength, and that the ignorant, rough, or vicious men among whom he grew to manhood felt — not always consciously, perhaps — the sway of both. These people, admirers of brute force though they were, would assuredly not have fallen with such complete self-surrender under the dominion of this powerful hand, had it not been for the corresponding superiority of the head and the heart by which it was controlled. A combination so striking had naturally led Lincoln's schoolmates to lay their boyish differences before him; and, as he advanced in years, it caused his associates to appoint him umpire of their sports, arbitrator of their disputes, referee of their unavoidable fights, and authority in general. The decisions, let us add, were not only remarkable for their fairness, but for the promptness, as well, with which they were enforced by the judge. He did not hesitate, moreover, to act in this capacity without waiting for an invitation from the persons most concerned. Rushing between two fighting men, he would fling them apart and insist upon settling their quarrel for them amicably. Good feeling, indeed, pervaded most, if not all, of young Lincoln's muscular activities. Such advantages as he possessed over others were so rarely abused, on the one hand, and were so commonly employed with credit, on the other, that an account of his prowess in the ring, which did not emphasize the facts, would be misleading.[53] To understand the Lincoln of this period, one must bear in mind that side by side with his pugilistic victories were these less palpable, but possibly more important, triumphs of character. "It is excellent to have a giant's strength," and excellent to use it as this giant did.

To the end of his life, Mr. Lincoln evinced an almost childish pride in his superior physique. As he stood, during the Civil War, watching, from the Potomac front of the Treasury, a forest on the Virginia hills fall before the blows of a regiment of Maine lumbermen, he exclaimed: —

"I don't believe that there is a man in that regiment with longer arms than mine, or who can swing an ax better than I can. By jings! I should like to change works with one of them."[54]

Indeed, the strength that had contributed to his early distinction among the settlers of the backwoods was displayed to the more refined associates of his later career frequently enough, though not always opportunely. Whenever an ax happened to be within the President's reach, his hand grasped it in some exhibition of dexterity or endurance. Thus, after he had insisted on shaking hands, one day, with a considerable number of the sick and wounded soldiers in the City Point hospital, when those who were with him expressed fears that he might be disabled by the exertion, he is said to have answered, "The hardships of my early life gave me strong muscles." Then, stepping through the open doorway, he took up a large, heavy ax that lay near a log, and, chopping vigorously, sent the chips flying in all directions. Presently he stopped and, with arm extended at full length, held out the ax horizontally by the extreme end of the handle. "Strong men, who looked on," so runs the tale, "— men accustomed to manual labor — could not hold the same ax in that position for a moment."[55] At another time, some officers and newspaper correspondents were returning with him from the Navy Yard, where they had gone to view the testing of certain new artillery inventions. As they sat on the steamer discussing what they had seen, the President caught sight of some axes that hung outside of the cabin. Walking over to where the implements were, he said: —

"You may talk about your Raphael repeaters and your eleven-inch Dahlgrens, but I guess I understand that there institution as well as anything else. There was a time when I could hold out one of these things at arm's length."

Whereupon, he took down one of the axes and held it as has been described. Several of the party tried to imitate him, but none succeeded. "When I was eighteen years of age I could do this," said Mr. Lincoln, on a similar occasion, to General Egbert L. Viele, "and I have never seen the day since that I could not do it." This was, in fact, one of his favorite feats. He seemed to enjoy the discomfiture of those who made unsuccessful efforts to equal it, no less than the admiration that it never failed to excite in the beholders.[56]

Mr. Lincoln's triumphs of physical strength led him into the practice of almost unconsciously comparing himself, in this respect, with other men. The habit is well illustrated in an incident related by Governor John Wesley Hoyt, for many years secretary and manager of the Wisconsin State Agricultural Society. He escorted

Lincoln, in the autumn of 1859, through the fair of the association, at which the Illinois visitor had made the address. They spent some time in one of the tents, watching the performance of a "strong man," who tossed about huge iron balls, catching and rolling them on his arms and back with remarkable brawn and agility. The exhibition appeared to interest the orator of the day so intensely that, at its conclusion, the manager introduced the athlete to him. Mr. Lincoln stood looking down upon the man, who was very short, as if wondering that one so much smaller than he could be so much stronger. Then he said abruptly, in his quaint fashion, "Why, I could lick salt off the top of your hat." [57] Nor was this the only occasion on which he remarked smallness of stature.[58] His first meeting with Stephen A. Douglas, in the Illinois legislature of 1834,[59] was memorable not, as might be expected, for any impression which the "Little Giant's" genius made upon him, but for his comment on the undersized Vermonter as "the least man" that he had ever seen.[60]

So, in Congress, during the winter of 1848, when another small great man, Alexander H. Stephens of Georgia, moved Mr. Lincoln to tears by "the very best speech of an hour's length" that he had heard, he did not, in writing about it to his partner, Mr. Herndon, forget to describe the speaker as "a little, slim, pale-faced, consumptive man." [61] The diminutive orator and his tall admirer met seventeen years later, at the Hampton Roads Conference, under strangely changed conditions — the one as an envoy of the dying but still struggling Confederacy, the other as the President of the Union. A momentous meeting, this. Upon its issue depended peace or continued bloodshed. Yet Mr. Lincoln was not so much engrossed in the serious questions under consideration as to put aside entirely his interest in Mr. Stephens's size. The little commissioner had protected his frail body against the midwinter cold with a profusion of overcoats and wraps, which, after reaching the River Queen's warm cabin, he peeled off, layer by layer. As the wearer finally emerged, the President is said to have remarked in an aside to the Secretary of State, who was with him, "Seward, that is the largest shucking for so small a nubbin that I ever saw." [62] This particular nubbin, meagre though it was, the speaker held in high esteem; still, here, as in the case of Douglas, he appears to have had a complacent sense of his own more ample proportions.[63]

The sight of a tall man usually aroused in Mr. Lincoln a desire to know whether he or the other had the more inches. This hobby he sought to gratify, in season and out, concern, as it might, a chance visitor from the country, or a dignified Senator. Indeed, at what was, perhaps, one of the most impressive moments of his life, when face to face with some of the leading public men of the day, the question, "Who is the taller?" seemed — if one may judge solely by what happened — to be uppermost in his mind. He had just responded in a few formal words to the official notification of his first nomination for the presidency, brought to his Springfield home by the committee of the Chicago Convention; and he had started, under the guidance of the chairman, the Hon. George Ashmun, to make the rounds of the delegation, for personal introductions. The party included such men as William M. Evarts, Carl Schurz, George S. Boutwell, John Albion Andrew, Gideon Welles, Caleb B. Smith, William D. Kelley, Francis P. Blair, Sr., David K. Cartter, and Norman B. Judd; but his eye rested upon the most commanding figure of all, that of Edwin Dennison Morgan, then Governor of New York and chairman of the National Republican Executive Committee. Before him Mr. Lincoln stopped first and, with a cordial greeting, said: —

"Pray, Governor, how tall may you be?"

"Nearly six feet three," answered the great man from the Empire State.

An embarrassing silence that followed was relieved by

Judge Kelley, the delegate from Pennsylvania, who was somewhat of a poplar, himself. "And pray, Mr. Lincoln," said he, "how tall may you be?"

"Six feet four," answered the candidate, taking the benefit of a doubtful fraction. Whereupon the Judge, as he relates, bowed and said:—

"Pennsylvania bows humbly before New York, but still more humbly before Illinois. Mr. Lincoln, is it not curious that I, who for the last twelve years have yearned for a President to whom I might look up, should have found one here in a State where so many people believe they grow nothing but 'Little Giants'?"[64]

Mr. Lincoln was not usually content, as in this instance, to take the word of tall men as to their height. So important a matter, it appears, could be determined to his satisfaction by actual measurement only. This, Congressman John Sherman learned to his surprise, as he paid his respects to the President-elect, on the evening after Mr. Lincoln's arrival in Washington. "When introduced to him," says Mr. Sherman, "he took my hands in both of his, drew himself up to his full height, and looking at me steadily, said, 'You are John Sherman! Well, I am taller than you. Let's measure.' Thereupon we stood back to back, and some one present announced that he was two inches taller than I. This was correct, for he was six feet three and one half inches tall when he stood erect. This singular introduction was not unusual with him, but if it lacked dignity, it was an expression of friendliness and so considered by him."[65]

Dignity! The pomp and circumstance of the White House itself did not abate Mr. Lincoln's fondness for measuring. How deeply rooted this trait was, may be gathered from the following typical scene, described by one who happened to be present. On one of the President's public audience days, a stalwart caller, evidently from the rural West, approached Mr. Lincoln awkwardly and managed to explain that, being on a visit to the Capital, he desired before leaving to see the President, and to have the honor of shaking hands with him. Mr. Lincoln, as he smilingly complied, surveyed the big man from head to foot and said, in his playful way: —

"I rather think you have a little the advantage of me in height. You are a taller man than I am."

"I guess not, Mr. President," replied the visitor; "the advantage cannot be on my side."

"Yes, it is," was the rejoinder. "I have a pretty good eye for distances, and I think I can't be mistaken in the fact of the advantage being slightly with you. I measure six feet three and a half inches in my stockings, and you go, I think, a little beyond that."

As the other still politely demurred, Mr. Lincoln said, "It is very easily tested." Rising from his chair, he placed a book edgewise against the wall, just higher than his head. Then, turning to his visitor, he bade him, "Come under." This the granger hesitated to do, his countenance the while wearing a bewildered yet half-smiling expression that, we are told, was comical to see.

"Come under, I say," repeated the President in a more peremptory tone, and the visitor slowly complied. When Mr. Lincoln, in his turn, stepped under the book, he was found to have fallen a trifle short of the other's measurement.

"There," said he, "it is as I told you. I knew I could n't be mistaken. I rarely fail in taking a man's true altitude by the eye."

"Yes, but Mr. President," said the man, to the merriment of the company, "you have slippers on and I boots, and that makes a difference."

"Not enough to amount to anything in this reckoning," was the reply. "You ought at least to be satisfied, my honest friend, with the proof given that you actually stand higher to-day than your President." [66]

Even more averse to Mr. Lincoln's yard-stick than this modest citizen was the senior Senator from Massachusetts.

"Sumner," said the President, "declined to stand up with me, back to back, to see which was the taller man, and made a fine speech about this being the time for uniting our fronts against the enemy and not our backs. But I guess he was afraid to measure, though he is a good piece of a man. I have never had much to do with Bishops where I live; but, do you know, Sumner is my idea of a Bishop."[67]

A palpable hit, this, when we recall the imposing presence and the massive frame of the cultured Bostonian, who, after towering for years above his contemporaries, was evidently not willing to surrender, in an idle moment, the physical preëminence in which he, too, took not a little pride.[68] Perhaps his eye had become as practiced "in taking a man's true altitude," as the President's. If so, it gave warning that when the loosely jointed figure before him unfolded to its full height,[69] "Old Abe" would, in one respect at least, prove to be Charles Sumner's superior.

The scholarly statesman from the East, no less than the man of the people from the West, owed something of that subtle, indefinable force which issued in mastery over their fellows, to mere physique. However slight this debt may have been, they did not fail to recognize it — each in his characteristic way. Sumner, whether he gave to the world an oration with carefully studied pose and gesture, or privately employed his powers of persuasion in furthering one of the lofty aims of his career, was ever conscious of the advantage that lay in his commanding figure, and he improved it to the utmost. Lincoln, rarely, if ever, self-conscious, made no such application of his strength and stature; but the exhibitions of them that he scattered through his life abundantly manifest his half-serious, half-joking sense of their importance. This appreciation of a superiority, purely physical, by leaders so unlike in temperament and training, is sufficient to warrant the attention that has been given here to a seemingly unessential matter. Moreover, it is no mere coincidence that the three most forceful personalities that have directed the fortunes of the American people from the President's chair were embodied in frames of uncommon size and vigor. Their habits of command, confirmed early in life by ability to enforce their wishes, armed them with the irresistible powers of control by means of which they triumphed in great crises of our nation's history. The heaviest demands of this nature were, beyond a question, laid upon Abraham Lincoln, and he, consistently enough, was, of all the Presidents, the tallest and sturdiest.

CHAPTER II

LOVE, WAR, AND POLITICS

LINCOLN'S quickly acquired ascendancy, such as it was, over the people of New Salem, received formal confirmation almost as speedily. In less than ten months from that lazy summer day on which, as he himself described it, the young stranger had lodged in the place like a piece of floating driftwood, he was singled out by his neighbors for the choicest honor then within their gift — a military command. The Black Hawk War, narrowly averted during the preceding year, had broken out in the spring of 1832, spreading panic along the Illinois frontier. Rock River valley in the northern part of the State, once the hunting-ground of the united Sac and Fox Indians, was overrun by a band of their warriors under the famous old leader for whom history has named the struggle that ensued. He had, the previous summer, in accordance with existing treaties, ceded the land to the government, and had removed with his people beyond the Mississippi. But Black Hawk's inveterate hatred of the Americans, engendered by wrongs not altogether imaginary, and kept alive, since the war of 1812, by the Englishmen in Canada, had aroused him to one final raid for the recovery of his home. Having recrossed the river at the head of his so-called British band, — for most of the Sac and Fox nations were in favor of peace, — he held the lives and property of the settlers in his hands. At this juncture, Governor Reynolds called for volunteers to drive the Indians back over the Mississippi. Among the first to respond was a company from New Salem that included Abraham Lincoln and many of his Clary's Grove friends.

A. Lincoln.

On their way to the rendezvous at Beardstown, the volunteers halted to elect a captain. The office was sought by two candidates, Abraham Lincoln and William Kirkpatrick. The latter, as the owner of a sawmill and as a person of standing in the community, considered the honor to be his due, particularly as he who disputed it with him was a newcomer and a mere hired man. Lincoln had, in fact, upon his arrival in the neighborhood, done an odd job or two in Kirkpatrick's mill. To the proprietor's unfair treatment of him, on that occasion, may be ascribed the workman's keen desire to defeat him in a public contest. Upon hiring Lincoln, Kirkpatrick had promised to buy for him a hook with which to move some heavy logs; but finding that by reason of the young man's strength and skill the work was done as well with a common hand-spike, he had agreed, at Lincoln's suggestion, to give him the two dollars that the hook would have cost. When pay-day arrived, Kirkpatrick had refused to keep his promise. The trick rankled in Lincoln's memory. As soon as he heard of the mill-owner's ambition for military rank he said to his friend Green: —

"Bill, I believe I can now make Kirkpatrick pay that two dollars he owes me on the cant-hook. I'll run against him for captain."

The election that followed was characteristic in its simplicity. The candidates stood apart; the voters, together. At a signal, the latter stepped over to the man whom they severally preferred. Three out of every four of them went promptly to Lincoln.[1] Whereupon the minority, who stood with his competitor, left their candidate one by one to join the successful party. This continued until Kirkpatrick stood almost alone. His punishment had been severe. "Damn him," muttered Lincoln to his friend, "I've beat him. He used me badly in our settlement for my toil." The more audible impromptu speech in which the new Captain thanked his company was probably expressed in language less unparliamentary. It has not been preserved, but a minute of the speaker's gratification has. Recalling the event, in that frank little third-person autobiography of 1860, Mr. Lincoln wrote: —

"He says he has not since had any success in life which gave him so much satisfaction."

And with reason, for this election meant far more to him than the humbling of an influential man who had wronged him. It was the first formal public recognition of his ability to lead.[2]

How creditably the young officer conducted himself may be determined only after an inspection of the material at his command. A motley company it was, every man of it equipped after his own fashion, and intent upon maintaining, in behavior as well as in appearance, the frontiersman's cherished individuality. Having joined his neighbors, on equal terms, for an expedition against the Indians, he became restive under discipline whenever, in his good judgment, it did not bear directly upon the affair in hand. This prejudice against subordination he had, it is true, overcome sufficiently to participate, on the democratic plan described, in the choice of a captain; but with his vote probably went the private reservation to obey that officer or not as occasion might suggest. Thus far, the men of Lincoln's company differed from the rest of Governor Reynolds's hastily gathered army in no important particular. Beyond this, however, lay a marked variation in degree, if not in kind. The volunteers from New Salem savored strongly of Clary's Grove. Untrained, disorderly, even mutinous, they distanced the other companies in their violation of rules, and soon won the distinction of being a "hard set of men." Their Captain once recalled that his first order to one of them was answered by, "Go to the devil, sir!" The officer hastened to the manual instead, so that no time might be lost in making soldiers out of his unpromising recruits.

The task of compelling obedience from such men, difficult under the best of conditions, must have taxed to their utmost the faculties of a captain no less deficient than they in military training. How Lincoln pieced out his ignorance and saved the official dignity from disaster is illustrated by the droll anecdotes with which he was accustomed, some years later, in the post-office of the House, to amuse his fellow Congressmen. One of these stories dealt with his first attempt to drill the awkward squad.[3] They were marching with a front of about twenty men across a field, when it became necessary to pass through a narrow gateway. "I could not for the life of me," said he, "remember the proper word of command for getting my company endwise so that it could get through the gate. So, as we came near the gate, I shouted, 'This company is dismissed for two minutes, when it will fall in again on the other side of the gate!'"[4] It was not so easy, be it said, for Lincoln to gloss over all his shortcomings. He failed, in one instance at least, to understand that he who would command must first learn to obey. Hence, shortly after his company had joined the main body of the army, we find him in disgrace for disobedience of a general order. This decree, issued while the horses were making a precarious crossing over the Henderson River, prohibited, for obvious reasons, the discharge of firearms within fifty paces of the camp limits. Deliberately ignoring the order, our Captain fired his pistol within ten steps of the camp. He was promptly deprived of his sword, and was placed under arrest for the day.[5]

About a week later, Lincoln was again subjected to punishment, but this time for the misdeeds of his men. They had, upon their arrival near the seat of war, been received into the United States service. The military prestige of the nation appears, however, to have restrained their unruly spirits no more than had that of the state. When the army was about to march in search of the Indians, one bright May morning, Captain Lincoln directed the orderly sergeant to parade his company. They failed to respond to the officer's calls, and the sounds that issued from beneath some of the blankets gave intimation of what soon proved to be the terrible truth. These valiant men had, during the night, made a sortie, on their own account, upon an enemy that, more powerful than the Sacs or the Foxes, had laid them low. The warriors from New Salem were dead — drunk. Investigation revealed that they had broken into the officers' stores, and had stolen enough liquor to render marching, a few hours later, an unreasonable proposition. Indeed, all the efforts of their mortified commander, who of course had been kept in ignorance of the spree, failed to maintain them on their feet long enough to start with the other troops. Some time after the army had marched, he managed to set his besotted ranks in motion ; but as stragglers dropped here and there along the road, to finish their interrupted slumbers, the company did not overtake the main body before nightfall. Then Captain Lincoln was again placed under arrest, with orders to carry for two days — oh, cutting mockery! — a wooden sword.[6] The punishment was in keeping with the opera bouffe element that runs through the incident. Yet, there is no reason for assuming that the young officer, keen of humor though he was, found aught in the affair, at the time, but chagrin. This failure to maintain control over his men, together with his own violation of discipline, a few days before, must have made clear to him that he had now to face entirely new problems in leadership.

New problems may sometimes be solved in old ways. So must have thought this captain of volunteers, for he sought to establish his military authority not by applying the unfamiliar regulations in the articles of war, but by employing the means that had already stood him in such good stead. Courage, skill, and strength had secured to him at home a certain ascendancy over these rough fellows. Why not, he may have asked himself, hold that ascendancy in camp by further exhibitions of these qualities? Opportunities were plentiful enough in the sports with which the soldiers tried to relieve the hardships of the campaign, and in which Lincoln appears, as was his wont, to have excelled them all. This was especially so in wrestling. With a handkerchief knotted around his waist, he would jump into the ring, on notice however short, to uphold the reputation of his company. The volunteers from New Salem believed that no man in the army could throw their Captain, a faith which he shared, and in which he took not a little pride. Indeed, long after his ambitions had undergone a change, he was fond of recalling these triumphs. They had a prominent place among the reminiscences with which he entertained his congressional friends. Telling them once about a champion of the southern Illinois companies who challenged him, Mr. Lincoln said: —

"He was at least two inches taller than I was, and somewhat heavier, but I reckoned that I was the most wiry, and soon after I had tackled him I gave him a hug, lifted him off the ground, and threw him flat on his back. That settled his hash."[7]

Lincoln continued to settle the hashes dished up for him by his enthusiastic followers, until a certain Dow Thompson, not otherwise known to fame, was pitted against him. On the day appointed, the respective supporters of the men, having wagered their money and valuables upon the result, formed a ring for the contest. Lincoln's confidence in his ability to throw Thompson underwent a change after the first few passes. Turning to his friends, he said: —

"This is the most powerful man I ever had hold of. He will throw me and you will lose your all, unless I act on the defensive."

The New Salem champion appeared, in fact, to be outclassed. He managed to keep his feet for some time, but he was at last fairly thrown. Two falls out of three were to decide the match, so the wrestlers tried another bout. The second differed somewhat from the first. Lincoln fell heavily, pulling Thompson to the ground with him. As both went down, this looked like a "dog-fall," and it was so declared by Lincoln's friends. The adherents of Thompson, on the other hand, as warmly claimed it to be a fair fall. A general fight seemed imminent, but before the angry partisans could come to blows, Lincoln, who had regained his feet, rushed between them, and said to his supporters: —

"Boys, give up your bets; if he has not thrown me fairly, he could."

This magnanimous course put an end to the quarrel, while it left Lincoln's reputation as a wrestler not seriously impaired. For his men, though they paid their bets in obedience to his commands, refused to concede that he had been defeated, or that any athlete in the army was his match.[8]

The pride of Lincoln's troopers in their Captain went far toward reconciling them to his authority. He was, in fact, the only officer whom they learned to obey. Moreover, "they were fighting men," as one historian says, "and but for his personal authority would have kept the camp in a perpetual uproar." Even Lincoln's control was, before he got through with them, put to a severe strain, — the severest that can come to an officer, be he recruit or veteran, — open mutiny. This is how it happened. After the disgraceful rout known as "Stillman's defeat," Governor Reynolds and his army started in hot pursuit of the Indians. The savages, as they fled, left ghastly traces of their presence, here and there, in sacked homes and murdered people; but, applying their skill in woodcraft, they confused their trail so well that their pursuers sought them, for some time, in vain. The volunteers, unaccustomed to the consequent privations, became exasperated against the enemy and unruly toward their officers. During one of these fruitless marches, a weary and hungry old Indian wandered into camp. He professed to be a friend of the whites, and showed a safe-conduct signed by General Cass. This declared him to have done good service and to be faithful to the government. Disregarding the pass, some of the Sangamon volunteers, actuated by their recently inflamed hatred of the red man, and recalling, no doubt, the frontiersman's maxim, that the only good Indian is the dead Indian, rushed upon the refugee, determined to kill him. At this juncture, Captain Lincoln, stepping between them and their victim, knocked up the leveled muskets.

"Men," said he, his voice ringing above their shouts, "this must not be done. He must not be shot and killed by us."

For a moment it seemed as if the speaker, as well as the creature that crouched behind him, was in danger. Then the courage and resolution in the young officer's attitude gained the mastery. Beneath his fixed gaze the mutinous group sullenly fell back with murmurs of disappointment and vengeance.

"This is cowardly on your part, Lincoln!" cried one of them.

"If any man thinks I am a coward, let him test it," was the reply.

"You are larger and heavier than we are," said another.

"This you can guard against. Choose your weapons," rejoined Lincoln.

To this the mutineers made no answer. They had never before seen him so aroused. There was nothing left for them but submission. One by one they slunk away, and left the Indian in peace. How imminent had been his danger may be inferred from the fact that one of his race, aged and blind, who threw himself upon the mercy of another company, a few weeks later, was murdered by the enraged soldiers. To oppose such men, be it said, in the height of their frenzy, was beyond the ability of most militia officers. Captain Lincoln, however, knew the crowd with which he had to deal. It was only by sinking the officer and asserting the man that he could have hoped for a real conquest. He might, it is true, have enforced obedience by recourse to military discipline; but the influence over this rough citizen-soldiery, which he so highly prized, would probably have been lost to him forever. As it was, neither his courage nor his authority was again questioned; for, as he himself afterwards declared, he had, at the risk of his life, finally established both.[9]

The force of character manifested in these incidents is sufficient to account for the inexperienced militia captain's sway over men whom no one else could handle; yet the respect and even the affection with which, before the close of the campaign, his conduct inspired them, contributed somewhat, no doubt, toward this result. Tactfully taking the middle ground between that of the commander and the comrade, he did not let "the boys" forget that he was their superior, although none of them entered more keenly than he into their pleasures or their troubles. Here was a captain of volunteers, indeed! When the duties of the day had been disposed of, he was always ready to join the men in their pastimes; when fatigues or hunger discouraged them, — for the marching was hard and the commissary too often missing, — he gathered them at night about the camp-fire, to turn their faultfinding into laughter over his inexhaustible flow of jests and stories; finally, when injustice threatened their welfare, he became so watchful of their comfort, so tenacious of their rights, that, in the language of one of the men, he "attached officers and rank to him, as with hooks of steel." The volunteers, be it known, had for some time suffered under the discriminations in favor of the regular troops, that inevitably arise from the employment of the two branches in the same service. The militia had, indeed, been accepted by the government; but it was a State body, under State control, none the less, and it accordingly did not escape the customary prejudice. Abuses continued, until Captain Lincoln, one day, received an order that appeared to be improper. He obeyed it, but, improving the opportunity, went directly to the regular officer, who had issued it, and protested against the injustice to which his men had been subjected. Lincoln is said to have stated the case in good, set terms, concluding with: —

"Sir, you forget that we are not under the rules and regulations of the War Department at Washington; are only volunteers under the orders and regulations of Illinois. Keep in your own sphere and there will be no difficulty, but resistance will hereafter be made to your unjust orders. And, further, my men must be equal in all particulars — in rations, arms, camps, and so forth — to the regular army."

This demand was effectual. The wisdom, if not the justice, of acceding to it had been made clear to the regular officers; and they discontinued, from that time, their unfair treatment of the volunteers. As for the militiamen themselves, they, naturally enough, regarded him who had thus championed their cause, with devotion.[10]

The victory over the epaulets at headquarters was not less satisfactory than had been our Captain's little private campaign for the mastery of his own men. Their surrender to him, at discretion, was — as we now view it — of far deeper significance than the subsequent capture of Black Hawk and all his savages. The so-called war would, in fact, like the other struggles of its class, be well-nigh forgotten to-day, if it were not for the few participants who became eminent.[11] And certainly, to none of these was the brief experience so momentous as to the raw youth whose task of leading seventy recruits was destined to be followed, within a few decades, by the supreme command, at one time, of over a million soldiers.

Lincoln's apprenticeship to discipline had, it should be added, in those early days, a two-fold character. When the volunteers, after five weeks of service, demanded their discharge, he was mustered out with his company.[12] As the new levies had then not yet arrived at the seat of war, Governor Reynolds appealed to the patriotism of the disbanded troops for a regiment of volunteers that would, in the interim, protect the frontier. Among those who reënlisted was the ex-captain from the Sangamon. He served then, and during a still later enlistment, as a private in an Independent Spy Company that was called upon to supply couriers, scouts, and skirmishers. Of his conduct in the difficult, and presumably dangerous, duties that were assigned to him, no record has been preserved, save in the few random recollections of his fellow soldiers. One of them recalls that whenever, on the march, scouts were to be sent out to examine a covert, in which an ambush might be concealed, Lincoln was the first man selected. Moreover, many of those who rode forward with him are said to have habitually found an excuse, as they neared the place, for dismounting to adjust their girths or their saddles, but "Lincoln's saddle," it is dryly added, "was always in perfect order."[13] He had probably learned, by this unusual inversion of military rank, how to receive orders as well as he had mastered the art of giving them. At all events, he was a faithful soldier to the end. For, when he was finally mustered out of service, a few weeks before the close of the war, it was not, as had been the case with so many of the volunteers, at his own wish, but in the general disbandment necessitated by the lack of provisions. Thus ingloriously terminated Abraham Lincoln's less than three months of soldiering, during which, as it happened, he caught sight of no enemy and took part in no battle. If this vexed the volunteer, he may have reflected, as he made his way back to New Salem, that it was, at least, as creditable to his courage to have saved an Indian as to have killed one. He had, moreover, engaged in sundry struggles with those who ranked above and those who ranked below him; he had tasted the sweets of office, and had felt its responsibilities; he had, in short, learned many new lessons in the rudiments of leadership. The campaign, it is true, as he himself once facetiously said, does not afford material for writing him "into a military hero"; yet the part that he had played in it gave indications, at least, of the stuff out of which heroes, military and otherwise, are sometimes developed.

The horizon of Lincoln's ambition had, even before the Black Hawk War, distinctly widened. To extend throughout the county the influence that he had attained over the village became, within a few months after he had taken his place behind Offutt's counter, one of his aspirations. In order to gratify it by the readiest means, he went, as the phrase goes, into politics. The road to public preferment did not then, as now, in Illinois, follow the devious windings of caucuses and conventions.[14] A straight course lay before candidates for elective offices, and as many as pleased entered the race. Each competitor, having merely announced that he intended to run, started off after his own fashion and made his way as best he could towards the winning post. These heats were not without rude jostlings — even collisions, for the runners were many and the posts few. But what would you have, when

> "The grave, the gay, the fopling, and the dunce,
> Start up (God bless us!) statesmen all at once."

This array of all the talents, moreover, usually scrambled for the same places — seats in the legislature. Sublimely ignorant of existing laws many of them were, to be sure, but this ignorance, as it left the prospective law-maker somewhat untrammeled in legislating according to the wants of his constituency, was not invariably regarded as a disability. Hence, the announcement one morning that the young clerk at the grocery store had become a candidate for the legislature was not so absurd, in the spring of 1832, as it might be to-day. Lincoln had, in fact, been "encouraged by his great popularity among his immediate neighbors" — so read the autobiographical notes — to offer himself as a representative of the people in the General Assembly.

The election was to take place late in the summer,

but he had issued at once, in accordance with custom, an "address" to the voters of Sangamon County. This was his first formal application to the public for political power. As such, the document, particularly its concluding paragraph, is of interest here.

"Every man," he wrote, "is said to have his peculiar ambition. Whether it be true or not, I can say, for one, that I have no other so great as that of being truly esteemed of my fellow men, by rendering myself worthy of their esteem. How far I shall succeed in gratifying this ambition is yet to be developed. I am young, and unknown to many of you. I was born, and have ever remained, in the most humble walks of life. I have no wealthy or popular relations or friends to recommend me. My case is thrown exclusively upon the independent voters of the county; and, if elected, they will have conferred a favor upon me, for which I shall be unremitting in my labors to compensate. But, if the good people, in their wisdom, shall see fit to keep me in the background, I have been too familiar with disappointments to be very much chagrined."[15]

How sincere was the writer's desire to be "truly esteemed" had been manifested, a few weeks later, at the outbreak of the war. Abandoning his canvass, before it was well begun, he had in response to the first call, as we have seen, marched off, with some of his neighbors, to the defence of the State.

The volunteer, upon his discharge, returned to New Salem with the politician's dearest attribute — a record, such as it was, of military service. That our ex-captain did not, then or thereafter, so far as is known, parade his sword for votes should be mentioned to his credit. This forbearance was especially noteworthy in the case of Lincoln's first canvass, which had been so interrupted by that very service as to leave the candidate, after his return from the front, but ten days for his contest. It was conducted, nevertheless, manfully on its merits. Seizing the few opportunities still open to him, he made little speeches in which, besides approving of certain popular local ideas, he declared himself to be "a Clay man," and in favor of Henry Clay's so-called "American system." Such national politics doomed his already heavily handicapped canvass; for the county, as well as the state and the country, was at that time overwhelmingly devoted to the policy of President Jackson. The Democratic leader's partisans, moreover, growing intolerant in their might, had adopted his proscriptive methods toward political enemies, who were to be "whipped out of office like dogs out of a meat house."[16] Yet this penniless and obscure young man, eager for office as he was, had the courage and self-reliance — let us say nothing of conscience — to take his first plunge into politics in accordance with his convictions and against the tide on which the victorious spoilsmen were carrying all before them. He went down, on election day, with the other Clay men, suffering his first and only defeat by a direct vote of the people. A glance, however, at the poll-book, reveals a crumb of comfort larger than usually falls to the lot of unsuccessful candidates. Of the thirteen men who ran for the legislature, four were elected, and Lincoln, running 158 votes behind his lowest successful competitor, stood eighth on the list. Somewhat different was the order in Lincoln's home, the precinct of New Salem. There, of the 290 voters who balloted for representatives, 277 voted for him and but 13 against him.[17] This almost unanimous support of his neighbors has been explained by Judge Stephen T. Logan, one of the rising young men of that day.

"The Democrats of New Salem," said he, "worked for Lincoln out of their personal regard for him. That was the general understanding of the matter here at the time. In this he made no concession of principle whatever. He was as stiff as a man could be in his Whig doctrines. They did this for him simply because he was popular — because he was Lincoln."

The strength of this hold upon the people may be appreciated to its fullest extent only when we remember that in the national election, a few weeks later, these same voters gave General Jackson a majority of 115 over Mr. Clay. Under such conditions, Lincoln's defeat was not without honor. Indeed, so extraordinary a local triumph at once established his standing among the Warwicks of the county, as a man to be reckoned with thenceforward.

During the two years following, Lincoln strove to prepare himself for the political career opened to him by his brilliant, if unsuccessful, start. The canvass had made clear to the candidate that he was at a disadvantage in two particulars, at least. The people of the county at large did not know him well enough, and — what may have been less evident to others, though it was even more deeply impressed upon him — he did not know enough to cope, on an equal footing, with some of the leaders whom he had encountered. The first of these deficiencies was largely overcome, strange as it may seem, through the kindness of a Democratic officer, the Surveyor of Sangamon County. This follower of Jackson, John Calhoun by name, so far forgot his "whole-hog" obligations as to admire the new "Clay man." He even went farther in his treason. Having persuaded Lincoln to study the rudiments of surveying,[18] he appointed him his deputy, and kept him so busy — for speculation in land was at its height — that the young man had ample opportunity not only to make many new acquaintances, but to win their confidence as well. The second deficiency was not so easily disposed of, though Lincoln's efforts to that end were untiring. Whether, as happened during this period, he picked up a living by doing odd jobs, keeping store, carrying letters, or laying out town lots, he invariably found time for the study of such newspapers, law books, and odd volumes as came within his reach.[19] Consequently when, during the summer of 1834, he again presented himself as a candidate for the legislature, he made, in this respect also, a better showing. Still, the homely, ill-clad young fellow must, in appearance at least, have fallen short of even Sangamon standards, simple as they were. "He wore," said a friend who had accompanied him in the preceding canvass, "a mixed jeans coat, clawhammer style, short in the sleeves, and bobtail — in fact it was so short in the tail he could not sit on it; flax and tow-linen pantaloons, and a straw hat. I think he wore a vest, but do not remember how it looked. He wore pot-metal boots."[20] This wardrobe had evidently not been greatly improved when Lincoln made his second appeal for the suffrages of the people, inasmuch as a certain doctor, looking him over contemptuously while he was on one of his electioneering tours, asked: —

"Can't the party raise any better material than that?"

"Go to-morrow and hear all before you pronounce judgment," said a common friend, who after the meeting on the following day inquired: —

"Doctor, what say you now?"

"Why, sir," was the answer, "he is a perfect take-in. He knew more than all of the other candidates put together."[21]

On election day Lincoln was found to have been chosen by a flattering plurality. He stood second on the list of four Assemblymen, and but fourteen votes below the first man.[22] This success was repeated in 1836, when he led the poll; in 1838, after he had become a lawyer, with his home at Springfield; and in 1840, when he made what, by his own choice, proved to be his last run for the office. The five canvasses themselves did not differ essentially from those conducted at the time by other young politicians of the neighborhood. In one respect, however, Lincoln appears to have made his contests distinctive. They afforded occasions, which he did not neglect, for the exercise of his aggressive faculties. Indeed, careful scrutiny of the few incidents that have here and there been chronicled reveals how the vein of mastery, which we have traced to this point, continued unbroken through the entire decade.

Lincoln's first canvass — in fact, his first appearance on the stump — was attended by a little scene that appropriately introduced the subduer of Clary's Grove to a community fully as capable of appreciating grit and muscle. A crowd of voters that had collected at Pappsville, getting full of whiskey and enthusiasm, began a general fight. Among those who were roughly handled was a follower of the New Salem candidate. Jumping from the platform, Lincoln rushed through the mêlée, seized his friend's assailant as if to make him "walk Spanish," tossed him off ten feet or so, resumed his place on the stand, and calmly began his little speech. This prelude, it is safe to say, did not lessen the warmth of his welcome from an audience akin to "the bare-footed boys," "the huge-pawed boys," or "the butcher-knife boys," who, in the elections of those days, so often held the balance of power.[23]

During the canvass of four years later, when Lincoln spoke at Mechanicsburg, he "jumped in and saw fair play" — so a bystander relates — for another friend who was getting the worst of it in a similar fight.[24] By that time, however, he had learned to use his tongue and his pen no less effectually than his hands in repelling an attack. Suiting the weapon to the occasion, he manifested, in those primitive electioneering encounters for the Assembly, something of the power and adroitness that in mature years distinguished his more ambitious efforts. None of the candidate's later triumphs excelled, in this respect, his victory, during the contest, over George Forquer, a politician of prominence and uncommon ability. A lawyer by profession, his words, as a speaker and as a writer, were weighted with the prestige which naturally attaches to one who had been member of the Assembly, Secretary of State, Attorney-General, and State Senator. He had recently deserted the Whig Party to join the

Jackson Democrats, a defection which the administration had rewarded with the lucrative place of Register of the Land Office at Springfield. This worthy might have sat for Hosea Biglow's portrait of Gineral C.: —

> "a dreffle smart man:
> He 's ben on all sides thet give places or pelf;
> But consistency still wuz a part of his plan, —
> He 's ben true to *one* party, — an' thet is himself."

Forquer's pretentious new house, from which projected a lightning-rod, — the only one in the county, — had been pointed out to Lincoln as he rode into town, one evening, with a few of his friends. They were unable to answer the young man's eager questions about the "new-fangled" rod. It was there to keep off the lightning. More than that none of them could say.[25] On the following day, in the debate which took place at the court-house, between the candidates for office, Lincoln made a good impression. In fact, his success was so marked that, as the audience was dispersing, the Democrats deemed it necessary to put forward one of their strong men to reply. This task was committed to Forquer, who, as he was not a candidate, had taken no part in the discussion. He responded to the call, nevertheless, with the vigor and skill of a practiced debater. Not content with what could be said in answer to Lincoln's arguments, the speaker sought to overwhelm the young man beneath a flood of personal abuse and ridicule. The onslaught was so severe that the candidate's friends trembled for their favorite. What could he say in rejoinder? Lincoln, evidently laboring under great excitement, stood a few paces distant, intently eyeing the speaker. At the conclusion of the attack, he remounted the stand to reply.

"I have heard him often since," writes his friend Joshua F. Speed, who was present, "in the courts and before the people, but never saw him appear and acquit himself so well as upon that occasion. His reply to Forquer was characterized by great dignity and force."

This praise was merited, if we may judge from the conclusion, which alone has been preserved.

"Mr. Forquer," said Lincoln, "commenced his speech by announcing that the young man would have to be taken down. It is for you, fellow citizens, not for me to say whether I am up or down. The gentleman has seen fit to allude to my being a young man; but he forgets that I am older in years than in the tricks and trades of politicians. I desire to live, and I desire place and distinction; but I would rather die now than, like the gentleman, live to see the day that I would change my politics for an office worth three thousand dollars a year, and then feel compelled to erect a lightning-rod to protect a guilty conscience from an offended God."[26]

Our Register and his rod had indeed drawn the lightning. The hit was a palpable one. It left the young candidate master of the field, from which his antagonist retired with a hurt that never entirely healed. When Forquer thereafter spoke in public meetings, his opponents usually found occasion to remind his audiences that he was the turncoat whom Abe Lincoln had accused of erecting a lightning-rod "to protect a guilty conscience from an offended God."[27]

The controversy with Forquer was typical of a canvass noted for its bitterness. Personal conflicts, not only between excited partisans, but even between the candidates themselves, disgraced the contest. In such a struggle, Lincoln, of course, could not hope to escape slander any more than he had avoided abuse. Vague charges against him and one of his colleagues were circulated by Colonel Robert Allen, a Democratic politician, who, for lack of argument, resorted to this shift for prejudicing the Whig cause. Lincoln's method of meeting the attack was in striking contrast with the violence to which similar acts, in the rough-and-tumble canvass of that year, gave rise. He sent Allen this letter, which is worthy of a place here, in full: —

NEW SALEM, June 21, 1836.

DEAR COLONEL, — I am told that during my absence last week you passed through the place and stated publicly that you were in possession of a fact or facts which, if known to the public, would entirely destroy the prospects of N. W. Edwards and myself at the ensuing election; but that through favor to us you would forbear to divulge them. No one has needed favors more than I, and, generally, few have been less unwilling to accept them; but in this case favor to me would be injustice to the public, and therefore I must beg your pardon for declining it. That I once had the confidence of the people of Sangamon County is sufficiently evident; and if I have done anything, either by design or misadventure, which if known would subject me to a forfeiture of that confidence, he that knows of that thing and conceals it is a traitor to his country's interest.

I find myself wholly unable to form any conjecture of what fact or facts, real or supposed, you spoke; but my opinion of your veracity will not permit me for a moment to doubt that you at least believed what you said. I am flattered with the personal regard you manifested for me; but I do hope that, on mature reflection, you will view the public interest as a paramount consideration, and therefore determine to let the worst come.

I assure you that the candid statement of facts on your part, however low it may sink me, shall never break the ties of personal friendship between us.

I wish an answer to this, and you are at liberty to publish both if you choose.

Very respectfully,

A. LINCOLN.

A remarkable production this, from a half-fledged backwoods politician, in the heat of an election contest! The refined irony of Lincoln's thrust — for a notorious perverter of facts was the Colonel — left this old campaigner as helplessly impaled upon its point as was the other veteran upon the barb of his own lightning-rod. Allen — need we say? — did not avail himself of the permission to publish the letter or an answer thereto. He was silenced. His son, finding the letter, long after the incident had been forgotten, gave to the public this further evidence of how "the young man," who was "to be taken down," exchanged rôles, on occasion, with the gentlemen in charge of the performance.[28]

The canvass of 1836, stirring as it was, did not put the candidates so much on their mettle as did that of 1840 — the *annus mirabilis* of American politics. The enthusiasm of "the hard-cider campaign," with its acres of mass-meetings, its processions, frolics, songs, free drinks, log-cabins, and coon-skins, pervaded, as elsewhere, the local elections in Illinois. State questions were lost sight of in national issues, such as they were, and Lincoln, besides his candidature for the Assembly, had a place on the Whig electoral ticket. Entering into the contest with his accustomed zeal, he was much in evidence throughout Illinois that year; yet what he said in debate and on the stump is, as was the case in previous struggles, largely a matter of conjecture.[29] On the other hand, some of the things that he did impressed themselves, firmly enough, in the people's memory.

The voters of 1840 flocked into political meetings not to learn and to reflect, but to shout, to scuffle, to laugh, and to sing. How cleverly Lincoln adapted himself to such an audience and, at the same time, crushed an opponent, with a turn of the wrist, as one might say, has been related by some of his associates. He was frequently opposed on the stump — so runs the story — by Colonel Dick Taylor, a demagogue with a weakness for sarcasm and fine clothes. Severely Democratic in theory, however, the Colonel took care to keep as much of his finery as possible out of sight, while he had his flings at the aristocratic pretensions of the Whigs, or warned "the hard-handed yeomanry" against "rag-barons" and "manufacturing-lords." Such taunts made up the stock of his inflated oratory, as usual, one day, when Lincoln, "to take the wind out of his sails," as he expressed it, slipped to the speaker's side and catching his vest by the lower edge, gave it a sharp pull. "It opened wide," says one of the narrators, "and out fell upon the platform, in full view of the astonished audience, a mass of ruffled shirt, gold watch, chains, seals, and glittering jewels." According to another veracious historian, the vest, when so rudely shaken, merely "opened and revealed to his astonished hearers" the Colonel's concealed grandeur. At all events, Lincoln, guiltless of linen and soft raiment, made the most of the situation. Pointing to the mortified orator, he exclaimed: —

"Behold the hard-fisted Democrat! Look, gentlemen, at this specimen of the bone and sinew. And here, gentlemen," — laying his large, coarse hand on his heart, and bowing, — "here, at your service, here is your aristocrat! Here is one of your silk-stocking gentry. Here is your rag-baron with his lily-white hands. Yes, I suppose I, according to my friend Taylor, am a bloated aristocrat."

After speaking of the demagogue's customary vaporings, he went on: —

"While Colonel Taylor was making these charges against the Whigs over the country, riding in fine carriages, wearing ruffled shirts, kid gloves, massive gold watch-chains with large gold seals and flourishing a heavy gold-headed cane, I was a poor boy, hired on a flat-boat at eight dollars a month, and had only one pair of breeches to my back, and they were buckskin. Now, if you know the nature of buckskin, when wet and dried by the sun, it will shrink; and my breeches kept shrinking until they left several inches of my legs bare, between the tops of my socks and the lower part of my breeches; and whilst I was growing taller they were becoming shorter, and so much tighter that they left a blue streak around my legs that can be seen to this day. If you call this aristocracy, I plead guilty to the charge."

Lincoln's humor and the discomfiture of his opponent were irresistible. Amidst Gargantuan peals of laughter, in which one of the audience "nearly broke his heart with mirth," was this elegant Democrat pilloried, in Sangamon County, for the rest of his career. As to "the young man," he had simply "taken down" one more lofty antagonist.[30]

There were times, during this extraordinary canvass, when raillery, as well as argument, failed to move a crowd; when, in fact, physical courage alone sufficed to control the turbulent spirits. It was on such an occasion, one evening, that Lincoln's friend, Edward Dickinson Baker, who already gave promise of the brilliant career that lay before him, addressed a hostile audience, in the Springfield court-room. The place happened to be directly below the law office of Stuart & Lincoln, in which the junior member of the firm lay listening, through a trap-door that opened above the platform. The speaker, as he warmed to his subject, denounced, with the impetuous eloquence that afterward made him famous, the dishonesty of Democratic officials. "Wherever there is a land-office, there you will find a Democratic newspaper defending its corruptions!" he thundered.

"Pull him down!" shouted John B. Weber, whose brother was the editor of the local administration sheet.

There was a noisy rush toward the platform, and, for the moment, it seemed as if Baker, who stood pale yet firm, would be punished for his temerity. Then, to the astonishment of the advancing crowd, a lank form dangled through the scuttle, and Lincoln dropped upon the platform between them and the object of their anger. After gesticulating in vain for silence, he seized the stone water-jug and shouted: —

"I'll break it over the head of the first man who lays a hand on Baker!"

As the assailants hesitated, he continued: —

"Hold on, gentlemen, let us not disgrace the age and country in which we live. This is a land where freedom of speech is guaranteed. Mr. Baker has a right to speak and ought to be permitted to do so. I am here to protect him, and no man shall take him from this stand, if I can prevent it."

The crowd receded, quiet was restored, and Baker finished his speech without further interruption.[31]

It was under somewhat similar circumstances, and during this same contest, that the muscular candidate interposed his commanding presence between some enraged Democratic partisans and another Whig orator. The speaker, in that instance, was General Usher F. Linder. He delivered before a large audience, in the Springfield State House, a spirited address, which was interrupted by threats and insults. Thereupon, Lincoln and Baker, who were present, mounted the platform and stationed themselves one on each side of him. As soon as the speaker had concluded, they passed their arms through his, and Lincoln said: —

"Linder, Baker and I are apprehensive that you may be attacked by some of those ruffians who insulted you from the galleries, and we have come up to escort you to your hotel. We both think we can do a little fighting, so we want you to walk between us until we get you to your hotel. Your quarrel is our quarrel and that of the great Whig Party of this nation; and your speech, upon this occasion, is the greatest one that has been made by any of us, for which we wish to honor, love, and defend you."

The three men walked unmolested through the crowd that, following them to the hotel, gave the orator, before it dispersed, three hearty cheers.[32]

The violence that marked "the hard-cider campaign" consistently extended to the very polls. On election day, word was brought to Lincoln that a certain railroad contractor, named Radford, had, in the interests of the Democrats, taken possession with his workmen of a polling-place and was hindering the Whigs from voting. Lincoln, seizing an ax-handle, made for the scene of action, on a run. "Radford," he said, as he opened a way to the ballot-box, "you'll spoil and blow, if you live much longer."[33]

The contractor, who knew the character of the man with whom he was dealing, did not stay to argue the question. He at once withdrew, somewhat — it must be admitted — to the disappointment of the candidate, who confided to his friend Speed that he wanted Radford to show fight, as he "intended just to knock him down and leave him kicking." Lincoln's "stern advice," as one writer terms it, was sufficient, however, to rout the heelers, and to secure the Whigs, that day, at least, against any further encroachments upon their rights.[34]

The spirit with which our campaigner plunged into conflict in behalf of his party, his friends, or himself, lost none of its vigor when the scene of his activities was transferred from the stump to the legislature. There, though one of the youngest and probably one of the least experienced of the members, he took his position, after the initiation of his first term, as if it were a matter of course, on the battle line. In the stirring session of 1836–37, county was arrayed against county, town against town. Their several representatives struggled for a prize, dear to every ambitious community — the State capitol. The seat of government was to be removed from Vandalia, but whither? Among the most strenuous claimants was Sangamon County, which had entrusted the task of securing this honor for Springfield to its Representatives and Senators. They constituted a notable group, — sons of Anak, all, — to whom was applicable, in more respects than one, their sobriquet, the "Long Nine";[35] and the longest of them was the member from New Salem. His colleagues, recognizing at the very outset his talent for leadership, assigned to him the management of their fight; for fight indeed it was. The opponents of Springfield were numerous and stubborn. Twice they prevailed so far as to lay the bill in its behalf on the table; but Lincoln contested every inch of the ground. "In those darkest hours," says one of his associates, "when our Bill to all appearances was beyond resuscitation, and all our opponents were jubilant over our defeat, and when friends could see no hope, Mr. Lincoln never for one moment despaired; but, collecting his colleagues to his room for consultation, his practical common-sense, his thorough knowledge of human nature, then made him an overmatch for his compeers and for any man that I have ever known." [36]

Holding his delegation well in hand, and casting its influence, on most questions, as a unit, Lincoln availed himself of the then current craze for "internal improvements" so as steadily to increase the Springfield following. To what extent he indulged in the reprehensible practice of trading votes, and whether or not he merited "the reputation of being the best log-roller in the legislature," may not be considered here. Suffice it to say that he did roll up the pledges for his bill, at every move, and that, shortly before adjournment, he carried the day for Springfield. This success, though much of it was due to Lincoln's skilful political manipulation, is to be ascribed, in part as well, to what may be best described as his personal magnetism. "He made Webb and me vote for the removal," says Jesse K. Dubois, one of the Whig Assemblymen, "though we belonged to the southern end of the State. We defended our vote before our constituents by saying that necessity would ultimately force the seat of government to a central position. But, in reality, we gave the vote to Lincoln because we liked him, because we wanted to oblige our friend, and because we recognized him as our leader." His party in the Lower House, remarkable as it must have seemed, had in fact, before the close of the session, begun to look for guidance to this new man. In that uneven contest of Sangamon against the field were manifested not a few of the qualities which parliamentary minorities look for in their captains.

Having demonstrated his ability to conduct an aggressive campaign, it remained for the Sangamon Chief, as Lincoln was now sometimes called, to prove his mettle on the defensive. An opportunity soon presented itself, inasmuch as somewhat of the animosity engendered by the struggle for the capitol outlived the legislature that dealt with the question. In the extra session, called during the following summer, the opponents of Springfield made a vigorous attempt to repeal the law which had established that town as the seat of government. The movement was led by General William L. D. Ewing, ex-United States Senator, who in a stinging address accused the "Long Nine" of having won their victory by "chicanery and trickery." Sparing neither invective nor sarcasm, he arraigned the members from Sangamon with a severity that called for immediate reply. Who would take up the gage flung down by this formidable antagonist — a man of culture, standing, and distinguished personal courage? Lincoln promptly did so. In a spirited speech, he defended the "Long Nine," and made countercharges of corruption against Ewing and his associates. So keen was this denunciation that the House believed the speaker, as one of the auditors reports, to be "digging his own grave." "This was the time," says that same friend, "that I began to conceive a very high opinion of the talents and personal courage of Abraham Lincoln." And with reason, for General Ewing, masterful and hot-tempered, would surely close such a controversy with a challenge. "Gentlemen," he said, turning to the Sangamon section, "have you no other champion than this coarse and vulgar fellow to bring into the lists against me? Do you suppose that I will condescend to break a lance with your low and obscure colleague?" What justification Ewing had, on that occasion, for so harsh a reference to his opponent's breeding cannot be determined, as there is no report of what Lincoln said, extant. The speech must have been effectual, however. "Our friend carries the true Kentucky rifle," was the comment of a Springfield editor, on Lincoln, at about that time, "and when he fires, he seldom fails of sending the shot home." [37] The weapon used on Ewing was doubtless double-barreled; for the scheme to have the Capital Law repealed fell to the ground, and the assailant of the "Long Nine" was so hard hit that the interference of friends alone prevented a duel.[38] Small wonder that the General did not approve of "this coarse and vulgar fellow," or that the Sangamon delegation was content to leave its standard in the hands of such a champion.

The force and fearlessness that had marked the reply to Ewing were not soon forgotten. Whenever thereafter, in the legislature or outside of it, the "Long Nine" were assailed, — and their enemies were numerous enough, — Lincoln was put forward to defend them. Once they were intemperately attacked by Jesse B. Thomas, a lawyer of ability and one of the most distinguished Democratic politicians in the State. While he spoke, Lincoln, who happened to be absent from the meeting, was sent for. Hastening to the court-house, in which the incident took place, the Sangamon chief mounted the platform after the speaker and made a reply, the language of which none of his auditors remembered, but the manner and effect of which were never effaced from their memories. Denunciation of Thomas, ridicule of his foibles, even mimicry of certain physical peculiarities followed one another, in rapid succession, amidst uproarious laughter and applause. So sharp was the onslaught that its object is said to have wept with vexation as he hurried from the scene. His emotion tempered the triumph of his adversary, who hunted him up, and, with characteristic good nature, apologized for the severity of the reply. This speech, like the invective against Ewing, has unfortunately not been preserved. The impression it made, however, in the political circles of Springfield may be inferred from the fact that it became a byword under the title of "the skinning of Thomas." From that time forward, moreover, but few Democratic orators, if we may judge from the records, cared to concern themselves with the iniquities of the "Long Nine."[39]

The judgment of Sangamon in the selection of its chief was vindicated, not alone by his successful battles in its behalf, but also by the action of his party. The Whigs, in the Assembly of 1837, as has been said, had begun to regard Lincoln as their head. In 1838, when the Lower House was organizing, they awarded him that distinction, beyond a doubt, by making him their candidate for the speakership. This was no small honor for a man of twenty-nine, particularly when that man was the "low and obscure" Lincoln; while his opponent, the Democratic nominee, happened to be no less a notability than that Ewing who had applied these epithets to him, a few months before. As the Whigs were in the minority, they of course did not elect their candidate. He maintained his place, nevertheless, at their head, and again received their votes for the office, in the legislature of 1840. Then, as in the former election, he was pitted against Ewing, and, because of the weakness of his party, with the same result. But the vital fact for us, the point which stands out above the flat details of these speakership contests, is the elevation of Offutt's gawky clerk, in an almost incredibly short period, to parliamentary leadership.

The steps by which Lincoln mounted to the mastery of his party in the legislature are not clearly defined. Nor is it easy to place one's hand upon the quality or qualities, in his make-up, which contributed most to that result. Courage, force, devotion, tact, and ready wit underlie the few narratives here set down; but as the incidents were selected with a view to illustration, rather than to historical completeness, they leave unnoticed other traits that deserve mention, even though they have not been severally crystallized in the heart of a good story. The political honesty that led Lincoln to cast his lot with a party in apparently hopeless minority; the loyalty that held him true to the interests of that party, when others turned their coats; the intellectual thoroughness and candor which rendered him formidable in debate, as well as influential in council; the extreme of self-reliance that rarely required assistance or advice, yet could receive without impatience what it did not want; the homely, unaffected good humor that expressed itself at every turn in a funny story or a sympathetic word, and won for him the title of "uncommon good fellow," even from men with whom he would neither smoke nor drink, — these also are some of the plus factors, as one might say, which in this his first political epoch already entered into the making of the master's character. He cannot, it is true, be said to have evinced, all in all, remarkable generalship, either on the stump or in the House. Indeed, if Lincoln's public career had closed with his last term in the Assembly, even local history might have found scant inspiration in those few electioneering episodes, or in the wild-cat legislation to which he contributed no unimportant part. As it is, however, the decade forms an essential link in the chain of our investigation. It may be termed the transition period from physical to intellectual power. Both held sway by turns, yet so conjointly that we can almost discern how the aggressive quality of the one was merged into that of the other. In this readjustment of his forces Lincoln, still held his own. Novel conditions speedily became familiar environment, and new men, great as well as small, took therein their proper places. As for the tall member from Sangamon, when he found his place, it was — need we add? — at the head.

Nor did Lincoln fail to maintain this ascendancy in several severe quarrels that took place outside of the legislature. Two, of a quasi-political nature, in which he became involved subsequent to his controversy with Ewing, afford further glimpses of his character, on its forceful side. The first of these encounters occurred during the summer of 1837, shortly after he had become a lawyer and had taken up his residence in Springfield, as the partner of a Black Hawk War comrade, Major John T. Stuart. The firm had been retained by a widow to prosecute a claim against a certain General James Adams, whom she accused of acquiring title to a ten-acre lot by the forgery of her deceased husband's signature. While the case was pending, the defendant, a chronic aspirant for public office, became a candidate for the place of probate justice. A few days before the election, he was unsparingly attacked for his conduct, in an anonymous handbill, which closed with the sentence: —

"I shall not subscribe my name, but hereby authorize the editor of the *Journal* to give it up to any one who may call for it."

Copies of the document having been scattered broadcast about the streets, they gave rise to a controversy, which was heightened rather than allayed by the election of Adams. He denied the charges in a long letter to the *Sangamon Journal*. The issue of the paper in which his communication appeared also contained a reprint of the original handbill, with an announcement by the editor that "A. Lincoln, Esq.," was its author. The quarrel raged for several weeks in the columns of the *Journal* and of the Springfield *Republican*. Step by step, Lincoln followed Adams up, exposing the seamy side of his career, and capping the climax with a copy of an indictment for forgery, found against him in Oswego County, New York, nineteen years before. An unscrupulous adventurer, this; yet the young barrister does not seem to have hesitated. In fact, the worse "the General's" character proved to be, as his past life was unfolded, the more fearless became his adversary's denunciations. Replying to Adams's flings at lawyers, Lincoln wrote: —

"He attempted to impose himself upon the community as a lawyer, and he actually carried the attempt so far as to induce a man who was under the charge of murder to entrust the defence of his life to his hands, and finally took his money and got him hanged. Is this the man that is to raise a breeze in his favor by abusing lawyers? . . . If he is not a lawyer, he *is* a liar; for he proclaimed himself a lawyer, and got a man hanged by depending on him. . . . Farewell, General, I will see you again at court, if not before — when and where we will settle the question whether you or the widow shall have the land."[40]

The widow did get the land, Adams was completely discredited, and one more scalp hung from the belt of the Sangamon Chief.

The second quarrel, like the first, mingled public with private motives, and grew, in similar fashion, out of an anonymous composition from Lincoln's pen. In the one case, as in the other, moreover, he manifested the fearless and masterful spirit with which we have by this time become familiar. But further than that the resemblance did not go; for Lincoln's exposure of a scamp like Adams had little in common with his unwarrantable attack upon James Shields. Shields was a brave, quick-tempered young Irishman, with a full share of his countrymen's taste for love and politics. An ardent Democrat of course, he had been elected to the Illinois Assembly even before observing the trivial formality of naturalization, and, a few years later, his services to the party had been rewarded with the place of State Auditor. The office gave him a certain prominence, which he is said to have made the most of in Springfield society. In truth, this gallant bachelor from County Tyrone was a very "lion among ladies." It is not surprising, therefore, that his social vanities, no less than his political flourishes, offered a tempting mark to the assaults of the Whigs. Their animus against the Auditor was intensified, during the summer of 1842, when the insolvent condition of the State treasury and the depreciation in the value of State Bank notes caused the Governor and his financial officers to issue a proclamation forbidding the payment of taxes in the almost worthless bank paper. As this was, practically, the only money in the hands of the people, they assailed the Democratic State government, from every quarter, with an outburst of indignation, which the Whigs — regardless of their own part in the extravagant improvement legislation that had given rise to the trouble — lost no opportunity of stimulating. The newspapers and leaders of the minority party were severe in their censure of the State authorities, among whom, by the way, the Auditor had rendered himself especially obnoxious. Upon him, in the midst of the denunciations, fell the heaviest charge of all; for it was directed by that same Kentucky marksman who seldom failed, as one of his admirers told us, "of sending the shot home."

The caustic humor that, from The First Chronicles of Reuben to "the skinning of Thomas," had now and then been so effectively employed by Lincoln in mastering an opponent, here again came into play. He contributed to the *Sangamo Journal* of September 2, edited at the time by his friend Simeon Francis, a singular composition. It purported to be A Letter from the Lost Townships, written by a Democratic widow who signed herself "Rebecca."[41] In robust country dialect, she denounced "these officers of State" as a hypocritical set, that ought to be supplanted in the places they disgraced by men who would "do more work for less pay, and take fewer airs while they are doing it." The "airs" of the Auditor had particularly aroused Rebecca's ire; for upon that functionary burst almost the whole torrent of her coarse ridicule.

"I seed him," she reports a neighbor as saying, "when I was down in Springfield last winter. They had a sort of a gatherin' there one night among the grandees, they called a fair. All the gals about town was there, and all the handsome widows and married women, finickin' about trying to look like gals. . . . I looked in at the window, and there was this same fellow Shields floatin' about on the air, without heft or earthly substances, just like a lock of cat fur where cats had been fighting. He was paying his money to this one, and that one, and t'other one, and sufferin' great loss because it was n't silver instead of State paper; and the sweet distress he seemed to be in — his very features, in the ecstatic agony of his soul, spoke audibly and distinctly: — 'Dear girls, it is distressing, but I cannot marry you all. Too well I know how much you suffer; but do, do remember, it is not my fault that I am so handsome and so interesting.' As this last was expressed by a most exquisite contortion of his face, he seized hold of one of their hands, and squeezed, and held on to it about a quarter of an hour. 'Oh, my good fellow!' says I to myself, 'if that was one of our Democratic gals in the Lost Townships, the way you 'd get a brass pin let into you would be about up to the head.'"

So much for ridicule; as to abuse, there was nothing in the letter more severe than this comment on a circular, issued by the Auditor: —

"I say it 's a lie, and not a well told one at that. It grins out like a copper dollar. Shields is a fool as well as a liar. With him truth is out of the question; and as for getting a good, bright, passable lie out of him, you might as well try to strike fire from a cake of tallow."

Fighting words these, as the writer must have known, especially when applied to a man of Shields's calibre.

Touched to the quick by the satire, and enraged by the attack upon his honor, the hot-blooded young Auditor did not conduct himself with that coolness which is alone effectual against such assaults. On the contrary, amidst the merriment of the town, he gave way to his fury after a fashion that must have gratified his assailant. More than that, it started the mischievous pens of two Whiggish and, we may add, waggish young ladies, Mary Todd and her friend Julia M. Jayne. Their interest in politics is accounted for by the fact that within the next few months they became respectively Mrs. Abraham Lincoln and Mrs. Lyman Trumbull. Moreover, what is more to the point, the former of these ladies was, at the time, conducting a clandestine renewal of her interrupted courtship with the author of A Letter from the Lost Townships, under the roof of Editor Francis. His hospitality opened to her the columns of the *Journal*, as well as his house, when she and her confidante, taking up the theme where Lincoln had left it, concocted a second letter. In this sequel, Shields's threats of vengeance appear to have frightened Rebecca into a proposal of marriage, by way of compromise. She prefers "matrimonial bliss" to "a lickin'"; but, if the Auditor persist in his demands for "personal satisfaction," she, on her side, as the challenged party, will insist on the choice of weapons. "Which bein' the case," she concludes, "I'll tell you in confidence that I never fights with anything but broomsticks, or hot water, or a shovelful of coals, or some such thing; the former of which, being somewhat like a shillalah, may not be very objectional to him. I will give him choice, however, in one thing, and that is, whether, when we fight, I shall wear breeches or he petticoats; for, I presume that change is sufficient to place us on an equality." But the affair terminated — that is to say according to the fair satirists — without bloodshed; for they closed their literary labors with some doggerel verses, celebrating the nuptials of the bachelor and the widow.

Not so peacefully disposed was the object of these attacks. In his veins, be it remembered, still flowed the ichor of Donnybrook. He was an expert swordsman, moreover, and in his youth had been an instructor in fencing. Smarting more than ever under a sense of injury, he sent his friend General John D. Whiteside, of Black Hawk War fame, to the editor, with a demand for the name of the author. If this was not complied with, Francis was himself to be held responsible. In his dilemma, the editor consulted Lincoln, who, about to leave town on the fall circuit, directed Francis to give his name, but to make no mention of the ladies. That the creator of "Rebecca" understood what the situation involved is evinced by the fact that he had sought out a certain dragoon major, who, broadsword in hand, drilled him in

> "fencing, and the use of arms,
> The art of urging and avoiding harms,
> The noble science and the mastering skill
> Of making just approaches how to kill."

As for Shields, following Lincoln to Tremont, he lost as little time as might be in sending Whiteside to him with a letter which, considering the state of society in the Springfield of that day and the writer's provocation, we are hardly inclined to ridicule. The missive, truth to say, conformed to Sir Lucius O'Trigger's rule, that when a man frames a challenge, he must "do the thing decently and like a Christian." It protested, temperately enough, against the "slander, vituperation, and personal abuse" in the Lost Townships articles, and concluded with: —

"I will not take the trouble of inquiring into the reason of all this, but I will take the liberty of requiring a full, positive, and absolute retraction of all offensive allusions used by you in these communications, in relation to my private character and standing as a man, as an apology for the insults conveyed in them. This may prevent consequences which no one will regret more than myself."

Lincoln's reply was singularly lacking in regard to the homely candor that is the particular charm of his correspondence. He wrote: —

"You say you have been informed, through the medium of the editor of the *Journal*, that I am the author of certain articles in that paper which you deem personally abusive of you; and, without stopping to inquire whether I really am the author, or to point out what is offensive in them, you demand an unqualified retraction of all that is offensive, and then proceed to hint at consequences. Now, sir, there is in this so much assumption of facts, and so much of menace as to consequences, that I cannot submit to answer that note any further than I have, and to add, that the consequences to which I suppose you allude would be matter of as great regret to me as it possibly could to you."

Shields rejoined, disavowing any intention of menacing Lincoln, asking whether he had written the articles in question, and repeating his request, if so, for a retraction of the offensive allusions. This letter Lincoln refused to answer unless Shields's first communication were withdrawn; but the demand met with no response.

By this time, the critical phase of the quarrel had been reached. The principals, as well as their representatives, treated one another with the top-lofty dignity which usage immemorial has, for such occasion, established. Lincoln, nevertheless, would gladly have withdrawn from the squabble, if this had been possible without discredit. To one of his friends, Dr. E. H. Merryman, who, with another, hastened to Tremont, in order to stand by him during the affair, he expressed himself as wholly opposed to dueling, and as willing to do anything to avoid a fight, that might not degrade him in the estimation of himself or of his friends.[42] Accordingly, in some instructions which he drew up for the doctor's guidance, he pledged himself, provided all letters were withdrawn and reparation were properly requested, to give this answer: —

"I did write the 'Lost Townships' letter which appeared in the *Journal* of the 2d instant, but had no participation in any form in any other article alluding to you. I wrote that wholly for political effect. I had no intention of injuring your personal or private character or standing as a man or a gentleman; and I did not then think, and do not now think, that that article could produce, or has produced, that effect against you; and had I anticipated such an effect, I would have forborne to write it. And I will add that your conduct toward me, so far as I know, had always been gentlemanly, and that I had no personal pique against you, and no cause for any."

The memorandum then prescribed the conditions under which, if the explanation were not accepted, the writer, as the challenged party, would fight. The meeting was to take place near Alton, on the Missouri side of the river, within the following two or three days.

"Weapons: — Cavalry broadswords of the largest size, precisely equal in all respects and such as now used by the cavalry company at Jacksonville.

"Position: — A plank ten feet long, and from nine to twelve inches broad, to be firmly fixed on edge, on the ground, as the line between us, which neither is to pass his foot over upon forfeit of his life. Next, a line drawn on the ground on either side of said plank and parallel with it, each at the distance of the whole length of the sword and three feet additional from the plank; and the passing of his own such line by either party during the fight shall be deemed a surrender of the contest."

This formidable document was read by Dr. Merryman to Shields's friend General Whiteside, but without the desired result; for, a few days thereafter, two parties, consisting of the principals, their seconds, surgeons, and other attendants, met on an island — Bloody Island,[43] if you please — in the Mississippi, below Alton. Upon reaching the ground, Shields found Lincoln already there, ax in hand and coat thrown off, clearing away the underbrush, for that fateful parallelogram. Before the duel could take place, however, Colonel John J. Hardin and Dr. R. W. English, common friends of the combatants, arrived upon the scene, and patched up a peace by persuading Shields to withdraw his letters and to accept the explanation that Lincoln had offered.

The duelists left the field in amiable spirits toward each other, as may be gathered from the reminiscences of an old resident of Alton, who, with others, stood at the ferry anxiously awaiting the issue. "It was not very long," said he, "until the boat was seen returning to Alton. As it drew near, I saw what was presumably a mortally wounded man lying on the bow of the boat. His shirt appeared to be bathed in blood. I distinguished Jacob Smith, a constable, fanning the supposed victim, vigorously. The people, on the bank, held their breath in suspense, and guesses were freely made as to which of the two men had been so terribly wounded. But suspense was soon turned to chagrin and relief when it transpired that the supposed candidate for another world was nothing more nor less than a log covered with a red shirt. This ruse had been resorted to in order to fool the people on the levee; and it worked to perfection. Lincoln and Shields came off the boat together, chatting in a nonchalant and pleasant manner."[44] Your votaries of "the code" might frown upon that playful device of the bleeding log. It set at naught the niceties of decorum, which are their meat and drink; yet how characteristic it was of at least one of those smiling gentlemen!

All the hot blood engendered by this affair did not, as might be supposed, cool off so readily. Two weeks later, we find Lincoln writing to his friend Speed:—

"You have heard of my duel with Shields, and I have now to inform you that the dueling business still rages in this city. Day before yesterday, Shields challenged Butler,[45] who accepted, and proposed fighting next morning, at sunrise, in Bob Allen's meadow, one hundred yards' distance, with rifles. To this Whiteside, Shields's second, said 'no' because of the law. Thus ended duel No. 2. Yesterday, Whiteside chose to consider himself insulted by Dr. Merryman, so sent him a kind of quasi-challenge, inviting him to meet him at the Planter's House, in St. Louis, on the next Friday, to settle their difficulty. Merryman made me his friend, and sent Whiteside a note, inquiring to know if he meant his note as a challenge, and if so, that he would, according to the law in such case made and provided, prescribe the terms of the meeting."[46]

Duel No. 3, suffice it to say,—for we have had enough of "the dueling business."—was, like No. 1 and No. 2, fought with the tongues and the pens of the combatants to a bloodless finish.

Having made his single appearance as a principal, and then as a second, on the so-called "field of honor," Lincoln quickly recovered his moral equilibrium. He appears to have become ashamed of his share in the quarrel, and to have refrained, for the most part, from discussing it with his friends. Several of them, in fact, record their failures to draw him into conversation on the subject. His partner, Mr. Herndon, reports this one voluntary reference to the duel: —

"I did not intend to hurt Shields unless I did so clearly in self-defence. If it had been necessary, I could have split him from the crown of his head to the end of his backbone." [47]

Lincoln's confidence in his power to vanquish Shields, no less than his freedom from animosity towards him, was further manifested shortly after the meeting, in a few words dropped to Usher F. Linder. As they stood together, near the Danville court-house, Lincoln picked up a lath and went through the broadsword manual. His friend, improving the occasion, asked why broadswords had been chosen for the proposed duel. The man with the lath answered: —

"To tell you the truth, Linder, I did n't want to kill Shields and felt sure I could disarm him, having had about a month to learn the broadsword exercise; and furthermore, I did n't want the damned fellow to kill me, which I rather think he would have done if we had selected pistols." [48]

The ghost of the duel still hovered over the scene. In the spring of the following year, Lincoln closed a letter on politics to Hardin with: —

"I wish you would measure one of the largest of those swords we took to Alton, and write me the length of it, from tip of the point to tip of the hilt, in feet and inches. I have a dispute about the length." [49]

Thereafter, Lincoln's friends respected his desire that the affair should not be spoken of, and it seemed to have been forgotten.

Greatly to Mr. Herndon's surprise, while on his visit in the Eastern States during the spring of 1858, to promote his partner's senatorial ambitions, he was frequently asked for an account of the so-called duel. Upon his return, the fact was reported to Lincoln, who sadly remarked: —

"If all the good things I have ever done are remembered as long and well as my scrape with Shields, it is plain I shall not soon be forgotten."[50]

The "scrape" was not so well remembered by the speaker's enemies as might have been expected. Two years later, the muckrake of a bitter opposition failed — if we may judge from the now available campaign literature of 1860 — to turn up the incident. So the "Party of Moral Ideas" was spared the mortification of defending its candidate's atrocities as a duelist.[51] During the Civil War, the story, having again made its rounds, returned to plague its hero, for the last time. A few weeks before his death, the President, together with Mrs. Lincoln, entertained a distinguished officer of the army. During the conversation, the visitor said: —

"Is it true, Mr. President, as I have heard, that you once went out to fight a duel for the sake of the lady by your side?"

"I do not deny it," answered Mr. Lincoln, with a flushed face, "but if you desire my friendship, you will never mention the circumstance again."[52]

This admission, which indeed was but the grudging half-truth of a man who wished to dispose of a distasteful topic, seems to warrant the oft-repeated claim that Miss Todd was responsible for all the obnoxious articles, and that her lover, to shield her, chivalrously avowed himself to be their author. Here is a pleasing fiction plentifully vouched for, which we should like to accept.[53] The facts, however, — weeds of fact will persist in springing up among the flowers of romance, — leave no ground for doubt as to the authorship of the first and most offensive of the letters; while those same dull realities make short work of the gallantry which, when pressed, merely consisted in acknowledging that authorship.

Still less defensible are the efforts usually made to gloss over Lincoln's conduct, at Shields's expense. The special pleading takes a wide range — as wide as the Mississippi itself, at the mile crossing, where, according to one story, the challenged party had, with grotesque humor, stipulated that the duelists should stand on opposite banks and fight with broadswords.[54] Somewhat on this order is the effort of Dr. Irelan — not by any means a through-thick-and-thin eulogist — to treat the affair as one of Lincoln's jokes. Says he: —

"Mr. Lincoln was absolutely opposed to dueling, and very well knew from the first that there would be no duel in this case. And here is where the ridiculousness of the whole thing appears. The gory Shields and his friends overlooked this entirely. The cavalry broadswords were procured, and these were of from thirty-six to forty inch blades; then, under Mr. Lincoln's requirement, the combatants were not only to stand the length of the two swords apart, but also six feet further, thus actually placing them at least twelve feet apart. With this arrangement, the most they could have done would have been to touch the points of their swords, if Shields could have measured half of that distance with his arm and sword. Lincoln had made these impossible provisions in full view of this funny side of the case. Even if the distance between the men had not been so preposterously great, the poor Irishman would have had no chance without crossing the board, which would have forfeited his life, while the long body and arm of Lincoln might have rendered his own position disagreeable. Mr. Lincoln's conduct in this matter was deliberate and premeditated, and this it was that took from him the odium of stooping to the savage and unchristian 'code.' With him, Mr. Shields's case began in fun, and ended in fun." [55]

A glance at the conditions, however, reveals that the distance of twelve feet mentioned by the Doctor was not to intervene between the combatants, but was, in fact, the length of the ten by twelve foot oblong within which the duelists, separated by the plank "on edge" only, were to fight. Dr. Irelan's misinterpretation of the terms is shared by the historians of Illinois, in whose opinion, also, the position "prescribed for the combatants on the field looks a good deal like the cropping out of one of Lincoln's irrepressible jokes; as if both were placed out of harm's way, and that they might beat the air with their trenchant blades forever and not come within damaging reach of each other." [56]

The fancy for separating the duelists by a river, or even by a dozen feet, does not, of course, extend to all the writers who laugh at poor Shields and his wrongs. The quarrel, in the eyes of one biographer, was "serio-comic"; another terms it "a silly fracas"; while a third dismisses it as "certainly a boyish affair"; still another thinks that "nothing but a tragedy could have prevented its being a farce"; a recent author would have us believe that the challenged party tried to avert a duel "by proposing the most absurd conditions"; and Lincoln's loyal secretaries, in view of the so-called "ludicrousness" of the incident, devote most of their chapter on the subject to the belittling of Shields, without, however, increasing the stature of their hero.[57] The amusing aspects of the story, on which these writers lay so much stress, appear, for the most part, to have escaped Lincoln's own usually keen sense of humor. He had realized, early in the progress of the broil, that he was on the wrong side of it. This alone must have been sufficient to sober him. At all events, as we have seen, he treated the affair seriously enough, and had the grace to be ashamed of his part in it ever afterward. No amount of laughter at Shields, whatever occasion that volatile gentleman may have afforded, relieves Lincoln of the onus which attaches to his attack upon the Auditor and to his acceptance of the challenge.

The difficulty with Shields constituted Lincoln's last personal quarrel. He had run the gamut from that first schoolboy fight with his fists to the preliminaries, at least, of what might have been a serious duel; and with it end our chronicles of his early encounters. Culled from the first thirty-three years of his life, they have been strung together, be it remembered, on the single thread of his masterful nature. Although the nobler, gentler traits have been thus practically disregarded, it would be manifest error to forget that they, too, entered into the fashioning of that strangely woven character, and that they became stronger and deeper as the man developed. Indeed, from this time forth, a mellower tone pervades his behavior.[58] How much of the change was due to the humiliation of the Shields squabble, to Lincoln's marriage with Miss Todd, which followed it by but a few weeks, to the requirements of a higher standing in his profession and in political circles, cannot, of course, be determined. We do know, however, that he never again became involved in a private quarrel. Holding his own — yes, more than holding his own — throughout the warmest controversies and fiercest struggles in his country's history, he is destined, as we shall learn, still to be master among men, to control them as firmly as in the frontier days of *Faustrecht*, and withal, so gently, that they do not know themselves to be controlled. Here is no simple achievement, yet it took the President but a moment once, and that when the turmoil was at its height, to explain the marvel, in part at least, by a simple formula. It was addressed to a young officer, who had been court-martialed for quarreling with one of his fellows: —

"The advice of a father to his son, 'Beware of entrance to a quarrel, but, being in, bear 't that the opposed may beware of thee,' is good, but not the best. Quarrel not at all. No man, resolved to make the most of himself, can spare time for personal contention. Still less can he afford to take all the consequences, including the vitiating of his temper and the loss of self-control. Yield larger things to which you can show no more than equal right; and yield lesser ones, though clearly your own. Better give your path to a dog than be bitten by him in contesting for the right. Even killing the dog would not cure the bite." [59]

A far cry this, from the Lost Townships diatribe and the rendezvous with broadswords on Bloody Island; yet the philosopher of 1862 may not, for all that, be thought less spirited than the Hotspur of 1842. What of true metal rang in the deeds of earlier times was not wanting in later days, though its form, as we shall see, was changed — changed, now and then, almost beyond recognition; for it became tempered and purified, in the fierce heat of a fire that all but consumed a nation.

CHAPTER III

GIANTS, BIG AND LITTLE

THE early encounters and controversies of Lincoln were insignificant when compared to the rivalry that existed, for almost twenty-five years, between him and Stephen A. Douglas. First as enthusiastic adherents of opposing parties, and later as acknowledged leaders of those parties, they so conducted themselves that the orbits of their political ambitions crossed and recrossed each other. The star of Douglas was generally in the ascendant. He became, successively, State's Attorney, member of the Illinois legislature, Register of the Land Office at Springfield, Secretary of State for Illinois, Judge of the Supreme Court of that State, member of Congress, and United States Senator. His rival's planet, on the other hand, showed, during that same period, the comparatively meagre glory of four terms in the State legislature and one in the Lower House of Congress. Yet the inferior light, swinging in season and out, across the pathway of the other, became steadily brighter in the reflected rays of the larger luminary, until suddenly they presented a singular phenomenon. The lesser became the greater, for while the one had grown, the other had diminished; and the rising orb, throwing off at last the borrowed beams, shone by its own intense power — so intense, indeed, that as its splendor spread, the waning star went out in total eclipse.

The political careers of these two men started at about the same time and place. When Lincoln entered upon his first term in the Illinois Assembly at Vandalia, he met in the lobby a shrewd little Vermonter, four years his junior, who, notwithstanding extreme youth and briefness of residence in the West, was conducting among the members of the legislature what proved to be a successful canvass for the office of State's Attorney for the first judicial district. The newcomer was Stephen A. Douglas. Identifying himself with the dominant party, he became as pronounced in his Democracy as Lincoln was in his Whigism. On opposite sides of the next Assembly, — both of them were elected to the legislature of 1836, — they clashed, from time to time, in tactics and debate. The antagonism thus started in Vandalia was transferred the following year to Springfield, where, within a few months of each other, the young men took up their residence. Here differences in character and temperament, rather than in party affiliations, acted as a bar to the friendship, or even to the esteem, that is not uncommon between contending politicians. If Douglas took one side of a question, Lincoln might safely be looked for on the other; and their rivalry soon became a recognized factor in the spirited local contests of the day.

The first of these encounters concerning which any details have been preserved took place during "the hard-cider campaign." At the very beginning of that memorable contest, one night in December, 1839, a group of disputatious young politicians sat around the stove in Joshua F. Speed's store. The argument, which is said to have been mainly between Lincoln and Douglas, was at its warmest when the latter sprang to his feet and said: —

"Gentlemen, this is no place to talk politics. We will discuss the questions publicly with you."

This informal challenge was followed within a few days by a resolution, which Lincoln offered in a meeting of the Whigs, inviting their opponents to a debate. The Democrats, accepting, appointed Stephen A. Douglas, John Calhoun, Josiah Lamborn, and Jesse B. Thomas to meet Stephen T. Logan, Edward D. Baker, Orville H. Browning, and Abraham Lincoln. These champions, for eight

S. A. Douglas

evenings, in the order named, defended and attacked by turns President Van Buren's independent treasury project, with an occasional tilt over the other economic questions on which their respective parties differed. "The great debate," as it was called, drew large audiences at the outset; but by the time Lincoln's evening, the last in the series, arrived, the attendance had considerably diminished. This had a chilling effect upon the speaker, yet he warmed up sufficiently to make what was considered the best address of all — so good, in fact, that it was published as a campaign document, not only in friend Francis's newspaper, but also in pamphlet form.[1] A glance through the speech reveals how keenly, at that time already, the "Sangamon Chief" was on the trail of his pet antagonist. The other Democratic speakers, it is true, were mentioned here and there, in refutation; but to Douglas fell the severest, and by far the largest share of Lincoln's attention. Here is a sample paragraph: —

"I return to another of Mr. Douglas's excuses for the expenditures of 1838, at the same time announcing the pleasing intelligence that this is the last one. He says that ten millions of that year's expenditure was a contingent appropriation, to prosecute an anticipated war with Great Britain on the Maine boundary question. Few words will settle this. First, that the ten millions appropriated was not made till 1839, and consequently could not have been expended in 1838; second, although it was appropriated, it has never been expended at all. Those who heard Mr. Douglas recollect that he indulged himself in a contemptuous expression of pity for me. 'Now he's got me,' thought I. But when he went on to say that five millions of the expenditure of 1838 were payments of the French indemnities, which I knew to be untrue; that five millions had been for the Post-office, which I knew to be untrue; that ten millions had been for the Maine boundary war, which I not only knew to be untrue, but supremely ridiculous also; and when I saw that he was stupid enough to hope that I would permit such groundless and audacious assertions to go unexposed, — I readily consented that, on the score both of veracity and sagacity, the audience should judge whether he or I were the more deserving of the world's contempt."[2]

This utterance was significant. Like the leading motive in the overture to a music-drama, it struck, at the very beginning of the Lincoln-Douglas struggle, a note that was destined to run through many similar scenes, in which these two were to be the principal actors.

During the canvass that followed the debate, Lincoln and Douglas stumped the State in the interests of their respective candidates, with equal enthusiasm.[3] Collisions between them were frequent, for the bearer of the Whig standard lost no opportunity of speaking from the same platform with the Democratic orator. In one of these debates, Lincoln charged Van Buren with having voted at the New York State Constitutional Convention of 1821, for negro suffrage with a property qualification. This Douglas denied. Whereupon, Lincoln, to prove his assertion, read, from Holland's Life of Van Buren, the Wizard of Kinderhook's own statement that he had so voted. Thus neatly cornered, "Douglas got mad," as the story goes, and jumped up to dispose of both the charge and the evidence, in characteristic fashion. Snatching the volume from the reader's hand, he exclaimed, "Damn such a book!" and hurled it among the audience.[4] In another of their encounters, Douglas had no occasion for so desperate a defence. On the contrary, he forced the fighting too ably for his antagonist. "Lincoln," says a friend of those days, "did not come up to the requirements of the occasion. He was conscious of his failure, and I never saw any man so much distressed. He begged to be permitted to try it again, and was reluctantly indulged; and in the next effort he transcended our highest expectations. I never heard, and never expect to hear, such a triumphant vindication as he then gave of Whig measures or policy."[5] But the victory of the canvass, so far as it concerned our two young campaigners, rested with Douglas. His opponent, it is true, was elected to the Assembly; yet the five electoral votes of Illinois, the real prize of the contest, remained in the Democratic column.

The next important conflict between the rivals was in a widely different field — as different, indeed, as hearts are from ballots. Yet love and politics — witness the Shields affair — were not so far apart as they might have been, in the Springfield of 1840. At that time, Miss Mary Todd, pretty, talented, and vivacious, had recently come from her Kentucky home to live with her sister, Mrs. Ninian W. Edwards. The hospitalities of the house were naturally extended by Mr. Edwards, one of the "Long Nine," to the leader of his delegation, so that Lincoln was a frequent visitor. He paid court to the fascinating little woman from his native State, and speedily became her accepted suitor. Lincoln's success, no less than the lady's charms, fanned the spirit of contention that already existed between him and Douglas. The little Vermonter, dashing and comely, followed his ungainly antagonist into the lists to dispute with him, as vigorously as in their political contests, the possession of this precious trophy. How the fight was conducted cannot — unfortunately for the romance of it — be told with the exactness of detail that usually makes such episodes entertaining. Says one old resident of Springfield: —

"As a society man, Douglas was infinitely more accomplished, more attractive, and influential than Lincoln; and that he should supplant the latter in the affections of the proud and aristocratic Miss Todd is not to be marveled at. He was unremitting in his attentions to the lady, promenaded the streets arm-in-arm with her — frequently passing Lincoln — and, in every way, made plain his intention to become the latter's rival."

This was merely — so some said — a flirtation on the part of Miss Todd to tease her lover. Others went so far as to say that Douglas made a proposal of marriage and was refused, "on account of his bad morals." According to still another account, she grew to prefer him, and would have accepted his offer if she had not given her promise to Lincoln. "The unfortunate attitude she felt bound to maintain between these two young men," relates the writer of this version, "ended in a spell of sickness. Douglas, still hopeful, was warm in the race; but the lady's physician, her brother-in-law, Dr. William Wallace, to whom she confided the real cause of her illness, saw Douglas and induced him to end his pursuit, which he did with great reluctance." So much for the doubtful incidents of the contest; but what of the result? Douglas withdrew, and Lincoln, after an otherwise not untroubled courtship, led Miss Todd to the altar.[6]

The private passage of arms between our politicians did not, of course, lessen their public antagonism. Yet, during the decade following the marriage, they had, it appears, no noteworthy encounters. This may have been due, in part at least, to the fact that Lincoln, diligently practicing his profession, found less time than previously for politics. He did, it is true, participate in conventions and campaigns — even emerging into public life, in 1847, for one term in Congress; but there is no evidence that these activities brought him into personal conflict with his brilliant adversary. Moreover, the uninterrupted rise of Douglas, during this same period, from the Illinois Supreme Court Bench to Congress, and thence to the United States Senate, carried him somewhat out of Lincoln's range. As the latter took his seat in the Lower House, the former entered upon his career in the Upper. The one, at the expiration of his term, returned to Springfield and the small-fry litigation of the Eighth Circuit, without having achieved distinction; the other soon became a figure of national importance.

Each success of the man whom he regarded as his particular rival added a pang to the ex-member's disappointment. The trophy of Miltiades would not let Themistocles sleep; and Lincoln, though he had come to look upon political affairs with comparative indifference, could not take his eyes off Douglas. So it happened that during the presidential canvass of 1852, when the Senator opened his stumping tour of the States, at Richmond, in a speech that was extensively republished, Lincoln obtained permission from the Scott Club of Springfield to deliver an answer, under its auspices.[7] The effort was not creditable. Depressed by the hopelessness of the Whig cause in Illinois, and carried away by his jealousy of Douglas, he descended to a tone unworthy of himself or of the occasion. Referring to the Richmond address, he said: —

"This speech has been published with high commendations in at least one of the Democratic papers in this State, and I suppose it has been and will be in most of the others. When I first saw it and read it, I was reminded of old times, when Judge Douglas was not so much greater man than all the rest of us, as he is now, — of the Harrison campaign twelve years ago, when I used to hear and try to answer many of his speeches; and believing that the Richmond speech, though marked with the same species of 'shirks and quirks' as the old ones, was not marked with any greater ability, — I was seized with a strange inclination to attempt an answer to it; and this inclination it was that prompted me to seek the privilege of addressing you on this occasion."[8]

Like the speaker's one failure during that very Harrison campaign, this defeat — as his friends regarded it — in the Pierce-Scott contest was destined to be followed by brilliant victories. But not at once, for Douglas was still rising toward the zenith of his power, and Lincoln's hour had not yet struck.

The "Little Giant," as the admirers of the Senator from Illinois fondly called him, had been a candidate, at Baltimore, for the Democratic nomination to the presidency, which had fallen, by way of compromise, to Franklin Pierce. That gentleman owed his selection largely to the bitterness of the struggle between the "Old Fogies," under such favorites as Cass, Marcy, and Buchanan, on the one hand, and "Young America," championed by Douglas, on the other. The youthful leader, though he had not himself attained the prize, had been strong enough to keep his powerful competitors from getting it. Here was glory enough for a first attempt, and Douglas emerged from the Convention still on the high-road to the White House. That road had, for many years, wound through the Southern States. It was dotted with the headstones of presidential aspirants, who had fallen beneath the slaveholder's whip; but surely this adroit politician, stepping off so firmly, would not fall. He advanced steadily enough while the growing differences between North and South could be turned into the primrose paths of compromise. Not only had the measures that secured the so-called Compromise of 1850 his support, but he had, at the same time, solemnly reaffirmed the great Missouri Compromise itself. "It had its origin," said he, "in the hearts of all patriotic men, who desired to preserve and perpetuate the blessings of our glorious Union — an origin akin to that of the Constitution of the United States, conceived in the same spirit of fraternal affection, and calculated to remove forever the danger which seemed to threaten, at some distant day, to sever the social bond of union. All the evidences of public opinion, at that day, seemed to indicate that this Compromise had been canonized in the hearts of the American people, as a sacred thing which no ruthless hand would ever be reckless enough to disturb."[9] Yet, within somewhat over four years, the speaker himself, of all men in the world, was guilty of that sacrilege.[10] At the command of the South, his own hand violated the hallowed instrument. The Compromise had served its turn — at least for the Slave States. Having enjoyed the benefits allotted to them by the compact, they viewed with alarm the prospect that the Free States were about to come into their share of it. This was to be prevented at all hazards. The lash cracked above the head of Douglas. He promptly responded, in his Kansas-Nebraska Bill, with the fateful amendment which declared the slavery restrictions of the Compromise "inoperative and void."

The storm of indignation, aroused in the North by the passage of the bill, swept its author home in the autumn of 1854 to defend himself before his constituents.[11] The people of Chicago, whom he first tried to address, gathered in an angry multitude and refused to hear him;[12] but elsewhere throughout the State, in the so-called Anti-Nebraska as well as in the Nebraska districts, his popularity secured to him large and respectful audiences. This tour was ostensibly in the interests of the party's State and Congressional tickets. In reality, however, it involved a strenuous bid for the endorsement of Douglas himself. His colleague, General Shields, who had supported him in the Senate, was to stand for reëlection before the next legislature. Hence the votes about to be cast, particularly those for members of that body, would afford the best immediate test as to whether or not he of the "ruthless hand" was sustained by the people.

With all his wonted skill and energy, Douglas threw himself into the struggle. Improving the opportunity offered by the large gathering of voters and politicians, at the State Agricultural Fair, in Springfield, he presented himself at the capitol, on the opening day, and made a speech. Like most of his utterances, it was specious but attractive. To answer it effectually would require ability of no mean order, and, as if by common consent of the several Anti-Nebraska elements, the task was assigned to his old antagonist, Abraham Lincoln. This selection appears, in fact, to have been made before Douglas had spoken. "I will mention," said the Senator in his opening remarks to the audience which crowded the hall of the State House, "that it is understood by some gentlemen that Mr. Lincoln, of this city, is expected to answer me. If this is the understanding, I wish that Mr. Lincoln would step forward and let us arrange some plan upon which to carry out this discussion."[13] Mr. Lincoln, as he happened to be absent at the moment, did not step forward then; but, on the following day, in the same place and before an equally large assemblage, he took a step forward that must have galled the great man's kibe. Aroused by the moral, no less than by the political obliquity of Douglas's course, Lincoln arose above the petty personalities which had disfigured his Scott Club address, and delivered a speech that evoked the praise of even the Senator's supporters. Douglas himself, as his frequent interruptions of the speaker indicated, was greatly disconcerted by the unexpected sweep and strength of the reply. Moreover, in his excitement and anger, the two hours before supper-time left to him for rejoinder were occupied to so little purpose that he closed with a promise to resume in the evening. Evening came and so did the audience, but not the "Little Giant." Whether he had tumbled into one of the seven-league boots that was putting a comfortable distance between him and the big giant, contemporary history saith not. It does relate that when he failed to return, his disappointed auditors drew the inevitable conclusion — and so may we.[14]

That the Senator should retrieve, unopposed, in other parts of the State, the ground he had lost in Springfield, was of course not on the program of the Anti-Nebraska leaders. They urged Lincoln to follow Douglas until, as one of them expressed it, he "ran him into a hole or made him halloo, 'Enough!'" Their champion was eager enough for pursuit, but to the "Little Giant," the prospect of continuing the combat had "no relish of salvation in 't." Douglas was cordial to his opponent when they met, a few days later, in Bloomington; but as soon as further debates were suggested, he became greatly irritated. "It looks to me," said he to Jesse W. Fell, who had made the proposition, "like dogging a man all over the State. If Mr. Lincoln wants to make a speech, he had better get a crowd of his own; for I most respectfully decline to hold a discussion with him."[15] To persist in this refusal, among a people whose rude sense of chivalry still delighted in the test of man to man, would have cost Douglas much of his hard-earned prestige. So we find him, twelve days after the Springfield debate, again sharing the platform with Lincoln — this time, in Peoria. Here, as at the Capital, the Whig's ambition to address large audiences — we say nothing of his confidence in his powers — led him to be content with one speech, while the Democrat had two, the opening and the close. Concerning this arrangement Lincoln quaintly said in his introduction: —

"I doubt not but you have been a little surprised to learn that I have consented to give one of his high reputation and known ability this advantage of me. Indeed, my consenting to it, though reluctant, was not wholly unselfish, for I suspected, if it were understood that the Judge was entirely done, you Democrats would leave and not hear me; but by giving him the close, I felt confident you would stay for the fun of hearing him skin me."[16]

But it proved, as they say in the East, to be "the other way round." Douglas got the flaying, and no one realized this more keenly than he himself. Going to his antagonist, after the meeting, — so one story runs, — he said:

"Lincoln, you understand this question of prohibiting slavery in the Territories better than all the opposition in the Senate of the United States. I cannot make anything by debating it with you. You, Lincoln, have here and at Springfield given me more trouble than all the opposition in the Senate combined."[17]

Then, throwing himself upon the other's magnanimity, he begged him to discontinue the pursuit. According to another tale, Douglas made a feigned illness the ground for his request.[18] At all events, the Senator's discomfiture, whether mental or physical, disarmed Lincoln. He granted the truce proposed by Douglas — both to abandon the field and to return to their respective homes. Accordingly, when, on the following day, they arrived at Lacon, where the next debate was to take place, Douglas excused himself from speaking, on the ground of hoarseness, and Lincoln declined to take advantage of his "indisposition." Thereupon, they separated, Lincoln going directly home, as had been agreed; but Douglas stopped at Princeton, where a chance meeting with Owen Lovejoy betrayed him into a violation of the compact.[19] This breach of faith should be borne in mind by him who would comprehend the characters of these adversaries; yet the little great man in retreat and crying, "Hold, enough!" while the big one stays his hand, is a still more significant spectacle.

The election that ensued was virtually a defeat for Douglas.[20] He beheld the majority by which he had twice been sent to the United States Senate crumble away; and when, during the following winter, the new legislature met in joint session to elect General Shields's successor, the choice lay in the hands of the Anti-Nebraska members. Their favorite, consistently enough, was Lincoln.[21] The champion who had so neatly unhorsed the Nebraska man, himself, on the local field, should have been granted his desire — so thought most of them — to continue the fight, in the national arena. Five of their number, however, as pronounced in their Democracy as in their opposition to Douglas, could not bring themselves to vote for a Whig. They supported Lyman Trumbull, while the Douglas Democrats voted first for Shields and then for Governor Joel A. Matteson.[22] After a number of ballots with varying but indecisive results, when Matteson's election became imminent, Lincoln directed his followers to unite upon Trumbull, who thus won the day. The new Senator, though in times gone by a political opponent of the Whig leader, now agreed with him in uncompromising antagonism toward Douglas and his Kansas-Nebraska legislation.

That was enough for Lincoln. If he himself might not follow Douglas into the Senate, the keen edge of his disappointment was tempered by the consolation of sending, in his stead, a David who was even less welcome than he to the diminutive Goliath.[23] Indeed, no sooner had the brilliant Trumbull taken his seat than he opened the attack that gave Douglas so much trouble; and throughout the stormy sessions which followed, the senior Senator from Illinois was sure to find his colleague in the van of his enemies — a constant reminder of that other inveterate opponent at home.

Busy as Lincoln was at the bar during the next few years, no move of the Democratic leader escaped his attention. When Douglas, still bidding for the presidential nomination that had twice slipped through his fingers, cast a defence of the Dred Scott decision into the southern scale beside the repeal of the Compromise, the speech did not long remain unanswered by his vigilant critic. Both addresses were made in Springfield, during June, 1857. At the time, the Senator's term had almost two years still to run, yet Lincoln's fancy appears to have carried him for a moment away from the important issues under discussion[24] to the day when Douglas could again be brought to book. Said he: —

"Three years and a half ago, Judge Douglas brought forward his famous Nebraska Bill. The country was at once in a blaze. He scorned all opposition, and carried it through Congress. Since then he has seen himself superseded in a presidential nomination by one indorsing the general doctrine of his measure, but at the same time standing clear of the odium of its untimely agitation and its gross breach of national faith; and he has seen that successful rival constitutionally elected, not by the strength of friends, but by the division of adversaries, being in a popular minority of nearly four hundred thousand votes.[25] He has seen his chief aids in his own State, Shields and Richardson, politically speaking, successively tried, convicted, and executed for an offence not their own, but his.[26] And now he sees his own case standing next on the docket for trial."[27]

The speaker might have added that when the trial took place, he hoped to conduct the prosecution.

Douglas gauged the full measure of his peril. He needed no Lincoln to point out that the Democracy of Illinois would not follow even his lead into the slave-holders' camp. And, if he should fail to carry his own State, what support could he expect from his party throughout the nation? At the same time, that party, or rather the dominating faction thereof, was committing itself more unreservedly, at every step, to the slavery cause. In this dilemma, Douglas seized the horn that presented itself first. He determined to preserve, above all things, his leadership at home, and, thus strengthened, to maintain it thereafter, as best he might, abroad. To accomplish the one purpose, without entirely losing sight of the other, he devised a straddle — "the great principle," as he called it, "of popular sovereignty." According to this doctrine, the people of a State or a Territory were free to have slavery or not as they might choose. Of course such a choice, so far as it would operate to exclude slavery from the Territories, was virtually barred by the Dred Scott decision, of which Douglas had warmly approved; but the inconsistency of his attitude gave him no concern, as long as it left him, like Hosea Biglow's "satty's factory" candidate, "frontin' South by North." That is to say, fairly on the track to the Senate, in 1858, and not turned too far away from the road that might lead to the White House, in 1860. When, in the winter of 1857–58, however, President Buchanan and other Democratic leaders sought to obtain the admission of Kansas into the Union, with a pro-slavery constitution that had not been properly submitted to the people of the Territory, Douglas found himself at the parting of the ways. Support of the scheme involved the surrender of "popular sovereignty," and his political ruin in Illinois, as well as in the other Northern States; opposition to it threatened similar disaster for his hopes in the South. With prompt decision, he took his stand against the President. Whereupon ensued the bitter struggle over Kansas that for a brief hour revealed Douglas at his best. To tell how brilliantly he fought in the Senate, for "the great principle," how manfully he bore himself under the heavy hand of the administration, how courageously he braved the abuse of old friends, and with what dignity he received the praise of lifelong enemies, would take us off the line of our narrative. Yet all this came near to having an important bearing on the fortunes of that particular enemy with whom we are most concerned.

Lincoln, as election time drew near, saw with chagrin not only that Douglas had recovered his popularity among northern Democrats, but that some of the most influential of the Republicans, also, began to regard him with favor. Such leaders of the new party as Greeley, Bowles, Wilson, Colfax, Banks, Burlingame, and Blair, dazzled by the hope of gaining so powerful an ally, counseled the Illinois Republicans to unite with the Douglas Democrats in returning him to the Senate.[28] This alliance would have committed the anti-slavery cause, in an important State, to the keeping of a politician who, to use his own phrase, cared not whether slavery was "voted down or voted up," and whose entire career, notwithstanding his course in the Kansas affair, should have rendered him an object of distrust to the Republican Party.[29] Its aid of Douglas, moreover, at the time, would have involved the gross betrayal of its own local leader; for Lincoln's sacrifices — to say nothing of his ability and his services — entitled his candidacy to the undivided support of his party. That this support should, even for a moment, be disputed with him by one against whom he and most of his followers had, all their lives, been arrayed, is its own commentary on the adroitness of Douglas.[30] So real seemed the danger that

Lincoln became greatly troubled. He was particularly disturbed over the course pursued by the editor of the New York *Tribune*. "I think Greeley," said he to his partner, Mr. Herndon, "is not doing me right. His conduct, I believe, savors a little of injustice. I am a true Republican and have been tried already in the hottest part of the anti-slavery fight, and yet I find him taking up Douglas, a veritable dodger, — once a tool of the South, now its enemy, — and pushing him to the front. He forgets that when he does that he pulls me down at the same time. I fear Greeley's attitude will damage me with Sumner, Seward, Wilson, Phillips, and other friends in the East."[31] Thereupon the faithful Herndon hastily journeyed toward the seaboard to reclaim the wise men of the East from following a misleading star. His mission was not entirely successful, for he found some of them wandering in a haze of expediency which all his earnest pleas in behalf of principle failed to dispel. Meanwhile, however, the atmosphere was clearing at home. Illinois Republicans could not bring themselves to "place any reliance," as Seward expressed it, "on a man so slippery as Douglas," and when their State Convention met at Springfield, on the 16th of June, 1858, they formally declared for the man on whom they could rely. Amidst great enthusiasm, and without a dissenting voice, was passed the resolution: —

"That Hon. Abraham Lincoln is our first and only choice for United States Senator to fill the vacancy about to be created by the expiration of Mr. Douglas's term of office."[32]

As Douglas had, with equal unanimity, been endorsed, though not actually nominated, eight weeks before, by the Democratic Convention, the two men now, for the first time in the course of their long rivalry, faced each other to do battle for the same high office.

With characteristic eagerness, Lincoln lost no time in beginning the contest. The evening of the day on which his nomination had been made, he addressed the

Convention in the speech which has since become famous because of its radical development of the text, "A house divided against itself cannot stand." But what at this moment interests us more than the issues under discussion is the fact that the speaker devoted most of his attention to his opponent, in person. Douglas subservient to the slave-owners, or Douglas in revolt against them, was pictured alike unworthy of northern confidence. Moreover, his recently acquired popularity among the Republicans, though it had signally failed to influence the Convention, appears still to have worried Lincoln. "There are those," said he, after speaking of the party's ambition to overthrow the southern régime, "who denounce us openly to their own friends, and yet whisper us softly that Senator Douglas is the aptest instrument there is with which to effect that object. They wish us to infer all from the fact that he now has a little quarrel with the present head of the dynasty, and that he has regularly voted with us on a single point upon which he and we have never differed. They remind us that he is a great man, and that the largest of us are very small ones. Let this be granted. But 'a living dog is better than a dead lion.' Judge Douglas, if not a dead lion for this work, is at least a caged and toothless one." [33]

A lion, indeed, but not of the sort described by Lincoln, did the people, three weeks later, make of the Democratic leader. Returning home to Chicago, with the glory of his gallant fight against the administration still fresh about him, he opened his canvass there on the evening of July 9, at a magnificent public reception. The speech made by the Senator on that occasion, from a balcony of the Tremont House, was a vigorous reply to Lincoln, of whom, in the flush of his pride, he spoke patronizingly as "a kind, amiable, and intelligent gentleman." [34] The speaker might have added "alert" to this catalogue of good qualities, for Lincoln was present at the meeting, and when Douglas had concluded, he announced, in answer to calls for a speech, that he would reply from the same place, on the following evening. At the time appointed the audience for the most part returned, but Douglas, not deigning to do so, went to a theatre instead. When he spoke in Bloomington, on the 16th of July, Lincoln was again a watchful auditor, and the Senator's speech in Springfield, the next day, was followed, within a few hours, by his opponent's rejoinder to the Bloomington address.[35] This continued, meeting after meeting. Yet, however closely Lincoln pressed Douglas, it soon became evident that the "Little Giant," with his plausible oratory and cleverly managed campaign machinery, had made the better start. Then Lincoln, recalling his old tactics at close quarters, challenged Douglas to a series of debates. In response, the latter, having accepted the proposition, stipulated that there were to be seven meetings, at places and on dates specified by him.[36] The terms, as further laid down by Douglas, gave him the advantage of opening and closing the series, of speaking eleven times to his antagonist's ten, and of having four openings and closes to Lincoln's three. That "amiable gentleman," however, was not entirely a stranger, as we have seen, to the idea of giving the great man odds, so he promptly accepted the conditions.[37]

What manner of man Stephen A. Douglas had become since those primitive Vandalia days, when he started with Lincoln in the race for political fame and fortune, is worthy of notice at this, a critical point in their course. The slight, boyish figure which, in 1834, had struck the big-boned young member from Sangamon as that of "the least man" in his experience, though no taller by 1858, had materially developed otherwise. A sturdy, thick-set frame, with broad shoulders and deep chest, gave evidence of physical vigor as clearly as the massive head, high forehead, flashing blue eyes, and firm, expressive mouth indicated intellectual strength. Whatever the shrewd, bold mind might plan, the body, with its extraordinary energy and powers of endurance, could evidently be relied on to carry out. Thus doubly fortified by nature, Douglas was an opponent to compel respect. Moreover, the remarkable public career which had borne him, while still young, from unfriended obscurity to the leadership of a great party, may be said to have schooled him in all the arts and accomplishments that make such a man formidable. With an exhaustive knowledge of our political history, and a grasp no less comprehensive of the problems that arise in party management, was combined an insight, well-nigh precise, into the shifting currents of popular favor. This store of wisdom was paralleled by the skill with which it was applied. No obstacle was long suffered to obstruct Douglas's progress. Questions of principle, of measures, and of men were all weighed alike in the balance of an ambition as inordinate as it was selfish. Yet, so artfully did he manage, that people, mistaking the self-seeking politician for the patriotic statesman, crowned him with successive honors.

A member of the Illinois legislature at the age of 23, State Supreme Court Judge at 28, Congressman at 30, United States Senator at 34, and a powerfully supported candidate for presidential nomination at the uncommonly youthful age of 39, Douglas was generally acknowledged, even some years before the period at which we have arrived, to be the ablest, as well as the most cherished, of the Democratic leaders. Indeed, a considerable element in the party looked for guidance to him, and to him alone. Through fair weather and foul it had clung to the man with a devotion that has not been surpassed in the history of the organization. For Douglas knew, as possibly but one other American ever did, how to captivate at once the heads and the hearts of the young men. They admired his sagacity, dash, fearlessness, and indomitable will; they loved him for the ardent, sunny temperament that manifested itself with equal readiness in a warm greeting or a personal service, in the reckless expenditure of his means, or in the good-fellowship of a convivial circle; but above all they exulted, as did many of their elders, over the power of his eloquence. Douglas was an orator by nature. He owed little or nothing of his triumphs in the Senate and on the stump to scholarship. Discarding humor, flights of fancy, and rhetorical ornament generally, he carried his hearers whithersoever he would on the flood of his earnest logic. A flexible voice, suited to his terse, vigorous English, and a manner which seemed to stamp every word as the utterance of an oracle, imparted to what he said all the force of which the statement was capable. Even the most audacious sophisms or perversions of fact — for Douglas never hesitated at either — owed a certain plausibility to this impressive delivery. It was in running discussion, however, rather than in the making of a formal speech — in spontaneous declamation, passionate invective, and impromptu reply, that he particularly excelled. Quick to seize upon the weakness in an opponent's argument, adroit at making the most of the strength in his own, expert in all the wiles and stratagems of controversy, unscrupulous about employing them to confound an adversary or mislead his hearers, he was conceded to be the best off-hand debater in the Senate during one of its brilliant epochs. The Upper House at the time held not a few orators who wrote their drafts on the bank of eloquence for larger amounts than Douglas could; but the flushest of them lacked so much ready change as he had always about him. His encounters with Sumner, Seward, Chase, Everett, Crittenden, Trumbull, Fessenden, Hale, Wilson, as well as other parliamentarians of their class, whether he met them singly or sustained an assault in force, had gained for him an almost unbroken record of forensic victories. These achievements had fixed the attention of the nation upon him as upon no other politician of the day. Small wonder that a man of his caliber grew arrogant. Recognizing no will but his own, he came to look upon opposition of any kind with ill-controlled passion. If to all this, finally, is added that twelve years in the Senate had led him to regard his seat as peculiarly his own, we may form some conception of what Lincoln undertook when, in the summer of 1858, he challenged Douglas to debate for the place.

No one realized to what heights Douglas had climbed more clearly than he who had pursued him so persistently. Lincoln's admission, not long before, of how wide a gap lay between them, makes a pathetic contrast to his disparagements of former days. "Twenty-two years ago," said he, "Judge Douglas and I first became acquainted. We were both young then — he a trifle younger than I. Even then we were both ambitious — I, perhaps quite as much as he. With me, the race of ambition has been a failure — a flat failure; with him, it has been one of splendid success. His name fills the nation, and is not unknown even in foreign lands. I affect no contempt for the high eminence he has reached. So reached that the oppressed of my species might have shared with me in the elevation, I would rather stand on that eminence than wear the richest crown that ever pressed a monarch's brow."[38] In an entirely different vein, though not less forcibly, Lincoln pointed out, at the beginning of the canvass, some of Douglas's further advantages over him. Said he: —

"Senator Douglas is of world-wide renown. All the anxious politicians of his party, or who have been of his party for years past, have been looking upon him as certainly, at no distant day, to be the President of the United States. They have seen in his round, jolly, fruitful face, post-offices, land-offices, marshalships, and cabinet appointments, chargéships, and foreign missions, bursting and sprouting out in wonderful exuberance, ready to be laid hold of by their greedy hands. And as they have been gazing upon this attractive picture so long, they cannot, in the little distraction that has taken place in the party, bring themselves to give up the charming hope; but with greedier anxiety they rush about him, sustain him, and give him marches, triumphal entries, and receptions beyond what even in the days of his highest prosperity they could have brought about in his favor. On the contrary, nobody has ever expected me to be President. In my poor, lean, lank face, nobody has ever seen that any cabbages were sprouting out. These are disadvantages all, taken together, that the Republicans labor under. *We* have to fight this battle upon principle, and upon principle alone." [39]

Whether much principle, by the way, could be introduced into a conflict with Douglas, the speaker, after twenty odd years of campaigning against him, was still in grave doubt. Having sounded the depths and shallows of his character, Lincoln had learned that when Douglas swore upon his honor — his political honor, at least — he was, as Master Touchstone might have said, not forsworn. Lincoln also knew how subtly this moral laxness wound, like a black thread, through the man's comings and goings; and how, in the stress of debate, sophistry, trickery, even falsehood were employed to establish his own position, or hopelessly to befog that of his opponent. It was in reference to this line of conduct that Lincoln once said: —

"Judge Douglas is playing cuttlefish, a small species of fish that has no mode of defending itself, when pursued, except by throwing out a black fluid, which makes the water so dark the enemy cannot see it, and thus it escapes."

Speaking, on another occasion, of the Judge's more dangerous qualities, he said: —

"It is impossible to get the advantage of him. Even if he is worsted, he so bears himself that the people are bewildered and uncertain as to who has the better of it." [40] The impossible, then, is what Lincoln was about to undertake.

As for Douglas, his ostentatious air of confidence in himself and his patronizing bearing toward Lincoln, on the stump, hardly manifested his real attitude. Upon receiving, at the Capital, a despatch, announcing that his old opponent had been chosen to run against him for the Senate, he had said to the group of Republican representatives gathered about him to hear it read: —

"Well, gentlemen, you have nominated a very able and a very honest man." [41]

A more emphatic, if not so dignified, form of the comment was that in which it had been expressed, privately, on several occasions: —

"Of all the damned Whig rascals about Springfield, Abe Lincoln is the ablest and most honest." [42]

Discussing the nominee with John W. Forney, Douglas had observed: —

"I shall have my hands full. He is the strong man of his party — full of wit, facts, dates — and the best stump-speaker, with his droll ways and dry jokes, in the West. He is as honest as he is shrewd; and if I beat him, my victory will be hardly won." [43]

In view of these opinions and of the previous encounters upon which they were based, it is not surprising that Douglas was loath now, even more than four years before, to meet Lincoln in debate. When the challenge was received, the Democratic leader said to certain of his political friends: —

"I do not feel, between you and me, that I want to go into this debate. The whole country knows me and has me measured. Lincoln, as regards myself, is comparatively unknown,[44] and if he gets the best of this debate, — and I want to say he is the ablest man the Republicans have got, — I shall lose everything and Lincoln will gain everything. Should I win, I shall gain but little. I do not want to go into a debate with Abe." [45]

Moreover, after agreeing to the proposed meetings — for there was no escape from them in 1858, any more than there had been in 1854 — he declared to some of his supporters who spoke slightingly of his antagonist: —

"Gentlemen, you do not know Mr. Lincoln. I have known him long and well, and I know that I shall have anything but an easy task. I assure you I would rather meet any other man in the country, in this joint-debate, than Abraham Lincoln."[46]

Whatever disquietude Douglas manifested, in these few instances, was not shared by his followers. Looking forward to the contest with assurance of success, they set no bounds, as was their wont, to partisan enthusiasm. Amidst their noisy demonstrations were heard boasts that Douglas would "use up and utterly demolish" Lincoln, that the country would shortly be treated to the spectacle of "the Little Giant chawing up Old Abe," and the like.[47] These things naturally cast a damper over Lincoln's friends. Somewhat disheartened, at the outset, by the prestige of Douglas's brilliant career, as well as by his unquestioned ability, they came to regard the approaching trial of strength with forebodings that were poorly concealed from their champion himself. He was, in fact, keenly alive to this lack of confidence. It showed itself in the comments of the Republican press, no less than in the talk of his supporters. One of them, Judge H. W. Beckwith of Danville, happened to greet him, on the street in Springfield, shortly before the first meeting. Inquiry as to the state of things in Vermilion County evoked the statement by the Judge that the leader's friends there awaited the coming debate with deep concern. This appeared to move Lincoln. The pained expression that passed over his face, however, quickly gave place to one of resolution. Then, in his half-serious, half-jocular way, he said, as he seated himself upon the steps of the Chenery House, before which they stood: —

"Sit down. I have a moment to spare and will tell you a story. You have seen two men about to fight?"

"Yes, many times."

"Well, one of them brags about what he means to do. He jumps high in the air, cracking his heels together, smites his fists, and wastes his breath trying to scare somebody. You see the other fellow, he says not a word" — here the speaker became very earnest and repeated, "you see the other man says not a word. His arms are at his side, his fists are closely doubled up, his head is drawn to the shoulder, and his teeth are set firm together. He is saving his wind for the fight, and as sure as it comes off he will win it, or die a-trying." [48]

There spoke the victor of Clary's Grove. He had learned that the principles of mastery do not vary, whether they are applied to a backwoods scuffle or a great political controversy.

The Lincoln-Douglas debates, as they are called, were the most remarkable exhibitions of their kind in the history of the country. Never before nor since have two of its citizens engaged in a series of public discussions which involved questions of equal importance. Personal and purely local differences were overshadowed, from the very beginning, by what the disputants had to say on issues so momentous that they were destined, within a few years, to plunge the country into civil war. Lincoln, accordingly, did not greatly exaggerate when he spoke, at Quincy, of the seven meetings as "the successive acts of a drama to be enacted not merely in the face of audiences like this, but in the face of the nation and, to some extent, in the face of the world." [49] To reconstruct these stirring scenes, in pen pictures, almost half a century after the curtain was rung down, is as much beyond our power as to do justice by the actors, in any summary of their speeches. Only a careful reading of the 263 pages in which the debates have been preserved will convey an adequate idea of how brilliantly, from the intellectual point of view, both conducted themselves. Now Douglas appears to prevail, now Lincoln. One page persuades us that slavery is constitutional, and that each commonwealth should be allowed to have "the institution," or not, as it elects. We turn the leaf, and lo! we are convinced that slavery is wrong, and ought, at least, to be restricted. The questions at issue in the debates, however, — their morals and their politics, — lie beyond the scope of our present inquiry. Look we then to the debaters themselves.

The jaunty manner in which Douglas had talked down to Lincoln, at the commencement of the canvass, in Chicago, had not left him when he opened the joint-meetings, in Ottawa. At some of the intervening Democratic rallies, he had, it is true, so far forgotten himself as to indulge in violent utterances against his opponent; but when they stood face to face again, he patted him on the back, as before.[50] And the caress was not the less gentle because it came between blows aimed at Lincoln's political record. Said Douglas: —

"In the remarks I have made on this platform, and the position of Mr. Lincoln upon it, I mean nothing personally disrespectful or unkind to that gentleman. I have known him for nearly twenty-five years. There were many points of sympathy between us when we first got acquainted. We were both comparatively boys, and both struggling with poverty in a strange land. I was a school-teacher in the town of Winchester, and he a flourishing grocery-keeper in the town of Salem. He was more successful in his occupation than I was in mine, and hence more fortunate in this world's goods. Lincoln is one of those peculiar men who perform with admirable skill everything which they undertake. I made as good a school-teacher as I could, and when a cabinet-maker I made a good bedstead and tables, although my old boss said I succeeded better with bureaus and secretaries than with anything else; but I believe that Lincoln was always more successful in business than I, for his business enabled him to get into the legislature. I met him there, however, and had sympathy with him, because of the uphill struggle we both had in life. He was then just as good at telling an anecdote as now. He could beat any of the boys wrestling, or running a foot-race, in pitching quoits, or tossing a copper; could ruin more liquor than all the boys of the town together, and the dignity and impartiality with which he presided at a horse-race or fist-fight excited the admiration and won the praise of everybody that was present and participated. I sympathized with him because he was struggling with difficulties, and so was I. Mr. Lincoln served with me in the legislature in 1836, when we both retired, and he subsided, or became submerged, and he was lost sight of as a public man for some years. In 1846, when Wilmot introduced his celebrated proviso and the Abolition tornado swept over the country, Lincoln again turned up as a member of Congress from the Sangamon district. I was then in the Senate of the United States, and was glad to welcome my old friend and companion."[51]

But the "old friend and companion," when he arose to reply, was in no mood for compliments. A bit of sarcasm was his only reference to the other's patronage.

"As the judge had complimented me," said he, "with these pleasant titles (I must confess to my weakness), I was a little 'taken,' for it came from a great man. I was not very much accustomed to flattery, and it came the sweeter to me. I was rather like the Hoosier with the gingerbread, when he said he reckoned he loved it better than any other man, and got less of it. As the Judge had so flattered me, I could not make up my mind that he meant to deal unfairly with me."[52]

It was a matter of fact, however, that Douglas had throughout, with the artfulness in which he knew no peer, so misrepresented Lincoln's career and misstated his principles as to place him almost entirely on the defensive. Purely defensive tactics, whether in physical or intellectual contests, rarely succeed. Hence the advantage, as the first debate closed, appeared to rest with the "Little Giant." Lincoln's speech, it is true, had been received with enthusiasm, and, as he left the platform, his excited supporters, lifting him upon their shoulders, had carried him, with songs and huzzas, to the place where he was to spend the night. Still, this happened in a Republican district, and his well-wishers elsewhere, as they read the report of the discussion in cold type, might with reason have renewed their fears for the result.

There was a change in the situation when next the champions met — at Freeport. Here Lincoln assumed the offensive, and thenceforth, to the end of the series, he frequently forced the fighting. Coolly parrying his antagonist's most dangerous blows, he countered with a force under which the redoubtable Douglas sometimes reeled. That gentleman's air of superiority soon disappeared. The pace became too hot for any such pretence. All his remarkable dialectic powers were called into play to combat a logic keener than his own and a straightforward persistence of purpose that no artifice could turn aside. When his sophisms were confuted and his untruths exposed, he had a way of introducing them over and over again in bewildering guises. Not Proteus himself took so many shapes before he gave up the truth. Nor was the little old man of the sea enmeshed, at last, in his fetters, more securely than was the "Little Giant" in the chain of reasoning that Lincoln so deftly wound around him. Twist and turn how he would, Douglas could not extricate himself. Losing his temper as he lost ground, he fell upon his adversary with personalities which the latter was not slow to return in kind. Then Douglas protested.

"Does Mr. Lincoln," said he at Galesburg, "wish to push these things to the point of personal difficulties here? I commenced this contest by treating him courteously and kindly; I always spoke of him in words of respect, and in return he has sought, and is now seeking, to divert public attention from the enormity of his revolutionary principles by impeaching men's sincerity and integrity, and inviting personal quarrels."[53]

To which Lincoln replied: —

"I do not understand but what he impeaches my honor, my veracity, and my candor; and because he does this,

I do not understand that I am bound, if I see a truthful ground for it, to keep my hands off of him. As soon as I learned that Judge Douglas was disposed to treat me in this way, I signified in one of my speeches that I should be driven to draw upon whatever of humble resources I might have — to adopt a new course with him. I was not entirely sure that I should be able to hold my own with him, but I at least had the purpose made to do as well as I could upon him; and now I say that I will not be the first to cry, 'Hold!' I think it originated with the Judge, and when he quits, I probably will. But I shall not ask any favors at all. He asks me, or he asks the audience, if I wish to push this matter to the point of personal difficulty. I tell him, No. He did not make a mistake in one of his early speeches, when he called me an 'amiable' man, though perhaps he did when he called me an 'intelligent' man. It really hurts me very much to suppose that I have wronged anybody on earth. I again tell him, No. I very much prefer, when this canvass shall be over, however it may result, that we at least part without any bitter recollections of personal difficulties. The Judge, in his concluding speech at Galesburg, says that I was pushing this matter to a personal difficulty to avoid the responsibility for the enormity of my principles. I say to the Judge and this audience now, that I will again state our principles as well as I hastily can in all their enormity, and if the Judge hereafter chooses to confine himself to a war upon these principles, he will probably not find me departing from the same course."[54]

This fairly indicates Lincoln's attitude. Thrice armed in the justice of his position, he held it with equal vigor, against argument or abuse, changing weapons as his adversary changed his, and evincing no animosity, even while he dealt the most telling strokes. His customary humor was, however, to a large extent, noticeable for its absence. When urged by his friends to introduce some of his witty illustrations and amusing anecdotes, so that audiences might applaud him as often as they did Douglas, he refused, saying: —

"The occasion is too serious. The issues are too grave. I do not seek applause, or to amuse the people, but to convince them." [55]

Moreover, beyond the cloud of local voters that enveloped the rude platforms in the Illinois clearings, he saw what these friends and what Douglas himself too often lost sight of, — the listening nation. To this larger forum Lincoln addressed himself. He was eager enough for the exalted office at stake; but what appealed as much, if not more, to his ambition, was the hope of overcoming his ancient rival, in the eyes of the whole country.

One incident of the debates is, in this connection, of particular interest. At the first meeting, Douglas challenged Lincoln to answer a series of seven interrogatories, based on the slavery problem. They were shrewdly calculated to entrap him into inconsistencies, or to elicit expressions of radical doctrine for which the people at large were hardly prepared. Lincoln did not formally reply at once, but during the interval between that and the following debate, he got ready a set of answers, remarkable for their blending of adroitness and candor. At the same time, as "questions" is a game that two can play, he framed four interrogatories, designed, in their turn, to embarrass Douglas. This was especially so of the one which read: —

"Can the people of a United States Territory, in any lawful way, against the wish of any citizen of the United States, exclude slavery from its limits, prior to the formation of a State constitution?" [56]

The question would bring the author of "popular sovereignty" face to face with the irreconcilable contradiction between his theory that the people of a Territory had the right to exclude slavery, or not, as they wished, and his defence of the Dred Scott decision, according to which they had no such right. Was it wise, however, to give

Douglas this opportunity for patching up the defect in his armor? "No," said the Republican leaders, to whom Lincoln submitted the questions, on the eve of the Freeport meeting, — unanimously, "No." Douglas, they said in effect, would not of his own accord, for fear of further offending the South, touch upon the subject any more than he found necessary. Consequently, his support of the decision might be attacked to advantage. On the other hand, argued they, if forced to give a categorical answer, he will say, "Yes," adhere to "popular sovereignty," declare that the decision is an abstract proposition dependent for its force upon local legislation, and thus gain a number of still doubtful votes.[57]

"If he does that," said Lincoln, "he can never be President."

"But," replied one of his friends, "he may be Senator."

"Perhaps," rejoined Lincoln; "but I am after larger game. The battle of 1860 is worth a hundred of this."[58]

His anxious supporters labored with him to the last moment before the debate opened, in the hope of persuading him to abandon that question. They protested, not unreasonably, against jeopardizing the present canvass for one that was two years distant; but their candidate, with the self-reliance that customarily followed his careful study of a subject, persisted in his purpose.[59] When the question was put, Douglas answered as had been predicted; and how accurately the effects of that answer[60] had been forecast by the questioner, we shall presently see.

Important as the debates were, they constituted but a small part of this memorable canvass. To consider all the elements that entered into the contest, and to credit each with its precise bearing upon the result, would be difficult, if not impossible. A number of speakers — aspirants for State offices and politicians generally — supported one or the other, as the case might be, of the senatorial candidates. The advantage, in this respect, owing to the eloquent aid of Trumbull, probably lay with Lincoln. It is agreed, on the other hand, that circumstances favored Douglas, and that nothing did this to so great an extent as the hostility of President Buchanan. The administration party's effort to compass the Senator's defeat, its nomination of a third State ticket to divide the Democratic vote, its virulent attacks upon him in the press, and its abuse of Federal patronage to punish his supporters, served merely to close up the ranks of those supporters, as they glorified the almost heroic courage with which he fought Republicans in front, and Buchanan Democrats in the rear. Moreover, the animosity of the President and his pro-slavery adherents against Douglas kept alive the sympathy of prominent Republicans, as well as other anti-administration leaders, throughout the country. They loved the "Little Giant" — somewhat as did those who cherished a nobler Democrat, of a later day — for the enemies he had made, and their influence brought him many times as many votes as Buchanan took. Indeed, a single favorable letter, penned at a critical point in the struggle, by Senator Crittenden of Kentucky, turned the wavering scale in enough districts to ensure the election of Douglas.[61]

But what Douglas himself accomplished and how close his competitor kept to him, through it all, are the striking features of the contest. From the midsummer evening on which it was opened by the Democratic candidate, in Chicago, to the night before election, when he tried, during a chill November storm, to deliver his closing speech, in that same city, Douglas made a fight as spirited as it was able. Traversing the length and breadth of the State, he spoke at all hours and places, regardless of weather or personal fatigue. In the one hundred working days between July 9 and November 2, he made, according to his own statement, one hundred and thirty speeches.[62] This vigorous campaign frequently necessitated traveling by night and speaking — for the most part, in the open air — several times on the same day; but the attendant hardships were alleviated, as much as could be, at every turn. Luxuriously fitted special cars, filled usually with a retinue of friends, carried him to many of his appointments, as one contemporary says, "like a conquering hero."[63] His approach was announced to the waiting crowds by salutes fired from cannon mounted on a platform car, and by the music of a brass band. Processions, banners, triumphal arches, decorations, receptions, serenades, fireworks, and the boisterous enthusiasm of the people — manufactured, when it failed to be spontaneous — stimulated Douglas, as would indeed have been the case with a man of weaker fiber, to strenuous exertion. Drawing upon all his resources, material no less than physical and intellectual, he cashed the obligations under which so many rested, for political favors, into a large campaign fund that was disbursed with a lavish hand. His own contributions, leaving him deeply in debt, drained his estate to the extent, it is said, of eighty thousand dollars.[64] This sum and Lincoln's subscription of five hundred dollars, or thereabouts, to the Republican fund, form a contrast, typical of differences between the candidates and their methods, that ran through the entire canvass.[65]

Neither enthusiasm nor the customary electioneering devices were lacking among Lincoln's followers, but their leader disliked "fizzlegigs and fireworks," to use his own phrase, as much as his competitor desired them. While the latter omitted no flourish that might gain a vote, the former relied, as much as his managers would let him, upon the stump; while the one was customarily driven through a town in the most elegant carriage to be obtained, the other was drawn about not infrequently on a farm-wagon; and, what was of the greatest importance, while Douglas enjoyed the best railroad facilities that money or influence could secure, Lincoln had to cover the same ground as he did, with scant favor. "At all points on the road where meetings between the two great politicians were held," relates Colonel Lamon, "either a special train or a special car was furnished to Judge Douglas; but Mr. Lincoln, when he failed to get transportation on the regular trains, in time to meet his appointments, was reduced to the necessity of going as freight. There being orders from headquarters to permit no passenger to travel on freight trains, Mr. Lincoln's persuasive powers were often brought into requisition. The favor was granted or refused according to the politics of the conductor. On one occasion, in going to meet an appointment in the southern part of the State — that section of Illinois called Egypt — Mr. Lincoln and I, with other friends, were traveling in the 'caboose' of a freight train, when we were switched off the main track to allow a special train to pass in which Mr. Lincoln's more aristocratic rival was being conveyed. The passing train was decorated with banners and flags, and carried a band of music which was playing 'Hail to the Chief.' As the train whistled past, Mr. Lincoln broke out in a fit of laughter and said, 'Boys, the gentleman in that car evidently smelt no royalty in our carriage.'" [66]

Another incident in point is recalled by Major Whitney. "Lincoln and I," says he, "were at the Centralia agricultural fair, the day after the debate at Jonesboro. Night came on and we were tired, having been on the fair grounds all day. We were to go north on the Illinois Central Railroad. The train was due at midnight, and the depot was full of people. I managed to get a chair for Lincoln in the office of the Superintendent of the railroad, but small politicians would intrude so that he could scarcely get a moment's sleep. The train came and was filled instantly. I got a seat near the door for Lincoln and myself. He was worn out and had to meet Douglas the next day at Charleston. An empty car, called a saloon car, was hitched on to the rear of the train and locked up. I asked the conductor, who knew Lincoln and myself well, — we were both attorneys of the road, — if Lincoln could not ride in that car; that he was exhausted and needed rest; but the conductor refused. I afterwards got him in by a stratagem. At the same time, George B. McClellan in person [then Vice-President of the road] was taking Douglas around in a special car and special train; and that was the unjust treatment Lincoln got from the Illinois Central Railroad."[67]

Nevertheless, as the struggle drew to a close, the favored candidate, vigorous as he was, almost succumbed to the strain, and his voice became so hoarse that it was painful to hear him. On the other hand, Lincoln, who, without making so many speeches, had probably endured all that Douglas had and more, appeared to be in prime condition. His voice was as clear, his eye as bright, and his step as firm as if he were about to begin, not to end, one of the severest of political conflicts.

The election, which took place on November 2, resulted in a virtual victory, but at the same time, an actual defeat, for Lincoln. His party, making heavy gains over its returns in 1856 when Buchanan carried Illinois, polled the largest popular vote and elected its State ticket. The Douglas men, however, profiting by inequalities in the apportionment of legislative districts, as well as by the fact that eight out of thirteen State Senators who held over were Democrats, had a majority, on joint ballot, in the legislature. When that body met in January, 1859, it accordingly reëlected Douglas.

Lincoln took his defeat as resignedly as could be expected. He was, as we have seen, not unprepared for such a result; yet this second check to his ambitions must have borne hard upon a man who once said that he "would rather have a full term in the Senate than in the Presidency."[68] The courageous, hopeful letters written by him, at about this time, do not — it is safe to say — reveal all his emotions. He felt, as he quaintly told a sympathetic friend, "like the boy that stumped his toe. — It hurt too bad to laugh and he was too big to cry."[69] The toe had, on this occasion, not been seriously injured, however, for the big boy was still in the running with the little one. Their names were thenceforward linked together in the public mind. Those who had watched the contest attentively agreed, for the most part, that Lincoln's failure had been as brilliant as Douglas's success. While the Senator had merely maintained the great prestige already established by him, throughout the land, his comparatively unknown opponent had leaped at one bound, as it were, into a national reputation. Some observers, in fact, undazzled by the Bengal lights of victory, recognized even then, what later judgment has confirmed, that the foremost campaigner of the Democracy had met his master.

After the conflict, Lincoln turned his attention again to his somewhat neglected private affairs. Urgent though these were, they did not — it is interesting to note — take his thoughts from the doctrines that he had combated, or from the man who had sought to uphold them. Douglas and "Douglasism," to use Lincoln's own word, were still at every turn the joint objects of his attacks. For, strange to relate, he deemed it necessary to oppose the Democratic leader anew, within, as well as outside of, the Republican ranks. Some members of the party, notwithstanding what the recent discussions had disclosed, persisted in the hope that the organization might yet march to power under the standard of the victorious Senator. Even a few of Lincoln's friends, for a brief period after his defeat, entertained this idea; but their leader — needless to say — lost no opportunity to counteract it. "Let the Republican Party of Illinois dally with Judge Douglas," said he, speaking at Chicago, in the spring of 1859. "Let them fall in behind him and make him their candidate, and they do not absorb him — he absorbs them. They would come out at the end all Douglas men, all claimed by him as having endorsed every one of his doctrines upon the great subject with which the whole nation is engaged at this hour."[70] As late as the midsummer of that year, we find the speaker expressing uneasiness at seeing his "friends, leaning toward 'popular sovereignty'" and toward its author, "the most dangerous enemy of Liberty because the most insidious one."[71] These warnings were reënforced by the conduct of the Senator himself. That wily politician, as soon as he had secured his reëlection, turned toward the South to regain the pro-slavery support which he had alienated at Freeport. His public utterances, about this time, particularly the speeches made on a southern tour that closely followed the debates, reveal how disastrous, if not fatal, his leadership might have been to the high aims of the Republican Party. But this peril passed over, with the approach of the fall elections, when party lines were again so sharply drawn that Lincoln and Douglas found themselves, as usual, in opposing camps.

At the request of the Ohio Democrats, Douglas visited that State, in September, 1859, to help them elect their local ticket. Similar invitations, addressed to Lincoln from various quarters in the North, had been declined; but, when the Buckeye Republicans asked him to come and answer the speeches of this man who was regarded as his particular antagonist, he complied. Following Douglas, by a few days, at Columbus and at Cincinnati, respectively, he made two effective speeches. They dealt not solely with what had been said at those places, but indeed, with most, if not all, of the important arguments made by the Democratic leader in his addresses and his contributions to the press since the debates. For now, more than ever, Lincoln tenaciously stuck to Douglas. No public word or act of the Senator escaped the notice of his indefatigable rival. After the Ohio election, which resulted in favor of the Republicans, Lincoln journeyed to Kansas. There as elsewhere, to judge from the reports of his speeches,— or rather from the fragments of several that have been preserved,— "popular sovereignty," together with the expounder of the doctrine, was still uppermost in his mind. And a few weeks thereafter, when he delivered at Cooper

Institute, in New York, the most elaborate address of his life, that same subject furnished a theme, and one of Douglas's speeches, a text. The oration at the metropolis was, in fact, a grand summing up of the controversy opened by Lincoln, as we have seen, somewhat over twenty months before, in the little western Capital. By a sort of political miracle, the arena in which the contestants then faced each other had, with unexampled rapidity, grown until it became coextensive with the entire country. A nation had been watching the men and weighing the merits of their quarrel. The time for a final decision between them was almost at hand.

When the Republican National Convention met at Chicago, in May, 1860, it passed over Seward, Chase, and other recognized leaders, who sought the presidency, to nominate Lincoln. This choice, though the causes and considerations which led to it were manifold, had its basis primarily on the record made by him in the fight against Douglas. For, sharp as had been that conflict between the two men, a still sharper one, to all appearances, impended between their political supporters. The Republicans and the northern Democrats, entering upon the most momentous presidential campaign of our history, had embodied in their respective platforms the principles at issue throughout the debates. Consequently, when they came to select candidates who were to stand upon these platforms, they naturally regarded the debaters themselves as, in one important sense at least, their logical standard-bearers. So Lincoln was named at Chicago, and five weeks later, the Democratic National Convention at Baltimore nominated Douglas.

But the second nomination was relatively a very different affair from the first. Lincoln received the unanimous vote of his party; Douglas was chosen by a mere rump. The Democracy had split across its middle, leaving the Senator from Illinois at the head of the northern half, and face to face with the fate foreseen by his competitor at Freeport. In the debate at that place, Douglas, as will be remembered, had been entrapped into an out-and-out declaration of his attitude toward slavery in the Territories. "It matters not," he had said, answering Lincoln's question, "what way the Supreme Court may hereafter decide as to the abstract question whether slavery may or may not go into a Territory under the Constitution, the people have the lawful means to introduce it or exclude it as they please, for the reason that slavery cannot exist a day or an hour anywhere, unless it is supported by local police regulations. Those police regulations can only be established by the local legislature; and if the people are opposed to slavery, they will elect representatives to that body who will by unfriendly legislation effectually prevent the introduction of it into their midst." [72] This rare sophism, "as thin," to use a Lincolnian illustration, "as the homeopathic soup that was made by boiling the shadow of a pigeon that had been starved to death," had nevertheless served Douglas's purpose with the Democrats of Illinois. But how had it affected his popularity with the party at large, and, above all, would it, as Lincoln had predicted, cost him the presidency?

The applause of the Senator's constituents over the subterfuge of "unfriendly legislation" had not subsided before a storm of protest arose in the South. Denunciations of Douglas and his "Freeport heresy," so-called, filled the pro-slavery press; adherents of Buchanan, pointing to the obnoxious avowal as conclusive evidence of apostasy, assailed him in rapidly increasing numbers, and, if possible, more bitterly than ever; while those of the southern leaders who might have overlooked his quarrel with the administration also raised their voices in condemnation of what they regarded as a betrayal of their dearest interests. In vain had Douglas hurried South, after the debate, with speeches that commended slavery. Fruitless were the addresses and pamphlets in which he had sought to defend his position. To no purpose had it been pointed out that he was pursuing the only course by which the Democratic Party could hope for success in the Free States. "His explanations explanatory of explanations explained," as Lincoln felicitously described them, appeared indeed to be "interminable"; yet all without avail. By that answer at Freeport, — a formal declaration at last of theories previously hinted at, — Douglas had destroyed what remained of his southern prestige. The slaveholders could have forgiven much in a man who throughout his entire career, more efficiently than any other northern politician, had fetched and carried for them; but this shifty doctrine, proclaiming "the institution" at the mercy of local laws, put forth as it was, on the eve of their last desperate civil campaign, had marked him for sacrifice. Hence the southern delegates to the Democratic National Convention were resolved — cost what it might — upon the overthrow of their once serviceable champion. His northern supporters, on the other hand, were as determined to make him their candidate. After a number of stormy sessions, in which the two factions drew farther and farther apart, the members from the "cotton States," together with their sympathizers from other sections, seceded to organize the pro-slavery convention that nominated John C. Breckinridge; and what was left of the National Convention chose Douglas to lead its forlorn hope.

So the "Little Giant" and the big one entered upon what proved to be their last contest. Douglas was heavily handicapped. His support in the South, as if it had not been sufficiently reduced by the disruption of the Democratic Party and the candidacy of Breckinridge, was still further impaired by the nomination, on a fourth ticket, of John Bell of Tennessee. Yet Douglas was game. Disregarding the wisdom and good taste that have, with rare exceptions, restrained presidential candidates from advocating their own election, he threw himself into the fight with all the energy which had characterized his previous campaigns. In an extensive tour through the country, he made many speeches, striking now at this competitor, now at that. His old opponent, however, for the first time in the history of their rivalry, was mute. Lincoln's cause was advocated by capable men enough, yet it must have irked him to remain at home inactive while Douglas, traveling from city to city, continued to state his side of their debate. The Democratic leader, in truth, presented no new arguments, and his old ones the Republican had, over and over again, refuted. Popular Sovereignty and the Freeport Doctrine — twin nostrums of an unscrupulous political quack — had, thanks to Lincoln, been exposed in all their futility. The time for shifts and delusions had passed. Symptoms of trouble multiplied on every hand. Columbia was sick — sick unto death. A black fever was upon her. Heroic treatment alone might save her. In this extremity, which of the two men — for the choice really lay between them — would the nation trust? The decision rested with the Northern States. Small wonder that, with a single exception, they turned from the charlatan and placed themselves in the hands of the master who had discredited him. Lincoln was elected. He led Douglas, at the polls, by about five hundred thousand votes; and in the Electoral College, his ballots were 180 to Douglas's 12.[73] What the result might have been had the candidate of the northern Democrats received the nomination of a united party, with but Lincoln and himself in the field, is, of course, purely a matter for speculation. The votes that were cast for Breckinridge and Bell, together with his own, would have given Douglas a majority on popular ballot; yet even so, his total from the electors would have been only 123, and whether or not he could have improved upon that figure, in a single-handed canvass against Lincoln, is beyond reasonable conjecture. In any event, defeated, North and South, he had ceased to be a vital factor in political calculations. All eyes were turned upon his successful rival; for the long race between Lincoln and Douglas was finished, and Lincoln had won.

When the President-elect, on inauguration day, stepped out upon the platform that had been erected in front of the eastern portico of the capitol, he found the senior Senator from Illinois among the distinguished men who sat awaiting him. Mr. Lincoln, as if to add to the novelty of his situation, was dressed in fine clothes, of which, for the moment, he appeared to be all too conscious. In one hand he held a new silk hat; in the other, a gold-headed cane. What to do with them perplexed him. After some hesitation, he put the cane into a corner; but he could find no place for the hat, which he evidently was unwilling to lay on the rough board floor. As he stood there in embarrassment, with the waiting multitude looking up curiously at him, his old rival came to his rescue. Taking the precious hat from its owner's hand, Douglas held it, while Lincoln took the oath of office and delivered his inaugural address.[74] The incident, simple in itself, forms a dramatic climax to the lifelong competition between them. As Lincoln stands forth crowned with the highest honors to which their conflicting ambitions had aspired, Douglas, in the background, humbly holds the victor's hat.

CHAPTER IV

THE POWER BEHIND THE THRONE

On the first roll-call at the Republican National Convention of 1860, no less than a dozen men received votes for the presidential nomination.[1] Among the distinguished party leaders and "favorite sons" thus honored, by far the most prominent, at the time, was William Henry Seward of New York. So greatly did he tower above all other aspirants that the keenest observers on the ground regarded his selection as a foregone conclusion. To him, perhaps, more than to any other member of the young organization was due the cohesion of its inharmonious elements;[2] to him those elements owed the most effectual expression of their common principles; and to him many of their representatives, as they gathered in convention at the opening of the great campaign, naturally looked for leadership.

Seward's brilliant career, extending over thirty years of political life, no less than his services to the new party, had fairly earned for him this distinction. Two terms in the upper chamber of the New York legislature, an equal period as Governor of that most difficult of commonwealths, and two terms — all but completed — in the United States Senate, had afforded him abundant opportunities for displaying executive and legislative talents of a high order. As a politician, he had won his spurs leading a minority in the New York Senate, during the days of the Anti-Masonic uprising; and when the Anti-Masons became Whigs, a few years thereafter, his capabilities for generalship had forthwith been recognized by the new associates, in a nomination to the governorship of his

State. Though defeated in the canvass which followed, he had, in the next election, as a candidate for the same office, won a splendid victory over the so-called Albany Regency — a powerful Democratic clique that had long controlled political affairs. This success had a significance more than local. It had carried Seward, before his thirty-ninth birthday, into the front rank of party leaders — an eminence that he was destined to maintain for many years. Entering the United States Senate amidst the stirring debates on the Compromise of 1850, he had taken advanced ground against the extension of slavery; and, in the fierce parliamentary conflicts to ensue, he had borne more than his share of southern abuse. With the disfavor of the South, however, had kept pace the approval of the North, where a following, influential, large, and steadily increasing, had looked to him, as to an oracle, for political guidance. When this section had merged its fortunes with those of the other anti-slavery factions to form the Republican Party, our Whig Senator from New York had been regarded generally throughout the country as the foremost champion of the new cause.

The day on which the Convention met at Chicago, Seward entered upon his sixtieth year. He was in his intellectual prime, however, and no other aspirant to the presidency appeared to be so amply qualified for the office. A college-bred man, his education had taken the direction of general culture rather than of profound learning. With habits of thought essentially philosophical was combined a grasp of practical matters that his long experience of public men and events could alone have developed. Seldom brilliant, but usually bright, he understood in a remarkable degree how to make the most of his acquirements, and, for that matter, of other people's as well. When his prolific mind failed to supply a needed thought or expedient, he adopted that of another so skilfully as to make it seem his own. No labor was too exacting for his industry; no obstacle could baffle his perseverance. A man "of cheerful yesterdays and confident to-morrows" — in him, more than in any other statesman of his times, the ardent hopefulness of youth blended with the wisdom of mature years. An untiring student, moreover, of history and literature, a lawyer of uncommon ability, and a thinker who lacked neither vigor nor imagination, he expressed himself, whether by tongue or pen, with equal felicity and force. As an orator, Seward ranked below the great triad — Webster, Clay, and Calhoun. He had neither their genius nor their commanding presence. In his slight stature, harsh voice, awkward gesture, and didactic manner were lacking the personal charm that contributed not a little to their triumphs; yet his thoughtful, unimpassioned speeches carried conviction as often, perhaps, as did their best efforts. Rising above the personalities which jangled the debates of the day, he maintained a dignity and amiability of temper that no provocation could disturb. To supporters, as well as to opponents, he seemed to say: —

> "Be calm in arguing; for fierceness makes
> Error a fault, and truth discourtesy."

In his personal intercourse with people Seward's courtly manners, his tact, and his social graces were not unimportant factors in the multiplication of his political friends. For, whatever else he may have been, he was still the politician. A party man, he believed that he could best attain his ends within one of the two great organizations that usually divide the country; but, when vital principles were at stake, he did not hesitate to express, in lofty periods, his own views, however much they might differ from those of his associates. In the actual practice, nevertheless, of political strategy, he was not above compromises or expedients which gave rise to charges of insincerity and time-serving. Though an admirer of John Quincy Adams to the point of veneration, he maintained for many years a close political association with Thurlow Weed. This was one of the enigmas in the man's complex character. That Seward's acts, now and then, fell considerably below his ideals, even staunch admirers could not deny; but they pointed out the limitations under which, as a party leader, he had to labor, and they held that these shortcomings were more than offset by repeated manifestations of patriotic statesmanship.

This outline may afford some conception of the man who, having left his seat in the Senate for his home at Auburn, sat among his friends while the Republican Convention was voting, and awaited with smiling confidence the news of his nomination. That news, as we know, never came. Instead of it, the wires brought the announcement of his defeat and of Abraham Lincoln's selection, on the third ballot. To explain this destruction of Seward's hopes, contemporary historians have assigned widely different causes. His radical utterances on the slavery question, particularly the speeches in which he foreshadowed the "irrepressible conflict" and declared that there was "a higher law than the Constitution"; his early indulgence toward the Catholics when they had asked to have the New York school fund divided, together with his uncompromising opposition to the so-called American principles of the old Know-Nothings; their consequent hostility to him, in considerable numbers, especially throughout the pivotal States of Pennsylvania and Indiana; his uniform support of liberal public expenditures which had led to extravagance — even corruption — on the part of political associates less scrupulous than himself; the ill-repute of these friends, who, under the boss-rule of Thurlow Weed, Seward's inseparable partner, had organized at Albany the most vicious lobby of the day; the antagonism of Horace Greeley, for many years devoted to Seward's political fortunes, but latterly embittered against him by feelings of wounded vanity, — each of these things has been credited with the overthrow of the New York Senator in the Convention. It would be nearer the truth to say that all contributed their share toward the creation of the opposition which, having faced Seward's plurality with but little coöperation at the outset, finally combined the required majority vote in support of his strongest competitor.

What causes and considerations of a positive character led to Lincoln's selection need not be considered here. He owed the nomination, in the opinion of the Seward men, to his weakness rather than to his strength. Their first outbursts of indignation characterized the affair as a triumph of unobjectionable mediocrity over greatness which had, of necessity, during a long series of public services, raised up many enemies to itself. They recalled that other National Conventions had sacrificed their most eminent leaders — as Webster had remarked, twelve years before, on a similar occasion — to the "sagacious, wise, far-seeing doctrine of availability"; but they could not, for all that, bring themselves at once to regard the overthrow of their idol with anything approaching to acquiescence.[3] A spirit of bitter protest pervaded the visits, letters, and newspaper comments which poured in upon Seward, from every direction. Their tenor may be inferred from what the Republican Central Committee of his own State addressed to him the day after the nomination had been made.

"The result of the Chicago Convention," wrote the Committee, "has been more than a surprise to the Republicans of New York. That you who have been the earliest defender of Republican principles — the acknowledged head and leader of the party, who have given direction to its movements and form and substance to its acts — that you should have been put aside upon the narrow ground of expediency, we can hardly realize or believe. Whatever the decision of this, or a hundred other conventions, we recognize in you the real leader of the Republican Party; and the citizens of every State and of all creeds and parties, and the history of our country will confirm this judgment."[4]

To this Seward replied: —

"I find in the resolutions of the Convention a platform as satisfactory to me as if it had been framed with my own hands; and in the candidates adopted by it, eminent and able Republicans with whom I have cordially coöperated in maintaining the principles embodied in that excellent creed. I cheerfully give them a sincere and earnest support."[5]

Similar sentiments were repeatedly expressed to his disconsolate friends, upon whom he urged the duty of foregoing their personal desires for the sake of the great cause. He, himself, magnanimously setting the example, engaged in the canvass with an energy and an eloquence that contributed not a little to its successful issue. Here was a general who did not sulk in his tent, while the war was on, even though the commander had deprived him of what so many told him and of what he himself believed to be his due. Seward bore himself, during those trying times, with rare dignity. Nevertheless, beneath his calm demeanor were hidden feelings of keen disappointment and humiliation — how keen, only those nearest to him could guess. When, in a letter to his wife, he described himself as "a leader deposed by my own party in the hour of organization for decisive battle," he compressed into a single phrase his sense of the injustice done him.[6] It is not surprising, therefore, that after the battle had been fought and the victory won, he should have looked upon Abraham Lincoln as wearing honors that belonged, of right, to William H. Seward.

A similar notion was entertained by the President-elect, himself. He had, for some time before the Convention, shared the prevailing opinion that the Senator from New York stood in the front rank of preferment. When, shortly after the debates of 1858, Jesse W. Fell, a politician of local prominence, had urged Lincoln to seek the nomination, he had replied: —

"Oh, Fell, what 's the use of talking of me for the presidency, whilst we have such men as Seward, Chase, and others, who are so much better known to the people, and whose names are so intimately associated with the principles of the Republican Party? Everybody knows them; nobody, scarcely, outside of Illinois, knows me. Besides, is it not, as a matter of justice, due to such men, who have carried the movement forward to its present status, in spite of fearful opposition, personal abuse, and hard names? I really think so."[7]

Not so, however, thought Fell and some of the speaker's other friends; for they persisted in their purpose until they succeeded in getting his consent to the steps that led to his nomination.

Even after the Chicago Convention had made Lincoln the Republican standard-bearer, he continued to speak of Seward as "the generally recognized leader" of the party. In truth, not many years had elapsed since the successful candidate had described himself to be "something of a Seward Whig";[8] and, on the very day of his nomination,[9] he determined, if elected, to give his powerful competitor the first portfolio in his cabinet.[10] Carrying out this resolution a month after the election, Lincoln sent Seward, with the formal tender of the office, a confidential letter, as sincere as it was deferential. Some assurance of the writer's good faith seemed to be in order, because of the newspaper rumors that the appointment was to be proffered as a compliment, with the expectation that it would be declined.

"I now offer you the place," wrote the President-elect, "in the hope that you will accept it, and with the belief that your position in the public eye, your integrity, ability, learning, and great experience, all combine to render it an appointment preëminently fit to be made."[11]

Seward accepted, though not without misgivings. His partner, Weed, after two days of consultation with Mr. Lincoln at Springfield, had returned home with most unsatisfactory conclusions as to the probable composition of the cabinet. It was to include, he inferred, Messrs.

Seward, Bates, Smith,[12] Chase, Cameron, Blair, and Welles. The first three had been Whigs, and the last four might be classified as former Democrats.

"I inquired," reports Weed, "whether, in the shape which the question was taking, it was just or wise to concede so many seats in the cabinet to the Democratic element in the Republican Party. He replied that as a Whig he thought he could afford to be liberal to a section of the Republican Party, without whose votes he could not have been elected. I admitted the justice and wisdom of this, adding that in arranging and adjusting questions of place and patronage in our State we had acted in that spirit, but that I doubted both the justice and the wisdom, in inaugurating his administration, of giving to a minority of the Republican Party a majority in his cabinet. I added that the National Convention indicated unmistakably the sentiment of its constituency by nominating for President a candidate with Whig antecedents, while its nominee for Vice-President had been for many years a Democratic representative in Congress. 'But,' said Mr. Lincoln, 'why do you assume that we are giving that section of our party a majority in the cabinet?' I replied that if Messrs. Chase, Cameron, Welles, and Blair should be designated, the cabinet would stand four to three. 'You seem to forget that *I* expect to be there; and counting me as one, you see how nicely the cabinet would be balanced and ballasted.'" [13]

This view of the matter failed to reassure Seward's friends. They were not disposed to accept the President-elect as a very heavy make-weight. What power, moreover, to keep his craft trimmed in the maelstrom of Washington politics, at that particularly threatening period, could they expect from an untried man who, to use the language of one of his biographers, "had just been so freakishly picked out of a frontier town to take charge of the destinies of the United States"?[14] His seeming inefficiency to meet the approaching crisis should have led him, they thought, to make up his cabinet under the advice of the New York statesman, —

> "That sacred seer, whose comprehensive view
> The past, the present, and the future knew."

Aided by harmonious assistants, Seward might then be relied on, said his admirers, to save the administration, and perhaps the country, from disaster. As the virtual, if not the nominal head of the new government, why should not the Secretary of State, like the British Prime Minister, be allowed to choose his own colleagues and to assign them their respective places? It was even urged upon Mr. Lincoln that he ought to visit Auburn and consult the great man's wishes; but, strange to relate, the President-elect did not do so.

These efforts to secure what was termed a Seward cabinet were redoubled after the prospective Secretary of State had accepted the portfolio. His political associates earnestly opposed the appointment of Messrs. Blair and Welles, not only because they had been Democrats, but also on account of their personal antagonism to him. Even more objectionable to the Seward faction, however, than these two men, was Mr. Chase. His incompatibility with the Whig leader was so pronounced that one or the other, it was intimated to the President-elect, should be omitted from the cabinet. And all this time Seward's campaign against Chase, it should be said, was not more aggressive than that of Chase against Seward. Mr. Lincoln listened to what was said on both sides, but he made none of the desired changes. Indeed, it is a highly significant fact that, despite this and other equally bitter partisan struggles over the cabinet, to say nothing of certain contemplated changes, the list when he arrived in Washington was essentially what he had planned on the night of his election.[15] Still the Seward men persevered. A large delegation of them waited upon the President-elect, two days before the inauguration, to urge the exclusion of Chase. His faults and Seward's virtues having been dwelt upon at length, they announced as an ultimatum, what had previously been implied, that their leader would not sit in council with him. Whether or not Mr. Lincoln was prepared for this may be inferred from his answer, shortly before, to a friend who inquired about a rumored change in the list.

"Judd," said he, "when that slate breaks again, it will break at the top." [16]

Nevertheless, the attitude of the delegation appeared greatly to distress him. He expressed his esteem for both men, and said that the country wanted the hearty coöperation of all good citizens, without regard to sections. Here there was an ominous pause. Then, taking a paper out of a table-drawer, he continued: —

"I had written out my choice and selection of members for the cabinet after most careful and deliberate consideration, and now you are here to tell me I must break the slate and begin the thing all over again."

He had hoped, he said, to have Mr. Seward as his Secretary of State and Mr. Chase as his Secretary of the Treasury; but he could not reasonably expect to have things just as he liked them, so he had prepared an alternative list to meet their objections.

"This being the case, gentlemen," he added, "how would it do for us to agree upon a change like this? To appoint Mr. Chase Secretary of the Treasury, and offer the State Department to Mr. William L. Dayton, of New Jersey?"

The delegation, according to Lamon, who tells the story,[17] were "shocked, disappointed, outraged." Their indignation, it is needless to say, was not allayed by Mr. Lincoln's phlegmatic reminder that Mr. Dayton was an old Whig like Mr. Seward himself, from "next door to New York," nor by his suggestion that the latter might be Minister to England. Exit delegation; enter Seward, on the same day, with their last shot. In a brief and coldly formal note he asked "leave to withdraw" the ac-

William H. Seward

ceptance of his appointment.[18] Here was a crisis on the very threshold of the new administration! The withdrawal of this potent leader would not alone alienate many whose support, in the perilous condition of affairs, the President-elect had counted on; but it would also necessitate an entire reconstruction of his proposed cabinet. Yet Lincoln stood firm. Pondering over his answer for two days, he handed it to his private secretary, on the morning of inauguration day, with the characteristic remark, "I can't afford to let Seward take the first trick." Nor did he. The note was as short, almost to the word, as the one that had called it forth.[19] Without touching upon the questions at issue, the message merely expressed a strong desire that Seward should not persist in his purpose. "It is the subject," wrote Mr. Lincoln, "of the most painful solicitude with me; and I feel constrained to beg that you will countermand the withdrawal. The public interest, I think, demands that you should; and my personal feelings are deeply enlisted in the same direction. Please consider and answer by 9 o'clock A. M. to-morrow."[20]

On the following morning, the New York statesman, having had an interview with the President, duly returned to his allegiance. A few hours later, when the cabinet appointments were submitted to the Senate, Messrs. Chase, Blair, and Welles were still on the list; and, lo! Governor Seward's name, like Abou Ben Adhem's, led all the rest.

The tact and strength of will manifested by Lincoln in this first difference with Seward should have made some impression, one would suppose, on that astute leader and his no less sagacious advisers. They still, however, entirely misconceived the new President's character. The homely simplicity with which he had borne himself when visited at "his secluded abode," as one of them expressed it, "in the heart of Illinois," the candor with which he acknowledged his deficiencies, and the meekness with which he listened to innumerable counselors, bidden or otherwise, left most of the politicians firm in the opinion that the conduct of the coming administration would be in the hands of his strongest Secretary. Seward's one formidable rival for this supremacy some of them had, it was true, failed to exclude from the cabinet; but this was attributed to the influence which Chase had brought to bear, rather than to any masterful trait in Lincoln, himself.

The widespread notion of the President's weakness was shared by Seward, who, at the same time, concurred — need we add? — in the general estimate of his own superiority. From the day on which he first consented to become head of the State Department, he carried himself as if responsibility for the entire government were to rest on his shoulders. Having been the guiding spirit, unofficially, eleven years before, through General Taylor's brief presidency, how much more might he now expect to dominate an equally untried Executive who had called him to the most prominent place in his cabinet! They were to take office, moreover, under conditions that tended greatly to magnify Mr. Seward's importance. During the winter which elapsed between the time of Mr. Lincoln's election and his inauguration, the Southern States, one after another, made good their threats of secession; officers of the army and navy, resigning from the service in large numbers, turned their swords against the government; treason paralyzed every department at Washington; enemies of the Union — even in Mr. Buchanan's very cabinet — labored to destroy national authority; and the aged President, himself, looked on helplessly, for a time at least, as civil government buildings, forts, arsenals, lighthouses, ships, marine hospitals, and navy-yard, together with valuable munitions, were seized by the rapidly organizing Confederacy. While the country, demoralized North and South, thus drifted through those four long months into civil war, the man who had just been chosen to control its fortunes remained, owing to a singular defect in our system, powerless to avert the disaster. In this extremity Mr. Lincoln naturally turned to Mr. Seward. From his seat in the Upper House the Senator became, in certain respects, the eyes and ears, as well as the tongue, of the coming administration. His utterances were eagerly scanned by the people for indications of its policy, while the President-elect was no less keen for the confidential letters in which his prospective Secretary kept him informed as to the temper of parties and persons at the Capital. When loyal members of Buchanan's cabinet wished to give warning of the conspiracy in the President's council, they communicated with Mr. Seward; when the General commanding the army needed advice, he too conferred with him; when Mr. Lincoln desired to lay his views before the committee appointed by the Senate to devise a preventive for the impending quarrel, his suggestions were placed in the hands of the member from New York; and when conservative men, on both sides, sought a peaceful solution of the difficulty, they appealed to that same gentleman. In short, during this period, Mr. Seward was considered by many to be the man of the hour, and it is not too much to say that he occupied a position unique in the experience of American statesmen.

For a parallel we must turn to that stormy period in English politics when William Pitt the Elder, on the eve of entering office as Secretary of State, with the lead in the House of Commons, the supreme direction of the French war, and the control of foreign affairs, declared: —

"I know that I can save the country, and I know no other man can."

So in Mr. Seward's private letters to his wife, from Washington, during the winter of 1860–61, may be caught glimpses, here and there, of how entirely he believed himself to be the Providence of the incoming administration.[21] The day on which he accepted the first tender of the secretaryship, he wrote to Mrs. Seward: —

"I have advised Mr. L. that I will not decline. It is inevitable. I will try to save freedom and my country."

A few days later he wrote: —

"I have assumed a sort of dictatorship for defence; and am laboring night and day, with the cities and States. My hope, rather my confidence, is unabated."

In another letter we find: —

"I am trying to get home; but as yet I see no chance. It seems to me that if I am absent only three days, this administration, the Congress, and the District would fall into consternation and despair. I am the only *hopeful*, *calm*, *conciliatory* person here."

Still another reads: —

"Mad men North and mad men South are working together to produce a dissolution of the Union by civil war. The present administration and the incoming one unite in devolving on me the responsibility of averting those disasters. . . . Once for all, I must gain time for the new administration to organize and for the frenzy of passion to subside. I am doing this without making any compromise whatever, by forbearance, conciliation, magnanimity."

And shortly after the inauguration, he wrote to her: —

"The President is determined that he will have a compound cabinet; and that it shall be peaceful, and even permanent. I was at one time on the point of refusing — nay, I did refuse, for a time, to hazard myself in the experiment. But a distracted country appeared before me; and I withdrew from that position. I believe I can endure as much as any one; and may be that I can endure enough to make the experiment successful. At all events I did not dare to go home, or to England, and leave the country to chance."

These assertions seem painfully presumptuous, to-day. Early in March, 1861, not many persons — had the letters been made public — would have so regarded them.

All circumstances seemed to confirm Seward's high estimate of his value. On the day of Mr. Lincoln's arrival in Washington, the President-elect submitted to his prospective Secretary of State a copy of his inaugural address, as it had been privately printed before he left home. If Mr. Sewárd believed this honor to be exclusive, he was mistaken, for the document had been placed before several other public men.[22] None of them had ventured, however, upon anything like the thorough revision to which he subjected it. When the address was returned, on the following evening, it was accompanied by many suggestions, ranging in importance from the rejection or insertion of entire paragraphs to the change of a word.[23] The critic, defending the conservative tendency of his corrections, wrote: —

"Only the soothing words which I have spoken have saved us and carried us along thus far. Every loyal man and, indeed, every disloyal man, in the South, will tell you this."

By way of apology for the liberties he had taken, the writer explained: —

"I, my dear sir, have devoted myself singly to the study of the case — here, with advantages of access and free communication with all parties of all sections. I have a common responsibility and interest with you, and I shall adhere to you faithfully in every case. You must, therefore, allow me to speak frankly and candidly." [24]

This "common responsibility" the President-elect, unconscious of personal pride in the matter, seemingly recognized. He adopted, with nice discrimination, wholly or in part, such of the amendments as improved the address; and the deference with which he did so, together with his unassuming manner throughout the affair, could not have raised him in the eyes of his ambitious Secretary of State. Perhaps that gentleman recalled how under similar circumstances the great Webster had revised the inaugural address of the brave but inexperienced Harrison. If so, the parallel must have augured well for the later minister's influence over the incoming administration.[25]

As the rôle of "guide, philosopher, and friend" to this

seemingly simple provincial statesman devolved on Mr. Seward before the inauguration, how much more dependent upon him might he not expect Mr. Lincoln to become after they had entered office! A minority President, to use an epithet common at the time, was about to govern a dismembered nation, with the aid of a party hardly less divided. His cabinet lacked unity of purpose or principle, and its strongest members agreed in nothing so much as in mistrusting his leadership. He, himself, felt keenly the want of preparation for a task such as had never before confronted an American Executive. Not one revolution, but two, piled up perplexities around him; for the sweeping changes among office-holders, required by the situation, troubled him, at first, almost as greatly as did the action of the seceding States. In the confusion, Mr. Lincoln, of necessity, entrusted much to his confidential advisers, and especially to his Secretary of State. That functionary bade fair, then, more than ever, to become the power behind the Throne, greater than the Throne itself. For his talents, brilliant as they were on public occasions, shone with their greatest splendor when he employed them to enforce his views, in private conference. At cabinet meetings, or at informal interviews with the President, these powers were, from the very beginning, exerted with frequent, though not uniform, success. During those first few weeks Mr. Lincoln seemed, so far as the public could see, to yield himself up — as did one President before him and one after — to the charm of Mr. Seward's persuasiveness. The influence of the State Department was believed to be paramount, and the journalist who, before the inauguration, had spoken of the coming régime as "the New Yorker with his Illinois attachment," thus coarsely expressed the popular opinion.[26]

"It is certain," wrote another keen observer, "that his *ego et rex meus* style of speaking about himself and Mr. Lincoln created a general belief at Washington that he would be the Wolsey of the new administration, with 'law in his voice and honor in his hand'; while others would be subordinate and the President himself little more than a figurehead." [27]

People of all classes soon formed the habit of applying to Mr. Seward the titles — foreign to our polity though they are — of Premier and Prime Minister. Under these designations the working head of the British government forms the cabinet, advises the selection and resignation of his colleagues, dictates policies, passes upon important matters in all departments, stands between the throne and the cabinet, dispenses enormous patronage, acts at times as a leader of his party in Parliament, and answers for his conduct, in the main, not to the sovereign, but to the representatives of the people. The first of these functions Seward had, somehow, as we have seen, failed to perform; but he plunged into the others, as nearly as might be, with a spirit befitting the Pitt of the first Republican administration.

The Secretary of State, patterning in a way after Jefferson and Jackson, succeeded, for several weeks at the outset, in preventing regular cabinet meetings. Greatly to the annoyance of his colleagues, he held that only such members as were particularly concerned in whatever might be under consideration should be invited to consult with him and the President. Accordingly, as occasion required, some or all of them were convened in council, on special notice from himself. This procedure, though short-lived, served to confirm for the time his pretensions to unlimited jurisdiction. He busied himself in matters that properly pertained to his cabinet associates; nor did he hesitate, upon the demands of a sharp-set political following, to claim the right of controlling appointments in departments other than his own. "The consequences were," records the then Secretary of the Navy, "that confusion and derangement prevailed to some extent at the commencement by reason of the mental activity, assumptions, and meddlesome intrusions of the Secretary of State in the duties and affairs of others, which were, if not disorganizing, certainly not good administration. Confidence and mutual frankness on public affairs and matters pertaining to the government, particularly on what related to present and threatened disturbances, existed among all the members, with the exception of Mr. Seward, who had, or affected, a certain mysterious knowledge which he was not prepared to impart. This was accepted as a probable necessity by his associates, for he had been in a position to ascertain facts which it was intimated he could not perhaps well disclose. It early became apparent, however, that the Secretary of State had ideas and notions of his own position and that of his colleagues, as well as of the character and attitude of the President, that others could not admit or recognize."[28] This sketch of the situation, though it may have been slightly colored by the recollection of Mr. Welles's own particular grievances, is in effect, correct. On the other hand, justice to Mr. Seward requires us to say that his motives were patriotic, and that some at least of his so-called "meddlesome intrusions" had the President's sanction.

Secretary Seward's activities outside of his department naturally led to misunderstandings. These embarrassed the administration, at times, not a little; but the President patiently smoothed them over, and continued to defer in many, if not in all things, to Mr. Seward's wisdom. That gentleman's evident purpose, however, to run the government had not escaped Mr. Lincoln's notice. While apparently ignoring his aspirations, the President, like the practiced wrestler of his youthful days, found time to take the measure of the man who, according to common report, was to occupy in fact, if not in form, the place to which he, himself, had been elected. When Mrs. Lincoln, ever vigilant for her husband's fame, repeated to him the boast of the Secretary's friends that Mr. Seward was the power behind the throne and could rule the President, he answered: —

"I may not rule, myself, but certainly Seward shall not. The only ruler I have is my conscience — following God in it — and these men will have to learn that yet."[29] A lesson was near at hand.

The first vital question to occupy the attention of the new government had, in fact, developed a wide difference of opinion between Mr. Lincoln and his Secretary of State. It concerned the stone pentagon at the entrance to Charleston harbor, in which Major Anderson and his command were practically besieged by the South Carolina troops. The batteries surrounding Fort Sumter had grown so formidable, and the post was, in many essentials, so weak, that it had become daily less tenable. Yet the President was hardly prepared to receive, on the morning following his inauguration, Major Anderson's report[30] that the garrison, unless succored, would in a few weeks be reduced to starvation, and that relief, with a view to holding the place, could not be effected by "a force of less than twenty thousand good and well-disciplined men." This estimate was accompanied by those of the nine other officers in Fort Sumter, who, while differing as to figures, agreed that a considerable land and naval expedition would be required.[31] No such adequate force was ready or could be made ready in time. Accordingly, Lieutenant-General Scott, the commander-in-chief, who had at once been consulted by Mr. Lincoln, reported on the night of that same day: —

"Evacuation seems almost inevitable, and in this view our distinguished Chief Engineer (Brigadier Totten) concurs."[32]

But the President did not concur. He had promised the nation, a few hours previously, in his inaugural address, that the power confided to him would "be used to hold, occupy, and possess the property and places belonging to the government." How could he, then, before the words had well reached the people, abandon, without a struggle, an important stronghold! The situation presented a problem as perplexing in its political as in its military aspects. So he turned to his cabinet for counsel.

Mr. Lincoln's civil advisers were, at first, almost a unit in adopting the conclusions of the experts at army headquarters. There was an exception, however, in the person of Postmaster-General Blair, a Democrat of the Jacksonian school, who was as earnest in advocating firm measures toward South Carolina as had been his father, twenty-eight years before, in upholding the strong hand with which President Jackson had put down sedition in that same State. Following this example, Montgomery Blair, previous to his entry into the cabinet, as well as on every available occasion thereafter, had urged upon the President the necessity of holding Fort Sumter at any cost. He alone among his associates appears to have fully recognized the inconsistency of reversing, at the very earliest test, the policy which Mr. Lincoln had so positively affirmed upon taking office.[33] The President, himself, was keenly alive to his predicament. "When Anderson goes out of Fort Sumter," said he, "I shall have to go out of the White House."[34] He believed, indeed, as he explained to Congress, some months later, "that to so abandon that position, under the circumstances, would be utterly ruinous; that the necessity under which it was to be done would not be fully understood; that by many it would be construed as a part of a voluntary policy; that at home it would discourage the friends of the Union, embolden its adversaries, and go far to insure to the latter a recognition abroad; that, in fact, it would be our national destruction consummated. This could not be allowed."[35] Yet his views were supported, apparently, by only the youngest and least distinguished member of the cabinet. None of the eminent soldiers or statesmen to whom Mr. Lincoln first looked for advice were in accord with the President's attitude; and the least acquiescent, perhaps, of them all was his Secretary of State.

Mr. Seward had throughout the preceding winter indulged the hope of averting civil war and of reconciling existing differences, without ultimately sacrificing the Union. How this was to be accomplished is not clear to us; nor could it, in the nature of things, have been clear to that statesman himself. His policy, as vaguely stated, weeks before, in the Senate, was "to meet prejudice with conciliation, exaction with concession which surrenders no principle, and violence with the right hand of peace."[36] Such tactics would, he believed, keep the wavering Border States loyal to the Union, stem the current of revolution in the cotton belt, and eventually bring the seceders back to their allegiance, by way of a convention in which their demands might, somehow or other, be satisfied. That these ends were to be attained, and through his instrumentality, was Seward's fixed idea. For weeks after the signs of the times must have discouraged a less buoyant leader, he persisted in his course. As late as March 8, 1861, he is reported to have said,[37] in effect: —

"I have built up the Republican Party, I have brought it to triumph, but its advent to power is accompanied by great difficulties and perils. I must save the party, and save the government in its hands. To do this, war must be averted, the negro question must be dropped, the irrepressible conflict ignored, and a Union party to embrace the Border Slave States inaugurated. I have already whipped Mason and Hunter in their own State. I must crush out Davis, Toombs, and their colleagues in sedition in their respective States. Saving the Border States to the Union by moderation and justice, the people of the cotton States, unwillingly led into secession, will rebel against their leaders, and reconstruction will follow."[38]

Mr. Seward's plans and expectations, it should be added, would, in his opinion, come to naught, if force were employed against the secessionists.[39] He had, accordingly, urged Mr. Lincoln to omit from the inaugural address that promise "to hold, occupy, and possess the property and places belonging to the government"; but without avail. The conflict in policy, thus revealed before the men had even entered office, reached deeper than at first appears. Not only did Mr. Lincoln deem it the President's duty to hold the possessions of the nation, but his rugged logic also recognized, as a necessary corollary, that he was under like obligations to reclaim any property of which it had been deprived. He had so expressed himself in the original draft of the address. Upon a friend's advice, however, the clause declaring a purpose to recapture what was seized had been omitted — not on account of any change in his intention, but because the announcement, at the time, might have needlessly irritated the South.[40] And this he desired to avoid no less earnestly than Mr. Seward. Indeed, the President and his Secretary of State had the same goal in mind, though they disagreed materially — as we have seen — over the path by which it should be reached.

With the weight of opinion among his advisers squarely against holding Sumter, Mr. Lincoln might have been justified in adopting their views. Such a step, it is true, would have been repugnant to his sense of duty. On the other hand, a relief expedition, in the face of all this opposition, — military as well as political, — was equally out of the question. Perplexed beyond measure, the President put off his decision and sought more light. The technical objections of the military men he was, of course, unprepared to meet. So the reports were referred back to General Scott, for further consideration; while army and navy officers, with special knowledge on the subject, were summoned before the cabinet, in frequent consultation. What followed makes one of the most entertaining chapters in the genesis of the war. Nevertheless — except so far as concerns the relations between Mr. Lincoln and Mr. Seward — a few lines must suffice for it here. The commander-in-chief, reaffirming his conviction that the fort could be neither provisioned nor reënforced, submitted an order of evacuation for the President's signature.[41] Instead of signing this, Mr. Lincoln requested his cabinet officers, respectively, to furnish him with written opinions as to whether, under the circumstances, an attempt to provision Fort Sumter was wise. In their answers, Mr. Blair, as before, said emphatically — yes; Mr. Chase said — yes, with reservations; Messrs. Smith, Bates, Welles, Cameron, and Seward said — no. The most urgent counsel for retreat still came from the Department of State. Mr. Seward argued, with his customary elaboration, that a relief expedition, whether successful or otherwise, would precipitate civil war; and, as this contention had the support of his four last-mentioned associates, he confidently expected the President to follow his lead.[42]

So sanguine was Mr. Seward of imposing his ultra-conciliatory policy upon the administration that he had, from the start, conducted himself as if the abandonment of Sumter were assured. This was notably the case in his dealings with the commissioners sent to Washington by the Provisional Government of the Confederacy.[43] Presenting themselves, on the advent of the Lincoln régime, they had sought to open diplomatic relations with it through the State Department. The head of that office, whom they then, in common with so many people, North and South, took to be the head of the administration as well, was — they were aware — committed to peace and concession. The commissioners' hopes, therefore, no less than their pretensions as ambassadors from what was ostensibly a foreign country, led them to Mr. Seward's door. He declined to receive them, and asked the President for instructions. Profiting by Mr. Buchanan's error, under somewhat similar conditions, Mr. Lincoln directed his Secretary neither to recognize the envoys officially, nor to hold any communication with them whatever. Whereupon several eminent intermediaries were impressed into service. Perhaps the most active among these was Justice Campbell of the United States Supreme Court.[44] Although a Southerner, who was shortly to join the secessionists, his exalted rank and apparent loyalty to the Union secured him Mr. Seward's respectful attention. Their interviews were chiefly about Fort Sumter, which, the Secretary gave the Judge to understand, would be evacuated within a few days. This welcome news Campbell lost no time in carrying to the commissioners and in writing to Jefferson Davis.

Meanwhile, Mr. Lincoln continued to study the situation, in his own way. Consulting with military and naval men whenever he could snatch a few moments from other cares, trying, by the reënforcement of Fort Pickens in Florida, to take the sting out of possible failure in South Carolina, studying Anderson's resources,[45] sending trusty observers to Charleston and Sumter, drawing information from executive departments, weighing chances in the Border States, gauging southern passions, testing northern sentiment, — all this got him ready, by the close of March, for the decision that could no longer be deferred. On the 29th of the month he again, at a cabinet meeting, took the written opinions of his ministers. Out of the six who were present, three — Blair, Chase, and Welles — now agreed with the President's homely dictum that they should "send bread to Anderson." Bates, who had previously been against provisioning the fort, was non-committal. Smith favored evacuation, on purely military grounds. Seward, standing alone, still advised "against the expedition in every view."[46] When the cabinet adjourned, Mr. Lincoln, who had practically reached a conclusion before it assembled, directed Secretaries Cameron and Welles to enter upon relief preparations.[47] The order for the expedition to sail was withheld several days, however, and while the issue seemed to hang in the balance, Mr. Seward continued his opposition. Even after the final command was given, he found it "difficult to believe" that the President's policy, and not his, had prevailed.[48]

Mr. Lincoln's decision left the Secretary of State in an embarrassing position. The North, for the moment, looked askance upon the all-powerful statesman whose plans, predictions, and promises were thus, despite his most strenuous efforts, discredited. The South, taking its cue from Justice Campbell and the Confederate commissioners, accused him of duplicity. A similar charge spread against the Lincoln government itself, which, the secessionist leaders insisted, was wholly under Mr. Seward's control. That such was not the case, the shrewdest of them had, for some time, more than conjectured; and that the Secretary of State acted in good faith, when he said he would have his way with Sumter, is established beyond reasonable doubt.[49] But the very facts which acquit the minister of double-dealing convict him, as clearly, of grave indiscretion. He had taken upon himself to speak conclusively in an important matter, while it was under the consideration of his chief, who alone had authority to pronounce the decisive word.[50] Such presumption would, of course, have been out of the question, for a politician of Seward's experience, had he not, even after four weeks of close intercourse with Lincoln, committed the unpardonable blunder in statecraft. That is to say, he still entirely miscalculated the caliber of the man he sought to rule.

In the whirl of events, the Secretary's dazzled vision mistook the President's lack of knowledge for incapacity; his indecision, for executive incompetence; his modesty, for weakness. The ship of state seemed to be drifting on to the rocks, and a stronger hand — so thought Mr. Seward — was needed, forthwith, at the helm. He had, as we have seen, embarked in the administration with the expectation of directing its course. The notion had apparently been confirmed, not only by public opinion, but also by the deference with which the President treated him. Nevertheless, as the Sumter incident advanced, the Secretary realized that his power was far from complete.

How to make himself supreme, once for all, and, at the same time, rescue the country from civil war, had occupied a few of the feverish hours which preceded that final decision to relieve the fort. Something had to be done, and quickly, too. Perhaps the readiest expedient might have been that by which Cardinal Gaetano supplanted his Pope, the pious and unworldly Celestine. Messer Gaetano, so the story runs, contrived, soon after the Pontiff's consecration, to fill the sacred chamber, at night, with voices that called, as if from Heaven, "Resign, Celestine! Resign!" Whereupon the simple monk, already distracted by ecclesiastical intrigues for which he was so ill-adapted, took the wily Cardinal's advice to abdicate, and turned "toward his secluded abode," in the heart of the mountains; while Gaetano succeeded him, as Boniface VIII.

This trick answered well enough for mediæval politics, but our Secretary of State had to dip deep down into his mind for a more modern device. So he summoned Mr. Lincoln to surrender the management of public affairs, in a memorandum entitled "Some Thoughts for the President's Consideration, April 1, 1861." The document, after declaring that the administration, at the end of its first month, was "without a policy, domestic or foreign," presented "Thoughts" that might serve for both. As "the policy at home," it set forth that the horde of applicants for local offices should be disposed of, without delay; that the issue before the country should be changed from a question of slavery to one of union; and that Sumter should be evacuated, but all other Federal points in the South defended. The "Thoughts" headed "For Foreign Nations" were vigorous, indeed. Explanations were to be required from Spain, France, Great Britain, and Russia, which all seemed to contemplate interference in American affairs. If the two first-named governments, more aggressive than the others, did not return satisfactory answers, Congress was to be convened, and war was to be declared against them.[51] A spirit of antagonism against European intervention was, at the same time, to be aroused in Canada, Mexico, Central America, and the continent, generally. "But whatever policy we adopt," read the concluding "Thoughts," "there must be an energetic prosecution of it. For this purpose, it must be somebody's business to pursue and direct it, incessantly. Either the President must do it himself, and be all the while active in it, or devolve it on some member of his cabinet. Once adopted, debates on it must end, and all agree and abide. It is not in my especial province; but I neither seek to evade nor assume responsibility."[52]

Never before had an American cabinet minister penned a document so extraordinary. Its unwisdom — wild as some of the suggestions were — did not exceed its effrontery.[53] The plan to unite the discordant sections of the United States by leaving their differences unsettled, and plunging the whole continent into a series of foreign wars on sentimental grounds, reads like the desperate contrivance of a panic-stricken mind.[54] The implication that Mr. Lincoln was unequal to his duties and should turn over the most important of them to a sort of dictator, could have been addressed by Mr. Seward only to a President whom he believed to be totally lacking in strength of character. His error was corrected without further delay. Before the last fish was hooked or the last cuckoo hunted, on that All Fools' Day, he had Mr. Lincoln's written reply. The President, with his customary disregard of self, ignored the insult, and with tact, not less delicate, refrained from comment on the fantastic scheme for European wars. His Secretary was informed that he would find the domestic policy of the administration outlined in the inaugural address,[55] and its foreign policy in the despatches sent abroad by the State Department. As to the exercise of absolute authority, suggested in Mr. Seward's closing propositions, Mr. Lincoln said: —

"I remark that if this must be done, I must do it. When a general line of policy is adopted, I apprehend there is no danger of its being changed without good reason, or continuing to be a subject of unnecessary debate; still, upon points arising in its progress I wish, and suppose I am entitled to have, the advice of all the cabinet."[56]

Having quietly settled the question of supremacy, Mr. Lincoln put the "Thoughts" away among his personal papers, where they remained until his private secretaries, years after both statesmen had passed from the scene, published them to an astonished world. Excepting Mr. Nicolay, nobody else apparently knew of their existence, for the one to whom they were addressed never, it is believed, spoke of them, not even to the Secretary of State himself. If that gentleman, when he received his answer, had any lingering doubts as to the President's superiority over him, they must have been dismissed when he realized how entirely Mr. Lincoln disdained to take advantage of a weapon which, in the grasp of most politicians, would, under the circumstances, have been used to destroy the maker. If ever public man held a formidable rival in the hollow of his hand, here was an instance of it. Yet Gulliver, setting down unharmed the Liliputian who had tormented him, behaved not more gently than did the President toward this presumptuous minister.[57]

Thus ended Seward's dream of domination. All his romantic notions of saving the country *aus eigner Macht*, so freely expressed in those confidential letters to his wife, had to be revised, and we find him presently writing to her: —

"Executive skill and vigor are rare qualities. The President is the best of us."[58]

In the public eye, however, the Secretary of State still held sway. His defeat on the Sumter question was soon lost sight of among the stirring scenes which crowded thick and fast upon that incident. There ensued, moreover, no apparent change in his control of the foreign department; he was, as before, entrusted occasionally with duties that should properly have fallen to one or another of his colleagues; and his cordial, almost constant, association with the President created the impression that his influence had increased rather than diminished.[59] Even public men high in office continued to believe for a time that Mr. Seward practically ran the administration, an idea which some of them, in fact, never quite abandoned.

As late as 1873, this view was advanced on a notable occasion by the Hon. Charles Francis Adams, our Minister at the Court of St. James during the Civil War. He favored the New York legislature, shortly after the great statesman's death, with a memorial address, which attracted widespread attention, not so much for its appropriate eulogy of Mr. Seward as for its disparagement of Mr. Lincoln. The President, according to this orator, was so inferior to the Secretary of State "in native intellectual power, in extent of acquirement, in breadth of philosophical experience, and in the force of moral discipline," that he allowed his minister to direct the affairs of the nation in the Executive's name. Lincoln, asserted Mr. Adams, had consequently reaped honors which he owed for the most part to Seward's labors, and which it was the duty of history to reapportion.[60] Here was manifest error; but panegyric, especially when pronounced upon a recently departed leader by a loving follower, has its privilege. Hence the address, notwithstanding its semi-official character and the eminence of its author, might have been lightly passed over by the historian of to-day if it had not, at the time it was delivered, evoked an important reply. This was published by ex-Secretary Welles, upon the request of Montgomery Blair, the only other surviving member of the Lincoln cabinet.[61] They agreed that the eulogist had entirely misapprehended the relations between the two men, and that, whatever might be said of Mr. Seward's ability, the President, not he, had been master of the situation. "Indeed," wrote

Mr. Welles, "the whole language, tone, tenor, sentiment, and intent of the address are to elevate Mr. Seward and depreciate Mr. Lincoln; to award to the Secretary honors that clearly belong to the President; to make it appear that the subordinate controlled and directed the principal; that the Secretary of State was *de facto* President, and the President himself a mere *locum tenens*, incompetent for the place from the want of 'experience' and 'previous preparation.' Mr. Seward had influence in the administration, but not control. His mental activity, the 'marvelous fertility of his pen,' his proneness to exercise authority and to make himself conspicuous on every important subject and occasion, imposed on admiring and willing friends, who, like Mr. Adams, persuaded themselves that one so active and prominent must be the moving and directing spirit of the administration. . . . To those who knew Abraham Lincoln, or who were at all intimate with his administration, the representation that he was subordinate to any member of his cabinet, or that he was deficient in executive or administrative ability, is absurd."[62]

Upon this testimony and more like it, throughout Mr. Welles's monograph, we infer that the Secretary of State — appearances to the contrary notwithstanding — must have stepped back to the place so firmly yet courteously pointed out by the President, in the little private interlude which closed their first four weeks of office. From that time to the end, Seward knew Lincoln to be his master. With a grace peculiarly his own, the Secretary adapted himself to this unexpected development. His every action seemed to say, as did the fair penitent of the house of Capulet, —

> "Pardon, I beseech you!
> Henceforward I am ever ruled by you."

When his inclinations or purposes conflicted with those of his chief, he gave way — nay, more, he put forth all his powers to carry out Mr. Lincoln's wishes. "There is but one vote in the cabinet," the minister once declared, "and that is cast by the President." [63] How complete was the submission of the speaker, himself, may be gathered from a few well-known incidents.

Seward's senatorial career, particularly his experience on the Foreign Relations Committee, fitted him, in Mr. Lincoln's eyes, for the management of the State Department. In planning his administration, the President-elect had said: —

"One part of the business, Governor Seward, I think I shall leave almost entirely in your hands; that is, the dealing with those foreign nations and their governments." [64]

Nevertheless, Mr. Lincoln required important questions to be laid before him, and, when occasion demanded, he did not hesitate to take the guiding hand himself. This was the case a few weeks after the episode of the "Thoughts," when the British government recognized, with unseemly haste, the belligerency of the Confederate States. England's unfriendly attitude irritated Mr. Seward out of his habitual diplomatic composure to such a degree that the letter of instruction, which he wrote for Mr. Adams, our Minister in London, was more forcible than wise. Had the despatch, as it stood, been sent abroad and read, in accordance with custom, to her Britannic Majesty's Secretary of State for Foreign Affairs, serious difficulties with England might have ensued. This would hardly have suited the President's maxim, "One war at a time"; so, retaining the document, he subjected it to a critical revision. Striking out some of the most offensive expressions and modifying others, he transformed an international fire-brand into a harmless diplomatic note. When the paper was returned to the author, its erasures and interlineations must have recalled his labors of three months before, upon the inaugural address. If so, the difference in the circumstances, probably, did not escape him. Mr. Seward's changes had, properly enough, been suggested in a separate letter; the President's were made, without ceremony, on the draft itself. Mr. Lincoln's corrections, moreover, although they materially altered the letter, in its general tone and purpose, were, unlike Mr. Seward's, — with a few slight deviations, — literally observed. For the Secretary of State took his lesson in diplomacy as meekly as he had, a few weeks before, received one in politics.[65]

Seward's blunders in the Adams despatch were grave. Together with his Quixotic scheme for continental wars, they naturally impaired the President's confidence in his judgment on foreign affairs. As international problems of importance arose, Mr. Lincoln fell into the practice of consulting not only his Secretary of State, but other advisers, in the cabinet and out of it, as well. Chief among these was Charles Sumner. His position as chairman of the Senate Committee on Foreign Relations, his familiarity with diplomatic questions, his acquaintance with European statesmen, and his ripe scholarship rendered his opinions of particular value to the President. Mr. Lincoln even went so far as to call the Senator and the Secretary into council together. When, as happened in several instances, Sumner's views were opposed to Seward's, the President decided between them. And his decision was not always in the minister's favor. Mr. Seward's humiliation at this compulsory division of his functions with another was hardly alleviated by the fact that that other represented a wing of their party intensely inimical to him. Once, upon being answered by Mr. Lincoln with an opinion from Sumner, he hotly exclaimed that there were "too many Secretaries of State in Washington."[66] But such outbreaks were rare; and champ as he might, when the team was doubled, Seward stayed in the traces.[67]

What was true as to foreign matters was equally the case in domestic affairs. Here also Mr. Lincoln, whenever he saw fit to do so, exercised over Mr. Seward supreme authority. This is strikingly shown in one of the famous episodes of the war. Early in 1865, the President of the Confederacy was influenced by Francis Preston Blair, Senior, to appoint a peace commission for informal conference with the Federal government. President Lincoln, having directed Secretary Seward to meet the southern representatives, Messrs. Stephens, Hunter, and Campbell,[68] at Fortress Monroe, handed him written instructions which read: —

"You will make known to them that three things are indispensable — to wit: first, The restoration of the national authority throughout all the States; second, No receding by the Executive of the United States on the slavery question from the position assumed thereon in the late annual message to Congress, and in preceding documents; third, No cessation of hostilities short of an end of the war, and the disbanding of all forces hostile to the government.

"You will inform them that all propositions of theirs, not inconsistent with the above, will be considered and passed upon in a spirit of sincere liberality. You will hear all they may choose to say and report it to me. You will not assume to definitely consummate anything."[69]

With these — the orders of a master to his servant — Mr. Seward set out. Not many hours later, a despatch from General Grant,[70] who had received the southern commissioners within his lines at City Point, led the President to think that he, himself, might accomplish more than his Secretary of State. The fact that the mission had been formally confided to Mr. Seward, and with minute instructions, did not deter Mr. Lincoln from taking it out of his hands. Hastening after the Secretary, he joined him previous to the conference, and, without so much as by your leave, took the northern side of the discussion under his own direction.

Truly, Seward's over-zealous eulogist blundered in magnifying the subaltern at the captain's expense. Yet, not a few of Lincoln's biographers have erred as badly, in the opposite direction. Perhaps they thought to increase the President's inches by belittling the cabinet officer who stood so near him — or, did their eyes, full of Lincoln's dominating figure, fail to take in Seward's actual stature? Be that as it may, they render the greater man's fame no service by underrating the powers of the subordinate, whom — as we have seen — he bent completely to his will. Indeed, justice to Lincoln, no less than to Seward, requires that the Secretary receive full credit. The records of the State Department, during that most critical epoch in the nation's foreign affairs, bear abundant testimony to Mr. Seward's brilliant labors. Granting his occasional mistakes of method or policy, in coping with the trained diplomatists of Europe, our Secretary's severest critics among his own countrymen should at least acknowledge, as did Earl Russell, his foremost British opponent, that he evinced singular and varied ability. Only talents of a superior order could, in fact, have conducted the State Department through the dark hours of the Civil War. With a distracted country behind him, and the two most powerful governments of Christendom threatening from both sides, in ill-concealed hostility, Mr. Seward achieved results that fixed his place high, if not highest, on the roll of American foreign ministers.

No one, it is safe to say, appreciated the Secretary at his true value so accurately as the President. In his admiration of Mr. Seward, he overlooked the mistakes, supplemented the important labors, on occasion, with necessary touches of his own shrewd common sense, and kept the brilliant talents employed for the best interests of the country. Mr. Lincoln, it is true, privately contemplated, in at least two recorded instances, the removal of Seward;[71] but he gave his Secretary, none the less, unwavering public support. Of this aid Mr. Seward, now and then, stood greatly in need. When military reverses or administrative troubles came, he was, for a time, because of his reputed power in the government, held responsible by the people; while Radical leaders, taking advantage of every opening, tried in season and out to influence the President against him.[72] As these unrelated attempts all failed, Seward's enemies resorted to organized attacks. Early in September, 1862, a committee of prominent New Yorkers, led by the venerable son of Alexander Hamilton, called upon Mr. Lincoln ostensibly to urge "a change of policy." They represented, according to their own statement, not only the views of the dissatisfied Republican element in the Empire State, but of five New England Governors as well. The animus of their criticisms soon became apparent to the President, who, in the midst of the heated discussion that ensued, angrily exclaimed: —

"You, gentlemen, to hang Mr. Seward would destroy the government."[73]

Exit the wise men of Gotham — sadder, though not wiser, than when they came. For despite Lincoln's attitude toward them, the factional opposition against his Secretary of State lost none of its momentum. On the contrary, it made such headway by the middle of December that a caucus of Republican Senators voted to demand Seward's dismissal; but even these formidable enemies failed to break down the President's protection. With what courage and adroitness he defended Seward, and how thoroughly he put the attacking party to rout, will be told, with all its dramatic details, in the story of that other cabinet officer who shared the defeat. It is enough to say here that our powerful minister gladly found safety behind the man whom, not many months before, he had thought to thrust into the background. After the repulse of the senatorial cabal, moreover, Lincoln made short work of those who came to undermine the Secretary of State. He shielded Seward against all such assaults, and kept him secure in his high office to the end.

Small wonder that the respect, which the Secretary had early learned to show his chief, became mingled with a warmth of personal devotion that has not, in similar relations of our history, been surpassed. Renouncing his own aspirations, Mr. Seward dedicated himself, without reserve, to the President's political fortunes, as well as to the success of his administration, so far as it might be achieved by the State Department.[74] The minister's conduct, as the bond between the two men strengthened, said — or seemed to say — with old *Adam*: —

> "Master, go on, and I will follow thee,
> To the last gasp, with truth and loyalty."

To the last gasp, indeed. For when Lincoln was murdered, the assassins, as if their foul work might otherwise have been incomplete, struck another blow that was to send Seward after him. It failed to cut off the springs of life, and he was left behind to carry — in a sense — alone, the burden these two had so affectionately borne together. A few years Seward tarried. Then, full of days and honors, he too was laid at rest. On his tomb, in Fort Hill cemetery, at Auburn, those who loved him inscribed no word of all his triumphs. Looking back through the trying scenes of the war and seeming to see him again at the President's side, they recalled an epitaph that Seward, himself, had, in his prime, selected.[75] So they carved on the stone: —

"He was faithful."

Had the master whom the departed statesman served stood by, he might well have pronounced, as of old, the familiar formula: —

"Approved. — A. Lincoln."

CHAPTER V

AN INDISPENSABLE MAN

THE man who divided with Lincoln and Seward the highest honors in the Republican National Convention of 1860 was Salmon Portland Chase. He received on two of the three ballots for the presidential nomination the third largest number of votes. The figures, themselves, in comparison with those of the two foremost candidates, were small; for not even all the delegates from Ohio, his own State, gave Mr. Chase their support. Nevertheless, if the suffrages of the Convention had been based — to the exclusion of other considerations — upon national prominence, reputed ability, and party services, he would have stood second to Seward, alone. Like that eminent leader, Chase had twice been Governor of a great commonwealth, and had twice been elected to the United States Senate. In these high places his acts, no less than his principles, had embodied the finest aspirations of the Convention. Many of its members, indeed, who withheld from him their votes paid tribute privately to the merits of his illustrious career.

Chase belonged to that class of strenuous nation builders who, for lack of a better title, have been termed Western Yankees. After graduation from Dartmouth College, in his native State, he had resorted to the twin stepping-stones on which so many Americans have attained eminence — school-teaching and law. Admitted to the bar in his twenty-second year, he had taken up his residence in Cincinnati, with the business, literary, and social life of which he soon became actively identified.[1] Professional success, together with an honorable position in the community, were within the newcomer's reach, when he had seemingly brushed them aside by lending his talents to the small knot of despised Abolitionists who braved, in the early thirties, the pro-slavery prejudices of southern Ohio. Cincinnati's interests were so closely interwoven with those of the black belt beyond the river that her citizens, especially, held the reformers in detestation. As was to be expected, the young lawyer's course in allying himself with the so-called disturbers of the public peace had estranged influential friends and clients, who saw, or thought they saw, in this association his inevitable ruin.[2] At some risk to himself, he had, in the summer of 1836, confronted a mob on its way to attack James G. Birney; and, a few months thereafter, when that friend of the negroes was indicted for harboring a female slave, Chase had appeared in his defence. The fugitive, herself, despite the plea of the same foolhardy advocate, was returned to bondage, but her race had gained a champion. So frequently thereafter had Chase acted as counsel for fugitive slaves and those who befriended them that he had been derisively nicknamed "attorney-general for runaway negroes." The duties of this fanciful office, unprofitable as they were unpopular, he had cheerfully accepted; yet adverse decision upon decision had taught him that the anti-slavery cause was to be won, not at the bar, but in the forum.

To the field of politics, therefore, Chase had carried his ideals, only to find that there, as in law, they were heavy handicaps. Neither of the two great parties, Whigs nor Democrats, — he had tried them both, — was prepared, at the time, for anti-slavery principles. So, foregoing the preferment that his talents might have won for him in such powerful organizations, Chase had affiliated himself, usually as a master mind, with the unsubstantial factions — Liberty-men, Independent Democrats, Free-soilers, and what not — which struggled one after another to give the cause a political standing. When at last one of these bodies chanced to gain a foothold, there came to pass something like the miracle promised in the Scriptures, — he who had lost his life for his conscience's sake had found it. A dead-lock in joint session of the Ohio legislature, during the winter of 1848–49, had left the balance of power in the hands of two Independent Free-soilers; and so skilfully had they exercised it as to compel the election of Mr. Chase to the United States Senate. There, political accident as he was, without experience in public office, and without recognition by either of the two parties which divided legislative business, he had before the expiration of his term taken rank as a leader among such anti-slavery giants as Hale, Sumner, Seward, Wade, Hamlin, and Fessenden. When these men and others, equally eminent, established the Republican Party, Chase's enthusiasm for its principles, no less than his talent for political organization, had again carried him to his accustomed place in the front rank. Scarcely had he completed his senatorial labors, when he had led the Ohio branch of the new party to a victory that placed him in the Governor's chair. Through two administrations — for he was, as we have said, reëlected to the office — Chase had not only strengthened Republicanism in the State, but had abundantly contributed, as well, to its upbuilding in the Nation. His prestige seemed complete when, upon stepping out of the governorship, he had, by a large and spontaneous vote, been again elected to the United States Senate. Still flushed with this triumph, Mr. Chase had, a few months thereafter, sought yet higher honors at the Chicago Convention, only to go down, in his first signal defeat, before Abraham Lincoln.

The man from Illinois felt kindly toward the Ohio leader. Mr. Chase was one of the few distinguished statesmen who had sympathized with Mr. Lincoln in his memorable canvass for the Senate against Stephen A. Douglas. On that occasion, the Governor had, like Giddings, Corwin, Colfax, and Cassius M. Clay, come from beyond the limits of the State to aid the Republican candidate.[3] In Lincoln's mind, moreover, Chase was coupled with Seward as one of the two great captains who, having guided the anti-slavery hosts through the wilderness, were entitled to lead them into the promised land.[4] When the National Convention decided otherwise, it was a change of votes among Chase's adherents that had turned the scale in the Illinoisan's favor;[5] and when the latter was elected to the presidency, none of his rivals for the nomination had given him more loyal support than had the Senator-elect from Ohio. Add to these circumstances that the Westerner, Chase, though an Independent, was credited to the Democratic element in the new party, as Seward, an eastern man, represented the Whigs, and we comprehend why Mr. Lincoln, beginning the construction of his carefully balanced cabinet with the New Yorker, should assign the second place in it to the famous Ohioan.

No sooner had Seward accepted his appointment than Chase was summoned by telegraph to Springfield. Learning of his arrival, the President-elect, with the disregard of formality habitual to him, called on the visitor, at his hotel. "I have done with you," said Mr. Lincoln, "what I would not perhaps have ventured to do with any other man in the country — sent for you to ask you whether you will accept the appointment of Secretary of the Treasury without, however, being exactly prepared to offer it to you."[6] The other replied that he desired no cabinet office, and that, if he did, he could not easily reconcile himself to a subordinate one. Whereupon Mr. Lincoln explained that he had tendered the portfolio of State to Mr. Seward, as the generally recognized leader of the Republican Party, with the intention, if he declined, of offering it to Mr. Chase; but that, as it had been accepted, the next important post in the cabinet was probably at the visitor's command. "I replied," wrote Mr. Chase in his account of the interview, "that I did not wish, and was not prepared to say that I would accept that place if offered." He graciously added, however, that the appointment of Mr. Seward to the Department of State would remove his objections to a subordinate office, if he should conclude to accept one, under any conditions. "Everything was left open," to quote Mr. Chase, when the two men parted; but it was understood, throughout the country, that he would probably be Secretary of the Treasury. This prospect, as we have seen, was distasteful in the extreme to Seward's friends. They strove to shut Chase out of the cabinet — how earnestly and how fruitlessly has already been narrated. Nor were they the only opponents of the appointment. Yet Mr. Lincoln's esteem for the man, as well as his confidence in the political wisdom of the selection, suffered no diminution during the two months of partisan bickerings that intervened between their conference and the inauguration of the new administration. One of its earliest acts was to lay before the Senate the President's proposed cabinet — with the Treasury assigned to Mr. Chase.

That gentleman's attitude, however, was now found to have undergone somewhat of a change. The good temper with which he had laid aside his pretensions to the highest cabinet prize, in Seward's favor, must have been sorely tried by the efforts of that leader's friends to exclude him altogether. They had not succeeded in this, it is true, yet Seward's ascendancy over the incoming administration was generally conceded, and it boded no good to Chase's personal ambitions. Under these conditions, a place in the untried Lincoln's parti-colored cabinet — face to face as it was with a crisis, serious beyond measure — looked less inviting than ever to a Senator with his full term before him. In the Upper House, Chase could, unhampered, advance his principles and his political fortunes together. His private estate, too, which was not in a flourishing condition, might properly be improved, while he held a legislative office; but as Secretary of the Treasury, all roads to profit — professional or otherwise — would be closed to him. Moreover, — and this was of much importance to a person of Mr. Chase's temperament, — his pride had been piqued at the way in which the offer of the appointment originally came to him. "Had it been made earlier," he said, "and with the same promptitude and definiteness as that to Mr. Seward, I should have been inclined to make some sacrifices."[7] By the time the formal nomination reached the Senate, therefore, Chase had practically decided not to accept a cabinet office. He had, in fact, already taken his seat in the upper chamber; but happened, at the moment, to be absent. Learning upon his return that his name had been presented for the Treasury portfolio and unanimously confirmed, he hastened before the President to decline. What took place at that interview is not precisely known. Chase came, as Seward had a few hours before, with a refusal, on the very eve of sailing, to embark in Lincoln's shaky craft. Like Seward, Chase was somehow influenced by that raw captain, with his gently masterful ways, to reconsider, and like him, still, he stepped on board the following day, signed for the voyage.

As the ship which carried the fate of a nation cast loose from her moorings and stood out for the open sea, already churning in the teeth of the gathering storm, a stranger, glancing over her group of officers to discern by appearance, if he might, which one of them had been entrusted with so perilous a command, must have quickly passed over the uncouth-looking Lincoln to single out, from among those about him, the imposing figure of Salmon P. Chase. He looked the part. His tall, well-proportioned frame supported a massive head. Every line of the expressive face, from dome-like forehead to firm, smooth-shaven chin, described a curve of virile beauty. Nature has been so lavish to but few of our public leaders, and by none of them have personal advantages been borne with greater dignity. This stately presence was reënforced, moreover, by a mind as vigorous as it was cultivated. A

Edwin M Stanton

lover of literature, with three modern languages at command, a good classical scholar, — as college men go, — a well-trained lawyer of judicial temperament, a close reasoner, a master of exposition, a fluent writer, an earnest worker, Chase was equipped for any task that his restless ambition might impose. As an author of political proclamations and party platforms, he had no peer. To his talents in this direction the resolutions and address of the Liberty Party, at the Ohio State Convention in 1841; the platform adopted by the same organization in the National Convention of 1843; the Address to the People, published by the Southern and Western Liberty Convention of 1845; the resolutions and address adopted by the People's State Convention of Ohio in 1848; the National Free-soil platform of that year; the platform of the Free Democracy adopted at Pittsburg in 1852; and the Appeal of the Independent Democrats in Congress to the People of the United States [8] in 1854, bear abundant testimony. Equal distinction as an orator cannot be ascribed to Mr. Chase. A slight impediment in speech rendered him, like the great Hebrew emancipator, "of a slow tongue." He lacked, moreover, the wit, play of fancy, sympathetic fervor, and charm of persuasion so essential, ordinarily, to political eloquence. "Light without heat" was how a statesman who became one of his senatorial colleagues characterized Chase's utterances, and the speaker might have added, in this connection at least, that ancient definition of equity upon which the phrase was modeled — "mind without passion." The mental processes of the man, on the stump no less than in the Senate, were as dignified as his carriage. Disdaining, for the most part, the familiar devices of rhetoric and elocution, by which anti-slavery orators, during the generation before the war, usually appealed to popular emotions, he addressed himself to the calm judgment of his audiences, with a freedom from personal animus, a fidelity to clearly stated facts, and a force of logic, as refreshing in those heated days as they were convincing. When it is recalled, too, that he spoke with the earnestness of profound conviction and, perforce, with a deliberation which imparted to his words values almost oracular, we can comprehend why his speeches, despite their shortcomings, strengthened rather than impaired his hold on so high a place in party leadership. Not less important, withal, than Mr. Chase's intellectual attainments was a rich endowment of "that other wisdom," to use his own words, "whose name is courage." During the twenty years of vehement politics which intervened between the first convention of the Liberty-men and the triumph of the Republican Party, he had been faithful to principles, under conditions that put his pluck severely to the test. For, having determined a certain course to be the right one, he had pursued it with an energy well-nigh tireless, and a singleness of purpose which would brook no compromise. Deeply religious by temperament and training, he recognized in his creed an ever-present obligation to employ great powers righteously. Indeed, his private as well as his public life was governed by so pure a spirit of integrity, on so lofty a plane of duty, that men, not unmindful at the same time of his noble bearing, likened him to a Roman statesman, in the golden days of the ancient Republic.

The reverse of the medal was not so pleasing. Mr. Chase had the defects that too often accompany high qualities. Those very virtues, which so distinguished him, cast long shadows over his nature. Conscientious to an extreme, he looked upon the business of life in a mood that rendered his manner austere — at times, even stern. His chiseled features usually wore an expression, at least in public, of rigid reserve. The heavy, firmly pressed lips rarely relaxed, and the light of humor as seldom shone in the cold blue-gray eyes. When, at infrequent intervals, he did unbend, his efforts to be gay were not signally successful; and for that reason, perhaps, as much as any other, frivolity in public men met with his disapproval. A descendant of Puritans and Scotch Covenanters, Chase took himself, no less than his work, very seriously indeed. The mass of diaries and letters that he so carefully wrote, and, for the most part, as carefully preserved, reveal, in minute detail, with how stately a tread he must have walked among less decorous mortals. If he threw off his official robes now and then, to exclaim in the manner of Thurlow, "Lie there, Lord Chancellor!" we find no record of the fact. Given from early manhood, moreover, to habits of introspection, Chase became, in time, so self-centered and so egotistic as to lose that sense of proportion which saves men from overrating the importance of small things. Sensitive to an uncommon degree, and punctilious as to the forms of either social or official intercourse, he was swift to resent any lapse in the respect which he considered to be his due. For this martinet, though generally esteemed, had failed to attain popularity. Not only the people at large, but political associates as well, were, in the main, repelled by his unsympathetic personality. In fact, with possibly one or two exceptions, there sprang up between the great man and other leading Republicans no warm friendships. Such relations rest, by reason of their very nature, upon footings of equality, which Chase's assumption of his own superiority, together with his ever-pressing ambition to stand a little higher than those around him, put out of the question. He was genial enough, it is true, at his own fireside, toward the family that almost worshiped him, as well as toward the friends and politicians who were willing to do him homage. Especially was this so in the case of certain brilliant young men, whose devotion he repaid with affectionate patronage; yet hardly less cordial, it must be admitted, was the attitude of their "chief" — if we may use the title in which Chase delighted — toward the unscrupulous self-seekers, sycophants, and scamps, who easily played upon his vanity. An almost childish susceptibility to flattery so warped his judgment of character that he could with difficulty be brought to see faults in any of the persons who admired or supported him. And what, after all, if some of his followers were unworthy? — "'The immortal gods,'" he seemed to say, "'accept the meanest altars'; why not I?" Incense, whether burned by good men or bad, was equally grateful to his nostrils, even while it enveloped him in an atmosphere of adulation, through which the wisest path was not always discernible. Betrayed repeatedly into error by the imperious temper thus developed, Chase, as a rule, knew no will among his associates but his own. Indeed, the lesson of occasional subordination, important as it is to those who would command, he had entirely failed to learn. So imbued was he with a sense of his superiority, and so accustomed to its unquestioned recognition, that when, in his fifty-fourth year, he reluctantly became Mr. Lincoln's Secretary of the Treasury, he might most fitly have been described, as to certain minor aspects of his character, at least, by the homely word — spoiled.

Unfortunately for himself, as well as for the administration of which he formed a part, Mr. Chase's proneness to assert himself was, as in Seward's case, heightened by the conditions under which he entered upon his duties. Succeeding to the depleted treasury and the heavily increased national debt that constituted together an important contribution of the Buchanan régime to the Confederate cause, he found the credit of the government seriously impaired. Before measures for its restoration could be taken, the outbreak of the Civil War cut the country in two, swept the South with its wealth of staples out of the Union, paralyzed trade for a time, bankrupted many of the northern merchants, whose accounts were repudiated by their customers in the seceded States, and brought Mr. Chase — unprepared as he was by adequate training or experience — face to face with a problem as perplexing as any that has ever tried the sagacity of a finance minister. Sir Robert Peel's famous description of Baring, "seated on an empty chest, by the pool of bottomless deficiency, fishing for a budget," fitted the American Secretary to a nicety. How, under existing circumstances, he could raise funds for what proved to be the most costly military struggle in history, was the question. The average requirements throughout the war of over $2,000,000 a day could not be supplied, to any extent, by foreign loans. European bankers — some of them in sympathy with the Confederacy, others in doubt as to Union success — closed their coffers, at least during a considerable part of the conflict, against northern securities. Nothing, in consequence, was left to Mr. Chase, for a time, but the crippled resources of the loyal States. As even these means were in the hands of a people unaccustomed to direct taxation and prejudiced against public debt, some conception may be formed as to the magnitude of his task. That this was well performed must be conceded, notwithstanding adverse, and in the main valid criticism by experts on the economic soundness of certain measures. These measures served with others, be it remembered, to supply the government's seemingly unlimited wants — to outdo, in fact, the marvels of Fortunatus and his inexhaustible purse. For, from the money-bag in the chapbook romance, coin could presumably be taken out only through the opening by which it had passed in; but "the spigot in Uncle Abe's barrel," as Mr. Chase dolefully expressed it, was "twice as big as the bung-hole."

The rich stream, nevertheless, did not run dry, neither did it submerge the nation in that flood of financial disaster, which was feared by many Americans, and periodically predicted by the most influential organs of British public opinion. As it happened, these discouragements merely rendered more brilliant the eventual triumphs of the Treasury — triumphs due, in no small degree, be it said, to the patriotism of the northern people, the victories of Union armies, and the coöperation of a loyal Congress; yet credited, naturally enough, to the department of finance, and, above all, to the statesman at its head.

Never before had even he drunk so deeply of the sparkling cup. Men compared him with Turgot and Necker, with Hamilton and Gallatin. Indeed, some of his admirers, abroad as well as at home, indulged in extravagancies of praise that might have enlarged the self-esteem of a statesman less egotistic than Salmon P. Chase.

If anything was lacking to confirm the Secretary's belief in his own importance, it was supplied by the President himself. Mr. Lincoln had neither capacity nor taste for financiering. The science of dollars and cents is not likely to interest a man who defines wealth, as he did, to be "simply a superfluity of what we don't need." His business undertakings, in early life, had been signally unsuccessful, — to such a degree, in fact, that upon the occasion of his first election to the Illinois legislature, he had to borrow the money for a presentable suit of clothes, and his fare to the Capital. Twenty-six years later, a busy and what should, at the same time, have been a lucrative practice had not netted enough cash to defray the expenses of his inauguration journey.[9] So, by a significant coincidence, he had been under the necessity of traveling to Washington as he had to Vandalia, on a friendly loan. Lincoln's deficiency in what his friend and former partner, William H. Herndon, termed "money sense" was frankly summed up by the President himself one day, during a period of financial stress, when Chase desired to introduce to him a delegation of bankers, who were assembled to discuss an important phase of the money question.

"Money!" exclaimed Mr. Lincoln, "I don't know anything about money! I never had enough of my own to fret me, and I have no opinion about it any way."[10]

To another committee of financiers, that waited on him to find fault with the legal-tender law, he said: —

"Go to Secretary Chase; he is managing the finances."

In fact, the administration of the Treasury had, wisely, from the beginning, been entrusted entirely to the head of the department, who, as long as he supplied the required funds, was left, for ways and means, to his own fertile devices. Nor were those ways, in every respect, according to usage. The very first treasury bill, drawn by Mr. Chase and enacted by Congress, at its special session in July, 1861, empowered him solely to effect certain loans, though such authority had invariably been conferred theretofore upon the President and the Secretary of the Treasury, jointly. This innovation, involving an extraordinary transfer of executive functions, characterized all similar enactments during Chase's incumbency; yet Mr. Lincoln, with that freedom from self-assertion which is already so familiar to us, raised no objection. Contenting himself with some such comment as, "You understand these things — I do not," he adopted his purse-bearer's monetary recommendations, for the most part, as they were laid before him, without question. He even permitted Mr. Chase, it is said, to write some of the financial paragraphs in his messages. Be that as it may, whatever legislation the Secretary deemed essential was vigorously urged by the President, not only in his formal communications to Congress, but in his frequent conferences as well with the influential members of both Houses. This coöperation, together with a suggestion, now and then, modestly offered, made up the sum of the Executive's customary attention to the operations of the Treasury, which, despite its importance, was thus the only one of the great departments of the government not kept under his constant supervision.

Mr. Lincoln's practice of non-interference in financial affairs was not without its exception. But his single deviation from the rule — and only one authentic instance has come under the writer's notice — serves in more than a rhetorical sense to prove that rule. For it reveals how ignorant the President was concerning treasury matters, while it confirms our impression of the latitude habitually enjoyed by his able Secretary. On the other hand, the incident evinces how ready was the President, when aroused, to exercise his authority, even in so unfamiliar a field, with firmness. He was chatting one day in his office with his old friend, Marshal Lamon, when the conversation turned on the greenbacks, then for some time in circulation. Mr. Lincoln's visitor asked him whether he knew how the currency was made.

"Yes," answered the President, "I think it is about — as the lawyers would say — in the following manner, to wit: the engraver strikes off the sheets, passes them over to the Register of the currency, who places his earmarks upon them, signs them, hands them over to Father Spinner, who then places his wonderful signature at the bottom, and turns them over to Mr. Chase, who, as Secretary of the United States Treasury, issues them to the public as money, — and may the good Lord help any fellow that does n't take all he can honestly get of them!" Pulling a five-dollar greenback from his pocket, he said, with a twinkle in his eye, "Look at Spinner's signature! Was there ever anything like it on earth? Yet it is unmistakable. No one will ever be able to counterfeit it."

"But," said the Marshal, "you certainly don't suppose that Spinner actually wrote his name on that bill, do you?"

"Certainly I do; why not?" was the reply.

Mr. Lamon asked, "How much of this currency have we afloat?"

Mr. Lincoln stated the amount.

"How many times," continued his friend, "do you think a man can write a signature like Spinner's in the course of twenty-four hours?"

The smile left the President's countenance. He put the greenback into his pocket and walked the floor. After a while he stopped, took a long breath, and said: "This thing frightens me!" Summoning a messenger, he sent for the Secretary of the Treasury. Upon Mr. Chase's arrival, Mr. Lincoln explained the occasion of his alarm, and asked for a detailed description of how the money was handled in the process of manufacture. When the Secretary had complied with this request, the President expressed his opinion that there were not sufficient checks against robbery; but Mr. Chase insisted that the system had all the safeguards which he could devise. "In the nature of things," said he, "somebody must be trusted in this emergency. You have entrusted me, and Mr. Spinner is entrusted with untold millions, and we have to trust our subordinates." Words waxed warm between the two, when Mr. Lincoln said, with some feeling: —

"Don't think that I am doubting or could doubt your integrity, or that of Mr. Spinner; nor am I finding fault with either of you. But it strikes me that this thing is all wrong, and dangerous. I and the country know you and Mr. Spinner, but we don't know your subordinates, who are great factors in making this money; and have the power to bankrupt the government in an hour. Yet there seems to be no protection against a duplicate issue of every bill struck, and I can see no way of detecting duplicity until we come to redeem the currency; and even then, the duplicate cannot be told from the original."[11]

The President prevailed. As a result of the discussion, Mr. Chase made elaborate efforts to secure an improved system of checks against fraud or error. Calling upon the Chief of the Currency Bureau for the outline of a feasible plan, he submitted it, after revision by himself, to a special commission, consisting of the Acting Assistant Secretary, the Register, and the First Comptroller. Their report was, upon its receipt, referred back to them for further consideration; and Senator Sprague, because of his expert knowledge, was added to their number. The enlarged commission, however, merely confirmed the findings of its predecessor. Whereupon all the documents were placed, for final review, in the hands of the Assistant Secretary of the Treasury, who had recently returned from a study of the safeguards employed in the Bank of England and in the Bank of France. Upon his observations abroad and the suggestions of the commission were based a new body of rules for the Currency Bureau.[12]

Ample as was the scope of Mr. Chase's authority in financial matters, it failed to fill the measure of his administrative ambitions. He must have been dazzled with the power conferred upon him, in his own proper sphere; for he believed himself, again like Seward, capable of dominating other departments, as well. Particularly may this be said of the War Office, over which, throughout his cabinet career, he strove to exert a certain influence. "I have been studying the art of war," he once said. "I can find nothing in it but a calculation of chances and a quick eye for topography. Were I not so near-sighted, I would be tempted to resign my place as Secretary for a command in the field."[13] So persistently, indeed, was the martial purpose pursued, that no treasury duties, however exacting, were allowed to stand in its way. Nor did the hand on the purse relax, while the other hand reached for the sword. With both in his grasp, Chase would truly have been prepared

> "to advise how War may, best upheld,
> Move by her two main nerves, iron and gold,
> In all her equipage."

He might even have gathered strength enough for what he aspired to be — the essential genius of the conflict. His hopes in this direction Mr. Lincoln, still further, unavoidably fed. The President not only found it expedient, at times, to consult with the ever-ready Secretary of the Treasury on questions purely military; but he employed him also, as occasion required, on business which belonged within the province of the War Department. Other members of the cabinet, it is true, were called, now and then, to the relief of their colleague in that overburdened office; yet none of them, we may safely say, were so busy over its affairs as Mr. Chase. To him, and not to Secretary Cameron, was committed the task of framing certain official orders for the enlistment of troops; to his direction military matters in the western Border States were, during the earlier stages of the war, largely entrusted; and to his recommendations might have been traced important changes in the fortunes of more than one general officer. The confidential relations that he managed to establish with some of the commanders, no less than his familiarity with their operations in the field, led both the President and the Secretary of War to ask his aid, as a go-between, several times when misunderstandings or delicate personal questions arose. When it was deemed necessary, moreover, for a council of war to interrogate General McClellan about his plans, Mr. Chase performed the ungrateful office; when General McDowell, to his disappointment, was ordered back from Fredericksburg, during the Peninsular campaign, Chase was despatched to the front, with explanations; when Lincoln and Stanton made what our warlike Secretary of the Treasury termed their "brilliant week's campaign" against Norfolk, he accompanied them; and when the President held his momentous midnight conference, after Rosecrans's disaster at Chickamauga, he was one of the three cabinet ministers present. Mr. Lincoln, on several occasions, even went so far as to direct generals-in-chief to discuss their projects with Mr. Chase; and still that gentleman was far from satisfied.

Considerable as was the Secretary's part in these and similar transactions, they bore together but a small ratio to all the affairs of the War Department on which he volunteered assistance or advice. To decline the former and disregard the latter came as natural to the President, at some times, as to avail himself of them at others. Confident of his own strength, he held Chase, as we have seen, by a free rein; but whenever they got too far from their course, the lines stiffened, and one masterful twist of the wrist brought the honorable Secretary back to his work. Like Seward, Chase was made to feel the power which lurked in that slack hand; unlike him, he never became reconciled to its sway. From the very outset, the man in the Treasury chafed under whatever limitations were placed upon his authority, but without avail. How helplessly he kicked against the pricks, his own letters and diaries reveal, at every turn. A few extracts from among many instances may not be out of place here.

The administration, to begin with, had hardly gotten under way before Mr. Chase's impatience at what he called "the Micawber policy of waiting for something to turn up" found vent in a letter to the President.

"Let me beg you to remember," it read, in a style strangely suggestive of Seward's "Thoughts," "that the disunionists have anticipated us in everything, and that as yet we have accomplished nothing but the destruction of our own property. Let me beg you to remember, also, that it has been a darling object with the disunionists to secure the passage of a secession ordinance by Maryland. The passage of that ordinance will be the signal for the entry of disunion forces into Maryland. It will give a color of law and regularity to rebellion, and thereby triple its strength. The custom-house in Baltimore will be seized, and Fort McHenry attacked — perhaps taken. What next? Do not, I pray you, let this new success of treason be inaugurated, in the presence of American troops. Save us from this new humiliation. A word to the brave old commanding general will do the work of prevention. You, alone, can give the word."[14]

The "word" was not given; nor is it known what reply, if any, Mr. Lincoln made to this querulous message. Its tone was ominous, as well as discordant, for many other strictures, equally severe or severer, followed from the same pen. To a private correspondent, some months thereafter, Chase made this comment: —

"It has been an error, I think, to push forward our whole army when two thirds of it, skilfully handled, would have effected the objects gained by the whole. But the great defect in the operations of the war has been a lack of vigor and celerity in movement. To make up for this, we accumulate immense forces at particular points, and wait until the enemy retreats, and then occupy his deserted quarters!"[15]

To another he wrote, still later, in a similar strain:—

"We have not accomplished what we ought to have accomplished. We have put small forces where large forces were needed, and have failed to improve advantages—the advantages we obtained. We have preferred generals who do little with much, to generals who do much with little. We blame and praise with equal want of reason and judgment."[16]

In his diary he noted, at about the same time:—

"Ten days of battle and then such changes—changes in which it is difficult to see the public good. How singularly all our worst defeats have followed administrative cr—, no, blunders!"[17]

Those changes were evidently not made upon Mr. Chase's recommendations. Indeed, the President's repeated disregard of his finance minister's military opinions evoked that officer's bitter faultfinding. He ascribed disasters to the neglect of his advice; and successes, he as truculently traced to its influence.

What vexed Chase, withal, more than Mr. Lincoln's failures to heed his counsels, was the fact that suitable opportunities for giving them were so infrequent. Complaints on this score abounded in his letters, especially in those addressed to his friends at home. To one of them he wrote:—

"Since the incoming of General Halleck I have known but little more of the progress of the war than any outsider,—I mean so far as influencing it goes. My recommendations, before he came in, were generally disregarded, and since have been seldom ventured. In two or three conversations I did insist on the removal of McClellan, and the substitution of an abler and more vigorous and energetic leader; on the clearing out of the Mississippi, and the expulsion of the rebels from East

Tennessee, all of which might have been done. But, though heard I was not heeded." [18]

To another:—

"I am not responsible for the management of the war, and have no voice in it, except that I am not forbidden to make suggestions, and do so now and then, when I cannot help it." [19]

And to still another:—

"Though charged with the responsibility of providing means for the vast expenditures of the war, I have little more voice in its conduct than a stranger to the administration—perhaps not so considerable a voice as some who are, in law at least, strangers to it. I should be very well satisfied with this state of things, if I saw the war prosecuted with vigor and success. I am only dissatisfied with it because I cannot help thinking that if my judgment had more weight, it would be so prosecuted." [20]

To Governor Brough, after the terrible slaughter of the Wilderness and Spottsylvania Court House, Mr. Chase thus unburdened himself:—

"My anxiety is very great; but departmental administration allows me no voice in military matters—not even in those which most nearly concern the Treasury—and I can therefore only wait and pray and hope." [21]

There were cabinet meetings, it is true, but Mr. Chase's conception of how they should be conducted differed widely from that of the President. This disagreement the Secretary emphasized, in several spirited letters. One to Senator John Sherman read:—

"Since General Halleck has been here the conduct of the war has been abandoned to him by the President almost absolutely. We—who are called members of the cabinet, but are in reality only separate heads of departments, meeting now and then for talk on whatever happens to come uppermost, not for grave consultation on matters concerning the salvation of the country—we have as little to do with it as if we were heads of factories supplying shoes or cloth. No regular and systematic reports of what is done are made, I believe, even to the President — certainly not to the so-called cabinet. Of course we may hope for the best — that privilege remains. As outsiders, too, I suppose we may criticise, but I prefer to forego that privilege. It is painful, however, to hear complaints of remissness, delays, discords, dangers, and to feel that there must be ground for such complaints, and to know that one has no power to remedy the evils and yet is thought to have." [22]

To Horace Greeley our disgruntled minister wrote: —

"It seems to me that in this government the President and his cabinet ought to be well advised of all matters vital to the military and civil administration; but each one of us, to use a presidential expression, turns his own machine, with almost no comparison of views or consultation of any kind. It seems to me all wrong and I have tried very hard to have it otherwise — unavailingly." [23]

Commenting on foreign intervention in Santo Domingo and Mexico, he wrote to the Rev. Dr. Leavitt, one of the editors of the New York *Independent:* —

"Had there been here an administration in the true sense of the word — a President conferring with his cabinet and taking their united judgments, and with their aid enforcing activity, economy, and energy, in all departments of public service — we could have spoken boldly and defied the world. But our condition here has always been very different. I preside over the funnel; everybody else, and especially the Secretaries of War and the Navy, over the spigots — and keep them well open, too. Mr. Seward conducts the foreign relations with very little let or help from anybody. There is no unity and no system, except so far as it is departmental." [24]

That the people around the spigots paid so little attention to the important functionary at the funnel was especially irritating to the Secretary of the Treasury. He scolded, in turn, the successive heads of the War Department, on the score of extravagance; yet it should be observed that his customary attitude toward them was friendly. For here, as elsewhere, the prime offender, in his eyes, was Mr. Lincoln. To Secretary Cameron, Chase complained: —

"The want of success of our armies, and the difficulties of our financial operations, have not been in consequence of a want or excess of men, but for want of systematic administration. If the lack of economy, and the absence of accountability, are allowed to prevail in the future as in the past, bankruptcy, and the success of the rebellion, will be necessary consequences." [25]

After the War Department had, for a considerable time, been under Mr. Stanton's direction, Mr. Chase wrote to a friend, in Ohio: —

"Nothing except the waste of life is more painful in this war than the absolutely reckless waste of means. A very large part of the frauds which disgrace us may be traced to the want of systematic supervision; and yet what encouragement is there to endeavors toward economy? Such endeavors league against him who makes them all the venality and corruption which is interested in extravagance. Most, if not all, the bitter attacks made upon me have originated in the spite of the people whose interests were thought to be affected by my efforts to keep things in the right direction and under economical management." [26]

To another friend he thus lamented: —

"There has been enormous waste and profusion, growing out of high pay and excessive indulgence. All these causes tend to demoralization, and we are demoralized. I cannot go into particulars, but the instances abound. It is some consolation to me that my voice and, so far as opportunity has allowed, my example has been steadily opposed to all this. I have urged my ideas on the President and my associates, till I begin to feel that they are irksome to the first, and to one or two, at least, of the second." [27]

In a letter to General Hooker, the same busy correspondent thus frees his mind: —

"There has been a deal of talk about recalling you, and placing you in command of the Army of the Potomac, which one of the chaplains, in a recently published letter, calls, not altogether without reason, 'This poor, old, strategy-possessed army.' I wish it might be done. But, of course, my wishes go for little in such matters. What right, indeed, has a Secretary of the Treasury, whose business it is to provide money for the people to spend, to have any wishes at all about the results of the expenditure? Is not that exclusively the concern of the President and of Congress? I suppose I ought to shut my eyes and suppress my feelings, but really it is a little hard, when one *thinks* one *sees* how much might be economized of action, power, and resources, not to say something of what he thinks and feels." [28]

Hooker was but one of several officers to whom Secretary Chase disparaged the administration of which he, himself, formed a confidential part. Heedless of the impropriety, at times even the disloyalty of his course, he warmly condoled with the generals who brought him their grievances, real or fancied, against the President. Fruitless opposition to Mr. Lincoln's policy, in one instance, moreover, led Chase to the extreme of urging upon two of his military correspondents out-and-out insubordination. This misstep had its origin, to state it briefly, in the vexed question of emancipation. Mr. Chase persistently advised that commanders should be permitted to free and enlist the slaves within their lines; Mr. Lincoln decided otherwise. When the President, in the spring of 1862, annulled General Hunter's proclamation, it was in spite of Chase's earnest appeal to the contrary. So curtly was the Secretary brushed aside that he gave vent to his disappointment in even harsher terms than ordinarily. "I have never," he wrote to Greeley, "been so sorely tried, in all that I have seen in the shape of irregularities, assumptions beyond the law, extravagances, deference to generals and reactionists which I cannot approve . . . as by the nullifying of Hunter's proclamation." [29] But it was not in Chase's nature to accept a defeat; so we find him, a few weeks later, still trying to displace the President's policy by his own. In the course of a long letter to General Butler, at New Orleans, he wrote:—

"I shall express only my own opinions; opinions, however, to which I am just as sure the masses will and the politicians must come, as I am sure that both politicians and masses have come to opinions expressed by me when they found few concurrents. . . . If some prudential consideration did not forbid, I should at once, if I were in your place, notify the slaveholders of Louisiana that henceforth they must be content to pay their laborers wages. . . . It is quite true that such an order could not be enforced by military power beyond military lines; but it would enforce itself by degrees a good way beyond them, and would make the extension of military lines comparatively quite easy. It may be said that such an order would be annulled. I think not. It is plain enough to see that the annulling of Hunter's order was a mistake. It will not be repeated." [30]

On the following day, Chase wrote, in the same tenor, to General Pope, commanding the Army of Virginia. This letter closed with:—

"If I were in the field, I would let every man understand that no man loyal to the Union can be a slave. We must come to this. The public sentiment of the world, common-sense, and common justice, demand it. The sooner we respect the demand, the better for us and for our cause." [31]

With the unruly spirit that inspired these futile outbreaks now and then mingled something very like despair. For instance, shortly after Mr. Lincoln had reinstated General McClellan, in the teeth of vehement protests from Chase and others, this comment was confided to the diary:—

"Expenses are enormous, increasing instead of diminishing; and the ill-successes in the field have so affected government stocks that it is impossible to obtain money except on temporary deposit. . . . It is a bad state of things; but neither the President, his counselors, nor his commanding general seem to care. They rush on from expense to expense, and from defeat to defeat, heedless of the abyss of bankruptcy and ruin which yawns before us — so easily shunned yet seemingly so sure to engulf us. May God open the eyes of those who control us, before it is too late!"[32]

And a letter addressed, some months later, to Wayne McVeagh contained this outburst: —

"Oh, for a vigorous, earnest, thorough prosecution of this war! for a speedy and complete suppression of this rebellion! How often does the question come to me with terrific force! How much longer can the strain, which delay and extravagance make, be endured before the links of credit snap?"[33]

The precious links did not snap. On the contrary, as the war advanced, they became — with an occasional period of weakness — more firmly riveted together. But this fact apparently made no impression on the conduct of the minister who had them in his keeping; as he continued, to the end, his practice of petulant and, for the most part, bootless criticism. In season and out, in letters and private journals, in formal council and chance conversation, whether he addressed himself to members of the government circle or to rank outsiders, Chase was the severe — at times almost hostile — censor of the President and his administration.

In fairness to the Secretary of the Treasury, it must be conceded that his charges of extravagance were, especially during certain periods of unpreparedness at the outbreak of hostilities, warranted by the facts. It is true, moreover, that the operations of his department were, at times, embarrassed by lack of success in the field. And due weight should be given to the necessity under which he labored, or believed himself to labor, for combining military with financial authority, as other statesmen in the world's history had done before him. His chagrin at finding his martial activities repressed was therefore not surprising, particularly when we recall the temperament of the man, and the expectations which must have been fostered by what he was occasionally called upon to do in the War Department, no less than by the extraordinary powers conferred upon him in his own office. Yet these things do not justify, or even fully explain, the animus against the President, so apparent throughout Chase's cabinet career. For the seed of that antagonism we must look below the surface — into the very core of the matter.

Chase never entirely forgave Lincoln the latter's victory at the Chicago Convention. That a man so markedly his inferior in education and public achievements should have been preferred to him was as grievous to the Ohio statesman's self-love as it was irritating to his sense of equity. That this man, moreover, when he came to the presidency, should persist in actually running the administration, while his brilliant Secretary of the Treasury — so willing at every turn to relieve him of the burden — remained a mere head of department, hardly allayed the minister's resentment. The prejudice engendered in the defeated candidate took deeper root in the disappointed cabinet minister. Mr. Chase's failures, withal, to sway the President in military affairs — numerous and, at times, humiliating though they were — did not, by any means, make up the sum of his rebuffs. On such important subjects as privateering, early emancipation, concessions to the Border States, and martial law in places outside the field of hostilities, our Secretary, do what he would, could not save his cherished opinions from being swept aside. Here again, the character, or fancied character, of the chief who overruled him made his cup of subordination doubly bitter. The masterful Chase had met his master, yet he could not bring himself to the point of admitting it. Indeed, we find ourselves wondering, as he returns again and again to the charge, at his inability to realize how completely he was outclassed; but the riddle is read when it is remembered that his judgment of character was notably defective. This constituted what may be called the blind side of his make-up. He was, in fact, so near-sighted that the play of men's features, with their tell-tale disclosures, was lost upon him; and so self-centered, that what he seemed to see in other people was, too often, the mere reflection of his own prepossessions or prejudices. Thus misguided, — to say nothing of the concurrent circumstances, — Chase must inevitably have underrated Lincoln. The President — so thought his Secretary of the Treasury — had been elevated by a freak of fortune to a place which he was incapable of filling; and, by a similar chance, the minister, himself, had become enlisted under a chief who at every point in his bearing seemed to fall far below that courtly functionary's standards of statesmanship. Perhaps Mr. Chase, learned though he was, forgot that truly great rulers make their own standards. At all events, there was little, if anything, in Lincoln's simple demeanor, lack of culture, disregard of formality, and low-leveled humor to warn his Secretary of the transcendent genius for leadership that, almost unwittingly to itself, was working out a great destiny. Hence Mr. Chase presents the phenomenon of encountering at every turn a force stronger than his own, and failing entirely to recognize its existence. He had been a member of Mr. Lincoln's official family more than a year and a half, when he tactlessly asked a general officer, who had a grievance against the administration, what he thought of the President. The officer answered: —

"A man irresolute, but of honest intentions; born a poor white in a slave State, and, of course, among aristocrats; kind in spirit and not envious, but anxious for approval, especially of those to whom he has been accustomed to look up — hence solicitous of support of the slaveholders in the Border States, and unwilling to offend them; without the large mind necessary to grasp great questions, uncertain of himself, and in many things ready to lean too much on others."[34]

The sketch must have been in harmony with our Secretary's own views, for he transferred it carefully to his diary, with the endorsement that its author was "well read and extremely intelligent." In truth, Mr. Chase was not by any means the only eminent man at the Capital who mistook Lincoln's measure. Disparagement of the President was, at first, the rule rather than the exception. But as he coped with the problems of the war, one after another, sagacious men caught glimpses of the power that was bound up in his quaint, almost grotesque personality, and revised their estimates to somewhat like proper proportions. Not so, however, with Chase. He never even approached to justice in a conception of Lincoln, or, if he did, there is no evidence of it among his voluminous diaries and letters. When he committed to one of his journals, after their official connection had ceased, the admission, "I feel that I do not know him," Chase made his truest comment on Abraham Lincoln.

The President and his Secretary of the Treasury were, as far as their personal relations went, at no time heartily in sympathy with each other. As a matter of fact, one rarely finds two public men working together so earnestly for the triumph of the same principles who are, at once, so essentially dissimilar in social attributes as they happened to be. Lincoln's ways — unconventional in the extreme — grated upon the sensibilities of the dignified Chase. To the Secretary's fondness for forms, pride of intellect, distaste for humor, and serious, almost ascetic devotion to his tasks, must be ascribed, in a degree at least, the absence of cordiality between him and a President who made no secret of his ignorance, troubled himself not a whit about precedents, and was reminded, on all conceivable occasions, of stories hardly constructed according to classic models. Not the least of Lincoln's offences against the Chesterfield of his cabinet was the ill-concealed amusement with which he regarded that gentleman's displeasure at his levity. The President's bump of reverence appears to have been so exceedingly flat that the frowns of an important personage, however great, failed to abash him. Mr. Chase once told, with evident disgust, how an old-time crony of Lincoln in the Thirtieth Congress was permitted to interrupt a meeting of the cabinet. That body was in session one day, when the doorkeeper announced that Orlando Kellogg was without and wished to tell the President the story of the stuttering justice. Mr. Lincoln ordered the visitor to be ushered in immediately. Greeting Kellogg at the threshold with a warm grasp of the hand, the President said, as he turned to his cabinet: —

"Gentlemen, this is my old friend, Orlando Kellogg, and he wants to tell us the story of the stuttering justice. Let us lay all business aside, for it is a good story."

So statesmen, as well as affairs of state, waited while the humorous Kellogg spun his yarn and Lincoln had his laugh.[35] Another cabinet meeting, perhaps the most momentous in the history of the administration, was disfigured, according to Mr. Chase's diary, by similar merriment. The President had called his advisers together in order to lay before them his draft of the first Emancipation Proclamation. But before proceeding to this weighty matter, he mentioned that Artemus Ward had sent him his new book, and that he desired to read to them a chapter which he had found to be especially funny. Whereupon Mr. Lincoln regaled his assembled ministers with the High-Handed Outrage at Utica. It was read with effect, for Mr. Chase reports that his colleagues, as well as the President, "seemed to enjoy it very much." Our diarist excepts the saturnine Stanton, but says nothing about his own disrelish of the performance. From another source, however, we learn of disapproval so plainly stamped upon Chase's countenance that Lincoln, eyeing the solemn-faced Secretary of the Treasury as he read, laughed more heartily than ever. In fact, the gentleman's distress became in itself an object of boisterous hilarity, "and Lincoln," we are told, "seldom lost an opportunity to entertain himself and others in this direction." [36] Mr. Chase naturally felt aggrieved on such occasions. They hardly served to place him at his ease with the President, or to render more agreeable to either an intercourse that, at its best, never reached far beyond the limits of official requirements.

In strong contrast to the distant relations between Lincoln and Chase was the cordial good-fellowship which the President evinced toward Seward. The Secretary of State appears to have been especially congenial to his chief. For Mr. Lincoln, of all men, could appreciate a cabinet minister who, whatever may have been his failings, submitted loyally, in the main, to superior authority, fomented no quarrels, and adapted a cheery, resourceful disposition, with rare felicity, to the President's moods. Seward's influence with Lincoln was notably greater than that of Chase — greater, in fact, than that of any of his colleagues; but not nearly so great, be it said, as was at the time generally believed. Great or small, however, the prestige thus enjoyed by the Secretary of State became particularly galling to the man in the Treasury. From their earliest days in the Senate, these two leaders, notwithstanding their common dislike of slavery and their previous coöperation on fugitive slave cases, had been, in a sense, opposed to each other. They had joined hands, it is true, in the parliamentary struggle against southern domination; but the Democratic tendencies of the one, and the Whig partisanship of the other, had stood in the way of a friendship that, even under more favorable conditions, would have been practically impossible to men of such conflicting personalities. They had been associated together in the Upper House for several months, when Chase wrote:—

"I don't know what Seward will do. I have never been able to establish much sympathy between us. He is too much of a politician for me."[37]

And within a few weeks, following, the Senator from Ohio complained to his New York colleague of the abuse, "without any stint," to which he had been subjected by the latter's friends. Antagonisms aroused at about that period were not allayed, even after Chase and Seward had sunk their political differences, for a time, in the formation of the new Republican Party. They became, as we have seen, rivals for the presidential nomination of 1860; and when that prize, as well as the election, went to Lincoln, they were again pitted against each other in a race for the ascendancy over a seemingly weak Executive. How he pressed them both into his cabinet, despite powerful opposition to such an association, has also been told. We need only add, for a clear comprehension of what ensued, that there, Chase, the champion of the radical anti-slavery men on the one extreme, and Seward, the representative of the conservative element in the party on the other, were at variance more than ever.

In their official intercourse, it is true, these two ministers maintained a proper decorum. They even coöperated, now and then, amicably together; but in private, the Secretary of the Treasury pursued his more favored colleague with criticisms, no less censorious than those he so freely visited on the President. To such a degree did Chase carry this faultfinding, that he could not even withhold a comparatively mild expression of it from Seward's partner and intimate friend, Thurlow Weed. "I told him," records Mr. Chase in his diary for September 15, 1862, "I did not doubt Mr. Seward's fidelity to his ideas of progress, amelioration, and freedom; but that I thought he adhered too tenaciously to men who proved themselves unworthy and dangerous, such as McClellan; that he resisted too persistently decided measures; that his influence encouraged the irresolution and inaction of the President in respect to men and measures, although personally he was as decided as anybody in favor of vigorous prosecution of the war, and as active as anybody in concerting plans of action against the rebels."[38] These charges, with others equally telling, constituted the basis of a widespread hostility to the Secretary of State; for Chase's blows against that officer, from within the cabinet, had evoked more than an echo outside. Indeed, almost every important occurrence appears to have multiplied Seward's enemies. Assuming him to be the controlling factor of the administration, people held him responsible — how mistakenly has been shown elsewhere — for whatever displeased them in its policy. The government's unpopular measures, no less than its errors and mishaps, its disasters in the field and reverses at the polls, were laid chiefly at his door. So strong, in fact, ran the current of condemnation, through the summer and autumn of 1862, that it bade fair to sweep him out of the cabinet. Toward this end the anti-slavery or Chase wing of the Republican Party, encouraged, if not actually inspired, by the Secretary of the Treasury, especially labored. These Radicals were irritated out of all patience by the slow-paced conservatism which held the preservation of the Union above the abolition of slavery; yet they might have taken pains to look higher than the State Department for the source of their disappointment, had not Mr. Seward so unreservedly identified himself with the President's policy that it was generally ascribed to him. Some of the Secretary's utterances, moreover, gave grave offence to the anti-slavery leaders. They determined that nothing short of his removal from the cabinet would salve their wounded dignity, and, at the same time, save their cause, by affording Chase the opportunity of succeeding to the influence over Lincoln which Seward was supposed to be exerting.

Accordingly, one evening shortly after the third session of the Thirty-seventh Congress had begun, a secret caucus of Republican Senators, convened for the purpose, adopted by a small majority a resolution demanding that the President dismiss Mr. Seward. Upon second thought, with a view, perhaps, of securing a larger vote, or of rendering less offensive this unprecedented intrusion on Executive authority, a substitute requesting the reconstruction of the cabinet was proposed, and almost unanimously carried. In fact, what had been a considerable minority dwindled to one dissenting voice — that of Preston King, Senator from New York. He hurried from the meeting to inform Seward, who as promptly, with characteristic tact, sent the President his resignation.

"What does this mean?" asked Mr. Lincoln in pained surprise, as he read the note; and Senator King, entering at the moment, answered the question. It must have seemed to the sorely tried President as if his supporters vied with his opponents to complicate his difficulties. He called upon Seward later in the evening to talk the matter over, and in the course of the discussion the Secretary remarked how relieved he would feel to be freed from official cares. "Ah yes, Governor," was the rejoinder, "that will do very well for you; but I am like the starling in Sterne's story, 'I can't get out.'"[39] And he determined that Seward should not "get out" either. On the following morning a formidable committee of nine — Senators Collamer, Sumner, Fessenden, Wade, Trumbull, Grimes, Harris, Howard, and Pomeroy — waited upon the President with the resolutions of the caucus. In the conference that ensued, the Secretary of State was denounced by most of the delegation as the evil genius of the government, and Mr. Lincoln was urged to have done with him. "While they seemed to believe in my honesty," said the President, describing the interview to the cabinet after his homely fashion, "they also appeared to think that when I had in me any good purpose or intention Seward contrived to suck it out of me unperceived."[40]

Having given the Senators no encouragement beyond an invitation to return in the evening, Mr. Lincoln summoned his advisers, narrated what had happened, and made a similar appointment with them. The situation was critical. To antagonize the senatorial leaders of his party in the darkest days of the war by refusing to make the change they desired, might deprive the President of coöperation that was vital to the success of his administration. To comply with their request, on the other hand, would cost him not only the services of a valued minister, but the support of that minister's followers as well. In either event, to use a Lincolnian phrase, "the thing would all have slumped over one way." The dismissal of Seward, under the circumstances, would involve, moreover, a shameful surrender to Chase, and what was of greater importance than all else, a surrender of Executive power and prerogative at the summons of a legislative cabal, acting without even the semblance of constitutional authority. Here was a supreme test of Lincoln's mastership. In the very nature of the case, he could seek no counsel among his customary advisers. The crisis had to be met, at least as far as tactics went, single-handed; and that somehow reminds us again of Lincoln's early days. It is a far cry from the White House back to Clary's Grove; yet, as the representatives of the caucus file into the Executive Mansion for their evening conference, we recall a scene in the backwoods settlement, — a mêlée of men, an angry onset, and a cool, muscular young fellow who stands braced against a wall to receive their combined attack.

When the Senators entered the President's room, they were taken aback at finding all the members of the cabinet, except Mr. Seward, seated around their chief; and the cabinet, it must be said, were as greatly surprised over the meeting as the committee. Thus confronted, the two parties, with Lincoln acting as a sort of moderator, entered upon a full and free discussion. The Senators made a brisk attack upon the administration, and upon the Secretary of State, in particular; the President's counselors defended themselves, as well as their absent associate, with spirit. The attitude of the Secretaries was indicated by Mr. Stanton. "This cabinet, gentlemen," said he, "is like yonder window. Suppose you allowed it to be understood that passers-by might knock out one pane of glass, — just one at a time, — how long do you think any panes would be left in it?"[41] Seward's cause had become, perforce, that of his colleagues. They were obliged, by the logic of events, to stand as a unit between him and his assailants. Even Chase, brought to bay, was forced into turning, after a fashion, against the men who had come to strengthen his position. He found himself in a predicament. To agree with the Senators, in their attacks upon Seward or the administration, though he had made the identical criticisms to them and to others, was, in that presence, obviously out of the question. To take ground effectively against these charges, without stultifying himself, was, under existing conditions, equally impossible. So he joined with his fellow ministers, as best he could, protesting angrily, the while, against his dilemma, and expressing regret that he had come. The rest of the meeting, however, talked itself frankly into a better understanding. Before it was dissolved, late in the night, Lincoln asked the committee: —

"Do you gentlemen still think Seward ought to be excused?"

On a formal vote, but four of the eight Senators present — Wade was absent — answered, "Yes."[42] As the visitors were leaving, one of them, unable to conceal his chagrin at Chase's apparent double-dealing, said privately to the President, yet with considerable feeling, that the Secretary of the Treasury had spoken in a different tone elsewhere.[43] This Lincoln knew well enough. He also knew what was perhaps beginning to dawn on the minds of the astute statesmen who had participated in this remarkable controversy — his trap had been sprung, and Chase was fairly caught.

Overnight reflection revealed to the Secretary of the Treasury how untenable his position had become. His own withdrawal from the cabinet was apparently the sole retreat open to his ruffled dignity. So, the next morning, when the President and some of his advisers met for further consultation, Mr. Chase offered his resignation. He held the paper in his hand, but made no motion to deliver it. Whereupon Mr. Lincoln, we are told, "stepped forward and took it with an alacrity that surprised and, it must be said, disappointed Mr. Chase."[44] Then the meeting was at once dismissed. There was no further need of discussion. From that moment the President saw his way clear before him. With the resignations of the rival leaders in his hands, he was master of the situation. He might retain them both, by treating their withdrawal as a joint affair, and making the readmission of the one dependent upon that of the other; or, if the cabinet was to be reconstructed after all, he would be free, with both of them out, to make such appointments as should still preserve the balance between their respective factions. "Yes, Judge," said Lincoln to Senator Harris, who came upon him as he stood with Chase's letter in his grasp, "I can ride on now, I 've got a pumpkin in each end of my bag."[45] Having delivered himself of this bucolic figure, so nicely expressive of the turn that affairs had taken, the President sent each of the Secretaries a note, addressed to them jointly, declining to accept their resignations. "After most anxious consideration," he wrote, "my deliberate judgment is that the public interest does not admit of it. I therefore have to request that you will resume the duties of your departments respectively."[46] Seward, promptly taking his cue, answered the following morning: —

"I have cheerfully resumed the functions of this department in obedience to your command."

Chase's lines were not so simple. Realizing that he had blundered into a false exit, when last on the scene, he wrote: —

"Will you allow me to say that something you said or looked, when I handed you my resignation this morning, made on my mind the impression that having received the resignations both of Governor Seward and myself, you could relieve yourself from trouble by declining to accept either, and that this feeling was one of gratification. . . . I could not, if I would, conceal from myself that recent events have too rudely jostled the unity of your cabinet, and disclosed an opinion too deeply seated, and too generally received in Congress and in the country, to be safely disregarded, that the concord in judgment and action, essential to successful administration, does not prevail among its members. . . . A resignation is a grave act — never performed by a right-minded man without forethought or with reserve. I tendered mine from a sense of duty to the country, to you, and to myself; and I tendered it to be accepted. So did, as you have been fully assured, Mr. Seward tender his. I trust, therefore, that you will regard yourself as completely relieved from all personal considerations. It is my honest conviction that we can both better serve you and the country at this time as private citizens than in your cabinet." [47]

Before the letter could be despatched, word came to the writer from Seward that he had returned to his post. This completely disarmed Chase. He would have been pleased at the removal of the Secretary of State, or even at the retirement of Seward and himself; but that his rival should be restored to power, while he returned to private life, was hardly to his taste. After another day of perplexity, Chase wrote to the President, also withdrawing his resignation. He enclosed the unsent letter, however, and accompanied his reluctant surrender with reservations that boded no good to the future peace of the administration. Here the episode closed, but it presents a dramatic coincidence that should not be overlooked. The same sagacity, adroitness, and mastery over men with which Lincoln had covered Chase's entrance into the cabinet, under a storm of opposition from Seward's friends, had been as successfully employed two years later to protect Seward, in his turn, against the assaults of Chase's followers, reënforced though they were by a senatorial caucus of exceptional influence. Both the great ones had thus found shelter from each other, under the President's ample shield. Yet the Secretary of the Treasury, strange to say, still failed to discern what had become so evident to his colleague of the State Department, — that the man who could do such things was their superior in fact, no less than in station.

Ere the winter had elapsed, Mr. Chase again measured his strength against that of the President. The occasion arose out of the rejection, by the Senate, of a treasury nomination. Mark Howard, selected by the head of the department to be a Collector of Internal Revenue for the First District of Connecticut, had, through the opposition of Senator Dixon from that State, failed of confirmation. In somewhat of a rage, Mr. Chase urged Mr. Lincoln to renominate his candidate, — who, by the way, was giving satisfaction under a temporary appointment, — or at least, to await the Secretary's selection of an equally suitable person; but under no circumstances to appoint any one recommended by the offending Senator. That gentleman, be it said, had acted entirely within his rights in securing Howard's rejection; and Mr. Lincoln had no intention of disciplining him for so doing. Nor was the President prepared, however much he may have agreed with his Secretary in the general theory of appointments, to disregard the wishes of influential legislators. He wrote to Mr. Chase: —

"After much reflection, and with a good deal of pain that it is adverse to your wish, I have concluded that it is not best to renominate Mr. Howard for Collector of

Internal Revenue, at Hartford, Connecticut. Senator Dixon, residing at Hartford, and Mr. Loomis, Representative of the district, join in recommending Edward Goodman for the place; and, so far, no one has presented a different name. I will thank you, therefore, to send me a nomination, at once, for Mr. Goodman." [48]

Upon receipt of the letter, Secretary Chase penned this curt reply: —

"Finding myself unable to approve the manner in which selections for appointment to important trusts in this department have been recently made, and being unwilling to remain responsible for its administration, under existing circumstances, I respectfully resign the office of Secretary of the Treasury." [49]

But before the message was sent, Senator Dixon called at the Treasury Department. He was in so conciliatory a mood that a compromise was easily effected. Both parties agreed to submit the matter at issue to the President for his further consideration, with the understanding that Chase should not insist on the renomination of Howard, while Dixon and Loomis should claim no recognition in the making of a substitute appointment.[50] The Secretary, laying his resignation aside, accordingly wrote Mr. Lincoln the purport of the interview, instead. So nettled was he, however, at the President's willingness to act counter to his wishes that he could not forbear, though the occasion had passed, to close the letter with this ultimatum: —

"My only object — and I think you so understand it — is to secure fit men for responsible places, without admitting the rights of Senators or Representatives to control appointments, for which the President and the Secretary, as his presumed adviser, must be responsible. Unless this principle can be practically established, I feel that I cannot be useful to you or the country in my present position." [51]

The covert threat of resignation was apparently unheeded by Mr. Lincoln. It was enough for him that the quarrel, in which he had no personal interest, had been settled, without alienating either the Secretary or the Senator. As to the rest, a favorite maxim guided his course — he never crossed Fox River until he reached there.

It might seemingly have been better for all concerned had the President departed, in this instance, from his practice, sufficiently to arrive at an understanding with Mr. Chase on the issue thus raised. Yet a glance reveals how impracticable such a step would have been. The Secretary of the Treasury took the ground, not without some show of justice, that, as he was held responsible for so important a department, all appointments to its numerous places of trust, no less than removals therefrom, should be under his sole control. He insisted, in short, that his substantially unrestricted sway over financial matters ought to include the rich patronage of the office, as well. This claim Mr. Lincoln allowed to an unusual degree. Indeed, so often did he defer to Mr. Chase's desires that the Secretary became incapable of recognizing a reasonable exception. Consequently when, on rare occasions, personal or political considerations moved the President to insist on nominations or dismissals contrary to the minister's wishes, that gentleman's unruly temper made things as disagreeable as circumstances allowed. At such times Lincoln sought to attain his ends with the least possible friction. Badgered by office-seekers as no American Executive had been before him; holding the balance between conflicting sections of a discordant party, largely by means of his appointments, and dependent upon the good-will of every element in that party, as only a President can be during a great civil war, he would not — in fact, could not — surrender to Chase the entire patronage of the Treasury, which, it may be added, was then more extensive, perhaps, than that of all the other civil departments combined. On the other hand, Mr. Lincoln, both on account of this Secretary's value personally, and because of the powerful wing that he represented, wished to avoid a rupture. So the man in the Treasury, usually, had his way with the offices; the man in the White House, now and then, had his. In either event, the question of absolute control over appointments lay flickering between them, ready, at the slightest poke among the smouldering embers, to leap into flame again.

The Howard incident had hardly closed, when a new squabble about patronage arose. Deeming it necessary to make sweeping changes in his department at San Francisco, Mr. Chase invited the three California Congressmen, Messrs. Low, Sargent, and Phelps, to his office, one evening, and informed them of the fact. He declared his determination to remove the leading treasury officers and to supply their places with men whose names he announced. His visitors, taken by surprise and believing his purpose to be irrevocable, offered no objections; but, as they left the building, they gave free vent to their anger. A few days thereafter, these Representatives, Congress having adjourned, left for home by way of New York. Upon their arrival at the metropolis, Mr. Phelps took passage for San Francisco, while his colleagues tarried in the city. Before they were ready to sail, a despatch from Mr. Lincoln recalled them to Washington. He had just learned, to his surprise and vexation, how summarily Mr. Chase was about to fill the most important Federal offices on the Pacific coast. For not only had the members of Congress from that section, as we have seen, been practically ignored by a mere pretence at consultation, but the President, himself, had also been kept in the dark. Upon the return of Messrs. Low and Sargent, the Secretary's plans were speedily revised. It was too late, in the absence of Mr. Phelps, to consider the appointments as Mr. Lincoln had intended; but he broke Chase's carefully constructed slate, and that stiff-necked minister's feelings, as the President afterwards said, were "exceedingly hurt" in the process.

Shortly after the California affair, another clash of authority arose between Lincoln and Chase, over a treasury office on the Pacific coast. Victor Smith, a friend of the Secretary, had, at his request, been made Collector of Customs in the Puget Sound District. The appointee was eccentric, and deft, to a notable degree, in the gentle art of making enemies. So wide-spread grew his unpopularity that Congressmen, Federal officers, and private citizens of influence united in demanding his removal. Not content with the letters and petitions which they had poured into Washington, the people, deeply aroused, sent a deputation all the way from Puget Sound — a formidable journey in 1863 — with charges against Smith. The accusations were referred by the President, for investigation, to the Secretary of the Treasury, who, throughout the clamor, had stood stoutly by his friend. But before Mr. Chase had time for a report, he was called away from the Capital, on business. During his somewhat protracted absence, the outcry from the scene of the trouble became well-nigh intolerable; and Mr. Lincoln was forced to the conclusion that the public interests required Smith's immediate dismissal. Steps in this direction had already been taken, when Mr. Chase returned. He found that a note had been received at the department, from the President, ordering a Collector's commission for Henry Clay Wilson, as Smith's successor. The man so appointed, however, had recently died. As soon as Mr. Lincoln discovered the fact, he wrote to Mr. Chase, recalling the order and directing a commission to be made out for Frederick A. Wilson, instead. Accompanying the first formal message was a private letter from the President, which read: —

"I address this to you personally rather than officially, because of the nature of the case. My mind is made up to remove Victor Smith as Collector of the Customs at the Puget Sound District. Yet in doing this I do not decide that the charges against him are true. I only decide that the degree of dissatisfaction with him there is too great for him to be retained. But I believe he is your personal acquaintance and friend, and if you desire it I will try to find some other place for him." [52]

Mr. Chase felt that both he and his Collector had been grievously wronged. "I had not thought it possible," he replied, "that you would remove an officer of my department without awaiting the result, although somewhat delayed, of an investigation, directed by yourself; and appoint a successor, for whose action I must be largely responsible, without even consulting me on the subject." He restated, at some length, what he deemed to be his rights in such matters, and concluded with:—

"The blank commission which you direct me to send you is inclosed; for to obey your directions, so long as I shall hold office under you, is my duty. It is inclosed, however, with my most respectful protest against the precedent, and with the assurance that if you find anything in my views to which your own sense of duty will not permit you to assent, I will unhesitatingly relieve you from all embarrassment, so far as I am concerned, by tendering you my resignation." [53]

Here was a new coil for the weary President to unravel. Smith had to go, even though he had become "so intertwined," to use his own high-sounding words, "in the fibers of the government" that his removal from office was "an impossibility." [54] At the same time, Lincoln could not afford to let the little Collector carry the big Secretary of the Treasury out with him. So the President, ordering his carriage, drove to Chase's house. What followed between the two men we will let Lincoln himself relate, as he once did to an acquaintance:—

"I went directly up to him with the resignation in my hand, and, putting my arm around his neck, said to him, 'Chase, here is a paper with which I wish to have nothing to do; take it back and be reasonable.' I then explained to him what had occurred while he was away. I told him that the man whom I had appointed happened to have been dead several weeks; that I could n't replace the person whom I had removed, — that was impossible, — but that I would appoint any one else whom he should select for the place.[55] It was difficult to bring him to terms. I had to plead with him a long time, but I finally succeeded, and heard nothing more of *that* resignation."[56]

A few days thereafter, Mr. Chase found a satisfactory candidate, whom Mr. Lincoln promptly appointed.

Meanwhile, a customs collectorship of more moment — in fact, the most important on the list — was hatching trouble between the President and his Secretary of the Treasury. They found in Hiram Barney, Collector of the Port of New York, a veritable germ of irritation. He was one of Chase's most valued supporters. As a political lieutenant, Barney had, in years gone by, won the Radical leader's good-will; as a friend, he had by his private kindnesses laid that gentleman, more recently, under heavy and somewhat peculiar obligations. Mr. Chase was therefore highly gratified when, in the spring of 1861, the President, who knew and liked Mr. Barney, appointed him, largely if not entirely of his own accord, to the management of the New York Custom House. This post, beset with difficulties under the best of conditions, was soon rendered particularly trying by conflicts between the opposing Republican factions. Conservatives accused Barney of running the Custom House in the interests of the anti-slavery men; while Radicals found fault with him for not using his patronage more freely than he did to strengthen the Chase element. Between these two fires the Collector's health became impaired. In the autumn of 1863, he asked to be relieved from a thankless position; but neither Lincoln nor Chase would hear of his retirement. As the time, however, for the next presidential canvass drew near, the attacks upon him grew fiercer than ever. They presently developed into charges of corruption and incompetency, which a Congressional Committee undertook to investigate.[57] Meanwhile Mr. Lincoln had come to the conclusion that both Mr. Barney and the public service might benefit if the resignation, rejected a few months before, were revived and accepted. He said so to Mr. Chase, and called upon him for his coöperation; but the Secretary answered with the warmth that had become habitual on such occasions: —

"I am to-day fifty-six years old. I have never consciously and deliberately injured one fellow man. It is too late for me to begin by sacrificing to clamor the reputation of a man whom I have known for more than twenty years, and whose repute for honesty has been all that time unsullied. I shall not recommend the removal of Mr. Barney, except upon such show of misconduct, or incapacity, as makes it my duty to do so. In such a case I shall not shrink from my duty. I pretend no indifference to the consequences, personal to myself, which you refer to as likely to follow this avowal on my part. But the approval of my own conscience is dearer to me than political position, and I shall cheerfully sacrifice the latter to preserve the former."[58]

Four weeks later, Lincoln, disturbed by the misbehavior of an officer high in the Collector's favor, again suggested the wisdom of Barney's retirement from the Custom House. Assuring both the Secretary and the Collector of his continued confidence in the latter, he offered Mr. Barney the mission to Portugal.[59] But the Collector declined to withdraw voluntarily, while under fire; and his friend at the head of the department sustained him in this position. Chase "was very angry," said the President, describing the interview which followed, "and he told me that the day that Mr. Barney left the New York Custom House, with or without his own consent, he, Chase, would withdraw from the Secretaryship of the Treasury. Well, I backed down again."[60] There the matter rested, pending the investigation. Before the committee had concluded its labors, however, Mr. Lincoln returned to the charge.

Nothing, indeed, had been disclosed to Mr. Barney's personal dishonor; yet the irregular and, in some instances, corrupt practices traced to some of his subordinates, together with a steadily growing dissatisfaction over his management, confirmed the President's purpose to make a change in the office. Mr. Chase again protested, but less vehemently than before; and while the question was still, in a sense, unsettled, came the succession of events that put an end to the jangling relations between Lincoln and his refractory minister.

Mr. Chase's persistent hostility toward the chief who was entitled to his support should, before we go further, be traced back to its one overmastering impulse — his own ambition to become President. Had all the other causes of irritation been removed, this aim would still have left him in an attitude of uncompromising antagonism. In fact, it alone accounts for whatever in the man's conduct might otherwise be inexplicable.

> "Such men as he be never at heart's ease,
> Whiles they behold a greater than themselves."

An aspirant for the nomination in 1856, and again in 1860, Chase had entered Mr. Lincoln's cabinet with the fixed idea that he, not the President, ought to be the standard-bearer of their party in 1864. It is said that a man once bitten with desire for our highest office is never — if it remain ungratified — wholly healed. This craving, when thwarted, appears to gnaw like the worm which dieth not, and to burn like the fire which is not quenched. Chase's attack of "the White House fever," as Lincoln in speaking of him called it, raged until 1872 — within a year or so of his death; but at no time was it so acute as during these cabinet days. His course in seeking to supplant Mr. Lincoln while a member of the President's official household has been severely commented on, and not without reason. Granting his fitness for the place to which he aspired, as well as the validity of his claim to the highest rewards within the gift of his party, and disregarding all questions concerning his personal disloyalty, we cannot overlook the impropriety which arose the moment he gave free range to an ambition, so dependent for its success on the reverses of the very administration that he was in duty bound to sustain with all his strength. "A man may be *either* a Minister or an agitator," said Lord Palmerston concerning a restlessly ambitious member of his cabinet; and even Chase's genius, as has been seen, failed to carry him with credit through the anomalous situations that resulted from his attempt to be both, at the same time. Nor could his ordinarily well-poised sense of justice deter him from the unfair criticism and factious opposition into which he allowed himself to be betrayed by his rivalry of the President.[61]

Mr. Chase began his canvass for the nomination betimes. He scattered the seeds of his discontent with Mr. Lincoln broadcast. Indeed, the letters that have supplied us with instances of the Secretary's hostility constituted but a small part of the correspondence by which he sought at once to blight the President's prospects, and to bring his own to fruition. He made it a point to cultivate cordial relations with generals and politicians who had, for one reason or another, become unfriendly to Mr. Lincoln; and, what is more reprehensible still, he did not hesitate to fan the flames of their resentment. That such conduct was "incompatible" — to use one of Chase's own phrases — "with perfect honor and good faith," appears never to have entered his mind. Nor did he see the inconsistencies into which he was carried by his almost childish eagerness. Declaring his affection for the President, he exerted himself, as far as his dignity permitted, to compass that leader's political overthrow; and affirming his indifference to the highest office, he pushed his chances for it through every avenue not barred by his own peculiar code of public ethics. He even availed himself of the prevalent prejudice against reëlecting a President; for, since Jackson occupied the White House, no man had been chosen to a second term. As early as the autumn of 1863, Chase wrote to his son-in-law, ex-Governor Sprague: —

"If I were controlled by merely personal sentiments, I should prefer the reëlection of Mr. Lincoln to that of any other man. But I doubt the expediency of reëlecting anybody, and I think a man of different qualities from those the President has will be needed for the next four years." [62]

The writer — it is perhaps unnecessary to add — believed himself endowed with all the gifts in which he fancied the Executive to be lacking.

Despite his Secretary's unfavorable opinion, Lincoln ardently desired a reëlection. Aside from his own ambition, which alone was keen enough to stimulate him in that direction, it was clearly his duty to do what with propriety he might toward remaining at the head of affairs. How long the life-and-death struggle for the Union would last, or with what result, no man could, in 1863, foresee. Under the most favorable conditions, part, if not all, of another term might be required for bringing the war to a triumphant close, and restoring the country to its former prosperity. The hope of seeing his efforts thus crowned had sustained the President's steps in the thorny path over which he was even then leading the nation. To be deprived of his command halfway, with the goal perhaps in sight, would have been a disappointment, indeed. He deemed himself, moreover, better fitted than any other man — Mr. Chase to the contrary, notwithstanding — for the completion of what he had begun. Discussing the matter with a friend, he said, in one of his favorite figures:

"I am only the people's attorney in this great affair. I am trying to do the best I can for my client — the country. But if the people desire to change their attorney, it is not for me to resist or complain. Nevertheless, between you and me, I think the change would be impolitic, whoever might be substituted for the present counsel." [63]

On another occasion, he expressed this opinion in the oft-quoted apothegm: —

"I don't believe it is wise to swap horses while crossing a stream." [64]

Lincoln's confidence in the wisdom of his reëlection was at first not generally shared by leading members of his own party. Some, like Chase, thought him unfit for the office. In this "fellow of infinite jest," with his easy-going moods, his seeming lack of executive talents, and his apparent incapacity to grasp the momentous problems of the war, they failed to discern

"The kindly-earnest, brave, foreseeing man"

that the whole world, wise after the event, now knows him to have been. Others, playing politics with the very life of the nation at stake, insisted on forcing out of the game a President who, after a masterful fashion of his own, had brushed their hands aside in filling this office or adopting that policy. Here, surely, was not an encouraging outlook for a renomination. "Of the more earnest and thoroughgoing Republicans in both Houses of Congress," writes a member, "probably not one in ten really favored it." [65] The spirit of faction, too, was bitter, even for those overwrought days. What might be called the Radical Anti-Slavery wing of the party — at least, certain politicians and editors who believed themselves to represent that wing — cried aloud against the renomination. Lincoln's cautious, conservative methods, particularly his course in subordinating the slavery question to whatever concerned the preservation of the Union, had aroused their vigorous opposition. They demanded a candidate who would push the war more vigorously, perhaps more sternly, in this, as well as other directions; and they declared Mr. Chase to be that man. Our Secretary met them coyly halfway. Hoping to combine in his favor all these elements of opposition to the President, he permitted a committee of Senators, Congressmen, and prominent citizens to enter upon a formal canvass for his nomination.

The movement in behalf of Chase was headed by Senator Samuel C. Pomeroy of Kansas, who presently issued the secret circular that is known in history by his name.[66] This document — though Chase had no hand in it — was entirely in his vein. It declared that the reëlection of Lincoln was "practically impossible"; that "the cause of human liberty and the dignity of the nation" suffered from his "tendency toward compromises and temporary expedients"; that "the application of the one-term principle" was essential to the safety of our institutions; that in the Hon. Salmon P. Chase were to be found "more of the qualities needed in a President, during the next four years," than were "combined in any other available candidate"; and that all those "in favor of the speedy restoration of the Union, on the basis of universal freedom," should at once form local organizations to promote his nomination. Many copies of the circular were sent out by mail. They were marked "Confidential," it is true, but before long they found their way into the newspapers, much to Mr. Chase's embarrassment. He thereupon, at once, wrote to the President, disavowing any knowledge of the circular, before its appearance in the public prints, but admitting his connection, as a candidate, with the Pomeroy Committee. "If there is anything," he added, "in my action or position which, in your judgment, will prejudice the public interest under my charge, I beg you to say so. I do not wish to administer the Treasury Department one day without your entire confidence. For yourself I cherish sincere respect and esteem; and, permit me to add, affection. Differences of opinion as to administrative action have not changed these sentiments; nor have they been changed by assaults upon me by persons who profess themselves the special representatives of your views and policy. You are not responsible for acts not your own; nor will you hold me responsible except for what I do or say myself."[67]

Mr. Lincoln, with characteristic deliberation, delayed

his answer a week. Then he wrote — and the letter is worth quoting almost entire: —

"I was not shocked or surprised by the appearance of the letter, because I had had knowledge of Mr. Pomeroy's committee, and of secret issues which, I supposed, came from it, and of secret agents who, I supposed, were sent out by it, for several weeks. I have known just as little of these things as my friends have allowed me to know. They bring the documents to me, but I do not read them; they tell me what they think fit to tell me, but I do not inquire for more. I fully concur with you that neither of us can be justly held responsible for what our respective friends may do without our instigation or countenance; and I assure you, as you have assured me, that no assault has been made upon you by my instigation, or with my countenance. Whether you shall remain at the head of the Treasury Department is a question which I will not allow myself to consider from any standpoint other than my judgment of the public service, and, in that view, I do not perceive occasion for a change."[68]

This seeming indifference of the President to his Secretary's rivalry, as well as Mr. Lincoln's failure to respond to that gentleman's professions of affection, greatly mortified Mr. Chase. He had, to be sure, been retained in the cabinet under conditions that would ordinarily have warranted his dismissal; but the relations between him and his superior were, from that time, less cordial even than ever.

Lincoln's attitude toward Chase's electioneering projects reveals the President at his full stature. It affords a view of the master, patient in his strength, under circumstances that would have tried the nerves of an Iron Chancellor. When his friends, advising at the very outset against a cabinet made up of convention rivals, predicted that some of the aspirants would continue antagonistic to him, he is reported to have replied: —

"No, gentlemen, the times are too grave and perilous

for ambitious schemes, and personal rivalries. I need the aid of all of these men. They enjoy the confidence of their several States and sections; and they will strengthen the administration."[69]

To the Secretaries themselves he said:—

"It will require the utmost skill, influence, and sagacity of all of us to save the republic. Let us forget ourselves, and join hands like brothers to save the republic. If we succeed, there will be glory enough for all."[70]

How deaf one of them was to this appeal the President had soon to discover. Yet he allowed neither his disappointment nor the resulting perplexities to modify his high opinion of Chase's value in the Treasury Department. Although Mr. Lincoln, as the minister complained, may never have expressed to him sufficient appreciation of his services, the President certainly did so, without reserve, to others. "Of all the great men I have ever known," said he, after weighing the Secretary's shortcomings, "Chase is equal to about one and a half of the best of them."[71] When Lincoln's supporters, moreover, called his attention to the practices by which the man in the Treasury was advancing his political fortunes, at the expense of the administration,[72] he told them:—

"I have determined to shut my eyes, so far as possible, to everything of the sort. Mr. Chase makes a good Secretary, and I shall keep him where he is. If he becomes President, all right. I hope we may never have a worse man."

Then, turning to the less pleasing aspect of the affair, he continued:—

"I have observed with regret his plan of strengthening himself. Whenever he sees that an important matter is troubling me, if I am compelled to decide in a way to give offence to a man of some influence, he always ranges himself in opposition to me and persuades the victim that he has been hardly dealt with, and that he would have arranged it very differently. It was so with General Frémont, with General Hunter when I annulled his hasty proclamation, with General Butler when he was recalled from New Orleans, with these Missouri people when they called the other day. I am entirely indifferent as to his success or failure in these schemes, so long as he does his duty at the head of the Treasury Department." [73]

These citations, furthermore, would be incomplete without one of those homely stories whereby the President was wont to point his remarks. He narrated it to Henry J. Raymond, when the famous editor called his attention to the danger that might arise from Chase's candidacy. "Raymond," said he, "you were brought up on a farm, were you not? Then you know what a 'chin fly' is. My brother and I were once plowing corn on a Kentucky farm, I driving the horse, and he holding the plow. The horse was lazy; but on one occasion rushed across the field so that I, with my long legs, could scarcely keep pace with him. On reaching the end of the furrow, I found an enormous 'chin fly' fastened upon him, and I knocked him off. My brother asked me what I did that for. I told him I did n't want the old horse bitten in that way. 'Why,' said my brother, 'that 's all that made him go!' Now, if Mr. Chase has a presidential 'chin fly' biting him, I 'm not going to knock him off, if it will only make his department *go*." [74]

Only a true leader of men could so regard the competition of a powerful subordinate.

It should not be supposed, however, as some eulogists of the President would have us think, that he was too big to regard Chase's pretensions with any uneasiness. Lincoln never underrated an opponent. He owed his victories as much to his careful measurement of the men with whom he had to deal as to any other single thing. The disaffection of many influential Republicans, during 1863, was painfully apparent to him. He realized how strong might be Chase's chances for the nomination, if the Secretary could combine upon himself the support of these leaders and of their constituencies. Somewhat of this apprehension was revealed in the President's discussion of the situation with Colonel A. K. McClure, the Pennsylvania journalist and politician, at the White House, one evening, while the Chase canvass was at its height. The Colonel belittled the movement, but failed to imbue Mr. Lincoln with his confidence in the President's renomination. Their talk lasted well into the night. As the visitor, after several futile attempts to take his leave, reached the door, Lincoln called him back and asked, with a twinkle of the eye: —

"By the way, McClure, how would it do if I were to decline Chase?"

The Colonel, surprised at the novel suggestion, inquired as to how that could be done.

"Well, I don't know exactly how it might be done," answered Mr. Lincoln, "but that reminds me of a story of two Democratic candidates for Senator in 'Egypt,' Illinois, in its early political times. That section of Illinois was almost solidly Democratic, as you know, and nobody but Democrats were candidates for office. Two Democratic candidates for Senator met each other in joint debate, from day to day, and gradually became more and more exasperated at each other; until their discussions were simply disgraceful wrangles, and they both became ashamed of them. They finally agreed that either should say anything he pleased about the other, and it should not be resented as an offence; and from that time on, the campaign progressed without any special display of ill-temper. On election night the two candidates, who lived in the same town, were receiving their returns together; and the contest was uncomfortably close. A distant precinct in which one of the candidates confidently expected a large majority was finally reported with a majority against him. The disappointed candidate expressed great surprise, to which the other candidate answered that he should not be surprised, as he had taken the liberty of declining him in that district, the evening before the election. He reminded the defeated candidate that he had agreed that either was free to say anything about the other, without offence; and added that, under that authority, he had gone up into that district and taken the liberty of saying that his opponent had retired from the contest; and therefore the vote of the district was changed, and the declined candidate was thus defeated. I think," concluded Lincoln, with one of his hearty laughs, "I had better decline Chase." [75]

It was evident to Colonel McClure that the President then seriously considered the question of inducing Chase to decline, and that what he said in jest he meant in sober earnest.

For some months Lincoln was uncertain how the defeat of Chase might be accomplished. When the way was not clear before him, he could sit still with better grace than any man that had occupied the presidential chair. Throughout 1863, therefore, he made no public sign. To the surprise of all observers, his ambitious Secretary was suffered to push the work of opposition against him without let or hindrance. By the time Chase formally announced himself to be a candidate, however, in January, 1864, Lincoln began to bring his forces into action. "He did this," says the old campaigner last quoted, "with a degree of sagacity and method that would have done credit to the ripest politician of the age." The President's friends in New Hampshire, Chase's native State, led off at their local convention by voting "Abraham Lincoln to be the people's choice for reëlection." Some weeks thereafter, a Republican caucus of the legislature in Ohio, Chase's State by adoption, followed with a similar resolution; and Rhode Island, where Senator Sprague, Chase's son-in-law, held sway, lost no time in arraying itself on the side of the President. From all quarters, indeed, as the winter advanced, came the call for his renomination. In local committees, Union League clubs, State legislatures, and State conventions, — wherever Republican politicians in close touch with the voters came together, Lincoln was proclaimed to be the party's choice.[76] How much of this was due to a skilful manipulation of his supporters, how much to the spontaneous esteem of the people, and how much to a reaction against Pomeroy's ill-advised circular, we may never know. Suffice it to say that the season was hardly over before our Secretary found himself swept by the current of Lincoln's popularity into a formal withdrawal from the contest.

The sincerity of Chase's request[77] "that no further consideration be given" to his name was open to question. One of the Secretary's supporters describes the letter of withdrawal as a "word of declination diplomatically spoken in order to rouse their flagging spirits."[78] And there are indications that some of Chase's adherents, as well as he, himself, still indulged hopes, all his disclaimers to the contrary notwithstanding, of somehow diverting the nomination from Lincoln. Indeed, his comments on the President during the spring of 1864 were especially censorious. It is not surprising, therefore, all things considered, that some of Mr. Lincoln's friends who had become inimical to the Secretary of the Treasury should have regarded him at the time with increased bitterness. Of this hostility the Blairs furnished a notable instance. They had, from almost the beginning of the administration, been at feud with Chase. He was a Radical, they were Conservatives; he made no secret of how lightly he regarded the President, they held Mr. Lincoln in high esteem; he strove to discredit and supplant his chief, they were as zealous, though not a whit more tactful, in that chief's support. Montgomery Blair in the cabinet, and General Francis P. Blair, Jr., on the stump or in Congress, lost no opportunity for assailing their common enemy. Like their father, Francis Preston Blair, Sr., "Old Hickory's" friend and kitchen counselor, they belonged to the Jacksonian school of politicians — aggressive, intense, uncompromising. "The Blairs," said Montgomery, "when they go in for a fight go in for a funeral." They undertook, in Chase's case at least, to make the boast good. Young Frank's attacks upon the Secretary from the floor of the House culminated, on April 23, in a speech which assailed him with extraordinary violence. "Nobody is simple enough," said General Blair, "to believe that the distinguished Secretary has really retired from the canvass for the nomination to the presidency, although he has written a letter declining to be a candidate. That letter was written because the 'strictly private' circular of the Pomeroy Committee unearthed his underground and underhand intrigue against the President. It was such a disgraceful and disgusting sight to make use of the patronage and power given him by the President, against his chief, that even Chase got ashamed to occupy such a position publicly. For that reason his letter was written. He wanted to get down under the ground and work there in the dark as he is now doing." The speaker accused Mr. Chase of disunion sentiments, reiterated charges that the Secretary of the Treasury was "sacrificing a vast public interest to advance his ambition," and asserted that corruption pervaded the banking as well as the southern trade operations of the finance department.[79]

This speech, whatever may have been its provocation, was in certain particulars nothing short of scurrilous. Upon hearing of it, Chase gave way to what one of his friends termed "Achillean wrath." His fury was due mainly to the fact that directly after it was delivered, seemingly on the very day, indeed, the President had revived Blair's commission as Major-General, and had sent him to the front in command of an army corps. This left no doubt in the Secretary's mind that the assault had been made with Mr. Lincoln's approval. So the inevitable resignation was again to the fore, but wise friends counseled delay. Two of them waited upon the President. He expressed his disapproval of the speech in no uncertain language, and emphasized the injustice of holding the Secretary of the Treasury particularly responsible for the trade regulations which had been adopted in cabinet council. As to Blair's commission, he explained that the General had resigned from the army on taking his seat in Congress, with the understanding that the resignation might be withdrawn at his own pleasure, if he should desire to reënter the service. A command had accordingly been secured for Blair, at his request, several weeks before, and it was merely the necessary formality of his reinstatement that had taken place on the day of the unfortunate attack. "Within three hours," added Mr. Lincoln, "I heard that this speech had been made, when I knew that another beehive was kicked over. My first thought was to have canceled the orders, restoring him to the army and assigning him to command. Perhaps this would have been best. On such reflection as I was able to give to the matter, however, I concluded to let them stand. If I was wrong in this, the injury to the service can be set right."[80] With this explanation Mr. Chase was fain to be content, or at least to seem so; but the barbs of the Blairs still rankled in his heart. That these inveterate enemies, moreover, enjoyed, without apparent diminution, the protection, even the affection, of the President, hardly served to improve the Secretary's temper. He looked upon Mr. Lincoln as an accomplice of his traducers, after the fact, and only the unanimous advice of his friends kept him at his post.[81]

Meanwhile, popular sentiment in favor of the President's renomination became more and more pronounced. The loyal people of the country understood him better than did the Washington politicians or the single-minded Radical leaders. From all walks of life came demands that he should have another term. Laborers, farmers, mechanics, merchants, and scholars, alike echoed Professor Gray's dictum, "Homely, honest, ungainly Lincoln is the representative man of the country."[82] As delegation after delegation was instructed in his favor, the President's renomination appeared to be a foregone conclusion; but the opposition did not entirely abandon the field, so Lincoln kept his eye warily on it. Within two weeks of the date set for the convention, when one of his supporters sought to relieve his anxiety by pointing out that a majority of the delegates were committed to him, he replied: —

"Well, McClure, what you say seems to be unanswerable, but I don't quite forget that I was nominated for President in a convention that was two thirds for the other fellow." [83]

These misgivings were, of course, groundless. The Union-Republican National Convention of June 7, 1864, proved to be not at all "for the other fellow." In fact, strenuous efforts to win over a few delegates for Mr. Chase from the almost solid Lincoln column failed. General Grant, it is true, on the roll-call received the 22 votes of the Missouri Radicals, — cast under peremptory instructions, — but even these were quickly transferred to Mr. Lincoln, in order that he might have the honor of a unanimous nomination, on the first ballot.

The President's brilliant victory in the Baltimore Convention hardly improved the already sharp-set temper of his finance minister. Chase would not, indeed could not acknowledge a master. He was as ready as ever to try conclusions with Lincoln; and the occasion, his final one,— for we have now reached the last of these remarkable encounters, — soon presented itself. Early in June, John J. Cisco, Assistant Treasurer of the United States at New York, proffered his resignation, to take effect at the close of the month. This office was surpassed in importance, financially speaking, by that of the Secretary of the Treasury, alone. To appoint a satisfactory successor accordingly became a matter of weighty consideration; especially because politics, as well as finance, had to be taken into account. So we find Mr. Chase, at the President's request, consulting on the subject with the New York members of the Upper House, particularly with Senator Edwin D. Morgan, who was regarded as representing, in a way, the commercial interests of the metropolis. The Senator and the Secretary agreed successively upon three prominent bankers, who each, in turn, declined the office. Thereupon, Mr. Chase decided to name Maunsell B. Field, an Assistant Secretary of the Treasury, who had previously been Mr. Cisco's deputy. This met with Senator Morgan's spirited opposition. He urged that Mr. Field was not competent for the place, and that his appointment would be hurtful to the interests of their party in New York. He presented, at the same time, the names of three highly esteemed citizens, any one of whom the Secretary was assured would be acceptable. But Mr. Chase could not be moved from his selection. As Field was one of his favorites, all personal objections nettled the Secretary; and as the office was one involving confidential relations with the head of the department, these efforts to apply outside political requirements were peculiarly offensive to him. Having made sure that Field's nomination would be confirmed by the Senate, Mr. Chase, without further ado, laid it, on June 27, before the President. Mr. Lincoln answered on the following day: —

"I cannot, without much embarrassment, make this appointment, principally because of Senator Morgan's very firm opposition to it."

The writer referred to the men whose names had been last submitted by the Senator, and closed with: —

"It will really oblige me if you will make choice among these three, or any other man that Senators Morgan and Harris will be satisfied with, and send me a nomination for him." [84]

The Secretary of the Treasury, however, was more determined than ever to resist what, as in former instances, he deemed to be an encroachment upon his prerogatives.

He replied by note, asking for a personal interview. Receiving no answer, he despatched to Mr. Cisco, the same day, an earnest request that the Assistant Treasurer retain his place, for "at least one quarter longer"; and sent to the President another letter, setting forth his reasons for selecting Mr. Field. To this Lincoln rejoined: —

"When I received your note this forenoon, suggesting a verbal conversation in relation to the appointment of a successor to Mr. Cisco, I hesitated, because the difficulty does not, in the main part, lie within the range of a conversation between you and me. As the proverb goes, no man knows so well where the shoe pinches as he who wears it. I do not think Mr. Field a very proper man for the place, but I would trust your judgment and forego this were the greater difficulty out of the way. Much as I personally like Mr. Barney, it has been a great burden to me to retain him in his place, when nearly all our friends in New York were directly or indirectly urging his removal. Then the appointment of Judge Hogeboom to be general appraiser brought me to, and has ever since kept me at, the verge of open revolt. Now the appointment of Mr. Field would precipitate me in it unless Senator Morgan and those feeling as he does, could be brought to concur in it. Strained as I already am at this point, I do not think I can make this appointment in the direction of still greater strain. The testimonials of Mr. Field, with your accompanying notes, were duly received, and I am now waiting to see your answer from Mr. Cisco."[85]

This answer came within a few hours. It averted — or seemed to avert — the impending crisis. For the Assistant Treasurer, as requested, withdrew his resignation.

Here the incident should have closed, but Mr. Chase felt that the President had not treated him with the consideration which was his due. A cabinet minister who had rendered such signal service as he, and whose value was emphasized by hosts of admirers, ought, once for all, to have complete control over his own department. It shall be that, thought he, or nothing. Mr. Lincoln, he told himself, could not get along without him, — certainly not in June, 1864, when the financial outlook was blacker than it had been at any time since Sumter fell. Gold was rising by leaps and bounds, with the national credit, for a brief period, badly shaken; a deficit of eighty millions, despite heavy taxation, foreshadowed the placing of still heavier burdens upon the people; and the Treasury was called upon to satisfy a regularly recurring demand for the almost fabulous sum of one hundred million dollars a month. Now was the time to discipline the President to some purpose; for all those previous resignations — however Chase may, in each instance, have been conciliated — had evidently failed to advance the Secretary's authority one step. Accordingly, his next letter to Mr. Lincoln read, in part: —

"The withdrawal of Mr. Cisco's resignation, which I inclose, relieves the present difficulty; but I cannot help feeling that my position here is not altogether agreeable to you; and it is certainly too full of embarrassment, and difficulty, and painful responsibility, to allow in me the least desire to retain it. I think it my duty, therefore, to inclose to you my resignation." [86]

This message greatly troubled the President. It is said to have disturbed him more than any matter that concerned him personally in the course of his whole administration; but he saw that to treat this resignation, under the circumstances, like its predecessors, would involve a virtual abdication of his proper functions in favor of his refractory minister. Secretary Chase had jogged the elbow of Fate once too often. In the expressive language of a foreign idiom, he had become impossible. On the following day, therefore, Mr. Lincoln wrote to him: —

"Your resignation of the office of Secretary of the Treasury, sent me yesterday, is accepted. Of all I have said in commendation of your ability and fidelity I have nothing to unsay; and yet you and I have reached a point of mutual embarrassment in our official relations, which it seems cannot be overcome or longer sustained, consistently with the public service."[87]

So the overstrained bond between these two remarkable men was snapped at last.

That Chase should cease to manage the Treasury was regarded on all sides as a public calamity. "Mr. President, this is worse than another Bull Run defeat!" exclaimed the Register of the department, when he learned of Mr. Lincoln's purpose. "Pray, let me go to Secretary Chase and see if I cannot induce him to withdraw his resignation. Its acceptance now might cause a financial panic."

"I will tell you how it is with Chase," was the reply. "It is the easiest thing in the world for a man to fall into a bad habit. Chase has fallen into two bad habits. One is that to which I have often referred. He thinks he has become indispensable to the country; that his intimate friends know it, and he cannot comprehend why the country does not understand it. He also thinks he ought to be President; he has no doubt whatever about that. It is inconceivable to him why people have not found it out; why they don't, as one man, rise up and say so. He is, as you say, an able financier; as you think, without saying so, he is a great statesman, and at the bottom, a patriot. Ordinarily he discharges a public trust, the duties of a public office, with great ability — with greater ability than any man I know. Mind, I say ordinarily, for these bad habits seem to have spoilt him. They have made him irritable, uncomfortable, so that he is never perfectly happy unless he is thoroughly miserable, and able to make everybody else just as uncomfortable as he is himself. He knows that the nomination of Field would displease the Unionists of New York, would delight our enemies, and injure our friends. He knows that I could not make it without seriously offending the strongest supporters of the government in New York, and that the nomination would not strengthen him anywhere or with anybody. Yet he resigns because I will not make it. He is either determined to annoy me, or that I shall pat him on the shoulder and coax him to stay. I don't think I ought to do it. I will not do it. I will take him at his word." [88]

The tidings that Secretary Chase had resigned once too often brought a cloud of eminent protestants to the White House. Most urgent among these were the members of the Senate Committee on Finance, who came in a body. They too believed, for the most part, that the withdrawal of Chase from the Treasury Department, at that time, would be a misfortune. Some of them, moreover, let it be seen that they did not hold the President free from blame for the rupture. Lincoln received the Senators cordially. A frank discussion ensued.[89] He recounted, incident for incident, the story of his painful relations with this minister, who seemed incapable of understanding that the President, not his Secretaries, must command; and nothing urged by the Senators could move him from his conclusion that Mr. Chase's usefulness as a cabinet officer was at an end. "I will not longer," said Lincoln, "continue the association. I am ready and willing to resign the office of President, and let you have Mr. Hamlin for your President; but I will no longer endure the state I have been in." [90] This was sufficiently emphatic. The Committee withdrew, and on the following day their Chairman, William Pitt Fessenden, became, amidst enthusiastic approval, Chase's successor.

No one, it is safe to say, was more surprised at the turn affairs had taken than the whilom Secretary of the Treasury, himself. He had confidently expected the President to put this resignation through the course of its numerous predecessors. That Mr. Lincoln took a different tack was greatly to his disappointment. There is even a tinge of bitterness in the regrets confided to his diary. "I had found," writes Mr. Chase, commenting naïvely on the President's final letter, "a good deal of embarrassment from him; but what he had found from me I could not imagine, unless it has been caused by my unwillingness to have offices distributed as spoils or benefits, with more regard to the claims of divisions, factions, cliques, and individuals, than to fitness of selection."[91] Yet the writer — as this same diary abundantly indicates — would gladly have resumed those embarrassments. When a friend told him how kindly the President had spoken of him, a few days before the resignation, Chase sadly replied that such expressions of good-will, had they reached him in time, would have averted the trouble;[92] and when the new Secretary repeated to his predecessor what Mr. Lincoln had conceded concerning appointments, Mr. Chase made lamentation after this fashion: —

"Had the President, in reply to my note tendering my resignation, expressed himself as he did now to Mr. Fessenden, I should have cheerfully withdrawn it."[93]

Even after Chase had retired from the department, his supporters did not despair of his return. The most potent among them, Charles Sumner, once suggested to the ex-Secretary that the President would perhaps recall him, as Louis XVI had twice recalled Necker. To which Chase replied: —

"That might be if Mr. Lincoln were King and not politician."[94]

Before the year was out, however, that politician evinced how immeasurably he towered above the statesman who had so persistently antagonized him, by nominating Mr. Chase to the Chief-Justiceship of the Supreme Court.[95]

Three months after the appointment, Lincoln entered the eastern portico of the capitol for his second inauguration. If his thoughts, as he stepped upon the platform, reverted to the incidents of that other ceremony which had taken place on the same spot, just four years before, he may have missed the defeated rival, who then came forward to hold the President's hat while he took the oath of office. Douglas, indeed, had closed his last earthly canvass; but another proud opponent of the victorious Magistrate stood beside him, as if to take the "Little Giant's" place. It was Salmon P. Chase. By virtue of his new office, he administered the oath and held the book for Abraham Lincoln to kiss.

CHAPTER VI

THE CURBING OF STANTON

EDWIN MCMASTERS STANTON made the third member of Mr. Lincoln's great cabinet triad. Unlike Seward and Chase, he brought to the government neither the experience nor the prestige that commonly results from a long period of public service. Engrossed in the practice of his profession at the bar, he had managed in his maturer years to eschew active politics,[1] until his brilliant work before the Supreme Court had secured to him, early in 1858, a retainer as special counsel for the United States on what were called the California Land Cases. So ably had these been conducted that President Buchanan, less than two years thereafter, appointed him Attorney-General. In that capacity Mr. Stanton had straightway become the most forceful of those advisers who saved from disgrace the closing days of a crumbling administration. The courage and skill with which he had opposed the intrigues of the secessionists in the cabinet gained for him — Democrat though he was — the confidence of leading Republicans. His ardent patriotism, indeed, seemed to outrun party fealty. He had gone so far as to hold secret conferences with Seward, Sumner, Wilson, Dawes, Howard, Ashley, and others, who have borne testimony to the value of his services, especially during the critical period that directly preceded Mr. Lincoln's inauguration. After that event, Mr. Stanton, having resumed his practice in Washington, became an anxious observer of the new government.

Notwithstanding his timely coöperation, while Attorney-General, with Republican Senators and Congressmen,

Stanton looked askance at the man whom they had elevated to the presidency. The two had met, several years before, under conditions that left no favorable impression in the recollection of either. As associate counsel with George Harding, in the famous reaper case of McCormick *vs.* Manny, they had appeared for the defendant, before Judges McLean and Drummond, in the United States Circuit Court, at Cincinnati. When the trial began, it was found that the plaintiff had but two advocates, E. N. Dickerson and Reverdy Johnson, the leader of the Maryland bar. They expressed their willingness to have the three counsel of the other side heard, if Mr. Dickerson, who was to make the argument on the mechanical phases of their case, might speak twice and Mr. Johnson once. This the attorney who had charge of the defence of course declined. He preferred to withdraw a representative, — but which one was it to be? Mr. Harding, then at the zenith of his fame as a patent lawyer, had been retained especially to make the technical argument. Choice for the forensic address, therefore, lay between Lincoln and Stanton. The latter was selected, to Mr. Lincoln's keen disappointment. He had looked forward to an active participation in the trial, not only on account of the important interests involved, but also because he was glad of the chance to measure his strength against that of the renowned Baltimore pleader. Lincoln's chagrin, moreover, was greatly intensified by Stanton's behavior. It is not true, as has been generally reported, that the man from Springfield was elbowed out of the case by his eastern colleague; but there can be no doubt that what at best was a mortifying experience for Lincoln became doubly so by reason of the other's rudeness. Our prairie lawyer, though he ranked high at home, made a poor impression upon Stanton, who described him, in his acrid way, as a "long, lank creature from Illinois, wearing a dirty linen duster for a coat, on the back of which the perspiration had splotched wide stains that resembled a map of the continent." What was worse, Mr. Stanton made no secret of his disdain. The object of it overheard him inquiring, —

"Where did that long-armed creature come from, and what can he expect to do in this case?"

So gross, indeed, were the discourtesies to which Lincoln was subjected from this quarter, that his magnanimous soul for some time harbored bitter feeling. "I have never been so brutally treated as by that man Stanton," was his comment on the affair; and low as was this gauge of Stanton's breeding, it corresponded closely enough with that worthy's estimate of Lincoln's ability.[2]

The relations between the two men underwent no improvement, even when the humiliated associate of a few years before became President. What dislikes are so deep-rooted as those for which no adequate reason can be given? And what public man of his day was so good a hater as Edwin M. Stanton? His recent connection, moreover, with Buchanan's somewhat discredited régime, together with his vehement, impatient patriotism, hardly served to temper his opinion of Mr. Lincoln, or of the new administration's temporizing policy.[3] In view, too, of the faultfinding and distrust which then marked the conduct of those who stood nearest to the President, it is not surprising that an outsider, so prejudiced as Mr. Stanton, should indulge in adverse criticism. We are not prepared, however, for the harsh expressions that he scattered through his private letters, in the spring and summer of 1861.

"No one," wrote he to Major-General John A. Dix, "can imagine the deplorable condition of this city, and the hazard of the government, who did not witness the weakness and panic of the administration, and the painful imbecility of Lincoln."[4]

To ex-President Buchanan he writes: —

"A strong feeling of distrust in the candor and sincerity of Lincoln personally and of his cabinet has sprung up. If they had been merely silent and secret, there might have been no ground of complaint. But assurances are said to have been given and declarations made in conflict with the facts now transpiring, in respect to the South, so that no one speaks of Lincoln or any member of his cabinet with respect or regard."

In other letters to Buchanan, Stanton charges the administration with "peculation and fraud," the trend of affairs is supposed to have excited "distrust in every department of the government," "it is said that Lincoln takes the precaution of seeing no strangers alone," it is believed that "in less than thirty days Davis will be in possession of Washington," there are "reports of the trepidation of Lincoln" after the Baltimore riot, "it is certain that the administration is panic-stricken for some cause," and so on. During the week that was ushered in by the defeat at Bull Run, Mr. Stanton wrote: —

"The imbecility of this administration culminated in that catastrophe; and irretrievable misfortune and national disgrace, never to be forgotten, are to be added to the ruin of all peaceful pursuits and national bankruptcy, as the result of Lincoln's 'running the machine,' for five months. . . . It is not unlikely that some change in the War and Navy Departments may take place, but none beyond those two departments until Jeff Davis turns out the whole concern."

This correspondence was not given to the public until some years after the war.[5] Even then, several of the letters to Mr. Buchanan were charitably suppressed by his biographer, because they were so violent in their denunciations. Mr. Stanton, however, at the time, made no secret of this hostility. His irritation, when quickened by discussion, found vent among friends, in coarse epithets. According to at least two chroniclers, he spoke of the President as "a low, cunning clown."[6] According to another, he habitually referred to Mr. Lincoln as the "original gorilla," and "often said that Du Chaillu was a fool to wander all the way to Africa, in search of what he could so easily have found at Springfield, Illinois."[7] Mr. Stanton went so far, it is reported, as to join the advocates of a revolutionary scheme, by means of which a military dictator was to displace the President. In short, from the day of their first meeting in Cincinnati, until deep into the first year of the war, he looked upon Mr. Lincoln with contempt.

What change, if any, Mr. Stanton's attitude had undergone by January, 1862, is not known. Howbeit, on the 13th of that month, the President, brushing personal feelings aside, nominated him to succeed Simon Cameron as Secretary of War. Though Stanton had been a supporter of Breckinridge, the southern Democratic candidate in the canvass of 1860,[8] he had, thereafter, as we have seen, given signal evidence of his fidelity to Union principles. The time, moreover, had come for breaking down the partisan barriers which divided northern patriots, so that the government might call to its aid friends of the Constitution in whatever party they might be found. This, of course, rendered Mr. Stanton's aggressive Democracy an advantage, in Mr. Lincoln's eyes. It was, in fact, one of the considerations which determined his selection. The appointment, which had been urged by Secretaries Seward and Chase, as well as by the retiring incumbent, had the approval, too, of Radical members in both Houses of Congress. It was promptly accepted and as promptly confirmed.

The elevation of Mr. Stanton to an important place in the Lincoln cabinet was a surprise to the nation. And his consent to associate himself with that administration aroused the still greater wonder of his own friends. One of them, who knew from frequent outbursts of scorn how the appointee regarded the President, referred to this feeling when he asked the new Secretary: —

"What will you do?"

Mr. Stanton, ignoring the purport of the question, answered, among other things: —

"I will make Abe Lincoln President of the United States."[9]

To another old friend he wrote, in confidence: —

"I hold my present post at the request of a President who knew me personally, but to whom I had not spoken from the 4th of March, 1861, until the day he handed me my commission. I knew that everything I cherish and hold dear would be sacrificed by accepting office. But I thought I might help to save the country, and for that I was willing to perish."[10]

To Mr. Buchanan he wrote: —

"My accession to my present position was quite as sudden and unexpected as the confidence you bestowed upon me in calling me to your cabinet, and the responsible trust was accepted in both instances from the same motives, and will be executed with the same fidelity to the Constitution and laws."[11]

The letters state what the conversation implies. Together they indicate the spirit in which Mr. Stanton entered upon his office. He clearly believed himself summoned, a second time, to strengthen the hands of an impotent President.

However grossly Edwin M. Stanton may have misjudged Mr. Lincoln, his confidence in himself was well founded. A glance at the new war minister's burly, thickset body revealed something of the force coiled within. His leonine head, with its mass of black, curling hair and long, slightly grizzled beard, gave promise of strength, which the keen, bespectacled eyes, no less than the full, resolute lips, appeared to confirm. In a physique capable, despite chronic asthma, of almost unlimited endurance, he nourished an intellect trained to equally sustained labor. "It is by work that we govern," said a powerful king, and Stanton was in this particular equipped to be a ruler of men. He brought to his undertakings a degree of energy which, according to contemporaries at the bar, had no parallel. Neither his knowledge of the law, comprehensive though it was, nor an eloquence that evoked praise from eminent advocates, had contributed so largely to his successes as the ardor, persistence, quickness of perception, executive swing, and promptitude of action with which he plunged into the conduct of a case. When complicated details were to be mastered, night and day seemed to him as one. In fact, had testimony on this point been required, any of his associates might have said concerning him, as Cecil did of Raleigh, "I know that he can toil terribly." Intense earnestness marked Stanton's every act. His enthusiasm for any cause which he had espoused would allow of no divided attention. So sharply, indeed, were all his faculties focused upon the purpose of the hour, that he is to be classed among the one-idea men of history. Whatever came between him and his goal encountered an iron will. He was not to be swerved to the right, or to the left; nor could he easily be reconciled to a backward step, however expedient. The tenacity of conviction which, at times, characterized his conduct must be ascribed — after due allowance for a masterful temper — to religious feeling. Like the Roundhead and Covenanter leaders to whom he has been compared, Stanton not only discerned the hand of the Lord in human affairs, but also believed himself, on more than one occasion, to be an instrument of the divine will. This may account, too, for the emotional quality in an otherwise practical nature. Extremes of reason and passion were here strangely commingled. Quick to penetrate through the husks of a fraud into the very nubbin of things, he was even more swiftly moved by relentless wrath to insist upon exposure and punishment. That brief career in Buchanan's cabinet had been long enough to demonstrate his almost savage hostility towards official dishonesty, as well as his moral courage to grapple with treason in high places. Above all, he evinced a loyalty to the Union that rose above the partisan creed of a lifetime — that might, in fact, demand of him, and not be denied, any sacrifice, however great.

So strong a character is seldom free from the defects almost inherent in its rugged structure. As Mr. Stanton's drafts on his own powers were invariably honored, he was unsparing in his demands upon others. Niggardly of praise and caustic in criticism, he set up a high standard of achievement, with no charity for those who fell below it. This led him to underrate most of the persons with whom he came in contact, while it may be doubted whether any one enjoyed his unqualified confidence. Slow to recognize what was good in a man, he not infrequently gave way, over slight shortcomings, to violent outbursts of anger. His very earnestness, at times, even when there were no such provocations, rendered him offensively aggressive. Tact had but a small place in Stanton's make-up. He drove his wedge broad end foremost. Not only was he lacking in the grace that sometimes transforms an enemy into a friend, but he was equally incapable of controlling a temper that, on more than one occasion, changed a friend into an enemy. After his brusque, impulsive manner, he scorned ceremony or etiquette. With rude hands he brushed aside whatever stood in his way. He might have sat for these lines in a notable portrait of Gladstone: "Side issues, risks, the feelings of friends, the prejudices of the day, the lions in the path — all would be either ignored, or only recognized to be thrust aside, when he had some great end immediately in view; and thus he has been looked upon by many as a sort of Juggernaut, who, to attain his end, would drive remorselessly over the bodies of men."

When thwarted, Stanton's rage, taking note of neither time, place, nor person, expressed itself with cutting precision; and his disregard of what was thought, or said, about him, in return, rendered him an anomaly in public life. Though careless of popularity, he loved deeply the few upon whom he bestowed his affections. If these might be credited, there was nothing of the bear about this fierce Orson but his skin. They have recalled how easily his mood shifted from storm to sunshine, and how tenderly his heart responded to humble suffering. But at this very point the corresponding shadow in the portrait is darker than elsewhere; for the unfortunates, who, with or without cause, excited his dislike, were not safe against insult, injustice, and even persecution. Some of the man's personal prejudices would not have been pounded out of him if he had been brayed in a mortar. Even when shown that he had erred, Stanton could with difficulty be induced to modify his antagonisms. He rarely made amends, and it may be doubted whether he ever brought himself to say, "I was wrong." His firmness degenerated, at times, into sheer obstinacy; his enthusiasm, into intolerance; his strength of will, into arrogance. No one who knew the man courted an encounter with him. Only a master of masters could control such an embodiment of force.

At the time of his appointment, Mr. Stanton had, in some degree, manifested most, if not all, of these traits. They boded no good for the harmony of the cabinet, nor for the President's authority. So thought the friends who warned Mr. Lincoln that nothing could be done with such a man, unless he were allowed to have his own way. There appeared to be abundant ground, moreover, for their comforting prediction that "Stanton would run away with the whole concern." Strangely enough, the President showed no alarm. He was merely reminded of a little story.

"We may have to treat him," said he, "as they are sometimes obliged to treat a Methodist minister I know of out West. He gets wrought up to so high a pitch of excitement in his prayers and exhortations, that they are obliged to put bricks into his pockets to keep him down. We may be obliged to serve Stanton the same way, but I guess we'll let him jump awhile first."[12]

The ability and self-sacrificing patriotism with which the appointee administered, from the outset, the affairs of his office, secured to him the President's unreserved confidence. "I have faith," said Mr. Lincoln, speaking of the new minister and another, "in affirmative men like these. They stand between a nation and perdition." He not only permitted Mr. Stanton largely to control the details of the War Department, but in matters of general policy as well, he frequently deferred to that officer's judgment. Men of such dissimilar temperaments, however, working together toward a common end in wholly unlike ways, naturally had frequent differences of opinion. Their very earnestness bred trouble. Mr. Stanton, moreover, conducting his department solely with regard to military requirements, could not fail to clash with a President who had to face the complex problems of a civil war, in their political as well as their strategic aspects. But Mr. Lincoln fathomed the man with whom he had to deal. When a misunderstanding arose, he ignored the Secretary's flashes of temper, and fixed his attention on the question at issue. Indeed, the President exercised tact enough for both of them. Whether he withdrew from a position because it was proved to be wrong, or maintained it because it was right, he seldom failed to treat Mr. Stanton with delicate consideration.[13] How far this consideration went is an interesting subject for inquiry, particularly in view of the not uncommon opinion that the fiery war minister dominated the President. Such incidents as gave rise to this belief were neither numerous nor conclusive; yet in them may be discerned the grain of truth from which the error sprouted.

Throughout the entire period of the war, Mr. Lincoln was beset, early and late, by people who wanted personal favors in matters that properly fell under the jurisdiction of the War Department. Those who came with an appeal from Mr. Stanton's decision were sometimes received as was Judge Baldwin of California. He applied for a pass through the lines to visit his brother in Virginia. As both of them were Union men, there seemed to be no good reason why it should not be granted.

"Have you applied to General Halleck?" inquired the President.

"Yes," answered the Judge, "and met with a flat refusal."

"Then you must see Stanton," said Mr. Lincoln.

"I have, and with the same result," was the reply.

"Well, then," rejoined the President, with a smile, "I can do nothing; for you must know that I have very little influence with this administration."[14]

The same answer, though sympathetically uttered, concluded an interview with a soldier's widow who asked for a sutler's appointment, which the Secretary of War had, under the regulations, refused.[15] In fact, this whimsical disclaimer of "influence" with the administration became one of Mr. Lincoln's favorite resources.[16] Commenting on the remark, at the time, to a cabinet officer, he said: —

"I cannot always know whether a permit ought to be granted, and I want to oblige everybody when I can; and Stanton and I have an understanding that if I send an order to him that cannot be consistently granted, he is to refuse it, which he sometimes does. And that led to a remark which I made the other day to a man who complained of Stanton, that I had n't much influence with this administration, but expected to have more with the next."[17]

This explanation accounts, too, for much, if not all, of Secretary Stanton's seeming insubordination, in the instances that follow.

If an applicant for military favors went, at the outset, to the White House, rather than to the War Office, he may have received from the President a penciled request in his behalf, addressed to Secretary Stanton. Sometimes this was granted, but it was as often curtly or angrily refused. Occasionally passes signed by Mr. Lincoln were confiscated by order of the War Department, upon presentation; and, in certain instances, even more formal documents were not safe against the Secretary's destructive fingers. This fact, one enterprising trader learned to his disappointment. He had pursued the President, in season and out, for a pass through the lines and a treasury license to buy cotton. How persistent he was may be inferred from Mr. Lincoln's complaint of his class, in general: —

"Few things are so troublesome to the government as the fierceness with which the profits in trading are sought."

This particular trader must have brought more than fierceness to bear upon the harassed President, for he finally received the coveted permit.

"You will have to take it over to Stanton for countersigning," said Mr. Lincoln.

The happy man, hastening to the War Department, handed the document to the Secretary. Mr. Stanton, taking advantage of military conditions that warranted a refusal, showed his deep-seated contempt for speculators by tearing the paper into shreds and stamping upon them. Our trader returned to the President in a rage, and told him what had occurred. Mr. Lincoln, feigning surprise, asked him to describe exactly how the Secretary had acted. Then, after a moment's pause, he said: —

"You go back and tell Stanton that I will tear up a dozen of his papers before Saturday night." [18]

The Secretary of War made the most of the discretion reposed in him. He insulted Congressmen and bullied traders, impartially, when they brought orders of which he could safely disapprove. Indeed, — if an anecdote to which the Hon. George W. Julian has given currency may be relied on, — he did not, in his fits of anger, spare the President himself. This story illustrates, better than any other, the popular war-time impression concerning the relations between the two men. For that, if for no other reason, it should be taken into an account which seeks to explain the origin of the belief that Mr. Stanton was master. A committee of western men, we are told, headed by Congressman Owen Lovejoy of Illinois, called on the President to urge that the spirit of national unity might be promoted in the army by the mingling of eastern and western troops. The plan, on its apparent merits, as well as because it was presented by a warm personal and political friend, interested Mr. Lincoln, who wrote a note to the Secretary of War, suggesting a transfer of some of the regiments. As the scheme seemed impracticable to Mr. Stanton, he refused to carry it out.

"But we have the President's order, sir," said Mr. Lovejoy.

"Did Lincoln give you an order of that kind?" asked the Secretary.

"He did, sir."

"Then he is a damned fool!" was the response.

"Do you mean to say the President is a damned fool?" asked the Congressman in amazement.

"Yes, sir, if he gave you such an order as that."

Returning to the Executive Mansion, Mr. Lovejoy reported the result of the conference.

"Did Stanton say I was a damned fool?" asked Mr. Lincoln, at the close of the recital.

"He did, sir; and repeated it."

"If Stanton said I was a damned fool," concluded the President thoughtfully, "then I must be one; for he is nearly always right, and generally says what he means. I will step over and see him." [19]

Nor was this the only occasion on which Messrs. Julian and Lovejoy had reason to infer that the man in the War Office dominated the man in the White House. They called on the President at another time to urge a certain army appointment for the son of a man who had befriended Lincoln in the days of his poverty. The President promptly endorsed the application and sent them with it to Mr. Stanton, who as promptly said, "No."

"Let us give his qualifications," suggested one of the Congressmen.

"I do not wish to hear them," was the reply. "The

position is of high importance. I have in mind a man of suitable experience and capacity to fill it."

When the callers, still persisting, reminded the Secretary that the President wished their man to be appointed, he retorted: —

"I do not care what the President wants; the country wants the very best it can get. I am serving the country regardless of individuals."

Returning to the White House, the Congressmen reported their failure, but Mr. Lincoln gave them no comfort.

"Gentlemen," he said, "it is my duty to submit. I cannot add to Mr. Stanton's troubles. His position is one of the most difficult in the world. Thousands in the army blame him because they are not promoted, and other thousands out of the army blame him because they are not appointed. The pressure upon him is immeasurable and unending. He is the rock on the beach of our national ocean against which the breakers dash and roar, dash and roar, without ceasing. He fights back the angry waters and prevents them from undermining and overwhelming the land. Gentlemen, I do not see how he survives, — why he is not crushed and torn to pieces. Without him I should be destroyed. He performs his task superhumanly. Now do not mind this matter, for Mr. Stanton is right and I cannot wrongly interfere with him." [20]

Taking advantage of this purely impersonal attitude of the President, his war minister did not hesitate, when the circumstances warranted, to oppose what Mr. Lincoln wanted for old friends as stubbornly as he planted himself in the path of political favorites. A case in point grew out of the so-called Coles County riot.[21] Some southern sympathizers, living near Charleston, Ill., had brought about a quarrel, at that place, with a party of Federal soldiers home on furlough. In the shooting that ensued, eleven officers and privates had been killed or wounded. Whereupon the military authorities, having arrested a number of the rioters, had held fifteen of them prisoners, in Fort Delaware. Their release had, from time to time, been sought by influential Illinoisans, but without success. At last, it occurred to the friends of the prisoners that what the politicians had failed to accomplish might be arrived at through the instrumentality of Mr. Lincoln's cousin and one-time playmate, Dennis Hanks. So behold Dennis, in a new suit of store clothes, presenting himself at the Executive Mansion, on what might be called a diplomatic mission. He was affectionately received by the President, who gravely handed him the official record in the Riot Cases to read. Then, as if to continue the joke, Mr. Lincoln sent him to confer on the subject with the head of the War Department. Luckily for cousin Dennis, the choleric Stanton was not to be found. That officer came to the White House presently, however, for a discussion in which President, Secretary, and citizen Hanks took part. Adopting the garrulous petitioner's own version, Mr. Stanton pointed out how heinous were the crimes of the rioters, and declared that "every damned one of them should be hung." Even Mr. Lincoln's query, "If these men should return home and become good citizens, who would be hurt?" failed to move the Secretary from his position that the prisoners ought to be severely punished. This opinion the President declined, at the time, to overrule. So Dennis's errand came to an inglorious close. He soon returned home, where his visit to the President was, ever afterward, drawn upon for stories that were not always consistent with one another. The envoy, of course, carried away an unfavorable impression of Mr. Stanton, whom he described as a "frisky little Yankee, . . . in a spike-tailed coat." After the great conference, when the Secretary had left the room, Dennis said, as he relates: —

"Abe, if I 's as big as you, I would take that little feller over my knee and spank him."

To which Mr. Lincoln rejoined, with a laugh, that he

guessed Stanton was a bigger man than he, in some respects.

"I asked Abe," recalled Dennis, on another occasion, "why he did n't kick him out. I told him he was too fresh altogether."

And the President is said to have replied: —

"If I did, Dennis, it would be difficult to find another man to fill his place." [22]

Nevertheless, in the sequel to this episode, Mr. Stanton's domination was found, after all, to be apparent rather than real. He demanded — not without reason — that the rioters should have short shrift before a military court; but to this the President would not consent. After carefully examining the evidence, Mr. Lincoln directed the prisoners to be returned to Coles County, where those of them who had been indicted were to be surrendered to the civil authorities, and the rest were to be discharged. The required order, it is perhaps needless to say, was promptly issued by the Secretary of War.

All of Mr. Stanton's arrests were not so defensible as the Charleston ones. Indeed, it became necessary, at times, to interpose between him and the objects of his severity. How to secure these unfortunates substantial justice, without impairing the Secretary's authority, or perhaps losing his services entirely, tried the President's good-humored tact to the utmost. Such a problem presented itself during the presidential canvass of 1864. The votes of the Pennsylvania troops were, in conformity with an act of legislature, to be cast in the field, under the eyes of State commissioners. That some of these officers should be Democrats, if the election were to have even a semblance of fairness, was obvious; but for reasons which were equally clear, prominent members of the minority party could with difficulty be prevailed upon to accept the appointments. At this juncture, Governor Curtin got Colonel A. K. McClure to help him complete the list. The Colonel applied, among others, to Jere

McKibbin, who, at the suggestion that he visit the army as a commissioner, instantly said: —

"Why, Stanton would put me in Old Capitol Prison before I was there a day. He hates our family for no other reason that I know of than that my father was one of his best friends in Pittsburg, when he needed a friend."

McClure assured him that the Secretary of War would not attempt any violence against a man who held Governor Curtin's commission. Yet it was only after the Colonel had pledged himself to protect McKibbin, if he got into any difficulty, that the latter consented to serve. He duly left Philadelphia for the front, with the other commissioners. They had not been gone two days, when McClure received from McKibbin a Washington despatch which read: —

"Stanton has me in Old Capitol Prison. Come at once."

The Colonel hastened to make good his promise. Arriving at the Capital late in the night of that same day, he obtained an immediate interview with the President. Mr. Lincoln knew of Stanton's grudge against the McKibbins. He had encountered it on several previous occasions, when Jere's brothers, who were officers in the army, would have lost well-merited promotions but for the President's interposition. It was not surprising, therefore, to find this last act of enmity, as a glance at the papers revealed, utterly without justification. A "stupid blunder," was Mr. Lincoln's comment. He appeared to be greatly distressed over the affair, and proposed to release McKibbin at once on his parole. This did not satisfy the Colonel, who urged that the commissioner should be discharged. But the President replied: —

"It seems hardly fair to discharge McKibbin unconditionally without permitting Stanton to give his explanation. You know, McClure, McKibbin is safe, parole or no parole, so go and get him out of prison."

With this the Colonel had, for the time, to be content. He prevailed upon Mr. Lincoln, however, to appoint an hour the following morning, at which they might meet the Secretary of War to have the parole discharged. Then hurrying to the Old Capitol Prison, with the President's order, he had the commissioner released. On the next day, at the time agreed upon, Colonel McClure sat in the President's room, awaiting Mr. Stanton. The Secretary entered, pale with anger.

"Well, McClure," he exclaimed, "what damned rebel are you here to get out of trouble, this morning?"

"Your arrest of McKibbin," replied the Colonel, "was a cowardly act. You knew McKibbin was guiltless of any offence, and you did it to gratify a brutal hatred."

The Pennsylvanian, having given further vent to his indignation in terms no less severe, demanded a final discharge of the prisoner. To this, Mr. Stanton, who had been excitedly walking the floor, answered, in his most offensive manner: —

"I decline to discharge McKibbin from his parole. You can make formal application for it if you choose; and I will consider and decide it."

"I don't know what McKibbin will do," hotly rejoined McClure, "but if I were Jere McKibbin, as sure as there is a God, I would crop your ears before I left Washington."

Mr. Stanton made no reply. He abruptly turned and left the room. Whereupon the President, who had been a silent auditor, said, in his jocular way: —

"Well, McClure, you did n't get on very far with Stanton, did you? But he 'll come all right. Let the matter rest."

A formal request, however, for the discharge of the parole was sent, at once, to the Secretary of War, who as formally replied, in an autograph letter, that the application, having been duly considered, "could not be granted consistently with the interests of the public service." Mr. McKibbin outlived Mr. Stanton, yet he died a prisoner on parole.[23]

Mr. Lincoln made no secret of his anxiety to avoid conflicting with his irascible Secretary, whose objection to a measure was, at times, frankly assigned as a sufficient reason for its rejection. This was the case when Major-General Nathaniel P. Banks, commanding the Department of the Gulf, sought to extend his authority by having that of his division commander, Major-General E. R. S. Canby, curtailed. The latter officer had been appointed to the Military Division of West Mississippi, constructed out of the departments of Arkansas and the Gulf, in the spring of 1864, directly after Banks's unsuccessful Red River campaign. General Banks chafed under the arrangement. But his administrative abilities were held in such high esteem by the President that several expedients were tried for keeping him contentedly at his post, where he was expected to play an important part in reorganizing the Louisiana state government. As he persisted, however, in his appeals to be relieved of Canby's authority, Mr. Lincoln finally dismissed the matter, with a refusal which read in part:—

"I know you are dissatisfied, which pains me very much; but I wish not to be argued with further. I entertain no abatement of confidence or friendship for you. I have told you why I cannot order General Canby from the Department of the Gulf — that he whom I must hold responsible for military results is not agreed." [24]

And with this Banks had to rest content.

On several of the numerous occasions when the President found it necessary to thwart Mr. Stanton's wishes, he did so in a way which tended to confirm, rather than to remove, the impression that the Secretary controlled him. An instance of this is preserved in another letter — one of Mr. Lincoln's characteristic pleas for mercy. His oft-mentioned clemency was not limited to northern offenders. He could not bring himself to regard the soldiers of the Confederacy with the bitterness evinced by his Secretary of War, whose uncompromising hostility toward those who had taken up arms against the Union had repeatedly opposed itself to the President's desire that certain penitent prisoners should be set free. This wish was finally embodied in the following communication to Mr. Stanton: —

"I am so pressed in regard to prisoners of war in our custody, whose homes are within our lines, and who wish to not be exchanged, but to take the oath and be discharged, that I hope you will pardon me for again calling up the subject. My impression is that we will not ever force the exchange of any of this class; that, taking the oath and being discharged, none of them will again go to the rebellion; but the rebellion again coming to them, a considerable percentage of them, probably not a majority, would rejoin it; that, by a cautious discrimination, the number so discharged would not be large enough to do any considerable mischief in any event, will relieve distress in at least some meritorious cases, and would give me some relief from an intolerable pressure. I shall be glad, therefore, to have your cheerful assent to the discharge of those whose names I may send, which I will only do with circumspection."[25]

This tactful presentation of the matter accomplished as much as would have resulted from a positive mandate. The Secretary responded: —

"Mr. President: Your order for the discharge of any prisoners of war will be cheerfully and promptly obeyed."[26]

Another illustration of how Mr. Lincoln, to use one of his own phrases, "plowed around" this sometimes obstructive minister is supplied by John Adams Kasson, who represented an Iowa district in Congress during the latter half of the war. His constituents desired him to procure promotion for the gallant Colonel James A. Williamson, commanding the Fourth Infantry Regiment of that State. The officer deserved the higher rank, but it was difficult of attainment. Letters and petitions poured in upon Mr. Kasson. He was given to understand that his failure to obtain the promotion might cost him his reëlection. The case was laid before the President, who valued this particular Congressman both as a personal friend and as one of the administration's most zealous supporters. It would not do to lose him for a brigadier's commission. Accordingly, at the first Iowa resignation of the rank desired, Mr. Lincoln signed an order upon Secretary Stanton to make the favorite colonel a brigadier-general. Pleased with his success, Mr. Kasson presented himself, with the order, at the War Department. He did not realize what difficulties were still in his way, or how fiercely the Cerberus at the portals to military preferment resented the intrusion of civilians. What followed is best told in Mr. Kasson's own language.

"Mr. Stanton," he says in his Reminiscences,[27] "was seated on the sofa, talking with a friend, and his immediate clerk was standing at a neighboring desk, with his pen in hand. As I advanced, taking off my hat, Mr. Stanton turned to me to hear what I had to say. I told him my errand, and handed him the President's order. He glanced at it, and said, in an angry tone, 'I shan't do it, sir; I shan't do it!' and passed the paper up to his clerk. Utterly amazed at his words, and indignant at his tone, I inquired why he refused to obey the President's order. 'It is n't the way to do it, sir, and I shan't do it.' I was going on to speak of the merits of the officer, and of the proceeding, my wrath rising, when he cut me off with 'I don't propose to argue the question with you, sir; I shan't do it.' Utterly indignant, I turned to the clerk and asked to withdraw the paper. 'Don't you let him have it, sir,' said Stanton; 'don't let him have it.' The clerk, whose hands were trembling like an Eastern slave before his Pasha, withdrew the document which he was in the act of giving to me. I felt my indignation getting too strong for me, and putting on my hat and turning my back to the Secretary, I slowly went to the door, with set teeth, saying to myself, 'As you will not hear me in your own forum, you shall hear from me in mine.' A few days later, after recovering my coolness, I reported the affair to the President. A look of vexation came over his face, and he seemed unwilling then to talk of it, and desired me to see him another day. I did so, when he gave me a positive order for the promotion of the colonel to be a brigadier, and told me to take it over to the War Department. I replied that I could not speak again with Mr. Stanton till he apologized for his insulting manner to me on the previous occasion. 'Oh,' said the President, 'Stanton has gone to Fortress Monroe, and Dana is acting. He will attend to it for you.' This he said with a manner of relief, as if it was a piece of good luck to find a man there who would obey his orders. The nomination was sent to the Senate and confirmed."

Soon after this occurrence, when the House was debating a motion concerning the investigation of the Old Capitol and the Carroll prisons, Mr. Kasson carried out his threat.[28] Describing what he termed Secretary Stanton's "arbitrary habit of mind," he denounced this war-lord for his tyrannical course and his disobedience toward his chief. To substantiate the latter accusation, the speaker related to an attentive audience his own experience with Mr. Stanton. The story not only helped to swell the overwhelming vote in favor of the resolution, but it also gave the widest publicity to what was considered an authoritative insight into the peculiar relations existing between Mr. Lincoln and the head of the War Department.

There is at least one other anecdote of how the President "plowed around" Stanton to reach a military appointment. In this instance, he had to encounter not only the Secretary's cogent objection to civilian interference in such matters, but that alert minister's equally sound rule as well, against the transfer of volunteer officers to the regular army. So, when a number of prominent public men came to the White House one day to urge such a transfer of Captain John J. S. Hassler, who was serving with credit in the Thirty-first New York Regiment, Mr. Lincoln threw up his hands in mock agony and said: —

"Gentlemen, I can do nothing. That rests entirely with Mr. Stanton, but I can go over and join in a request to Mr. Stanton to have Captain Hassler appointed in the regular army."

The Secretary of War received the petitioners with an absolute refusal. Similar requests, it was explained, came to him in such numbers that to comply would result in leaving the volunteer regiments almost without officers. An ironclad rule had therefore been made against such transfers, and he declined to break it under any condition. Returning from the War Office, the delegation met Adjutant-General Townsend, to whom they related the whole affair.

"I think I can fix it for you," he said. "Let it be understood by the President that Mr. Hassler will step across the street and enlist as a private in the regular army, at the same time resigning his commission as an officer of volunteers. He can then at once be promoted."

When the plan was laid before Mr. Lincoln, he smilingly assented, but Stanton had no smile for the officer who shortly brought him the papers for Hassler's promotion in the regular army. He is said to have given the man "one of those through-and-through looks with which it was his habit to chastise in silence those who had done something they knew was not right," and then he signed the document.[29]

The Secretary of War did not always hold himself so well in hand. There were times when his spleen made serious trouble, — when, in fact, he did not spare even his cabinet colleagues. It was then that the President's touch could be especially delicate, as he evinced in the handling of a certain disagreement between Secretary Stanton and Postmaster-General Montgomery Blair. Mr. Lincoln settled the question at issue adversely to his hot-headed war minister, yet he again skilfully avoided a struggle with him. The Blair-Stanton feud was of long standing. It had antedated the war, and had caused the Postmaster-General bitterly to oppose Mr. Stanton's appointment to a cabinet office. As they were both men of aggressive temperament, they naturally did not work harmoniously when, later, their department duties brought them into relations with each other. Several attempts, at the same time, to involve the President in the quarrel were without avail. "I learned a great many years ago," he once said, referring to a controversy carried on by two prominent Republicans, "that in a fight between man and wife, a third party should never get between the woman's skillet and the man's ax-helve." How Mr. Lincoln managed the cabinet belligerents was illustrated, during the summer of 1864, when Mr. Stanton refused Mr. Blair's request to issue certain orders that would facilitate the postal service within the lines of the army. The orders had been drafted at headquarters, under General Grant's supervision, but he waited for Secretary Stanton's sanction. As this was withheld, because it would "accommodate Mr. Blair," an appeal to the President followed. After reading the Postmaster-General's letter of complaint, and having questioned the bearer, Colonel Absalom H. Markland of the army mail service, he said:—

"If I understand the case, General Grant wants the orders issued, and Blair wants them issued, and you want them issued, and Stanton won't issue them. Now, don't you see what kind of a fix I will be in if I interfere? I'll tell you what to do. If you and General Grant understand one another, suppose you try to get along without the orders, and if Blair or Stanton make a fuss, I may be called in as a referee, and I may decide in your favor." [30]

The contemplated changes were made without the orders, and nothing further was heard about this particular difference.

The foregoing instances of Secretary Stanton's alleged insubordination, or excessive power over Lincoln, are the only ones worthy of record that have come to the writer's notice. They are not all, it is true, supported by documentary evidence; yet the standing of the narrators, — with perhaps one exception, — certain corroborative circumstances, and the entire absence of conflicting testimony entitle them to credit. As much cannot be said, however, for many of the anecdotes of Mr. Stanton's mastery, in which the newspaper and magazine press have abounded. Now and then, one of these apocryphal tales has found its way into some historical work of authority, where it has served, more than its fellows, to keep alive an exaggerated conception of the Secretary's influence over the President. A typical case is to be found in the Personal Memoirs of General Grant. He speaks of Mr. Stanton as "a man who never questioned his own authority, and who always did in war time what he wanted to do." In connection with this statement, it is related that Mr. Lincoln, on the occasion of his visit to the captured city of Richmond, issued permission to "the body, calling itself the Legislature of Virginia, to meet for the purpose of recalling the Virginia troops from the Confederate armies." The summons for a meeting which, according to the illustrious author, "immediately" afterward appeared in the local newspapers, "went very much further than Mr. Lincoln had contemplated, as he did not say the 'Legislature of Virginia,' but 'the body which called itself the Legislature of Virginia.' Mr. Stanton," continues Grant, "saw the call, as published in the northern papers, the very next issue, and took the liberty of countermanding the order authorizing any meeting of the legislature, or any other body, and this notwithstanding the fact that the President was nearer the spot than he was."[31] The story is incorrect. Mr. Lincoln did, on April 6, 1865, while at City Point and after several interviews with Judge Campbell, the Confederate Assistant Secretary of War,[32] write to Major-General Godfrey Weitzel, in command at Richmond: —

"It has been intimated to me that the gentlemen who have acted as the Legislature of Virginia, in support of the rebellion, may now desire to assemble at Richmond, and take measures to withdraw the Virginia troops and other support from resistance to the general government. If they attempt it, give them permission and protection."[33]

But the call to the members of the legislature was not published, even in Richmond, until April 12, three days after the President had returned to Washington. He then found that Judge Campbell had gone beyond the authority conferred, and had — we quote Mr. Lincoln's criticism — assumed the President to "have called the insurgent Legislature of Virginia together, as the rightful legislature of the State, to settle all differences with the United States."[34] This misconstruction gave the President pause. He found disapproval, moreover, within the cabinet, of any plan for reconstruction that even seemed to recognize the political elements of the Confederacy. Most strenuous in opposition was Secretary Stanton, who earnestly advised Mr. Lincoln to revoke the City Point instructions. This the President concluded to do, especially as the recent surrender of the Virginia troops to General Grant had removed all occasion for the meeting. Mr. Lincoln, accordingly, brought the incident to a close, on the evening of April 12, by telegraphing to General Weitzel, from the Capital, that the permission to assemble was withdrawn. Strange to say, General Grant, himself, the following day, despatched from Washington to the commander at Richmond certain supplementary instructions. To this extent the Lieutenant-General, rather than the Secretary of War, figures officially in the correspondence.[35] So far from countermanding the President's orders was Mr. Stanton, that none of the messages concerning the Virginia legislature even went through the customary form of carrying his signature.[36]

The Secretary of War never successfully opposed his will to that of the President in any matter concerning which his chief had reached a definite purpose. Yet Mr. Lincoln made no display of his authority. He even, as we have seen, turned it over at times to Mr. Stanton; or, anxious to avoid a conflict, exercised it with all the delicacy of which he was capable. Few, if any, of the world's great captains could have managed this truculent lieutenant with so little friction. To that end, concession, persuasion, and diplomacy were freely intermingled. When they failed, however, the President asserted his mastery with a vigor before which the Secretary's passion and obstinacy had to give way.

This was the case in the autumn of 1864, after compulsory military service had been introduced. To fill their quotas, without drawing too heavily on their own citizens, some communities voted liberal bounties, by means of which their agents obtained recruits wherever they could be found. One of these agents, Colonel Huidekoper, representing a Pennsylvania district, evolved a crafty scheme. Learning that some Confederate prisoners at Rock Island, Ill., were about to be released and enlisted for our frontier service, he secured permission from Mr. Lincoln to pay them bounties so that they might be credited to his county.[37] When Huidekoper presented the President's order for the credits at the War Department, Mr. Stanton refused to obey it. Indignant and disappointed, the Colonel reported this to Mr. Lincoln, who repeated the order, but without effect. Then the President, himself, visited the War Department, and the Secretary called in his Provost-Marshal-General, James B. Fry, to state the facts.

"I reported to the two high officials," says General Fry, who relates the incident, "as I had previously done to the Secretary alone, that these men already belonged to the United States, being prisoners of war; that they could not be used against the Confederates; that they had no relation whatever to the county to which it was proposed they should be credited; that all that was necessary toward enlisting them in our army for Indian service was the government's release of them as prisoners of war; that to give them bounty and credit them to a county which owed some of its own men for service against the Confederates would waste money and deprive the army, operating against a powerful enemy, of that number of men, etc."

"Now, Mr. President," added Stanton, "those are the facts, and you must see that your order cannot be executed."

Mr. Lincoln, who had sat attentively listening, with his legs crossed, said, in a somewhat positive tone: —

"Mr. Secretary, I reckon you'll have to execute the order."

Stanton replied with asperity: —

"Mr. President, I cannot do it. The order is an improper one, and I cannot execute it."

Mr. Lincoln, eyeing Stanton fixedly, rejoined with an emphasis that clearly showed his determination: —

"Mr. Secretary, it will have to be done."

"Stanton," concludes Mr. Fry, "then realized that he was overmatched. He had made a square issue with the President and been defeated, notwithstanding the fact that he was in the right. Upon an intimation from him I withdrew, and did not witness his surrender. A few minutes after I reached my office, I received instructions from the Secretary to carry out the President's order." [38]

Here was a bitter leek for Mr. Stanton to eat, the more so because he had such good ground for his opposition. Indeed, not many days thereafter, Mr. Lincoln admitted to General Grant that the entire proceeding had been a blunder. Taking all the blame upon himself, in his own frank way, he especially exculpated the Secretary of War, and explained that before Mr. Stanton could convince him of his error, he had committed himself too far to recede.[39]

In determining the proportion of troops to be furnished

by each of the States, the War Department aroused considerable faultfinding. To all the complaints, whether justifiable or not, the brusque Secretary turned a deaf ear. He rigidly adhered to the assignment for New York, under the call of December 19, 1864, although Reuben E. Fenton, the newly installed Republican Governor of the State, went to Washington in person, to point out its inaccuracies. Failing to secure a reduction, Mr. Fenton appealed to the President, who, having listened to his argument, said: —

"I guess you have the best of it, and I must advise Stanton and Fry to ease up a little."

Then Mr. Lincoln wrote to the Secretary of War, on one of his little cards: —

"The Governor has a pretty good case. I feel sure he is more than half right. We don't want him to feel cross and we in the wrong. Try and fix it with him."

The War Department did "fix it," by a reduction of nine thousand from the number of men that had originally been required.[40]

The President's attitude toward Mr. Stanton on these occasions was supplemented, in comparatively trivial affairs, by an equally firm bearing. One instance of this, at least, should be cited. It indicates that Mr. Lincoln, notwithstanding his habitual disregard of ceremony, did not brook disrespectful treatment in an official matter, at the Secretary's hands. The head of the War Department, in the spring of 1862, sent to the Executive Mansion Edward Stanley's commission as Military Governor of North Carolina, with the request that the President should sign and return it. The document was sent back, but without the signature. Another attempt to have the commission completed met with the same fate. Then Mr. Stanton placed the scroll in the hands of Major William G. Moore, his private secretary, with instructions to call on Mr. Lincoln and ascertain whether he had any objections to signing it. When the document was presented by Major Moore, the President unrolled it and turned it about as if in search of something.

"Did Mr. Stanton say *where* I was to put my signature?" he asked.

"No, sir," answered the messenger.

"Can *you* tell me," continued Mr. Lincoln, striking the commission two or three times with his forefinger, "whereabouts on this paper I am to put my signature?"

Major Moore had not read the document. He now looked, and saw Mr. Stanton's name written in a bold hand directly below the body of the instrument, with the Adjutant-General's counter-signature to the left. He also saw, beneath the name of the Secretary, sufficient space for another signature; but he was a discreet young man, so he replied: —

"I don't see any place provided for your signature, Mr. President."

Then he sought to explain the omission. Interrupting him, Mr. Lincoln said: —

"Take the paper back to the Secretary of War, with my compliments, and say that the President will promptly sign any *proper* commission that may be sent to him for Governor Stanley or anybody else."

Hastening back to the War Department, Major Moore reported to his chief what had occurred. Mr. Stanton, as his secretary relates, showed considerable feeling over the matter. Ringing violently for the Adjutant-General, he directed him upon his appearance to draft another copy as quickly as possible. When this order had been obeyed, the commission made its fourth journey to the White House, whence it soon returned with the desired signature.[41]

In this episode President and Secretary appear, as far as habits go, to have exchanged places. For the volcanic Stanton — paradoxical though it may seem — had ideals of regularity, while Lincoln, who was deliberation itself, did not hesitate to sever red tape, if it lay across his path to a legitimate end. Occasionally these short-cuts led through the War Department, much to the annoyance of the man at its head. In fact, his stern adherence to established rules, and the President's proneness to set them aside, led to several sharp disagreements. On questions of mercy — at times, even of justice — their points of view were not in the same plane. With Lincoln's broad humanity, Mars, as he playfully called his war minister, had but little sympathy. The Secretary insisted — not without reason — that military discipline was endangered by the President's clemency, and by his too liberal interpretation of the laws. Nevertheless, pardons arrived at the War Office with irritating frequency. The head of the department delayed, argued, protested, blustered, threatened, and — obeyed.[42] To do the last was especially hard for him when he believed that Mr. Lincoln had been imposed on. Such an instance is recalled by Henry Laurens Dawes, who during the war represented a Massachusetts district in Congress. His constituents were interested in a quartermaster from his State, who had been sentenced to five years in the penitentiary for gambling with government money. The convict's influential neighbors, together with a prominent physician and the prison doctor, signed a petition for his pardon, on the ground that his health had become seriously impaired, with every prospect of a speedy death unless he were released.

"I took this petition," says Mr. Dawes, in whose hands the document had been placed, "to Mr. Lincoln, who, after carefully reading it, turned to me and said, 'Do you believe that statement?' 'Certainly, I do, Mr. President, or I should not have brought it to you.' 'Please say so here on the back of it, under these doctors.' I did as requested, adding, 'And because I believe it to be true I join in this petition.' As I signed my name he remarked, 'We can't permit that man to die in prison after that statement,' and immediately wrote under it all, 'Let this man be discharged. A. L.' He handed the paper back to me, and told me to take it to the War Office and give it to Mr. Stanton. He saw at once something in my countenance which led him to think that I had already encountered some rough weather in that quarter, and had little relish for more. He took back the paper, and smiling, remarked that he was going over there pretty soon, and would take it himself."

What followed was related the next day, by the President, to two Michigan Representatives, in response to their appeal for the pardon of a deserter who had been sentenced to death. He told them how, on the preceding day, he had granted a petition for the discharge of a convict, and how, when he had taken the order to the War Department, Mr. Stanton had refused to execute it.

"He told me," concluded the President, "that it was a sham, and that Dawes had got me to pardon the biggest rascal in the army, and that I had made gambling with the public funds perfectly safe. I could n't get him to let the man off. The truth is, I have been doing so much of this thing lately that I have lost all influence with this administration, and have got to stop."

On learning from his fellow Congressmen what had happened, the member from Massachusetts hastened to the White House, and asked the President whether the pardon had been issued.

"He replied that it had not," writes Mr. Dawes, continuing his narrative, "and then recounted, in his quaint way, the scene in the War Office, much as it had been already repeated to me. I said to him that I could not afford to have this matter rest on any uncertainty. 'Retain this pardon, send a messenger to Albany, and make certain the truth or falsity of this statement — at my expense, if we have been imposed upon.' His reply was, 'I think, if you believe it, I will. At any rate, I will take the risk on the side of mercy.' So the pardon went out."

When Mr. Dawes, after the adjournment of Congress, returned to his home, one of the first to greet him on the street was his "dying" quartermaster. The man's appearance of robust health left small room for doubt that Mr. Stanton's intuitions had been correct.[43]

The President's ever ready sympathy went out, in the same impulsive way, to a handsome young lady who called on him, in dire distress. She had been married to a lieutenant in a Pennsylvania regiment, who had been compelled to rejoin his command the day after the wedding. He had then secured a leave of absence for a brief honeymoon journey with his bride; and on the tour had failed to see a War Department order requiring all absent officers to rejoin their regiments by a certain day, under penalty of being treated as deserters. Upon returning home, after the specified date, he had found a notice of dismissal from the service. His young wife, leaving her husband prostrated by the disgrace, had hastened to Washington, where she told her simple story to the President.

"Mr. Lincoln," she pleaded, in conclusion, "won't you help us? I promise you, if you will restore him, he will be faithful to his duty."

The President, who had listened with a somewhat amused smile on his furrowed face, said:—

"And you say, my child, that Fred was compelled to leave you the day after the wedding? Poor fellow, I don't wonder at his anxiety to get back, and if he stayed a little longer than he ought to have done, we 'll have to overlook his fault this time. Take this card to the Secretary of War and he will restore your husband."

Later, as the young lady left the office of the War Department, where she had been curtly dismissed with a rebuke by the Secretary for troubling the President, she met Mr. Lincoln, on his way in.

"Well, my dear," he asked, "have you seen the Secretary?"

"Yes, Mr. Lincoln," she replied, "and he seemed very angry with me for going to you. Won't you speak to him for me?"

"Give yourself no trouble," was the answer. "I will see that the order is issued."

Within a few days the lieutenant was reinstated; and not long thereafter, on the field of Gettysburg, he redeemed with his life the young wife's pledge.[44]

Another officer, Captain Edward W. Andrews, who had been dismissed from the service unjustly, as he thought, by Secretary Stanton, appealed to Mr. Lincoln for redress. The incident illustrates at once the Secretary's zeal and the President's manner of checking it, when carried beyond the limits of propriety. The offence which had aroused Mr. Stanton's ire had been committed during the presidential canvass of 1864, while Captain Andrews, as Assistant Adjutant-General and Chief-of-Staff to General William W. Morris, was stationed in the defences of Baltimore. The Captain, a Democrat who favored the election of General McClellan, had, when attending a political meeting of his party, one evening, been called upon persistently for a speech.

"Forced to say something," as he afterward explained, "I contented myself with a brief expression of my high regard for McClellan as a soldier, and a statement of my intention to vote for him. I made no reference to Mr. Lincoln, and soon left the hall."

On the following day, when the occurrence was reported to the Secretary of War, he indignantly commented on the Captain's conduct, and, without formally assigning a reason, ordered him to be mustered out of the service. Captain Andrews, who had been unwavering in his loyalty to the Union, determined not to suffer this disgrace without a protest. Going to Washington, he sent a personal friend, a Republican member of Congress, to ask the President whether the commission had been revoked by his order.

"I know nothing about it," was Mr. Lincoln's reply. "Of course Stanton does a thousand things in his official character which I can know nothing about, and which it is not necessary that I should know anything about."

When the case had been stated, he added: —

"Well, that's no reason. Andrews has as good a right to hold on to his Democracy, if he chooses, as Stanton had to throw his overboard. If I should muster out all my generals who avow themselves Democrats, there would be a sad thinning out of commanding officers in the army. No, when the military duties of a soldier are fully and faithfully performed, he can manage his politics in his own way. We've no more to do with them than with his religion. Tell this officer he can return to his post, and if there is no other or better reason for the order of Stanton than the one he suspects, it shall do him no harm. The commission he holds will remain as good as new. Supporting General McClellan for the presidency is no violation of army regulations, and as a question of taste — of choosing between him and me — well, I'm the longest, but he's better looking."

Captain Andrews did return to his post. He was not again molested by the Secretary of War.[45]

A private, equally guiltless of intentional wrong-doing, applied to the Secretary of War for relief from unmerited disgrace. He had been sent home from his regiment on sick furlough. At its expiration, his disability continuing, he had not rejoined his company for several weeks; but had regularly forwarded to his officers surgeon's certificates of his condition. These had probably miscarried, for upon his return to the army, as soon as he could travel, he had been surprised to learn that his name was on the rolls as a deserter. His fault having been a purely technical one, he had been permitted to go on duty; but the stigma remained on the records. The task of having it removed was entrusted to the young soldier's friend and neighbor, James F. Wilson, a Congressman at the time, from Iowa. He called on the Secretary of War, briefly explained the case, and presented the accompanying papers. Declining abruptly to receive them, Mr. Stanton said: —

"Ah, this is the case of a deserter, is it? I want nothing to do with it. We are having too many of them now. We had better make a few examples by shooting a deserter now and then. That might put a stop to the business."

To this outburst, Mr. Wilson answered: —

"Mr. Secretary, this is not the case of a deserter, except in the narrowest and most technical sense."

"That is what they all say," was the reply. "Every man of them, when caught, or in hiding and asking for relief, has some plausible excuse. I have no time to spare for the consideration of the cases of men who run away from their duty."

Having failed to impress upon the Secretary's mind the peculiar merits of the case, the Congressman declared that he should lay it before the President, who would no doubt restore the soldier to his place on the rolls. To which Mr. Stanton rejoined: —

"Go to the President, if you please. I will not consider the case, nor will I execute such an order."

Mr. Wilson, narrating the incident many years later, writes: —

"Proceeding at once to the Executive Mansion, I placed the papers in the hands of the President. He read them, and said, 'If the statements herein made are true, this soldier ought to be relieved; for he is in no proper sense a deserter. He seems to have done all that he could do to comply with the regulations governing such cases, and to discharge his duty. Are you sure that the facts are correctly stated?' To this question my answer was, 'I have personal knowledge that all of the material facts are true as stated in the papers you have read'; and I explained the sources of my knowledge. The President handed me the papers, requesting me to endorse on them the statement I had made, which I did, and, after signing my name to it, I handed the papers back to him. He was proceeding to endorse the proper order on them, when I requested him to stay his hand for a moment that he might be placed in possession of some further facts connected with the case. He complied with the request, and I gave him a circumstantial statement of my interview with the Secretary of War. It seemed to interest him. At its conclusion he made no remark, but endorsed and signed the order as requested. He then returned the paper to me, quaintly remarking, 'Your persistence in this case is right. There is the order, and I guess it will be obeyed.' I thanked the President, and was about to depart, when it occurred to me that another question and answer might be of some service. I asked him what I should do in case the Secretary of War should decline to execute the order. He promptly replied, 'Report the fact to me, but I guess he will obey that order. I know it is a small thing, as some would look at it, as it only relates to a private soldier, and we have hundreds of thousands of them. But the way to have good soldiers is to treat them rightly. At all events, that is my order in this case. Let me know what comes of it.'

"The result of this interview," continues Mr. Wilson, "was promptly reported to the Secretary of War. The papers were placed before him and his attention directed to the endorsement of the President. He read it and evidently was vexed, for with a noticeable degree of feeling he repeated the declaration that he would not execute the order. A circumstantial statement was then made to him of the interview with the President, nothing being omitted. This did not seem to affect the Secretary nor move him to compliance. After waiting a moment and seeing no indication of action on his part, I picked up the papers, remarking as I did so, 'Mr. Secretary, as you decline to obey the President's order to you, I will obey the one he gave to me, and report the result of this interview to him at once.' Leaving the Secretary's room, I proceeded down the stairway leading to the first floor of the department, intending to go directly to the Executive Mansion with my report of the foregoing interview, and ascertain the further purpose of the President. Before I reached the outer door of the department a messenger overtook me and said the Secretary desired to see me. Returning to his room, I found him apparently in better mood, and his manner greatly changed. He pleasantly requested me to give him the papers in the case, and I passed them to him. Without further remark he endorsed on them directions to the Adjutant-General to execute the President's order. This done, he turned to me and said, 'It seems to me that the President would rather have a fuss with anybody than miss a chance to do a kindness to a private soldier. But I suppose this case is all right. At all events, I like your dogged persistence in it, and we will be good friends.' And so we ever after were."

Mr. Lincoln's firmness in the matter was still further evinced, some days later, when, on learning from Mr. Wilson how it had terminated, he remarked: —

"Well, I'm glad you stuck to it, and that it ended as it did; for I meant it should so end, if I had to give it personal attention. A private soldier has as much right to justice as a Major-General." [46]

If the stern Stanton was disinclined to obey the President's orders when they related to men who had been unjustly treated, how much stronger must have been his repugnance toward the clemency that was extended to wrongdoers undergoing deserved punishment. An instance of this is outlined in two notes addressed to him by Mr. Lincoln. In the first the President wrote: —

"Mrs. Baird tells me that she is a widow; that her two sons and only support joined the army, where one of them still is; that her other son, Isaac P. Baird, is a private in the Seventy-second Pennsylvania Volunteers — Baxter's Fire Zouaves, Company K; that he is now under guard with his regiment on a charge of desertion; that he was under arrest for desertion, so that he could not take the benefit of returning under the proclamation on that subject. Please have it ascertained if this is correct, and if it is, let him be discharged from arrest and go on duty. I think, too, he should have his pay for duty actually performed. Loss of pay falls so hard upon poor families." [47]

That Mr. Lincoln's wishes were not, at the time, complied with may be inferred from the second note, sent many months later. Having restated Baird's case, the President wrote: —

"At the tearful appeal of the poor mother, I made a direction that he be allowed to enlist for a new term, on the same conditions as others. She now comes, and says she cannot get it acted upon. Please do it." [48]

This polite yet firm command finally won obedience. Baird was transferred to another regiment, and was permitted to reënlist.

When other means of staying the President's merciful hand failed, the Secretary of War had recourse to threats. So Mr. Lincoln informed his friend Joshua F. Speed, on the occasion of a visit to the White House, a few weeks before the assassination. Mr. Speed was present when two women appealed for the release, — the one, of her husband, the other, of her son, both of whom had been imprisoned for resisting the draft in western Pennsylvania.

"Where is your petition?" asked the President.

"Mr. Lincoln," replied the old lady, "I've got no petition. I went to a lawyer to get one drawn, and I had not the money to pay him and come here too; so I thought I would just come and ask you to let me have my boy."

"And it's your husband you want?" said he, turning to the young woman.

"Yes," she answered.

The papers in the case were, in response to the President's summons, brought to him by Charles A. Dana, the Assistant Secretary of War.

"General," said Mr. Lincoln, after counting the names of the prisoners, "there are twenty-seven of these men. Is there any difference in degree of their guilt?"

"No," was the answer; "it is a bad case and a merciful finding."

"Well," said the President, looking out of the window and seemingly talking to himself, "these poor fellows have, I think, suffered enough. They have been in prison fifteen months. I have been thinking so for some time, and have so said to Stanton, and he always threatened to resign if they are released. But he has said so about other matters, and never did. So now, while I have the paper in my hand, I will turn out the flock."

Then he wrote, "Let the prisoners named in the within paper be discharged"; and signed his name. Turning to the women, he said: —

"Now, ladies, you can go. Your son, madam, and your husband, madam, is free."[49]

The Secretary's threat to resign, it may be added, proved to be, like its predecessors — a sound and nothing more.

Thus Mr. Lincoln found it — using his own phrase — "necessary to put the foot down firmly," when Stanton would have forced shut the gates of mercy. But stronger pressure still had to be exerted, at times, to keep an open door in the War Department for the President's appointments. An instance of this has been recalled by former Vice-President William A. Wheeler. He relates that while in Congress, during the early days of the war, he applied to Mr. Lincoln, before leaving Washington at the close of a session, for the appointment of his friend, John A. Sabin, as additional paymaster. The President, assenting, directed his private secretary to take note of the matter. A few weeks later, Mr. Lincoln wrote to Mr. Wheeler that the appointment had been sent to the Secretary of War, who would notify Mr. Sabin to report for muster into the service. As no such notification was received, and as a letter of inquiry to the Secretary remained unanswered, the Congressman, upon his return to the Capital, waited upon Mr. Stanton and called his attention to the appointment.

"He had no recollection of the matter," says Mr.

Wheeler, "but told me, in his brusque manner, that Mr. Sabin's name would be sent in, with hundreds of others, to the Senate for its consideration. Earnestly I argued that Mr. Sabin had been appointed by the Commander-in-Chief of the army, and that it was unjust to ask him to wait, perhaps the whole winter, the tardy action of the Senate upon his nomination, and that he was entitled to be mustered in at once. But all in vain. I got but this reply from the iron Secretary, 'You have my answer; no argument.'[50] I went to the chief clerk of the department and asked him for Mr. Lincoln's letter directing the appointment. Receiving it, I proceeded to the White House, although it was after Executive hours. I can see Mr. Lincoln now as when I entered the room. He wore a long calico dressing-gown, reaching to his heels. His feet were encased in a pair of old-fashioned, leathern slippers — such as we used to find in the old-time country hotels, and which had evidently seen much service in Springfield. Above these appeared the home-made, blue woolen stockings which he wore at all seasons of the year. He was sitting in a splint rocking-chair, with his legs elevated and stretched across his office table. He greeted me warmly. Apologizing for my intrusion at that unofficial hour, I told him I had called simply to ascertain which was the paramount power in the government, he or the Secretary of War. Letting down his legs and straightening himself up in his chair, he answered, 'Well, it is generally supposed (emphasizing the last word) I am. What's the matter?'

"I then briefly recalled the facts attending Sabin's appointment," continues Mr. Wheeler, "when, without a word of comment, he said, 'Give me my letter.' Then taking his pen, he endorsed upon it, 'Let the within named J. A. Sabin be mustered in AT ONCE. It is due to him and to Mr. W. under the circumstances. — A. Lincoln.' He underscored with double lines the words 'at once.' Armed with this Executive mandate, I called on Mr. Stanton the next morning, who, on its presentation, was simply furious. He charged me with interfering with his prerogatives, and with undue persistence — perhaps as to the last, not without some force, for I had wearied with the delay and was a little provoked by what I regarded as the 'insolence of office.' I told him I would call the next morning for the order to muster in. I called accordingly, and handing it to me in a rage, he said, 'I hope I shall never hear of this matter again.'"[51]

The member from New York was always, thereafter, cordially received at the War Department; and none of his requests were again refused by the grim minister who presided there.

One more episode in this class must suffice. We are indebted for it to Josiah B. Grinnell, a member of Congress from Iowa during the latter years of the war. He called on Mr. Stanton to urge the advancement of Colonel Elliott W. Rice to the rank of brigadier-general. That sterling officer had not only shown himself worthy of the promotion, at the head of his regiment, the Seventh Iowa Infantry, but he had demonstrated his fitness for it as well, in the actual command of a brigade. The Secretary of War, however, according to his wont, regarded this application as an unwarrantable interference with his department.

"No use, sir," was his reply to Mr. Grinnell's importunities; "your case, sir, is like thousands. What we want now is victories, not brigadiers. We are in a crisis. I refuse, sir, to make a promise even to consider the wish of a civilian at such a time. I am sorry. My desk is loaded with business. I must say good-morning."

A second interview ended as abruptly as the first.

"No use," repeated Mr. Stanton, "in a civilian's talking to me on the subject, sir."

"Neither," replied Mr. Grinnell, "can I waive a civilian's rights."

"Then go to the President," said the Secretary sharply.

"That would be an offence," rejoined the Congressman.

"My regard for the Secretary of War would make that step a last resort."

"Get your request granted and I will resign," was Stanton's angry retort.

After another unsuccessful effort Mr. Grinnell did go to the President.

"What does Stanton say?" asked Mr. Lincoln.

"Nothing," was the answer, "will not even look up the papers."

"Yes, I know," responded the President, "the cases like yours are hundreds, and it disturbs him — even my hint that we may move up the boys and encourage enlistments. It is a very delicate question. Don't be impatient, but get on the right side of a very good officer."

When our undaunted Congressman next presented himself at the Executive Mansion, Mr. Lincoln said: —

"Stanton was fairly mad on the suggestion of promotion by civilians or members of Congress."

To which Mr. Grinnell replied: —

"I base my claim on the recommendations of superior officers in the field."

"You get the facts," suggested Mr. Lincoln, "and quietly say the President hopes your request will be granted."

There followed still another interview, as Mr. Lincoln was returning from a walk in which he had vainly tried to shift the weary burden of the cares that beset him.

"I cannot attempt to make Stanton over at this stage," he declared. "You will win, if patient."

But as they reached the White House door, the President asked: —

"Have you a slip of paper?"

Resting the scrap that had been handed to him against one of the columns, he addressed this note to Mr. Stanton:

"Sir, — Without an if or an and, let Colonel Elliott W. Rice be made a Brigadier-General in the United States army. — A. Lincoln."

Giving this to Mr. Grinnell, the President added: —

"Report, if necessary, from the War Office."

When the order was presented at the department, the Secretary muttered, as he tossed it into his waste basket:

"I will resign."

But as the Congressman turned to go, he said, with a smile: —

"Wait, Mr. Grinnell; come over and take dinner with me."[52]

Colonel Rice was duly commissioned a brigadier. Not long afterward, the member from the Fourth Iowa District secured a military appointment for one friend, and a promotion in the army for another, on demand. It is a noteworthy fact, moreover, that Mr. Grinnell, like Mr. Wilson and Mr. Wheeler, won by his spirit the arrogant Stanton's good-will, or a semblance thereof. For the Secretary of War may be said to have reversed, on occasion, the maxim of that other great minister, Cardinal Richelieu, and to have conciliated when he could not crush.

Military appointments of far greater importance than those of brigadiers and paymasters were made by the President in the teeth of Mr. Stanton's opposition. All the power at the war-lord's command was exerted in vain, at certain junctures, to prevent the advancement, severally, of Rosecrans, Hooker, and McClellan. The first of these became commander of the Army of the Ohio, under peculiar circumstances. When it was decided to remove General Buell from that place, the choice of the administration fell upon one of the Secretary's favorites, General George H. Thomas of Virginia. As soon as an order directing this change reached headquarters, at Louisville, the army was turned over to Thomas, who was, at the time, in command of the First Division.[53] That officer, however, as promptly, despatched a request to Washington for Buell's immediate restoration.

"General Buell's preparations," it read, "have been completed to move against the enemy, and I therefore respectfully ask that he may be retained in command. My position is very embarrassing, not being as well informed as I should be as the commander of this army and on the assumption of such a responsibility."[54]

Upon receipt of this appeal Buell was reinstated. But within a few weeks — after he had fought the indecisive battle of Perryville — dissatisfaction with his course revived, and led to his final removal. The selection of his successor gave Mr. Lincoln some trouble; for the Secretary of the Treasury, as well as the Secretary of War, had a candidate. Mr. Chase urged the appointment of General William Starke Rosecrans, whose successes in western Virginia and northern Mississippi had brought him into prominence. A blunt, impulsive soldier, indifferent to the opinions — on military matters — of civilians, however lofty, "Old Rosy," as the soldiers fondly called him, had failed to win Mr. Stanton's favor. So the Secretary of War hotly opposed his advancement and, with equal vehemence, advocated the appointment of Thomas, who had so magnanimously declined the command, several weeks before. The President, having listened patiently to both his Secretaries, said: —

"Let the Virginian wait. We will try Rosecrans."[55]

The details of the discussion have not been preserved, but Mr. Stanton's behavior, after he left the Executive Mansion, indicated how entirely his wishes had been ignored. Flushed with anger, he returned to his office, and said abruptly to an officer who had previously excited his wrath by suggesting the appointment of Rosecrans: —

"Well, you have your choice of idiots. Now look out for frightful disasters."[56]

Mr. Stanton then issued the orders which placed General Rosecrans, as General Buell's successor, in command of the newly constituted Department of the Cumberland.

Three months later, the President and the Secretary of War were again at variance over the selection of a commander — this time, for the Army of the Potomac. The noble but ill-fated troops composing that body had, after the disaster of Fredericksburg and the hardships of the so-called "mud march," regained the winter camp near Falmouth. Here their commander, Major-General Ambrose E. Burnside, humiliated by his failures and smarting under the criticisms of some of his lieutenants, had, on January 23, 1863, written the famous General Orders No. 8, disciplining nine officers, by the removal of five from the Army of the Potomac and the dismissal of four from the service.[57] The document had been presented to the President for his approval, with the consistent alternative of accepting General Burnside's resignation. That loyal officer, frankly acknowledging the lack of confidence in himself which he, however, resented in his subordinates, had twice before asked to be relieved from the command and to be retired to private life. His successor had therefore already been tentatively selected by Mr. Lincoln, and, strange to say, he was the man whom Burnside's orders had most severely marked for disgrace — Major-General Joseph Hooker.[58] In the important engagements of the Army of the Potomac, Hooker had gained unusual distinction. He had led divisions and corps with equal gallantry. There was no handsomer or braver officer in the service than "Fighting Joe," as the soldiers and war correspondents called him.[59] His commanding appearance and engaging manner, no less than his dash and skill, had rendered his presence on the field of battle an inspiration to the troops. These high qualities were in a measure offset, however, by the liquor habit, selfish ambition, a spirit of insubordination, an exaggerated idea of his own merits, and a proneness to belittle or to criticise adversely the acts of other officers. His unrestrained censure of his superiors, civil as well as military, after the battle of Fredericksburg, had moved General Burnside to say of him, in the orders submitted to the President: —

"General Joseph Hooker, Major-General of Volunteers and Brigadier-General U. S. Army, having been guilty of unjust and unnecessary criticisms of the actions of his superior officers, and of the authorities, and having, by the general tone of his conversation, endeavored to create distrust in the minds of officers who have associated with him, and having, by omissions and otherwise, made reports and statements which were calculated to create incorrect impressions, and for habitually speaking in disparaging terms of other officers, is hereby dismissed the service of the United States as a man unfit to hold an important commission during a crisis like the present, when so much patience, charity, confidence, consideration, and patriotism are due from every soldier in the field." [60]

In conjunction with this arraignment of Hooker, it should be said that Mr. Stanton had, for some time, opposed his elevation to an independent command. Notwithstanding the General's ability, courage, and personal popularity, his faults unfitted him, in the Secretary's opinion, for the control of the most important army in the service. When choice of a commander, in the event of Burnside's resignation, was nevertheless found to lie between Hooker and General George G. Meade, the head of the War Department took the position that the former was not to be appointed in any contingency. On the other hand, the President, recognizing the importance of making a selection that would be equally acceptable to the army and to the country at large, inclined toward "Fighting Joe." "Hooker does talk badly," he admitted, when his attention was called to that officer's indiscreet language concerning General Burnside and himself; "but the trouble is, he is stronger with the country to-day than any other man." [61] This strength was augmented by the friendship of Secretary Chase, who — again in opposition to Secretary Stanton — had, for some time, urged General Hooker's advancement.[62] In return for this support the General was expected to throw the weight of whatever military glory he might gain, in favor of Mr. Chase's presidential aspirations. As the intrigue came to the knowledge of Mr.

Stanton, his personal loyalty to Mr. Lincoln, no less than his distrust of General Hooker, rendered unavailing the repeated efforts that were made to remove his opposition. Whether or not he called the President's attention to the electioneering aspect of the matter is not known; but, in his eagerness to prevent the appointment, he is not likely to have omitted it. If the appeal to Mr. Lincoln's political interests was made, it failed, as had all other arguments, to move him from the conclusion that circumstances required the selection of Hooker.[63] The President, having declined to disorganize the already demoralized Army of the Potomac by approving of the drastic measures demanded by its commander, directed the Secretary of War to issue orders relieving General Burnside and assigning General Hooker to his place. When this decision was announced, Mr. Stanton's first impulse was to resign. Then cooler counsels prevailed. He not only remained faithfully at his post, but he also supported the new commander to the utmost of his power, until the defeat at Chancellorsville added the name of Hooker to the dreary list of generals who led the Army of the Potomac to disaster.

The operations of "this poor old strategy-possessed army" had been hampered, from time to time, by the necessity for defending Washington. The loss of the northern Capital, particularly in the earlier years of the war, would, from a diplomatic no less than from a military point of view, have been a serious blow to the Union cause. This fact was appreciated more keenly, perhaps, by the Secretary of War than by any other member of the administration. His anxiety on the subject previous to and during General McClellan's Peninsular campaign led to conflicts of opinion between Mr. Stanton and the President. As the affair involved their only recorded disagreements in important strategical matters, it has an interest beyond that created by the endless discussions over who was and who was not to blame for the failure of that expedition. During the winter of 1861–62, Mr. Lincoln, with a view to the protection of Washington while attacking Richmond, had advocated an early opening of the spring campaign by a direct march overland upon the Confederate Capital. This plan, though warmly approved of by Secretary Stanton and certain prominent military men, was as earnestly opposed by General McClellan, who urged an advance by way of the lower Chesapeake Bay with a base at Urbana. After much discussion, the plans were, with the consent of the President, submitted by General McClellan on March 8, 1862, to a council of division commanders. As eight of these out of twelve voted in favor of the Urbana route, Mr. Lincoln acquiesced.[64] Not so, Mr. Stanton, whose confidence in the general commanding the army was rapidly waning. McClellan's assurances that the movement would "not at all expose the City of Washington to danger," and that he regarded "success as certain by all the chances of war,"[65] did not satisfy the head of the War Department. He still objected to the project under which more than one hundred thousand troops were to be set afloat in wooden bottoms, to seek a battle-field many miles away, while the enemy lay fortified before the Capital.

"We can do nothing else," said the President, "than adopt this plan, and discard all others; with eight out of twelve division commanders approving it, we can't reject it and adopt another, without assuming all the responsibility in case of the failure of the one we adopt."

The Secretary took issue with Mr. Lincoln as to his method of computation.

"Who are the eight generals," he asked, "upon whose votes you are going to adopt the proposed plan of campaign? All made so since General McClellan assumed command, and upon his recommendation, influenced by his views, and subservient to his wishes, while the other four are beyond these influences, so that in fact you have in this decision only the operation of one man's mind."[66]

This clever, though not entirely correct analysis of the

vote reversed the odds of eight against four in support of McClellan so that they became four to one in favor of Mr. Lincoln's plan. Admitting the apparent force of the argument, he remained, however, steadfast in his decision to abide by the action of the council; and instructed Mr. Stanton to proceed with the preparations for the campaign. How chagrined the Secretary felt over his lack of influence was revealed at a conference held, about this time, with the Committee on the Conduct of the War. "He was thoroughly discouraged," says one of the members. "He told us the President had gone back to his first love as to General McClellan, and that it was needless for him or for us to labor with him, although he had finally been prevailed on to restrict McClellan's command to the Army of the Potomac."[67] One other crumb of comfort the disappointed Stanton had carried away from his discussion with the Executive. Their interview closed with the President's assurance that sufficient troops should be retained for the protection of the Capital. To this end, on the day the division commanders met, Mr. Lincoln ordered: —

"No change of the base of operations of the Army of the Potomac shall be made without leaving in and about Washington such a force as in the opinion of the General-in-Chief and the commanders of all the army corps shall leave said city entirely secure."[68]

When the evacuation of Manassas and Centreville, on the following day, rendered a change of plan necessary, General McClellan submitted the question with the President's order to four newly created corps commanders, Generals McDowell, Sumner, Heintzelman, and Keyes. They unanimously approved of his alternative route by way of the peninsula between the York and the James rivers, with a base at Fortress Monroe, providing, among other things, that the troops left in the forts on the Potomac and in front of the Virginia line to cover Washington should be "such as to give an entire feeling of security for its safety from menace." This required from 40,000 to 55,000 men, according to the several stipulations made by the corps commanders.[69] Their conclusions were, with General McClellan's concurrence, reported to the Secretary of War, who, responding with the President's assent, took occasion again to repeat the command, "Leave Washington entirely secure." [70]

Immediately after General McClellan had, with part of his troops, embarked for the Peninsula, alarm spread through the city at the rumor that it had been left inadequately guarded. Such neglect of orders, particularly in view of the stress laid upon them, was almost incredible. Nevertheless, Secretary Stanton at once called upon General James S. Wadsworth, Military Governor of the District of Columbia, to make a report of the forces left under his command for its defence. In reply, General Wadsworth stated that he had 19,000 available men, most of them "new and imperfectly disciplined." About 4500 of these were, under General McClellan's orders, to be sent to Manassas, Warrenton, and Budd's Ferry; while about 1500 were to join certain divisions, on their way to the Peninsula.[71] This report, together with a formal opinion secured from Adjutant-General Thomas and Major-General Hitchcock, military adviser of the War Department, to the effect that the force was "entirely inadequate," and that the President's requirements had "not been fully complied with," was laid by the Secretary before Mr. Lincoln.[72] Then followed an anxious conference at the War Office between the President and the chiefs of bureaus. They agreed with Mr. Stanton in the conviction that the Capital was not safe. At the conclusion of the meeting, the Secretary, under instructions from the President, retained McDowell's corps, which belonged to McClellan's army, but had not yet left for the Peninsula. This command, of about 36,000 men, consisting of Franklin's, McCall's, and King's divisions, was to have served as a flanking column. The withdrawal of the corps from the campaign, at the eleventh hour, was a shock to General McClellan, who regarded the part assigned to it as vital to the success of his operations. When the news of this change in his circumstances reached him before Yorktown, he at once — to borrow a phrase from a letter to his wife — "raised an awful row." [73]

In the despatches to the President and to the Secretary of War that followed one another in close succession, the General commanding protested against the action of the administration, and urgently requested that at least Franklin's division be restored to his command. Then arose the quarrel between McClellan and his superiors that has survived the principal disputants. The last word, in fact, has not yet been said; but the evidence is more than sufficient to prove that the commander brought this disappointment upon himself by his neglect of the President's orders. So Mr. Lincoln, after his kindly fashion, stated to General McClellan, whose complaints, however, that he had not been properly sustained in other respects, were entitled to consideration. Persisting in his appeals, he finally telegraphed to Secretary Stanton: —

"The reconnoissance to-day proves that it is necessary to invest and attack Gloucester Point. Give me Franklin and McCall's divisions, under command of Franklin, and I will at once undertake it. If circumstances of which I am not aware make it impossible for you to send me two divisions to carry out this final plan of campaign, I will run the risk and hold myself responsible for the results if you will give me Franklin's division. If you still confide in my judgment, I entreat that you will grant this request. The fate of our cause depends upon it." [74]

This extraordinary message brought the President to the War Office for another consultation. The reports on file there showed that the army sent to the Peninsula already consisted of more than 100,000 men.[75] How greatly it, in fact, outnumbered the force opposed to it was, of course, not known until some time afterward.[76]

But General McClellan's tendency to underrate his own strength and to exaggerate that of the enemy may have been taken into the account by the Secretary of War, who was once moved to say of him: —

"If he had a million men, he would swear the enemy had two million, and then he would sit down in the mud and yell for three." [77]

At the conference, Mr. Stanton insisted that General McClellan did not need the troops that had been detached from the expedition, and that they could not even be employed if they were restored. He objected, moreover, to the withdrawal of Franklin's division from McDowell's corps, on the ground that the entire force, by advancing over the shortest land route toward Richmond, so as to keep between Washington and the enemy, could aid General McClellan while protecting the Union Capital. This argument, although it was sustained by Adjutant-General Thomas, Quartermaster-General Meigs, Major-General Hitchcock, and Brigadier-General Ripley, Chief of Ordnance, failed to influence the President. Anxious to gratify McClellan and to give him all the support available, he overruled the head of the War Department, for the second time in the history of the Peninsular campaign, and directed Franklin's division to be shipped at once to the Lower Chesapeake.

"I yielded my opinion to the President's order," wrote Mr. Stanton to a friend; but how vigorously the order was carried out, he omitted to mention. Before our Secretary slept that night he telegraphed to General McClellan: —

"Franklin's division is marching to Alexandria to embark. McCall's will be sent if the safety of this city will permit. Inform me where you want Franklin to land. He will embark to-morrow and as quickly as possible." [78]

Without pursuing the narrative of the hapless operations that immediately followed, it may be added that when the troops, so persistently pleaded for as a flanking column, arrived below Yorktown, they floated idly in their transports, nearly a fortnight. At the end of that period, just as their disembarkation seemed "about completed," the besieged enemy was found, as at Manassas, to have vanished from the scene.

Two months of fruitless campaigning on the Peninsula ensued. They did not improve Stanton's opinion of McClellan. The General, moreover, at almost every step demanded reënforcements which the Secretary, for the most part, could not supply. Each fresh disappointment intensified McClellan's bitterness toward the administration, and toward his one-time friend, the head of the War Department, in particular. This feeling manifested itself in violent attacks upon Mr. Stanton. He became a target for the abuse of the General's military and political sympathizers, as well as for that officer's own insubordinate faultfindings. How far McClellan carried his insolence may be gathered from the message that he despatched to the Secretary of War, after the desperate battle of Gaines's Mill. It closed with: —

"I know that a few thousand more men would have changed this battle from a defeat to a victory. As it is, the government must not and cannot hold me responsible for the result. I feel too earnestly to-night. I have seen too many dead and wounded comrades to feel otherwise than that the government has not sustained this army. If you do not do so now, the game is lost. If I save this army now, I tell you plainly that I owe no thanks to you or to any other persons in Washington. You have done your best to sacrifice this army." [79]

When the message reached the military telegraph bureau of the War Department, Major Thomas T. Eckert, the officer on duty, was amazed at this sharp attack upon Mr. Stanton and, over his shoulder, upon the President himself. He forthwith laid the despatch before Colonel E. S. Sanford, Military Supervisor of Telegraphs, who, exceeding his authority, indignantly struck out the two closing sentences. Thus mutilated, a copy of the telegram was handed to the Secretary of War, and he carried it to the President. Neither of them knew how sharp had originally been the sting which Colonel Sanford's blue pencil left but partly extracted. Enough of the accusation against the government remained, however, to have, under any other administration, cost McClellan his command. Yet Lincoln's unparalleled forbearance was equal to the test. In his anxiety for the Army of the Potomac, he lost sight of the affront offered by its commander. Not so with Stanton; though moved by the danger to send the offending General assurances of his friendship and support, he was incapable of overlooking such an insult. He had, indeed, reached a state of mind that could be satisfied with nothing short of McClellan's removal. To this end, the Secretary of War joined hands in a powerful coalition with the Secretary of the Treasury, who had long before lost confidence in "Little Mac." Together they urged the President to recall that officer, and to give Major-General John Pope, commanding the recently constituted Army of Virginia, his post. Mr. Lincoln was not prepared, however, for so drastic a step. Instead of removing McClellan, he placed him, together with the other commanders in the field, under the orders of a newly commissioned General-in-Chief, Henry W. Halleck. This appointment, let us say in passing, was almost as distasteful to our truculent war minister as the President's refusal to dismiss McClellan. Stanton and Halleck cherished a mutual dislike, which dated from their professional encounters before the war, on opposing sides in certain of the California Land Cases. The Secretary is said to have "used some pretty strong language" concerning Mr. Lincoln's selection, when it was announced;[80] but he speedily established friendly relations with the new commander. They were soon in entire accord about McClellan, and when Halleck cast his influence into the already heavily weighted scale of that officer's declining fortunes, the President yielded.

Early in August, the Army of the Potomac was recalled from the Peninsula to be merged, corps by corps, in Pope's forces before Washington. General McClellan's chagrin over this inglorious close to his campaign was exceeded only by the keen humiliation that followed. Stripped of all but a nominal authority, we find him at Alexandria forwarding his beloved troops to another commander, and begging, in vain, for the privilege of joining them on the battle-field. Then came General Pope's defeat at Second Bull Run. To what extent, if any, that disaster may fairly be charged to the tardiness of McClellan's coöperation remains a moot point. It is sufficient for the purposes of this study to record that the administration, civil as well as military, was, at the time, almost a unit in deeming him partly responsible. The Secretary of War became especially incensed at his seeming disinclination to support Pope. While the two days' conflict was at its height, Mr. Stanton had prepared a letter to the President recommending General McClellan's immediate removal. This the Secretary had laid before some of his colleagues in the cabinet for their signatures, but its language was obviously too harsh even for their angry mood.[81] The protest was accordingly modified to read:—

"The undersigned, who have been honored with your selection as a part of your confidential advisers, deeply impressed with our great responsibility in the present crisis, do but perform a painful duty in declaring to you our deliberate opinion that, at this time, it is not safe to entrust to Major-General McClellan the command of any army of the United States. And we hold ourselves ready, at any time, to explain to you in detail the reasons upon which this opinion is founded." [82]

It was signed by Messrs. Stanton, Chase, Smith, and Bates. Mr. Blair favored McClellan; Mr. Seward happened to be absent. Mr. Welles had declined to add his name, not because he was out of harmony with his associates in the matter, but because he considered the manner of their proceeding "improper and disrespectful to the President."[83] This objection, as well as the promise made by the Secretary of the Navy to second his colleagues, verbally, at the next cabinet meeting, had caused them to withhold the paper.[84] Whether it ever came to Mr. Lincoln's knowledge, or not, has been left in doubt.[85] There can be no question, however, that he knew how embittered these men had become against McClellan. Indeed, the President himself said privately concerning the General: —

"He has acted badly towards Pope; he really wanted him to fail."[86]

So matters stood when Bull Run became, for the second time, a field of ill omen to the Union arms, and Pope's routed columns reeled back toward Washington.

A crisis confronted the government. Lee's victorious army was said to be pressing close upon the disorganized Federals, as they poured toward the city. The Capital seemed lost. Terror and confusion reigned on all sides. Halleck was unequal to the emergency; Stanton, preparing for the flight of the administration, directed all supplies in the arsenal to be shipped to New York; Chase gave orders for the removal of the money in the Treasury to the same place; and Pope, as he neared Washington, telegraphed, "Unless something can be done to restore tone to this army, it will melt away before you know it."[87] The situation called for masterly action. President Lincoln did not falter. He knew that there was but one man who had the love, as well as the confidence, of those defeated troops — one man who could restore them to discipline speedily enough to preserve the Capital. Turning a deaf ear to the public clamor against McClellan, setting aside most of his military advisers, and deliberately ignoring the nearly unanimous wish of his cabinet, Mr. Lincoln called upon the General to take command of the routed forces, as they reached the defences of Washington. An official order to this effect was issued in Secretary Stanton's name, though that functionary had not even been consulted in the matter.[88] His indignation found expression at a cabinet meeting, on the day of the appointment. "Stanton entered the council-room," reports Secretary Welles, "a few moments in advance of Mr. Lincoln, and said, with great excitement, he had just learned from General Halleck that the President had placed McClellan in command of the forces in Washington. The information was surprising, and, in view of the prevailing excitement against that officer, alarming. The President soon came in, and in answer to an inquiry from Mr. Chase, confirmed what Stanton had stated. General regret was expressed, and Stanton, with some feeling, remarked that no order to that effect had issued from the War Department. The President calmly, but with some emphasis, said the order was his, and he would be responsible for it to the country."

"In stating what he had done," proceeds Mr. Welles, "the President was deliberate, but firm and decisive. His language and manner were kind and affectionate, especially toward two of the members who were greatly disturbed; but every person present felt that he was truly the chief, and every one knew his decision, though mildly expressed, was as fixed and unalterable as if given out with the imperious command and determined will of Andrew Jackson."[89]

A spirited discussion ensued. Mr. Lincoln gave the reasons for his course. The cabinet disapproved. Even Postmaster-General Blair, McClellan's friend, appears to have reached the conclusion that the General could not then be wisely trusted with the chief command. Of course, the most strenuous objections came from the two ministers who had led the opposition. Mr. Chase expressed apprehensions that the reinstatement of McClellan would prove to be a national calamity. He went so far as to declare the appointment "equivalent to giving Washington to the rebels."[90] And Mr. Stanton's bitterness, according to one of his fellow Secretaries, can scarcely be conceived.[91] Their combined onslaught at last moved the President to say, as he did to Seward's senatorial foes, that he would gladly resign his place, but that he could not rescind the order. Then this remarkable meeting closed — closed as it had begun — with Abraham Lincoln master of the situation. The entire cabinet acquiesced in his decision. Even the two aggressive leaders, who had at one point been prepared to make McClellan's dismissal the price of their further service, bowed to the inevitable. The object of their hostility not only retained his command in the defences of the Capital, but what is more, when the reorganized army marched out a few days thereafter, on the Antietam campaign, he was still at its head. Secretary Stanton, let us add, disappointed and dispirited as he is said to have been, gave General McClellan, none the less, his loyal support.

About two years thereafter was enacted another significant cabinet scene, when the high-strung Stanton again tried to force the President's hand. The second occasion, like the first, was brought about, in a way, by a Confederate advance upon the Capital, and by the efforts of the Secretary to secure the removal of an obnoxious officer. This time, no less a person than one of his own colleagues, Montgomery Blair, had been marked for sacrifice. The Postmaster-General's antagonisms in the cabinet, it should be remembered, were not limited to Mr. Stanton. Secretary Chase, during his entire period — recently concluded — at the head of the Treasury Department, had found Mr. Blair, as we have seen, to be a thorn in his side; while the Postmaster-General's personal aggressiveness, as well as his conservative attitude toward slavery and reconstruction, had led to friction with still other associates. They might all, perhaps, have agreed with that newspaper correspondent who called him "the stormy petrel" of the administration. Mr. Blair had managed, moreover, to arouse the uncompromising hostility of Radical Republicans throughout the country. Their leaders had gone so far as to exact from the convention that renominated Mr. Lincoln, early in June, 1864, a resolution which, counseling harmony in the cabinet, asked by unmistakable implication for the dismissal of the man in the Post Office.[92] But the President made no sign of compliance. He was fond of Montgomery Blair, appreciative of his ability, and mindful of the obligations under which the Blair family had placed the Union cause, during the early days of the war. In the midst of this clamor, however, for the Postmaster-General's removal, he himself furnished an additional provocation, which Stanton was not slow to seize. When the Confederates, on their famous raid under Early, withdrew from before Washington, they plundered and burned the residence of Mr. Blair, in the suburbs. His misfortune, involving the destruction of a valuable library, stirred him — it was alleged — to severe criticism of the officers in command about the Capital. This General Halleck resented. He sent an indignant letter to Secretary Stanton: —

"It should be known," wrote the chief of staff, "whether such wholesale denouncement and accusation by a member of the cabinet receives the sanction and approbation of the President of the United States. If so, the names of the officers accused should be stricken from the rolls of the Army; if not, it is due to the honor of the accused that the slanderer should be dismissed from the cabinet."[93]

This communication Mr. Stanton forwarded, with a note, to the President, who addressed his reply to the Secretary of War. Mr. Lincoln's letter, after summarizing General Halleck's charges, read: —

"Whether the remarks were really made I do not know, nor do I suppose such knowledge is necessary to a correct response. If they were made, I do not approve them; and yet, under the circumstances, I would not dismiss a member of the cabinet therefor. I do not consider what may have been hastily said in a moment of vexation at so severe a loss is sufficient ground for so grave a step. Besides this, truth is generally the best vindication against slander. I propose continuing to be myself the judge as to when a member of the cabinet shall be dismissed." [94]

So masterful a treatment of the matter might have sufficed, but the President thought it was time to assert himself in another direction. At the next cabinet meeting he read to his astonished councilors the following curt lecture: —

"I must myself be the judge how long to retain in and when to remove any of you from his position. It would greatly pain me to discover any of you endeavoring to procure another's removal, or in any way to prejudice him before the public. Such endeavor would be a wrong to me, and, much worse, a wrong to the country. My wish is that on this subject no remark be made nor question asked by any of you, here or elsewhere, now or hereafter." [95]

A schoolmaster reprimanding a class of unruly boys could hardly have been more peremptory. Certainly, no President ever taught his cabinet its place in language that rang so true to the tone of absolute authority.[96]

One of these ministers especially needed a sharp word now and then. Secretary Stanton's temperament, as we have seen, rendered him anything but an easy instrument in any man's hand. His very faults partook of the rugged strength which, viewed at this distance, makes him stand out as the Titan of Lincoln's cabinet. That the President controlled so turbulent a force without sacrificing aught of its energy was perhaps his highest achievement in the field of mastership. This was due, primarily, of course, to his insight into Stanton's character. Few men, if any, had fathomed as truly the sterling qualities that lay beneath the failings of the great Secretary. For the real Stanton revealed himself to the President in the daily — at times hourly — meetings imposed upon them by the requirements of the war. Together they bore the anxieties and shared the joys of the struggle. Their coöperation in the absorbing work to which both had dedicated themselves established between the men, dissimilar as they were by nature, a bond of sympathy which even Stanton's headiness could not destroy. Indeed, Mr. Lincoln, treating the Secretary somewhat as a parent would a talented but high-strung child, — now humoring, now commanding, — appears to have risen above even a shadow of personal resentment, and to have overlooked an occasional opposition that, however violent might have been its outbursts, always yielded in the end to his authority. His esteem for Mr. Stanton not only suffered no impairment in these passages at arms, but stranger still, it ripened into affection. The President's protection went out unasked to the Secretary of War, as it did to his other councilors. Mr. Stanton's enemies — and he had a choice assortment of them — lost no opportunity for assailing him. When he was attacked publicly because of certain administrative acts, Mr. Lincoln, stepping between him and his critics, assumed the responsibility. When his detractors sought to undermine him privately with the President, they made no headway. At times, in fact, they found a tiger while beating the jungle for a deer, as happened to one who came with severe denunciations against the Secretary. "Go home, my friend," interrupted Mr. Lincoln, "and read attentively the tenth verse of the thirtieth chapter of Proverbs."[97] If the man turned to the text, he read: —

"Accuse not a servant unto his master, lest he curse thee, and thou be found guilty."

No better fate attended the efforts that were confessedly made to get Mr. Stanton out of the cabinet. So strong became the pressure in this direction that it aroused anxiety among his supporters. One of them, Judge E. R. Hoar, discussing cabinet appointments for the second administration, in November 1864, said to the President: —

"I hope, whatever is done, that Stanton will be retained in his position until the war is over."

To which Lincoln replied: —

"Mr. Stanton has excellent qualities, and he has his defects. Folks come up here and tell me that there are a great many men in the country who have all Stanton's excellent qualities without his defects. All I have to say is, I have n't met 'em! I don't know 'em! I wish I did!"[98]

The answer makes clear why the foes who sought the minister's overthrow, and the friends who urged his elevation to the Supreme Court bench, on the death of Chief Justice Taney, were alike unsuccessful. When this promotion was advocated by Bishop Simpson, the President replied: —

"If you will find me another Secretary of War like him, I will gladly appoint him."[99]

But Mr. Stanton himself contemplated a change. Bending at that very time under the terrible strain of his exertions, he looked forward longingly to a release from his place in the cabinet. When the Surgeon-General, alarmed over his condition, urged him to take a furlough, he said: —

"Barnes, keep me alive till this rebellion is over, and then I will take a rest — a long one, perhaps."[100]

In a similar strain, after several days on a bed of sickness, he wrote to Mr. Chase: —

"I am better now and again at work, but with feeble and broken health, that can only be restored by absolute rest from all labor and care. This I long for, and hope soon to have. Our cause is now, I hope, beyond all danger, and when Grant goes into Richmond my task is ended. To you and others it will remain to secure the fruits of victory."[101]

Upon the announcement, in the following spring, that

Lee was about to surrender, Mr. Stanton accordingly tendered his resignation. A letter which he handed to the President took the ground that this event would virtually end the war, and leave him free — with his work done — to give up his portfolio. Mr. Lincoln is reported to have been greatly moved. Tearing the resignation in pieces, and throwing his arms about the Secretary, he said, according to Mr. Carpenter, who tells the story: —

"Stanton, you have been a good friend and a faithful public servant; and it is not for you to say when you will no longer be needed here." [102]

The Secretary himself has left an account of the scene. He relates how the President, with tears in his eyes, put his hands on the other's shoulders, and said: —

"Stanton, you cannot go. Reconstruction is more difficult and dangerous than construction or destruction. You have been our main reliance; you must help us through the final act. The bag is filled. It must be tied, and tied securely. Some knots slip; yours do not. You understand the situation better than anybody else, and it is my wish and the country's that you remain." [103]

What could be answered to such an appeal? The Secretary of War once again bowed before a will stronger than his own, and cheerfully resumed his duties.

There was something more than mere obedience in this submission. The minister's heart had been touched as well as the President's. Stanton's distrust — even contempt — of Lincoln in 1861, had given way, by 1865, to entirely different sentiments. Like his associates in the cabinet, with possibly one exception, the Secretary of War had at last correctly gauged the President's intellectual and moral force. That this force, when exerted to the full, was well-nigh irresistible, he had, as we know, painfully learned by repeated but unsuccessful strivings to get his own way. No one had ever so worsted Edwin M. Stanton. He was outclassed. With his increasing respect for Mr. Lincoln's power came, naturally enough, something like a fair appreciation of the President's lofty character. Such magnanimity, devotion to duty, and homely sincerity could have but one effect upon a man of Stanton's intense nature. He began with reviling Lincoln, he ended with loving him.

Among the friends who desired the President's reëlection, none labored more loyally to that end than Mr. Stanton. Every available resource of the War Department was employed in Mr. Lincoln's interest. So earnest did the Secretary grow that on one occasion — Mr. Dana tells us — he became greatly vexed at the President's seeming indifference as to the result.[104] Still, Mr. Lincoln, as we know, was triumphantly reëlected. He had entered upon his second term, when Stanton's concern took another form — not new, but more marked than ever before. He became anxious for the President's personal safety. This was especially so while Mr. Lincoln was on his Richmond jaunt. When he telegraphed to the Secretary of War that he was about to visit Petersburg, which had just been evacuated, Mr. Stanton immediately replied: —

"Allow me respectfully to ask you to consider whether you ought to expose the nation to the consequence of any disaster to yourself in the pursuit of a treacherous and dangerous enemy like the rebel army. If it was a question concerning yourself only, I should not presume to say a word. Commanding generals are in the line of their duty in running such risks; but is the political head of a nation in the same condition?"[105]

Nevertheless, the President continued his excursion into Confederate territory; but he despatched thanks to the Secretary, and promised: —

"I will take care of myself."[106]

Eleven days later, that promise went by default. A capricious fate, which suffered him to walk the streets of an enemy's Capital unharmed, reached him in his own Washington; and Abraham Lincoln fell, wounded to death by John Wilkes Booth. A notable group watched around the bed on which he breathed his last. Among all the public men in the sorrowing company, no grief was keener than that of his iron war minister. None of them had tested, as Edwin M. Stanton had, the extraordinary resources of the stricken chief. It was fitting, therefore, that he, as "past the strong heroic soul away," should pronounce its eulogy: —

"There lies the most perfect ruler of men the world has ever seen." [107]

CHAPTER VII

HOW THE PATHFINDER LOST THE TRAIL

AMONG the public men who, at the outbreak of the Civil War, offered their services to the government, none was more warmly welcomed than Colonel John Charles Frémont. In him seemed to be happily combined two elements which the administration then greatly valued — political influence and military skill. His exploits as the "Pathfinder" who had conducted five exploring expeditions through the wilds of the far West, no less than his splendid canvass in 1856 as the first national standard-bearer of the Republican Party, singled him out for high command. Indeed, he was looked upon by many of his fellow countrymen as an ideal leader, for he brought to the Union cause what animated few of its captains — the inspiration that springs from a romantic career.

Frémont inherited through his father, a French refugee, the love of adventure. He was born, in fact, on one of several expeditions which his parents made among the southern Indians; [1] and the untimely death of that father, a few years thereafter, was due to exposure during a forest excursion. At school the boy evinced talents of a high order, yet there were early indications of a restive disposition. His formal education came to a sudden stop upon his expulsion from the college in Charleston, S. C., as he himself narrates, "for continued disregard of discipline." This somewhat sobered him, and years of earnest labor ensued. Teaching school at home in Charleston, cruising as an instructor of mathematics on a United States sloop of war, pursuing scientific studies, making railroad surveys among the Tennessee mountains, and taking part in a military reconnoissance of the Cherokee country, he acquired the experience that led to his appointment as second lieutenant in the United States Topographical Corps. Then followed government explorations of the region lying between the Mississippi and the Missouri rivers, in which the young officer served under Nicollet, the distinguished French scientist.

While at work in Washington upon a report of these expeditions, Frémont fell in love with Jessie Ann Benton, the gifted daughter of the Senator from Missouri. The young lady smiled upon the lieutenant's suit, but her parents were less cordial. So Frémont, displaying characteristic dash and impatience of restraint, eloped with her. This marriage has been described by a not too friendly critic as "the most brilliant achievement of his life." It certainly exerted a far-reaching influence upon the young subaltern's fortunes. Mrs. Frémont, a model of wifely devotion, was destined to share her husband's aspirations, in a notable degree; but what was of greater immediate importance — his new relationship to her father, together with his tastes and qualifications, fitted him providentially, as it were, into Senator Benton's long-cherished dream of western expansion. Through that statesman's influence, Lieutenant Frémont was commissioned to make his first exploration of the extensive and practically unknown country beyond the Missouri River. Four great expeditions to the Pacific slope followed. They brought Frémont international renown. His simple, straightforward reports, wherein he told

> "Of moving accidents by flood and field,
> . . . .
> Of antres vast, and deserts wild,
> Rough quarries, rocks, and hills whose heads touch heaven,"

charmed admirers of the romantic wherever these widely scattered narratives were read. Not less enthusiastic were eminent scientists of the day over the precision and variety of his contributions to our knowledge of this

J. C. Frémont

newly unfolded wonderland; and so serviceable, withal, were his observations that caravan after caravan of western emigrants laid its course across the prairies according to his charts.

Frémont was not merely a finder of paths. On the far side of his adventures he also found military and political distinction. Arriving in the Mexican province of California, on the third exploring expedition, while a revolution was in progress, he played a prominent rôle among the dramatic scenes which culminated in the winning of the country for the United States. Not less spectacular were other incidents that presently crowded upon one another in kaleidoscopic succession. Lieutenant-Colonel Frémont — he had risen to that rank — acted, for a brief period, as military commandant of the conquered territory. Becoming involved in a conflict for authority on the coast, between General Kearney and Commodore Stockton, he was convicted by court-martial of mutiny, disobedience of the lawful command of a superior officer, and conduct prejudicial to good order and military discipline. A sentence of dismissal from the army followed. But, in view of his valuable services, of the extenuating circumstances, and of a recommendation for clemency by a majority of the court, President Polk, although he approved of the findings as to the second and third charges, remitted the penalty. Whereupon Colonel Frémont, with popular sympathy on his side, resigned. Presently came the announcement that gold had been discovered in the new possessions. California, entering the Union, elected Frémont its first Senator; and, as if nothing might be lacking to complete the marvelous story, mines of apparently fabulous value were found on a grant which had been bought by him a year before Sutter's tail-race yielded up its golden secret. At the proper moment, moreover, though a southerner by birth and education, he declared himself to be a hater of slavery. That such a career should appeal to the popular imagination was inevitable. It presented so strong a promise of gallant leadership that the Republican National Convention of 1856 nominated Colonel Frémont for the presidency.[2] Having served but part of a short term in the Senate, he was practically untried in statesmanship. The absence, however, of a political record — that frequent bugbear of public men — rendered him, then, peculiarly available as the nominee of a party in process of formation from the remains of many parties; while his pronounced anti-slavery views supplied sufficient common ground on which these not entirely harmonious sections of the young organization could make their first vigorous fight for freedom. "Free speech, free press, free soil, freemen, Frémont, and victory!" was a favorite slogan, in the North, throughout that stirring campaign. The Republicans were defeated, but by so narrow a margin in some quarters that all signs gave promise of success within the near future. Their electors had carried eleven States; and their popular vote, aided by the Fillmore ballots, had left Buchanan a minority President. To Frémont largely went the credit of having made this breach in the Democratic columns. Long after the din of that canvass had ceased, he was looked upon with a certain sentimental regard by many of those who had worked and marched and sung and voted for him with so much enthusiasm.

One of these supporters was Abraham Lincoln. Though the candidate had not been his first choice for the nomination, he had labored in Illinois, with voice and pen, at the head of the Republican electoral ticket, for Frémont's election. Four years later, when Lincoln himself won the presidency, it was his purpose to find some appropriate station under his administration for the leader whom he had so zealously served. Frémont was talked of for a place in the cabinet, and then for a first-class foreign mission. The President had finally decided upon him as Minister to France, but in deference to Secretary Seward's plans, the appointment was not made. So it happened that when the beginning of the Civil War found Colonel Frémont abroad, he was still a private citizen. Hastening back to this country, he received from Mr. Lincoln the highest military commission within the President's gift — that of Major-General in the regular army; and on July 3, 1861, he was assigned to the command of the Western Department.[3]

The appointment was in accordance with Frémont's own preference. It was the most extensive and, as he believed, the most important department in the service.[4] It comprehended, together with Illinois and New Mexico, all the country west of the Mississippi as far as the Rocky Mountains; but this, unfortunately, was not to be the West of our explorer's experience — the West of prairie, forest, and cañon, of Indian stalking and Mexican skirmishing. The scene of action now lay, for the most part, in the Border Slave State of Missouri, where the intrigues and pitfalls of party strife were more to be dreaded than the hardships or dangers of Frémont's early days. His new path — to use his own language — "led out from among the grand and lovely features of nature, and its pure and wholesome air, into the poisoned atmosphere and jarring circumstances of conflict among men, made subtle and malignant by clashing interests."[5] Missouri was, in fact, already, to a certain extent, the center of those political complications which made it one of the vexatious problems of the war. Governor Jackson and Lieutenant-Governor Reynolds, supported by the General Assembly, had committed the State, as far as they could, to secession. A convention, on the other hand, summoned by the legislature with the expectation that it would complete their work, had remained loyal to the Federal government, by a strong majority. This loyalty, however, was not without important reservations; for it actuated patriots holding every shade of opinion, from Radicals, who would have no Union without immediate emancipation, to ultra-Conservatives, who demanded that slavery and the Union be saved together. Their "pestilent factional quarrel," as Mr. Lincoln once impatiently termed it, gave him more trouble in the State than the enemy. And how bitter this antagonism became may be inferred from the President's remark, "Either party would rather see the defeat of their adversary than that of Jefferson Davis." Yet these extreme partisans and the other Unionists, who differed from them in this or that particular, had one point of agreement — they all desired the success of the Federal cause. To combine such warring elements into an effective force against a common foe, was a problem for a statesman rather than for a soldier. It called for wisdom and administrative skill of a type so rare that we may well stop here to inquire more closely into the character of the man who was to undertake the task.

Frémont's personality was not less romantic than the story of his life. Moving in a material age, among practical matter-of-fact men, he exhaled, as it were, an atmosphere of bygone chivalry. The slender, well-knit frame, with its alertness of action and grace of bearing, could have belonged only to one who had spent many of his adult years in the saddle, close to nature. He was slightly above the medium height, but his habitual dignity of carriage made him seem taller; just as a full beard and long curling brown hair streaked with gray lent to his dreamy countenance an additional touch of the picturesque. The handsome weather-browned face, with its high forehead, deep blue eyes, and aquiline nose, gave index of mental vigor. What Frémont had done, however, more than what he looked, was stamped upon the world's valuation of him. His achievements as an explorer had called for so many manifestations of pluck, dash, self-reliance, energy, and perseverance that, in the popular fancy, he became invested with qualities well-nigh heroic. Nor did the man's intellectual accomplishments appeal less to the respect of educated people. His knowledge of the sciences rendered him a unique figure in politics. He spoke French and Spanish fluently, while his command of the English language, in speech no less than in writing, was scholarly. That he owed this culture largely to his own efforts is the more surprising, as it was accompanied by a refinement of manner to which our so-called self-made men are, for the most part, strangers. Courtly in demeanor, and amiable withal, he generally exercised a certain personal fascination over those who came into relations with him. But this power to attract men was, unfortunately, accompanied by no nice discernment into the characters of his admirers. Accordingly, we find Frémont, from time to time, surrounded by followers who were as unscrupulous in their designs as they were unblushing in their flattery. Vanity and ambition — twin products of such influences — colored the visions in which his imagination abounded. He chafed under authority at mature age, hardly less than during the days of his impetuous youth. In fact, a certain spirit of insubordination was the most conspicuous blemish of this otherwise amiable character. Like your true knight-errant, moreover, Frémont did not hesitate, on occasion, to be a law unto himself; and still further recalling the romantic ideal, he presently revealed a strong distaste for the details of administrative affairs. Nor was he lacking, as we shall see, in these respects only. When confronted by important questions that required a tactful, sagacious handling of things as they were, or a comprehensive grasp of things as they should be, he was destined to prove painfully ineffective. What had served for brilliant leadership in the limited field of western exploration, hardly met the requirements of a departmental command on the larger theater of our Civil War. In brief, though the glamour that enveloped him had concealed the fact, Frémont was unfit by nature and by training for the enormous responsibility laid upon him by Mr. Lincoln's appointment.

The new general's initial duties were of vital importance. His earliest efforts should obviously have been directed toward harmonizing the discordant factions which, as we have seen, distracted the Union cause in Missouri. That commonwealth was especially delicate ground. It put to a severe test the famous "Border State policy," by which the President labored to rescue Missouri, Kentucky, and Maryland from secession. "These all against us," said he, "and the job on our hands is too large for us. We would as well consent to separation at once, including the surrender of this Capital."[6] Whether the wavering sections could be induced to wheel into the Federal column turned largely, of course, on the question of slavery. Mr. Lincoln, accordingly, during the first period of the struggle, maintained a conservative attitude toward that institution. Laying aside his own deep sympathy for the bondmen, he strove to retain the support of loyal slaveholders in the Border States, and of their sympathizers in the North, by repeatedly declaring his controlling purpose to be the preservation of the Union. He went so far, indeed, as to proclaim that it was not the intention of the government to interfere with slavery, as such, in any of the Southern States. This policy — need we add? — had been adopted in good faith. That its sincerity should be generally unquestioned was, judging from the President's utterances, essential to the very existence of the country. He expected his subordinates, as a matter of course, to coöperate with him along a line so deliberately chosen; and upon none did this obligation more palpably rest than upon the commander of the Western Department.

But, almost from the day of his assignment, Frémont was a source of anxiety and embarrassment to the administration. He became, in fact, one of the keenest of Lincoln's disappointments. When, after three weeks of perhaps unavoidable delay, the General arrived at his headquarters in St. Louis, he found the department in a state of disorganization which energetic, though oftentimes misdirected, efforts improved too slowly. The regular forces of the enemy menaced him from several directions, small bands of bushwhackers spread through country districts the horrors of guerrilla warfare, and neighborhood feuds were responsible for private outrages of every kind. To meet the military needs of the situation, without losing sight of its political aspects, required the exercise of an unclouded judgment. That is precisely what Frémont, at this juncture, did not have. He was surrounded by a swarm of time-servers, who, for their own ends, played upon the weaknesses of a brave man. Their fulsome praise, together with the clamor of the Abolitionists, whose idol the "Pathfinder" still was, incited him to the one thing which, above all others, he should not have done. On August 30, 1861, Frémont issued his famous emancipation proclamation. This announced that owing to the lawless condition of Missouri, the General commanding "should assume the administrative powers of the State," and establish martial law. Having defined the limits of military occupation, the document proceeded: —

"All persons who shall be taken with arms in their hands within these lines shall be tried by court-martial, and if found guilty will be shot.

"The property, real and personal, of all persons in the State of Missouri who shall take up arms against the United States, or who shall be directly proven to have taken an active part with their enemies in the field, is declared to be confiscated to the public use, and their slaves, if any they have, are hereby declared freemen." [7]

To render this last startling clause operative, the author of it at once convened a military commission, which began to issue deeds of manumission.

By a stroke of his pen, so to say, Frémont had momentarily changed the issue before the country from Union to Emancipation. That the change might be fraught with danger to the Federal arms, and with perplexities beyond calculation to the already overburdened President who had reposed so much confidence in him, does not appear to have given the General any concern. That his act, withal, greatly aggravated rather than soothed the local irritation which he had been sent to allay, seemed equally unimportant to him. For, granting a set-back in the Western Department, he no doubt thought himself more than compensated, in the country at large, by a return of his old-time popularity. Frémont, in fact, now again loomed large in the public eye. His proclamation aroused the Radicals throughout the North to the highest pitch of enthusiasm; while many Unionists, who had not been so keen about slavery, applauded what looked at first sight like a crushing blow against the South. But Mr. Lincoln, stationed where he could see — and indeed where he had to deal with — both sides of the question, saw mischief alone in this extraordinary fiat. Immediately upon its appearance, the support which he had been so tactfully nursing in the Border States, especially in Kentucky, threatened to become antagonism; just as the embers of factional difference within the Republican Party itself, kept previously under control by his cool management, were stirred, no less suddenly, into a blaze of controversy. In the excitement that ensued, some of the President's best friends appeared to waver. Like his critics, they failed, for a time, to realize that however much Frémont's proclamation might please them, the impetuous hand which penned it had thereby sought to grasp not only the executive powers of the government, but the legislative and judicial functions as well.

This view was set forth, with Mr. Lincoln's accustomed force, in a confidential letter to his old friend, Senator Orville H. Browning, who had approved of the manifesto. Here, in part, is what the President wrote: —

"General Frémont's proclamation as to confiscation of property and the liberation of slaves is *purely political*, and not within the range of *military* law or necessity. If a commanding general finds a necessity to seize the farm of a private owner for a pasture, an encampment, or a fortification, he has the right to do so, and to so hold it as long as the necessity lasts; and this is within military law, because within military necessity. But to say the farm shall no longer belong to the owner, or his heirs forever, and this as well when the farm is *not* needed for military purposes as when it is, is purely political, without the savor of military law about it. And the same is true of slaves. If the general needs them, he can seize them and use them; but when the need is past, it is not for him to fix their permanent future condition. That must be settled according to laws made by law-makers, and not by military proclamations. The proclamation in the point in question is simply 'dictatorship.' It assumes that the general may do *anything* he pleases — confiscate the lands and free the slaves of *loyal* people, as well as of disloyal ones. And going the whole figure, I have no doubt, would be more popular with some thoughtless people than that which has been done! But I cannot assume this reckless position, nor allow others to assume it on my responsibility."[8]

The President, it should be observed, saw fit, in the following year, to shift his ground somewhat; but he did so deliberately, under vastly different conditions, and by his own act — not at the dictation of a usurping subordinate.

Meanwhile the clash of policy — to say nothing of authority — between Frémont and Lincoln required immediate attention. Something, moreover, had to be done at once in order that the General might be turned from his declared purpose to shoot prisoners. As soon as a copy of the proclamation reached the President, he despatched a special messenger to St. Louis with a "private" letter, which read: —

"Two points in your proclamation of August 30 give me some anxiety.

"*First.* Should you shoot a man, according to the proclamation, the Confederates would very certainly shoot our best men in their hands in retaliation; and so, man for man, indefinitely. It is, therefore, my order that you will allow no man to be shot under the proclamation without first having my approbation or consent.

"*Second.* I think there is great danger that the closing paragraph, in relation to the confiscation of property and the liberating slaves of traitorous owners, will alarm our southern Union friends and turn them against us; perhaps ruin our rather fair prospect for Kentucky. Allow me, therefore, to ask that you will, as of your own motion, modify that paragraph so as to conform to the first and fourth sections of the Act of Congress entitled, 'An act to confiscate property used for insurrectionary purposes,' approved August 6, 1861, and a copy of which act I herewith send you.[9]

"This letter is written in a spirit of caution, and not of censure. I send it by special messenger, in order that it may certainly and speedily reach you." [10]

Mr. Lincoln's first point was, as the parliamentarians say, well taken. That headlong threat of indiscriminate military executions had shared, without particular scrutiny, the plaudits bestowed upon the order of emancipation. Its unwisdom was, nevertheless, obvious to the President. And how accurately, although nine hundred miles from the scene of action, had he gauged the temper of the enemy! On the very day his letter was sent, General M. Jeff Thompson, Confederate Commander of the First Military District of Missouri, issued a retaliatory proclamation, in which he "most solemnly" announced that for every soldier of the State guard or of the southern army so put to death, he would "*hang, draw, and quarter* a minion of said Abraham Lincoln." [11] Yet Frémont could not bring himself frankly to acknowledge his error. On the contrary, we find him, six days later, defending his position, in an answer to the President. This missive ignored, with singular untruthfulness, Thompson's proclamation, and said as to his own:—

"I do not think the enemy can either misconstrue or urge anything against it, or undertake to make unusual retaliation." [12]

Having thus seemingly maintained his dignity, the

General seized an early opportunity to assure another Confederate officer, who demanded an explanation, that he did not intend to violate, under his proclamation, the usages of war.[13]

Point number two in Mr. Lincoln's letter was made with characteristic delicacy. There was — as we know — not a word about the General's presumptuous exercise of an authority which properly belonged to the government; nor was there more than a gentle reference to the troubles which his impulsive act had brought upon the Head of that government.[14] The President's self-restraint deceived Frémont, as it did so many other "big men," in 1861. Our "Pathfinder" managed not to find the kindness that had inspired the letter; but he did find — at least, he is credibly said to have found in it — an attempt to rob him of his newly enhanced popularity. Be this as it may, he felt strong enough to take issue with the Executive in defence of the proclamation. "Modify" that illustrious document! — not he. His wife, the daughter of the great Benton, advanced upon Washington to deliver Frémont's reply and, incidentally, to bully the President. That one of the so-called gentler sex should be sent on such a mission need not surprise us after we learn that during her stay at department headquarters she was described as "the real chief of staff." When it is remembered, moreover, that Jessie Benton had inherited a son's full portion of her distinguished father's aggressive personality, we tremble for poor Mr. Lincoln. "She sought an audience with me at midnight," said he afterwards, in a confidential chat,[15] "and taxed me so violently with many things, that I had to exercise all the awkward tact I have to avoid quarreling with her. . . . She more than once intimated that if General Frémont should decide to try conclusions with me, he could set up for himself."[16] Such a menace from such a source was significant. It must have reminded the President of the rumors which had persistently linked the name of the lady's husband with revolutionary designs. According to some, Frémont was to establish an independent Confederacy in the Northwest; while others — principally extreme Abolitionists, and his own personal followers — urged that he ought to be placed, as dictator, in absolute control of national affairs. Yet these mutterings do not appear to have greatly disturbed Mr. Lincoln. He took no formal notice of Mrs. Frémont's treasonable talk, nor of the insubordination that lurked on the under side of the written message which she brought.

In his letter to the President, General Frémont asserted the wisdom of the proclamation and his right to make it.

"This is as much a movement in the war as a battle," said he, "and in going into these I shall have to act according to my judgment of the ground before me, as I did on this occasion. If, upon reflection, your better judgment still decides that I am wrong in the article respecting the liberation of slaves, I have to ask that you will openly direct me to make the correction. The implied censure will be received as a soldier always should the reprimand of his chief. If I were to retract of my own accord, it would imply that I myself thought it wrong, and that I had acted without the reflection which the gravity of the point demanded. But I did not. I acted with full deliberation, and upon the certain conviction that it was a measure right and necessary, and I think so still."[17]

Frémont's request, whatever may be said of its wilfulness, looked shrewd enough. If he was playing politics, — and there is reason for so believing, — he could hardly have found a surer method of strengthening himself, in certain quarters, at Lincoln's expense. Should the President publicly order him to modify the proclamation, they might stand before the people as the champions of opposing policies. In that event, the advantage of positions would, to all appearances, — from a sentimental as well as from a moral point of view, — rest with Frémont. His pretensions could not, in the nature of things, fail to command Radical support; and the North at large, or, accurately speaking, a considerable part thereof, had already, by its first frank outburst of approval over the proclamation, seemingly indicated on which side its choice would lie.

Still Mr. Lincoln stood firm. True to the singleness of purpose that distinguished him at critical junctures, he adhered to his much-condemned policy. The prospect of Frémont's rivalry, with all its adventitious strength, was allowed to influence his course, in this respect, no more than had Frémont's contumacious letter or the threats of Frémont's messenger. On the day following her arrival in Washington, the President despatched an answer to St. Louis. Touching in his passionless way on the emancipation clause of Frémont's proclamation, he commanded it to be so modified as not to go beyond the Act of August 6, 1861, and directed a copy of the law to be published with his order.[18] This made up the issue between them precisely as the General had desired. It left his prestige with the Abolitionists unimpaired, and seemed to establish his status generally as the better — if not indeed the stronger — Republican of the two. Comparisons between Lincoln and Frémont were, in fact, now freely made to the President's disparagement. "He is not a genius," said Wendell Phillips, from the platform, some months later; "he is not a man like Frémont, to stamp the lava mass of the nation with an idea."[19] But it was in the first throes of their disappointment over the fate of the proclamation that the anti-slavery people were especially severe upon Lincoln. Great newspapers and influential men were equally unsparing in their censure. Some even went so far as to advocate the impeachment of the President, and to spread the talk of a military dictatorship under General Frémont. "I have never," wrote Judge Hoadly of Cincinnati to a member of the cabinet, "heard wilder or more furious denunciation than yesterday and day before found expression from the lips of cool men. Three times I was applied to, to join in getting up a public meeting to denounce the administration and support Frémont; and while no such disturbance will be permitted, I am nevertheless certain that there is here a perfect and, I am sorry to say, very angry unanimity in support both of Frémont's proclamation and of his action at St. Louis in other respects, expensive though it may have been. . . . General Frémont is thus far the favorite of the Northwest, because he has come up to the standard. And if the election were next fall, to displace him would be to make him President."[20] That Frémont's removal was commonly expected at the time is its own commentary on his behavior. But we have studied Abraham Lincoln to small purpose if we are prepared for such a sequel to the incident. The President, in fact, declared that he had "no thought of removing General Frémont on any ground connected with his proclamation." And this brings us to the reasons why the gentleman was, about seven weeks later, relieved of his command.

Troublesome to the administration as were Frémont's anti-slavery tactics, the General's military and executive blunders proved to be no less embarrassing. During the first eight weeks of his control in the Western Department, Missouri was the scene of two relatively important battles. They were both disastrous to the Federal cause, and in each instance he was severely blamed; for Wilson's Creek, as well as Lexington, is charged to Frémont's account. The former engagement was the culmination of a campaign that had begun before the General assumed command. While he tarried in New York, those precious weeks after his appointment, came appeals for reënforcements from southwestern Missouri, where General Nathaniel Lyon, with a wretchedly equipped force, faced twice his strength in State and Confederate troops. These calls for aid became more urgent on the arrival of Frémont at St. Louis. Letters, telegrams, special messengers, followed one another in quick succession. They continued, in fact, almost up to the hour — sixteen days later — when Lyon.

making his choice between a hazardous retreat and a desperate battle, attacked the enemy at Wilson's Creek.[21] In the ensuing action, — one of the bloodiest of the war, — the Union forces struggled vainly against overwhelming numbers, and the gallant Lyon fell at the head of his troops. He had seemingly been left to fight without guidance or succor from his superior officer. There is good reason to believe, however, that a message from Frémont, received on the eve of the battle, had instructed Lyon, in case he found himself too weak for his position, to fall back until reënforcements should meet him. Yet nothing was generally known, at the time, about this order, which has disappeared from the Official Records; and the Department Commander, when he testified in his defence before the Committee on the Conduct of the War, omitted, for reasons that can only be conjectured, to include a copy of the document among the despatches that he submitted with his testimony.[22] It is but fair to add that Frémont gave tardy orders for several regiments to join Lyon; though they did not — it should also be said — move in time to be of any service. Owing to a similar failure, the Union arms were again defeated in Missouri, under mortifying conditions, the following month, at Lexington. That place was held by Colonel James A. Mulligan, with a force of about 2800 Federals, when General Stirling Price appeared before it, with an army of State troops, which soon numbered over 20,000 men. Against these heavy odds the little garrison, confident that it would be relieved, held out through siege and assault for eight days. This gave General Frémont ample time in which to send the sadly needed reënforcements; but he again acted too slowly, and when several relief columns had been set in motion, their efforts to reach Colonel Mulligan were, by one fatality or another, rendered futile. Despairing of help, that officer, after a spirited resistance to the limit of his resources, surrendered.[23] Tidings of this disaster were received in the North with a cry of indignation against the General commanding the department. He was condemned on the face of it by the deadly parallel which people drew between Lexington and Wilson's Creek. To what precise extent these two reverses were justly laid at Frémont's door need not be determined here. Granting all the difficulties, however, under which he claims to have labored, it is the judgment of history that, with the means at his command, better generalship could have brought about different results in both actions.

Meanwhile, Frémont's exertions at headquarters to bring order out of chaos opened up a whole Iliad of woes. He worked hard, with insufficient means, to organize and equip an army for a great campaign down the Mississippi. But obstacles that would have tried a stronger man beset him on every side. His confused efforts to remove them laid a train of troubles which he might have avoided only by exercising administrative skill of the first order; and this, as we know, Frémont did not possess. Unfortunately, what the General lacked in that particular could hardly be supplied by the persons to whom he entrusted important duties. For his confidence was given not to the officers nearest to him in rank, but to a coterie of parasites, among whom he scattered commissions and contracts with a liberal hand. This gang of speculators, held together, as has been pithily said, by the cohesive power of public plunder, subordinated the welfare of the department to their own interests; and went so far, at times, as to crowd out loyal men from intercourse with the misguided commander. Frémont's methods not only seriously retarded his operations, but what proved right here to be of even greater moment, they, at the same time, estranged from him some of the most prominent Unionists in the State.

Among those who found fault with the General was Colonel Francis Preston Blair, Jr. Indeed, his voice most insistently of all cried, —

> "Fie on the chance that brings the righteous man
> Close-mated with the ungodly!"

He had the right to speak, if any one had. A member of Congress from St. Louis, as well as commanding officer in the First Volunteer Regiment of Missouri Light Artillery, he had done more than any other man to hold his State in the Federal columns. By common consent, the "unconditional Unionists" of that section looked upon him as their leader. Whatever he did was therefore invested with an importance of its own, regardless of the President's friendly attitude toward the Blair family. When their opinion had been taken, at the outbreak of the war, concerning the best man for Missouri, they had enthusiastically recommended their old friend and political favorite, Colonel Frémont.[24] As his nomination to the presidency, in 1856, was generally credited to Francis P. Blair, Sr., so his assignment, five years later, to the Western Department — as far as this may not have been Mr. Lincoln's spontaneous act — must be ascribed to the influence of that same redoubtable politician and his two no less strenuous sons. The older of these, Montgomery, who had become Postmaster-General, is even said to have been the sole advocate in the cabinet of Frémont's appointment. Be that as it may, the General had no sooner taken command than the Blairs, with the whole-heartedness so characteristic of the family, threw themselves into his service. Frank at St. Louis and Montgomery at Washington advised, planned, and labored for his success. But Frank's confidence in Frémont, rudely shaken by the affair of Wilson's Creek, became still further impaired by the disaster at Lexington, and by what he deemed the gross mismanagement at headquarters. His letters, after a time, to the Postmaster-General "were pervaded," said Mr. Lincoln, in the confidential chat to which reference has been made, "with a tone of sincere sorrow and of fear that Frémont would fail. Montgomery showed them to me," the President continued, "and we were both grieved at the prospect."[25] In a letter dated September 1, this correspondence reached its inevitable climax. Declaring the General "incapable of comprehending his position," Frank urged that he "should be relieved of his command, and a man of ability put in his place."[26] Such a dictum from the leader who had a few weeks before been Frémont's stanchest supporter could not fail to weigh heavily with the President. He found in what Colonel Blair wrote, moreover, striking corroboration of the charges and complaints that had assailed him from many sources; but Lincoln sometimes carried to an almost culpable extreme the loyalty with which he stood by the men to whom he had given his confidence. For a week — the very week, indeed, which followed the publication of that troublesome emancipation proclamation — he pondered, not the truculent commander's removal, but how best to sustain him in his place.

Frémont had evidently fallen into the hands of bad advisers. Concluding them to be responsible for most of these weak spots in the General's armor, the President set out to reënforce it, after his own informal fashion. He despatched two confidential representatives with instructions to look into the condition of things at St. Louis, and to give Frémont a little judicious counsel. The visitors were Postmaster-General Blair — who, by the way, had a West Point education — and Montgomery C. Meigs, Quartermaster-General of the army. They carried with them a letter written by Abraham Lincoln to his friend, General David Hunter, stationed at Chicago. It read: —

"General Frémont needs assistance which it is difficult to give him. He is losing the confidence of men near him, whose support any man in his position must have to be successful. His cardinal mistake is that he isolates himself and allows nobody to see him, and by which he does not know what is going on in the very matter he is dealing with. He needs to have by his side a man of large experience. Will you not, for me, take that place? Your rank is one grade too high to be ordered to it, but will you not serve the country and oblige me by taking it voluntarily?"[27]

General Hunter took the post of second in command at St. Louis, as the President had requested; but matters did not appear to mend. Like several experienced officers of high rank, before him, the newcomer failed to get on a confidential footing with his superior. Frémont's affairs, in fact, went from bad to worse, and complaints redoubled on every hand. The resources of the Treasury were strained by the exorbitant bills of the rascals who were looting the Western Department; while what Montgomery Blair saw but served to confirm the reports of maladministration, already in Mr. Lincoln's hands. The Postmaster-General, therefore, upon returning to Washington, expressed his opinion that the good of the service required Frémont's removal.

An acrimonious personal quarrel with the Blairs had meanwhile complicated the situation. Mrs. Frémont, after her arrival at the Capital, on that memorable mission in defence of the proclamation, had heard about the Colonel's criticisms. She indignantly denounced them, in her interview with the President, and subsequently made a written demand upon him for copies of all the faultfinding letters that had come from the West. These he politely declined to furnish without the consent of the writers. He was moved by the lady's heat, moreover, to explain that the Postmaster-General had been sent to St. Louis, as a friend of her husband; and he protested, with no uncertain tone, "against being understood as acting in any hostility" toward General Frémont.[28] But here the President, of course, found himself at a disadvantage. He could not show the confidential reports that made it his duty to investigate the affairs of the Western Department; nor could he prove how kindly — despite what had happened — he felt toward Frémont, by telling that officer's militant spouse about the message to Hunter. Mrs. Frémont naturally lost no time in reporting how things stood, to her

General, who, smarting under a sense of injury, ordered Colonel Blair's arrest. Notice of this was telegraphed to the War Department, with an intimation that charges in preparation would touch upon the Colonel's "insidious and dishonorable efforts to bring" the commander's "authority into contempt with the government, and to undermine" his "influence as an officer."[29] After an interval of ten days, Frank was, at his brother's request, released. He forthwith declared that he, in turn, would prefer charges against Frémont, who met this announcement with the rearrest of his now embittered critic. When Colonel Blair's formal accusations reached the authorities, they were found to be of a grave character. Charging General Frémont with neglect of duty, unofficer-like conduct, disobedience of orders, behavior unbecoming a gentleman, waste of the public moneys, and despotic courses, he supported this catalogue of his superior's sins with a still more formidable array of specifications.[30]

The tangle into which Missouri had, by this time, fallen, was a source of almost constant anxiety to the President. Determined upon having things set right, once for all, he hurried the Secretary of War to the scene, with power to act. Mr. Cameron, accompanied by Adjutant-General Thomas, overtook Frémont in the field, after he had started on his campaign. The Secretary of War, like the cabinet colleague who had preceded him, speedily arrived at an unfavorable conclusion. "I had an interview with General Frémont," he wrote to Mr. Lincoln, "and in conversation with him showed him an order for his removal. He was very much mortified, pained, and, I thought, humiliated. He made an earnest appeal to me, saying that he had come to Missouri, at the request of the government, to assume a very responsible command, and that when he reached this State he found himself without troops and without any preparation for an army; that he had exerted himself, as he believed, with great energy, and had now around him a fine army, with everything to make success certain; that he was in pursuit of the enemy, who he believed were within his reach; and that to recall him at this moment would not only destroy him, but render his whole expenditure useless. In reply to this appeal, I told him that I would withhold the order until my return to Washington, giving him the interim to prove the reality of his hopes as to reaching and capturing the enemy, giving him to understand that, should he fail, he must give place to some other officer. He assured me that, should he fail, he would resign at once."[31]

The reprieve was hardly warranted by what Mr. Cameron's investigations disclosed. A report drawn up under his direction by General Thomas, when they had returned to Washington, appeared — even after allowing for the hearsay nature of certain statements — to bear out the most serious among Colonel Blair's charges.[32] So severe was the Adjutant-General's censure that one might doubt his good faith, if it were not for the cloud of witnesses whose testimony against Frémont had, all this time, continued to pour in upon the administration. There could no longer be any question as to the President's duty. Even his much-enduring patience had well-nigh reached its limit. Frémont's time was up. Whatever might be the hapless General's grievances, his ability, or his deserts, the period of his usefulness in Missouri had plainly passed.[33] Aside from weighty considerations of public policy, moreover, General Thomas reported an instance of disobedience so flagrant that, under any other President than Abraham Lincoln, it would have brought the offender to immediate disgrace. Somewhat over a week, ran the story, after Frémont had received the President's order modifying his emancipation proclamation, two hundred copies of that very document as originally issued were sent, by the General's express commands, to eastern Missouri for distribution.[34] That there might be no doubt about so grave a charge, Frémont's order was quoted verbatim in the Adjutant-General's report. Yet this piece of extraordinary misconduct failed to elicit further official notice. Had Lincoln paid any public attention to it whatsoever, nothing short of Othello's sentence upon Cassio,

> "I love thee,
> But never more be officer of mine,"

could have done justice to the occasion.

In a wholly different spirit did the President approach Frémont's removal. We scrutinize his conduct, in vain, for traces of the personal resentment to which any other Executive would doubtless, under the circumstances, have given way. Even after Frémont's fate had been decided, Mr. Lincoln attached conditions that left the General ample chance for escape. With the order recalling him and appointing General Hunter temporarily to his command,[35] were enclosed private instructions for General Curtis, who, from St. Louis, was to manage the transfer. "If," wrote the President, "when General Frémont shall be reached by the messenger — yourself or any one sent by you — he shall then have, in personal command, fought and won a battle, or shall then be actually in a battle, or shall then be in the immediate presence of the enemy in expectation of a battle, it is not to be delivered, but held for further orders."[36] Whether this lenity was due to ordinary military foresight, to Secretary Cameron's promises, to the protests by Frémont's supporters against his repeatedly rumored removal, to mutterings in the army of resistance against such an order, to Lincoln's sense of justice, to his good-will toward the General, or to his practice of not displacing favorite commanders until they had fully manifested their incapacity, or whether these all and several entered into the President's motives, is matter for speculation only. The essential facts are that Mr. Lincoln, so far from trying to get rid of Frémont as a dangerous rival, did, to the very end, what lay in his power to save him; and that the General's downfall at last must be ascribed to circumstances which were as much under his control as they were beyond the President's. For, when the officer whom Curtis had sent overtook the "Mississippi Army" in the field, it had neither fought a battle, nor was it within striking distance of the enemy. The order of removal was therefore delivered; and Frémont relinquished his command with a dignity, as well as a subordination, so perfect that they compelled praise from many who had, not without reason, looked for different behavior.[37]

Though the expected outbreak among the western troops failed to occur, men and officers alike — with certain exceptions — deplored their commander's downfall. It was an excited camp to which Frémont addressed his farewell message. He may have lacked military capacity, but he possessed, in an eminent degree, one attribute, if no other, of good generalship — the art of endearing himself to his soldiers. Loud and bitter were their denunciations of the government; but more formidable still, as the news spread, became the outcry of disapproval from Frémont's political admirers. Their hopes centered in "the statesman-soldier" — to use Wendell Phillips's appellation — as in no other leader, during the autumn of 1861; and many of the extreme anti-slavery men among them could not or would not see that he had been at fault. "If Frémont has been guilty of mistakes, or even of crimes," wrote an able journalist, at the time, "there are a million men now living who will forgive him, in consideration of his proclamation and his deed of manumission — documents which will be as immortal as the Declaration of Independence."[38] What seemed to increase this obligation a hundredfold was the belief that he had fallen a martyr to the anti-slavery cause. Even public men who should have known better looked upon Frémont as a friend of freedom, sacrificed to appease the slave power. "Whatever may have been his acts, or omissions to act," wrote Senator Grimes, one of these blunderers, "there is no question in my mind that the real cause of his removal was the proclamation he issued, and which he failed to modify in accordance with the President's wishes. That was the great sin for which he was punished." [39] A similar view was voiced by Whittier, the laureate of Abolitionism, in the well-known lines: —

> "Thy error, Frémont, simply was to act
> A brave man's part, without the statesman's tact,
> And, taking counsel but of common sense,
> To strike at cause as well as consequence."

The rôle of picturesque victim to governmental injustice was, as we have seen, not new to Frémont. He had, in fact, mastered the part. So now, as at other monumental moments of his career, the "Pathfinder" rose, in certain eyes at least, to heroic stature. From influential Radicals, on all sides, came expressions of esteem for him, and of censure for the administration. Press, pulpit, and platform, together with both houses of Congress, made liberal contributions for a brief season to the work of exalting Frémont, while putting down Lincoln. How deeply, too, that spirit moved the people, in certain sections of the country, may be gathered from this letter, written by Richard Smith of the Cincinnati *Gazette* to his friend, Secretary Chase, a few days after the removal: —

"Could you have been among the people yesterday and witnessed the excitement, could you have seen sober citizens pulling from their walls and trampling under foot the portrait of the President, and could you hear to-day the expressions of all classes of men — of all political parties, you would, I think, feel as I feel, and as every sincere friend of the government must feel, alarmed. What meaneth this burning of the President in effigy, by citizens who have hitherto sincerely and enthusiastically supported the war? What meaneth these boisterous outbursts of indignation, and these low mutterings favorable to a Western Confederacy that we hear? Why this sudden check to enlistments? Why this rejection of treasury notes by German citizens? Why is it that on the 6th of November, 1861, not one dollar was subscribed here to the national loan? Why is it that it would not be safe to go into places where the Germans resort, and publicly express an opinion favorable to the President? Why this sudden, this extraordinary, this startling change in public sentiment, on 'change, in the street, in the banking-house, in the palace and the cottage, in country and city? Is it not time for the President to stop and consider whether, as this is a government of the people, it is not unsafe to disregard and override public sentiment, as has been done in the case of General Frémont? The public consider that Frémont has been made a martyr of. . . . Consequently he is now, so far as the West is concerned, the most popular man in the country. He is to the West what Napoleon was to France; while the President has lost the confidence of the people." [40]

For the moment, it did indeed look, in some quarters, as if Lincoln had reaped the whirlwind. But was this storm fierce enough to bear out Judge Hoadly's warning that to displace Frémont might result in making him President?

The next election was still three years distant. As this, for the time being, precluded political operations, Frémont's supporters directed their energies toward securing his restoration to active service. Some of his partisans in Missouri held secret meetings that did not stop short of planning treason in their favorite's behalf; but most of his friends throughout the North contented themselves with the orderly presentation of his case. They asserted that in a purely military command the General would do justice to his reputation; and this claim Mr. Lincoln, despite what had happened, was willing to treat with indulgence. So, after the first pressure upon the President had subsided, we find him, one day, calling into the Executive Chamber Henry C. Bowen, the proprietor of the *Independent*, who happened to be passing the open door, on his way to another office.

"Come in," said Mr. Lincoln, in his unceremonious way; "you are the very man I want to see. I have been thinking a great deal lately about Frémont; and I want to ask you, as an old friend of his, what is the thought about his continuing inactive."

"Mr. President," was the reply, "I will say to you frankly that a large class of people feel that General Frémont has been badly treated, and nothing would give more satisfaction, both to him and to his friends, than his reappointment to a command commensurate, in some degree, with his rank and ability."

"Do you think," asked Mr. Lincoln, "he would accept an inferior position to that he occupied in Missouri?"

"I have that confidence in General Frémont's patriotism that I venture to promise for him in advance," was Mr. Bowen's earnest reply.

"Well," said the President thoughtfully, "I have had it on my mind for some time that Frémont should be given a chance to redeem himself. The great hue and cry about him has been concerning his expenditure of the public money. I have looked into the matter a little, and I can't see as he has done any worse or any more, in that line, than our eastern commanders. At any rate, he shall have another trial." [41]

Shortly after this interview, when the Mountain Department was carved out of the steeps and forests of western Maryland, western Virginia, eastern Ohio, eastern Kentucky, and eastern Tennessee,[42] the command of it was appropriately enough assigned to the "Pathfinder." [43] Here he figured, not greatly to his credit, in the government's disastrous experiment of opposing to "Stonewall" Jackson the three independent departmental commands of Frémont, Banks, and McDowell. Their efforts to entrap that brilliant campaigner, in his dash down the Shenandoah valley, were a succession of failures; and naturally so, for only the most efficient coöperation of the Union generals could have secured a different finish to the intricate strategy imposed upon them from Washington. When at last it appeared as if Jackson might be caught between the converging columns of McDowell and Frémont, those officers were ordered to the only outlet through which the then retreating Confederates could escape from the valley. McDowell reached his appointed post in time; but Frémont arrived just too late, and their alert foe slipped between them. "Too late" has ever been a sorry commentary when the day is lost. What shall we say, then, of a general to whom it must be applied thrice within the year? Not a little, moreover, of this last failure was due to Frémont's constitutional disrespect for orders. According to his instructions from the President, he was to advance by a route that would have brought his line of march between the enemy and the southern exit from the valley, for which Jackson was headed. Taking what he believed to be a more practicable road, without notifying Mr. Lincoln of so important a modification of his orders, Frémont made a detour that led him several days' march away from the Confederate line of retreat, and brought him out, when he did reach the strategic point, in the rear of the enemy, just as the last of Jackson's troops were leaving that place.

Though Frémont failed, his reasons, as usual, were excellent. The road prescribed by the President had — we are told — been "obstructed"; it would have been "fatal" — in the General's opinion — to a line of supplies; and to have taken it — he asserted — must, under any conditions, have defeated the end in view.[44] When Mr. Lincoln said to Major Zagonyi: —

"General Frémont ought to have informed me of his plans, and of the reasons why he could not obey my orders"; he was answered: —

"Mr. President, I am instructed by General Frémont to say that he could not spare any of his officers, nor trust the telegraph; and, furthermore, to say that all the intelligence of his movements which has been placed in the office of the Adjutant-General has reached the enemy soon afterwards."[45]

But — it has been urged — there was still ample time, even after the detour, to cut off Jackson's worn-out and bedraggled forces. To which Frémont replies that the weather was so stormy, the roads so heavy, the men so weakened by fatigue and want of food, that a whole day had to be lost in resting them on the march.[46] All these things might be pleaded in mitigation before a court-martial. They are as dust in the balance, however, at the bar of military history, where commanders are judged, not by the plausibility of the reasons that they assign for their defeats, but by the victories that they have snatched, with straitened means, from unpropitious circumstance. Before this tribunal the Frémont of the Mountain campaign, like the Frémont who warred a hundred days in Missouri, stands condemned.

After Jackson's escape, the President realized his own share in the disaster. It was evident that the three divided commands, which had supported one another so loosely, should be united, at once, under one general in the field. This honor might properly have fallen to Frémont, the ranking officer of the group; but Lincoln, for obvious reasons, looked elsewhere. He selected Major-General John Pope, who had made a good record in the West, to lead the combined forces. They constituted, for the most part, the newly organized Army of Virginia. It was divided, to correspond with the former departments, into three army corps, under the command, respectively, of Frémont, Banks, and McDowell.[47] These officers were all Pope's seniors in the service. Banks and McDowell, nevertheless, bowed to the President's wishes; but Frémont, belying the good Mr. Bowen's "confidence" in his patriotism, declined — as Mr. Lincoln had surmised he would — to "accept an inferior position." On receipt of the order, the General forthwith telegraphed to the Secretary of War: —

"I respectfully ask that the President will relieve me of my present command. I submit for his consideration that the position assigned me by his recent order is subordinate and inferior to those hitherto conceded me, and not fairly corresponding with the rank I hold in the army. I further desire to call his attention to the fact that to remain in the subordinate command to which I am now assigned would virtually and largely reduce my rank and consideration in the service of the country. For these reasons I earnestly request that the President will not require the order to take effect so far as I am concerned, but will consent immediately to relieve me." [48]

This missive was a blunder. The ambitious man who penned it must have lost sight, for the moment, not only of what he owed to his country, but also of what he owed to himself.[49] He was plainly in the wrong on a question that involved no political differences, and that could, therefore, not so easily be befogged by partisan prejudice. Frémont had gone the whole length of his tether. There is no mistaking the hand that pulled him up short, though it was ostensibly that of Mr. Stanton. The Secretary of War answered promptly: —

"Your telegram requesting to be relieved from duty has been received and laid before the President, who directs me to say that Congress having by special resolution vested him with authority to assign the chief command between officers of the same grade as he might consider best for the service of the country, without regard to priority of rank, he exercised that authority in respect to the Army of Virginia, as he has done in other instances, in the manner which, in his judgment, was required for the service, and without design to detract from the 'rank and consideration' of any general.[50] General Pope was the junior in rank, but of the same grade not only of yourself, but also of Generals Banks and McDowell, neither of whom have considered their rank and consideration in the service of the country as a condition upon which they would withdraw from that service.

"The President regrets that any officer in the service

should withdraw from the service of his country, in any position where he is lawfully assigned by his commander-in-chief; but he cannot consistently with his sense of duty grant your request that an order, made according to his judgment for the welfare of the nation, should not be required to take effect, so far as you are concerned. The obligation of duty is the same upon all officers in the service, whatever their rank, and if there be any difference, it should be most readily observed by those of highest rank. Your request, therefore, to be relieved from your present command is granted.

"You will turn over your command and orders to the officer next highest in rank to yourself, and direct him to report to the department for further orders." [51]

A general's popularity must be deep-rooted indeed to survive such a blast.

Notwithstanding his misconduct and his failures, many of the Radicals clung to Frémont. He was still their champion — political and militant, the leader on whom they depended for the ultimate triumph of Abolition. They applauded him accordingly, without reservation, but their faith in his soldierly qualities, be it said, was no longer shared by the President. "I thought well of Frémont," he remarked, chatting confidentially one evening with a few friends. "Even now I think well of his impulses. I only think he is the prey of wicked and designing men, and I think he has absolutely no military capacity." [52] This opinion, though expressed more than a year after the Shenandoah campaign, was probably held by Mr. Lincoln at the conclusion of that fiasco; yet we fail to find among his open utterances a word that might hurt the General's sensitive pride or impair his reputation. Meanwhile Frémont's supporters left no stone unturned in their efforts to secure his restoration. From the East, as well as from the West, came delegations, petitions, letters, telegrams, and what not, urging that he be sent to the field at the head of another army, or be assigned to some responsible executive post under the administration. For a time, Mr. Lincoln readily disposed of these appeals. When, for instance, Congressman George W. Julian of Indiana, in the spring of 1863, expressed his regret that Frémont had not received another command,[53] the President replied that as he did not know where to place the General, he was reminded of the young man who, when advised by his father to take a wife, answered, "Whose wife shall I take?" Mr. Lincoln proceeded to explain that a suitable appointment could be provided for Frémont only by removing some other general, which he did not wish to do.

"I remarked," reports Mr. Julian, "that I was very sorry if this was true, and that it was unfortunate for our cause, as I believed his restoration to duty would stir the country as no other appointment could."

The President might have become reminiscent as to the General's stirring powers, but he contented himself with saying:—

"It would stir the country on one side, and stir it the other way, on the other. It would please Frémont's friends, and displease the Conservatives; and that is all I can see in the *stirring* argument."[54]

Mr. Lincoln replied after a similar fashion, some weeks later, when a St. Louis mass meeting "resolved" that Frémont and several other anti-slavery generals had been "systematically kept out of command." To the committee which presented these resolutions the President sententiously said that there were "more pegs than holes to put them in." The officers mentioned had, he added, placed themselves by their own actions in the positions they then occupied, and however willing he might be to send them to the field, it could not be done without working injustice to those whom they would displace.[55] This was unanswerable. It seemed as if, by a neat application of the physical law that inhibits two bodies from occupying the same space at the same time, Lincoln had effectually shelved Frémont or, more accurately speaking, fastened him to the shelf upon which the General had placed himself.

Still the extreme anti-slavery men were far from content to leave their idol in retirement. If there was no suitable post for Frémont, why — they queried — not create one? So said Horace Greeley, William Cullen Bryant, Parke Godwin, Peter Cooper, and other prominent citizens, who signed a memorial suggesting that the General should be commissioned to organize and command an army of negro troops. The delegation that carried the petition to the President was introduced by Senator Charles Sumner, to whom Lincoln, after the interviews, addressed his answer. This letter evinces how the President's good-will toward Frémont, no less than his desire to conciliate the General's powerful friends, brought him to the inconsistency of again contemplating the appointment of that officer to a military command. It reads, in part:—

"In relation to the matter spoken of Saturday morning and this morning — to wit, the raising of colored troops in the North, with the understanding that they shall be commanded by General Frémont — I have to say: —

"That while it is very objectionable, as a general rule, to have troops raised on any special terms, such as to serve only under a particular commander or only at a particular place or places, yet I would forego the objection in this case upon a fair prospect that a large force of this sort could thereby be the more rapidly raised;

"That being raised, say to the number of ten thousand, I would very cheerfully send them to the field under General Frémont, assigning him a department, made or to be made, with such white force also as I might be able to put in."[56]

Nothing came of this, however, for the enlistment of negro troops was entrusted, in good time, to safer men than the "Pathfinder."

Another notable attempt to get Frémont back into active service brought Wendell Phillips, the Rev. Moncure D. Conway, F. W. Bird, Dr. Howe, and others to Washington. Calling on the President, they requested him to remove Edward Stanley from the military governorship of North Carolina, on the ground that he was not acting in sympathy with the then recently issued proclamation of emancipation. Mr. Lincoln asked the delegation who was wanted in Stanley's place. They promptly answered, "Frémont."

"Gentlemen," said the President, "it is generally the case that a man who begins a work is not the best man to carry it on to a successful termination. I believe it was so in the case of Moses — was n't it? — who got the children of Israel out of Egypt, but the Lord selected somebody else to bring them to their journey's end. A pioneer has hard work to do, and generally gets so battered and spattered that people prefer another man, though they may accept the principle. Don't understand me as having, myself, the least objection to Mr. Frémont; but he is so associated with Abolitionism that many people object to the man, even though they go his way." [57]

Stanley's office, like the other coveted places, did not fall to Frémont; and his disappointed adherents grumbled more than ever. At last, applying Lincoln's biblical citation to the President himself, they diligently spread the opinion that he ought to give way, on the completion of his first term, to some other leader. Who that leader should be had become a fixed idea in the Radical mind.

By the spring of 1864, Union opposition to Lincoln's renomination centered chiefly around Frémont. He succeeded to what remained of the following which Secretary Chase, as we have seen, had wisely resigned. In fact, no sooner had the Ohio man actually withdrawn his candidature than the "Pathfinder's" little lightning-rod was pushed up into the presidential heavens. Frémont's name became a rallying-cry for such of the Radicals as were out of patience with the President's cautious attitude toward slavery; for such of the Conservatives as believed, or pretended to believe, that Lincoln's reëlection would be a menace to Republican institutions; and for such political and private malcontents, generally, as had been unavoidably created by the exigencies of a war administration. These discontented elements now drew together. With a view to influencing the regular Republican Convention[58] that was to meet at Baltimore on the 7th of June, they assembled on May 31, in Cleveland, for what they called a "Mass Convention." This body by acclamation nominated General Frémont for the presidency, and General John Cochrane of New York — a few dissenting — for the vice-presidency.

The candidates hastened to issue their letters of acceptance, which appeared three days before the Baltimore Convention. What Frémont wrote seemed tinged with the yellow of his grudge against Lincoln. The President was here accused of creating a schism in the party by not remaining "faithful to the principles he was elected to defend." His administration was severely arraigned for its "disregard of constitutional rights," for "its violation of personal liberty and the liberty of the press," its "abandonment of the right of asylum," its "feebleness," "want of principle," "incapacity, and selfishness." All of which led up smoothly enough to the General's ultimatum: —

"If the Convention at Baltimore will nominate any man whose past life justifies a well-grounded confidence in his fidelity to our cardinal principles, there is no reason why there should be any division among the really patriotic men of the country. To any such I shall be most happy to give a cordial and active support. My own decided preference is to aid in this way, and not to be myself a candidate. But if Mr. Lincoln should be nominated, — as I believe it would be fatal to the country to indorse a policy and renew a power which has cost us the lives of thousands of men, and needlessly put the country on the road to bankruptcy, — there will remain no other alternative but to organize against him every element of conscientious opposition with the view to prevent the misfortune of his reëlection."[59]

This shaft fell wide of the mark. So far as its effect upon the Baltimore Convention was concerned, it might as well never have been discharged. For that body renominated Abraham Lincoln by a unanimous vote, on the first ballot.

If the President felt aggrieved at Frémont's behavior, he made no visible sign. Yet the rancor of the General's attacks upon him and upon his administration was in striking contrast to the consideration with which the "Pathfinder" had uniformly been treated. Indeed, at this, the very climax of Frémont's opposition, Lincoln's sole recorded comment was a jest. It related to the Cleveland "Mass Convention," — "mass" in name only, of which William Lloyd Garrison, arch-Radical though he had been, said in the *Liberator*, "There never was a more abortive or a more ludicrous gathering held, politically speaking." Very few representative people attended; and the assembly, instead of numbering thousands as appears to have been expected, consisted, at no time, of more than four hundred men. When this disparity was mentioned by Congressman Deming, in a chat with the President, the number caught Mr. Lincoln's attention. Putting on his spectacles, he opened the bible on his desk, turned, after a moment's search, to the twenty-second chapter of the First Book of Samuel, and read in a waggish tone: —

"And every one that was in distress, and every one that was in debt, and every one that was discontented, gathered themselves unto him; and he became a captain over them: and there were with him about four hundred men."[60]

Auspicious as the President's comparison may, from the historical point of view, have been for Frémont, that leader, unlike the chieftain in the Cave of Adullam, did not become a ruler in Israel. Those who might have encouraged the General to "set up for himself," as Mrs. Frémont appears to have expressed it in 1861, understood him, and Lincoln too, somewhat better in 1864. Even the "Pathfinder's" old friends the Abolitionists refused —with certain notable exceptions—to follow him on this last and stoniest of his trails. They realized, as soon as the Democrats put forth their candidate and their platform, that emancipation would triumph, if at all, through Abraham Lincoln. Reluctantly, in some instances half-mutinously, his opponents within the party came to the support of the great statesman whose course they had condemned; but whose hold on "the plain people," and whose perfect mastery of the situation, had made him the indispensable man of the hour. As for Frémont, he found himself, before the canvass had rightly begun, that most humiliating of political spectacles — a nominee without a party. Nothing that he contrived could impart seriousness or dignity to his situation. When the issues between Lincoln and McClellan were sharply defined, moreover, his position of antagonism to the President became, for a loyal Republican leader, clearly untenable. So, early in the autumn, Frémont withdrew from the canvass.[61] Even this step, however, was taken with bad grace. For he was careful to explain that he retired "not to aid in the triumph of Mr. Lincoln," but to do his part "towards preventing the election of the Democratic candidate." As an illustration, perhaps, of how he would perform this extraordinary feat, the writer went on to say: —

"In respect to Mr. Lincoln, I continue to hold exactly the sentiments contained in my letter of acceptance. I consider that his administration has been politically, militarily, and financially a failure, and that its necessary continuance is a cause of regret for the country."[62]

With this last futile stroke at the man who had so completely routed him, Frémont disappears from the stage of national politics, disappointed alike in his ambition and his spite.

CHAPTER VIII

THE YOUNG NAPOLEON

THE dead level of disappointment which marked the opening operations of the Civil War, on the northern side, was relieved by one brief and comparatively brilliant campaign. This took place in upper western Virginia, where Federal troops drove less than their number of Confederates before them in a succession of engagements. Philippi, Laurel Hill, Rich Mountain, and Carrick's Ford were, it is true, mere skirmishes when viewed beside the great battles of the war that followed; but in the summer of 1861 they were hailed throughout the North as important victories. To judge by results, they were not so insignificant, either, as at first glance now seems to be the case. For that decisive little campaign shattered a Confederate army, rescued what before long became the State of West Virginia from secession, infused renewed courage into northern hearts, and formally introduced to Union men their first military idol — George Brinton McClellan. As Major-General in command of the Department of the Ohio,[1] that officer had won some of these successes, and had received credit for them all. Their moral effect on the country, be it said, was heightened not a little, at the time, by the trumpet-like tones of his proclamations, addresses, and despatches, which followed one another, during the campaign, in rapid succession.[2] Bulletins fell as thick as bullets. The General carried a portable printing-press, which worked overtime; and its output was disfigured by a vein of exaggeration, amounting occasionally — as we now perceive — to bombast. Amidst the jubilation aroused by his joyful tidings, however, and in the confusion of the gathering conflict, these productions were received at their face value. Even Lieutenant-General Scott, the venerable chief of the army, did not scrutinize them too closely. This sudden triumph of an officer who had once been numbered among the veteran's most promising subalterns so moved the old campaigner that he added his praise, without reserve, to the general acclaim. McClellan was easily the hero of the hour. His vigor of rhetoric, combined, as it seemed, with a genius for tactics, recalled to men's minds the conqueror of Austerlitz. Reversing history, in their enthusiasm, they fondly styled him the "Young Napoleon," though he was considerably older than Bonaparte had been at the close of his first campaign;[3] and in that same spirit they turned, as by one accord, toward the new prodigy, with high hopes of great achievements to come.

The North was still rejoicing over McClellan's victories, the thanks of Congress and the congratulations of the administration were still making the rounds of an applauding press, when the Union army under McDowell came to grief at the first battle of Bull Run. As the routed volunteers poured into Washington, in a state of almost total demoralization, their first need was evidently a new commander; and to provide one was President Lincoln's first care. His choice naturally fell upon the popular favorite, the only general officer who had, since the war opened, gained any distinction. It seemed to Mr. Lincoln, no less than to the country at large, that this picturesque soldier was destined to repair the disaster of July 21, and to lead the reorganized troops to victory. So McClellan received a hurried summons to the Capital. Upon his arrival he was assigned to the command of the newly created Division of the Potomac, by far the most responsible post in the field.[4]

This promotion, dazzling as it must have been even to the man so honored himself, did not rest upon those few successful weeks in western Virginia, alone. Some credit, however slight, should doubtless be conceded to his earlier

Geo B McClellan

history and training. A graduate of West Point shortly after the outbreak of the Mexican War, McClellan had seen active service before his twentieth birthday.[5] He had distinguished himself repeatedly, though only a second lieutenant of engineers, in General Scott's campaign; and that commander's attention was, on several occasions, called to the youthful officer's exploits. At the close of the Mexican War, Captain McClellan — he was so brevetted for gallantry — had entered upon eight busy years of varied official duties. Serving with his engineer company as an instructor at West Point, assisting Major John Sanders in construction work at Fort Delaware, exploring the country of the Upper Red River under Captain Randolph B. Marcy, making a military inspection of Texas as chief engineer on the staff of General P. F. Smith, surveying the coast of that State for the improvement of its harbors, exploring the Cascade Mountains to determine part of the proposed route for the Pacific Railroad, reconnoitering the West Indies in a secret search for a coaling station, and visiting Europe during the Crimean War as one of the three commissioners appointed to make military observations abroad, — he had won, in whatever task was assigned to him, golden opinions from his superiors. He had found time, moreover, during this period, busy as it was, to employ his pen with good effect. A general memoir on the island of Hayti, a monograph on railroad construction, Regulations for the Field Service of Cavalry in Time of War, a Manual of Bayonet Exercise which upon General Scott's urgent recommendation was adopted by the War Department as an official text-book, and a voluminous treatise on The Armies of Europe, besides a number of minor reports, all bear testimony to his ability no less than to his zeal.[6] But in times of peace army life usually fails to fill the measure of such a man's ambition. Resigning his commission in 1857,[7] Captain McClellan had become successively Chief Engineer of the Illinois Central Railroad Company, Vice-President of the same corporation, and President of the Eastern Division of the Ohio and Mississippi Railroad, with headquarters at Cincinnati. Hence, when the Civil War began, Ohio rather than New York or Pennsylvania—for his services were sought by both the latter commonwealths—had secured the honor of McClellan's enrollment. Promptly finding employment in military preparations at Columbus, he had been appointed by Governor Dennison Major-General of State Volunteers.[8] At the head of the local forces, he had straightway impressed those about him with a confidence in his skill that as speedily found its way to the National Capital. For, presto! in just three weeks, this militia officer had been commissioned—remarkable to relate—a Major-General of the United States Army.[9] In that capacity, he had presently conducted the campaign into western Virginia which made his name a household word all over the Union; and directly afterward, a symbol of security in Washington, when he reached there, during the week of Bull Run.

McClellan and Lincoln were not, at the time, strangers to each other. They had met before the war in the conduct of certain lawsuits, which concerned the one as an officer of the Illinois Central Railroad Company and the other as its counsel. On these occasions, the then unpolished lawyer had been an object of interest to the well-bred West Pointer, who many years later thus touched upon his early acquaintance with Mr. Lincoln:—

"More than once I have been with him in out-of-the-way county-seats where some important case was being tried, and, in the lack of sleeping accommodations, have spent the night in front of a stove listening to the unceasing flow of anecdotes from his lips. He was never at a loss, and I could never quite make up my mind how many of them he had really heard before, and how many he invented on the spur of the moment. His stories were seldom refined, but were always to the point."[10]

If memories of those Attic nights on the Eighth Judicial Circuit arose in the minds of the two men as General McClellan presented himself to President Lincoln at the White House, on the morning of July 27, 1861, there might also have been recollections not quite so agreeable. When Abraham Lincoln and Stephen A. Douglas had made their memorable canvass for the senatorship three years before, one of the "Little Giant's" most ardent supporters was George B. McClellan. As Vice-President of a railroad company which, for reasons of its own, favored Douglas, he had employed in the Senator's behalf all the influence and facilities at his command. Special trains — on occasion even McClellan's private car — had carried the Democratic champion to the scenes of the debates, while his opponent, in order to keep these appointments, had been reduced at times, as we have seen, to the necessity of begging rides on freight trains. This discrimination, though it had greatly angered Lincoln's friends, evoked, so far as we know, not a complaint from the man against whom it was directed. Nor does the closest scrutiny into his conduct reveal a trace of resentment. He had never, in all the ruck of frontier politics, learned how to nurse personal grievances. It goes without saying, therefore, that in the loftier sphere of the presidency his heart, big as it was, had no room for a private grudge. If any misgivings on this score troubled General McClellan when he made his first bow in Washington, they were speedily dispelled by Mr. Lincoln's cordial greeting. Neither mistrust for the past nor doubt of the future was allowed to mar the harmony of their meeting. The new commander glowed with the warmth of his reception. Touched by the President's kindness, he eagerly accepted the great dual task assigned to him of defending the Union Capital and taking Richmond.

McClellan seemed at first glance equal to the emergency. He entered upon the arduous labors of reconstructing, indeed of creating, an army with the prime requisite, bodily vigor. A muscular frame, deep-chested, broad-shouldered, full-throated, rendered him capable of physical exertions so long sustained that they aroused the admiration of those who had to keep up with him in a trying round of duties. His bearing, as he rode about Washington from post to post, was alert and soldierly. Though but slightly above medium height, length of body made him look tall in the saddle, while a good seat and a steady hand completed the impression of superb horsemanship. His every movement betokened dignity, every command perfect self-reliance. When with these externals are recalled the well-set, closely-cropped head, martial mustache, bronzed complexion, aquiline nose, and compelling blue eyes, we comprehend why many who saw him at the time pronounced him to be the beau-ideal of a military chieftain. His appearance, it may be said, gave promise of more than his talents were destined to fulfil, yet McClellan's powers were of no common order. A study of modern warfare in all its aspects, supplemented by a broad general scholarship, had admirably prepared him in the theory of military organization. Hardly less notable seemed the skill with which this knowledge was now employed. Indeed, McClellan's tireless energy, mastery of details, comprehensive discipline, and administrative grasp of what was needed to place the country on a war footing justified more nearly than in any other respects a comparison to the great Napoleon. Immeasurably inferior, withal, to the Corsican in military ability, as we shall see, the American surpassed him in character. McClellan was a man of good impulses, for the most part, in fact, of high ideals. The romantic — more precisely speaking, the sentimental — view of life appealed to his imagination. He plunged into a duty, as he saw it, with all the fervor of an emotional nature. That he did not always see clearly at critical moments must be conceded. Nevertheless, his integrity, courage, and fidelity to a trust, private or official, were in the main as deep-rooted as the religious feeling from which they sprung. A man of prayers, like so many who have led in the world's bitterest conflicts, he was, to a remarkable degree for a professional soldier, pure in thought and word and deed. Some fellow officer might fitly have applied to him, with perhaps a slight modification, that eulogy addressed by a comrade, full two hundred and fifty years before, to the first illustrious captain on Virginian soil: —

> "I never knew a warrior yet, but thee,
> From wine, tobacco, debts, dice, oaths, so free."

This resemblance to John Smith may be traced still further in McClellan's charm of manner. Richly endowed with the social virtues, he was so cordial, frank, and sympathetic, so courteous in demeanor, so buoyant of speech, that men were insensibly drawn toward him, even on first acquaintance. Not a few, after closer intercourse, came to hold him in affectionate regard; while the favored ones whom he admitted to his friendship repaid it with signal love and loyalty. This power to inspire devotion, this personal magnetism, is an important, if not an essential element of successful leadership. Measured according to that attribute alone, the first commander of the Army of the Potomac would easily have ranked as its greatest.

But McClellan fell short of heroic proportions. To what extent, the campaigns upon which he eventually entered all too clearly disclosed. In fact, before operations began, certain defects of temperament that contributed not a little to his failures showed themselves through the pomp and circumstance of military grandeur. The pace, as is usual in revolutionary times, was rapid — far too rapid for McClellan's equipoise. His sudden bound into fame had, as early as the west Virginian days, disturbed that nicety of balance, lacking which, no man can long maintain suitable relations with the rest of the world. We find him, then, already nursing an inordinate respect for his own importance, that grew by the flattery and hero-worship on which it was fed, until it had swelled, at the commencement of his Washington career, to a condition bordering upon exaltation. He believed himself "called" to a sacred mission. No "man of destiny" ever approached an allotted task in a profounder spirit of consecration. To McClellan's stimulated imagination it seemed as if Providence had fashioned him throughout his earlier life into an instrument of the divine will for the preservation of his country; and this notion unfortunately received apparent confirmation from the manner of his reception at the Capital. Our Camillus had been on duty there just one day, when he wrote to his wife: —

"I find myself in a new and strange position here — President, cabinet, General Scott, and all, deferring to me. By some strange operation of magic I seem to have become the power of the land."[11]

Another branch of the government paid its tribute, three days later, to the rising sun. Visiting the Senate, for the purpose of urging some special military legislation, McClellan "was quite overwhelmed," as he expressed it, at his treatment by the members. "I suppose," reads a message to the same fair correspondent, "half a dozen of the oldest made the remark I am becoming so much used to, 'Why, how young you look, and yet an old soldier!' It seems to strike everybody that I am very young. They give me my way in everything, full swing and unbounded confidence. All tell me that I am held responsible for the fate of the nation, and that all its resources shall be placed at my disposal. It is an immense task that I have on my hands, but I believe I can accomplish it. . . . When I was in the Senate chamber to-day, and found those old men flocking around me; when I afterwards stood in the library, looking over the capitol of our great nation, and saw the crowd gathering around to stare at me, I began to feel how great the task committed to me. Oh! how sincerely I pray to God that I may be endowed with the wisdom and courage necessary to accomplish the work. Who would have thought, when we were married, that I should so soon be called upon to save my country?"[12]

These are but specimens of the ebullitions in which the General's earlier private letters to his wife abounded. A dip, at random, into almost any of them, — for they have, since his death, been rather injudiciously published, — reveals at once the egotism of the writer, and the well-nigh unprecedented good-will lavished upon him at the start, by eminent public men. What wonder if the new wine of their adulation mounted to McClellan's head! He had not been in Washington long before the fixed idea that God had placed him there to save his country became tinged with the fatal delusion that it could be saved by him alone.

Here was a saviour of no common mold. Beside him all those other tutelary personages who surrounded the President seem to fade into insignificance. McClellan's own confidence in his star, to say nothing of the popular belief that he was about to do great things, had been frankly adopted by Mr. Lincoln himself. He petted the General in his simple, abnegating way, and did his best to satisfy that officer's innumerable demands upon the government. McClellan's engaging personality, moreover, was not without its wonted effect, for it stirred the great heart in the White House to a feeling of friendliness quite apart from mere official support. We have seen something of the President's amiable indulgence toward the statesmen who severally fancied that their names spelled the country's salvation; but none of them, it is safe to say, were treated with such consideration as was shown, in the beginning, at least, to the "Young Napoleon." McClellan's pretensions met with the utmost good humor. Flowers and invitations to dinner and kind words poured in upon him from the Executive Mansion, until even he, a very glutton for honor, turned aside to cry, "Enough!" "I enclose," reads one of those private letters to his wife, "a card just received from 'A. Lincoln'; it shows too much deference to be seen outside."[13] This complaisance hardly raised "A. Lincoln" in the eyes of his punctilious subordinate. To McClellan's straitened vision, the President differed but little from the country attorney, who had made entertainment on the western circuit, with stories that "were seldom refined." The homely manners, unconventional methods, and whimsical moods which misled, as we have seen, so many politicians naturally carried this soldier of aristocratic tendencies, far afield. He failed more grievously, perhaps, than any of them to comprehend the extraordinary man with whom they were dealing. The nearest that he could bring himself to expressing anything like appreciation was contained in a patronizing comment, — "The President is honest and means well." [14] He might have said, with equal grace,— "The President is a worthy dunce." For, to sum it all up, conformably with McClellan's academic standards, — and he knew no other, — Lincoln seemed to fall as far below the requirements of the situation as the General fancied himself to rise above them.

An officer who has fallen into such a frame of mind will not submit patiently to the supervision even of his commander-in-chief. So the President's natural interest in military matters, as the work of organization went on, greatly annoyed McClellan. It soon began to look as if the "full swing and unbounded confidence," in which he had exulted, might have its limitations after all. He chafed under Mr. Lincoln's questions, and had but a cold welcome for his suggestions. Nor was this the only source of irritation. Day by day the General's resentment of what he called "meddling" took a wider compass, until finally, not the Chief Executive alone, but the Lieutenant-General, most of the cabinet officers, and other public men, as well, appear to have fallen within the spreading circle of his displeasure. That something of this feeling should find expression in McClellan's private correspondence was to be expected. We are unprepared, however, for the spleen which has left its unseemly tracks among these posthumous revelations of the man's vanity.

"I am weary of all this," reads a letter to his wife, after the third week at the Capital. "I have no ambition in the present affairs; only wish to save my country, and find the incapables around me will not permit it."[15]

Who these incapables were may be inferred from other outbursts that followed. The first splutter of McClellan's rage was directed, in part at least, against his venerable patron and commander, General Scott, concerning whom the younger officer confided many complaints to the lady at home. Early in August he wrote: —

"The old General always comes in the way. He understands nothing, appreciates nothing."

On the following day he added, in the same strain: —

"General Scott is the great obstacle. He will not comprehend the danger. I have to fight my way against him."

A few days more brought an ultimatum in sight: —

"General Scott is the most dangerous antagonist I have. Our ideas are so widely different that it is impossible for us to work together much longer."

Then there was something very like a panic, with honors for the responsibility about evenly divided: —

"I am here in a terrible place. The enemy have from three to four times my force. The President, the old General, cannot or will not see the true state of affairs."

And so on, to the end of the chapter, when Scott's retirement made way for the last coveted promotion of his ambitious junior.

Painful as are these manifestations of McClellan's acerbity toward an illustrious chief, they do not quite move us to the sense of outrage with which we come upon his privately expressed ill-will — at times, even contempt — for Abraham Lincoln and the statesmen by whom the President was supported.

"I can't tell you," wrote the General at the beginning of October, "how disgusted I am becoming with these wretched politicians."[16]

Yet straightway he proceeded, in letter after letter, to enlighten his sympathetic correspondent on that very subject. A few extracts must suffice here.

"This getting ready," reads one lament, "is slow work with such an administration. I wish I were well out of it."

Then makes he moan after the following fashion: —

"I am becoming daily more disgusted with this administration — perfectly sick of it. If I could with honor resign, I would quit the whole concern to-morrow."

He does not quit, however, but remains for martyrdom: —

"I was obliged to attend a meeting of the cabinet at eight P. M., and was bored and annoyed. There are some of the greatest geese in the cabinet I have ever seen — enough to tax the patience of Job."

Not long thereafter he strikes a harsher note: —

"I have a set of men to deal with unscrupulous and false. . . . The people think me all-powerful. Never was there a greater mistake. I am thwarted and deceived by these incapables at every turn."

Meanwhile, like an alert tactician, McClellan countered with a little thwarting and deceiving of his own. For the same letter tells how he concealed himself in order "to dodge all enemies in shape of 'browsing' Presidents, etc."

This happened during November, by which time his scorn for the administration knew no bounds. "It is sickening in the extreme," he wrote, "and makes me feel heavy at heart, when I see the weakness and unfitness of the poor beings who control the destinies of this great country."

But enough of such vaporings, for the present. Happily, "the poor beings" who controlled were unaware how low they stood in their accomplished critic's private books, though he furnished the prime offender with grounds for more than a conjecture.

Mr. Lincoln had made it a practice, from the beginning, to pay informal visits at McClellan's headquarters.

Waiving, with characteristic self-surrender, all questions of etiquette, he hoped thus to keep in touch with military affairs at the least possible expenditure of the General's time. Before breakfast or after supper, as the case might be, the President would arrive with some such greeting as, "Is George in?" And it became a matter of comment that, if George was in, he did not always receive his distinguished caller promptly. Seemingly unconscious of any discourtesy, Mr. Lincoln waited with unruffled good humor, in McClellan's reception-room, among the "other common mortals," as one indignant chronicler expressed it, until the oracle was pleased to have him admitted.[17] More vehement still must have been the rage of a White House clerk, who tells how he accompanied his Chief, one evening, to the headquarters in H Street. "We are seated," he writes, "and the President's arrival has been duly announced, but time is being given him to think over what he came for. General McClellan is probably very busy over some important detail of his vast duties, and he cannot tear himself away from it at once. A minute passes, and then another, and then another, and with every tick of the clock upon the mantel your blood warms nearer and nearer its boiling-point. Your face feels hot and your fingers tingle, as you look at the man, sitting so patiently over there, whom you regard as the Titan and hero of the hour; and you try to master your rebellious consciousness that he is kept waiting, like an applicant in an ante-room." [18] On another occasion, Secretary Seward had the honor of sharing a snub with the President. Calling together at headquarters, one evening, they were told that the General was out, but would soon return. After they had waited in the reception-room almost an hour, McClellan came back. Disregarding the orderly who had told him about his visitors, he went directly upstairs. Whereupon Mr. Lincoln, thinking that perhaps he had not been announced, sent up his name; but the messenger returned with the information that the General had gone to bed. It is doubtful whether the President ever required or received an explanation of this gross misbehavior.[19] There was no appreciable change in his friendly attitude toward McClellan, but thenceforth most of their consultations took place at the White House. What happened concerning an appointment for one of these meetings nicely illustrates how Lincoln, at the time, regarded his inflated subordinate. The President had arranged a conference, to be held in the Executive Mansion, between General Ormsby M. Mitchel, Governor Dennison, and General McClellan. All but the last-named gentleman kept the engagement. After Mitchel and Dennison had, with perhaps some show of irritation, waited a long time, Mr. Lincoln said: —

"Never mind; I will hold McClellan's horse, if he will only bring us success."[20]

Meanwhile the President's forbearance was subjected to a still severer strain. As time advanced, it appeared to him, and indeed to a considerable portion of the loyal North, that the Army of the Potomac lingered longer than necessary in the camps about Washington. This splendid force had been due to an outpouring of men and means lavish beyond parallel. With unlimited confidence in McClellan, the people, as well as the administration, had determined that nothing should be lacking to his success. By common consent, moreover, it had been agreed that he should not be hurried; for Bull Run had sobered the nation, and the cry of "On to Richmond!" had, temporarily at least, fallen into disfavor. Relying besides upon the General's promise, when he assumed command, that the war should be "short, sharp, and decisive," the public watched in patience, through the late summer and early fall, while the army took shape under his skilful hands. Organization was then the order of the day. But there came a time, after months of elaborate preparations and imposing reviews, when the country began to grow restless again. On all sides arose demands for an advance of the army;

yet comparatively few of those who found fault with its inaction during October blamed McClellan. Professing himself eager to open the campaign, he charged his delays now to the government, now to the aged General-in-Chief, until, at last, one of these alleged obstacles was removed. Scott, bending beneath the weight of his infirmities, and smarting under the junior officer's repeated discourtesies, had, in August, asked to be retired.[21] This request was finally granted on the 1st of November, but not before McClellan, by representing that the Lieutenant-General stood in the way of a forward movement, had secured the intervention of Senators Wade, Chandler, and Trumbull. Their belief in the younger General's ardor was then still shared by Mr. Lincoln, as indeed by the nation at large. So, when the President appointed McClellan to the command of the whole army in Scott's place, his act met with general approval;[22] yet the eager patriots, who looked for an advance as soon as the new General-in-Chief got a free hand, were doomed to disappointment. Drills and parades and the work of getting ready went on as before. The beautiful autumn weather invited McClellan into Virginia, without response; while his vast host remained coiled around the Capital, like an overfed serpent, about to take its winter sleep.

Why did not the Army of the Potomac advance? Disciplined and equipped by perhaps the ablest military organizer on American soil, it excelled the force confronting it in resources, health, and efficiency. So formidable an array had never before been seen in the Western World. With fine enthusiasm, the troops chafed while awaiting the order to march. They longed to break camp for the enemy's country, and their many weeks of labor on a formidable chain of earthworks had gone far enough for them to feel that they would leave Washington a fortified city. When it is added that the Federals at this point outnumbered the Confederates by more than three to one, we may well ask the reason for further delay. A satisfactory explanation must be sought far below the surface of things, — in the purpose and disposition of the General commanding. His aim, as he expressed it at the very outset, was to carry matters "*en grand* and crush the rebels in one campaign." If this might be accomplished by a single decisive battle, so much the more to his liking. For McClellan evidently aspired to the strategic triumphs of a Turenne, rather than the bloody progress of a Tamerlane or a Bonaparte. He had accordingly set about the creation of an army which should be so overwhelmingly superior to that of the enemy as to demonstrate "the utter impossibility of resistance."[23] And here rose the rock upon which this talented officer eventually came to grief. A weakness for overrating his antagonist's strength and for underrating his own rendered him incapable of making a correct comparison. To such an extent was this carried that he persisted in demanding more men, and time for further preparations, long after the balance tipped heavily to his side. There was still room, it is true, for improvement in the Army of the Potomac, — as of what army might that not at any time be said? — but war, like politics, is the science of the attainable, and, all things considered, the troops were ready to move by December.

About the first of that month the President suggested an advance against the enemy encamped before Washington. A memorandum, which he handed to McClellan, asked a few pertinent questions about the situation, and outlined a plan of operations. After a delay of perhaps ten days, this paper was returned to Mr. Lincoln with brief answers inserted, in pencil; while the plan was dismissed somewhat after the same curt fashion. "Information recently," wrote the General, "leads me to believe that the enemy would meet us in front with equal forces nearly — and I have now my mind actually turned towards another plan of campaign that I do not think at all anticipated by the enemy, nor by many of our own people."[24] The information referred to was far from accurate. It is now known that the Confederates along the Manassas line numbered, at the time, about 47,000 effective men, whereas the Federals, according to McClellan's own showing, had a force of over 164,000 equipped and present for duty. Deducting 60,000 on garrison or other service, as he did, still left 104,000 with which to meet 47,000.[25] But the General, with something akin to infatuation, declared himself confronted by a force "not less than 150,000 strong, well drilled and equipped, ably commanded, and strongly intrenched."[26] To make headway against this fanciful host, he had insisted, a few weeks before, that the Army of the Potomac should be increased to an effective strength of 208,000 men.[27] McClellan's tendency to exaggerate did not escape Mr. Lincoln, who tried to correct it, we surmise, in his characteristic way. They were together one night when the General received a telegram from an officer commanding a regiment on the Upper Potomac. The despatch described in magniloquent language a desperate conflict that had taken place during the day, and closed with a list of casualties so small as to be out of all proportion to the alleged importance of the struggle. "The President," relates McClellan, "quietly listened to my reading of the telegram, and then said that it reminded him of a notorious liar, who attained such a reputation as an exaggerator that he finally instructed his servant to stop him, when his tongue was running too rapidly, by pulling his coat or touching his feet. One day the master was relating wonders he had seen in Europe, and described a building which was about a mile long and a half mile high. Just then the servant's heel came down on the narrator's toes, and he stopped abruptly. One of the listeners asked how broad this remarkable building might be. The narrator modestly replied, 'About a foot!'"[28] That there could be any personal application in the parable apparently never entered the listener's mind; but those who have made themselves familiar with Lincoln's tactful use of the little stories which this, that, and the other thing reminded him of, will find no difficulty in drawing the moral, though it was lost upon McClellan. He stood stoutly by his inflated estimates. How erroneous these were, the President had no means of demonstrating, nor was he favored with a hint of the new plan for which his suggestion had been so unceremoniously brushed aside. He waited for the General to speak, hoping against hope that the spell of inaction which brooded over the army might soon be broken. Still the oracle made no sign.

A fatal irresolution appears to have possessed McClellan. He was not willing to take the field until his ideal of completeness had been attained, nor could he bring himself to the unpopular course of going into winter quarters. In this latter respect only, the General-in-Chief recognized the existence of an aroused public opinion, which he would have done well to take carefully into account. No commander, worthy of the name, opens a campaign, under ordinary conditions, by cutting himself off from his base of supplies; and, in a free country, this base, whatever may seem to be its place on the theater of operations, really lies close to the hearts of the people. Without their continued support, the general cannot hope to succeed; for, sooner or later, their wishes compel attention — even to the point, at times, of becoming a controlling factor in his calculations. When McClellan, therefore, in the arrogance of military pride, refused to give the popular will that consideration to which it was clearly entitled, he showed himself lacking, as has well been said, "in those statesmanlike qualities that enter into the composition of a great general." [29] His failure, moreover, to set the army promptly in motion foreshadowed other deficiencies not less serious.

How urgent grew the need of military action, before the close of 1861, may be seen at a glance. A body of northern soldiers — the largest ever collected on this continent, was seemingly held in and around Washington by an inferior southern force, which, unmolested, had flaunted its flag for months in sight of the capitol; a chance encounter — the disastrous battle of Ball's Bluff — had confirmed a belief, among some, in the superior courage of the besiegers; railroad communication with the city, by way of the Baltimore and Ohio Railroad, was interrupted; and Confederate batteries, on the Virginia side of the Potomac, effectually closed the river to navigation. The humiliation, to say nothing of the trouble, produced by this condition of affairs, was none the less keen because McClellan, after repeatedly emphasizing the necessity for vigorous operations, continued merely to mark time. Within ten days of his arrival at Washington, he had delivered himself of a "memorandum" to the President, in which he said: —

"Our foreign relations and financial credit also imperatively demand that the military action of the government should be prompt and irresistible." [30]

No wiser words had, at the time, been uttered. Nevertheless, after four months of exhaustive preliminaries, his own course — the very reverse of what was prompt or irresistible — had brought both those important interests into jeopardy. Europe could not but respect a secession movement which seemed strong enough to keep the Union Capital so long in a state of partial siege. For it goes without saying that such prestige as could be extracted from the pitiful spectacle was made the most of by southern sympathizers abroad, and the Confederate government at home. Every day of inaction on the Potomac now favored the diplomatic hopes of Jefferson Davis, as it augmented among Abraham Lincoln's supporters an ever-present fear of foreign intervention.[31] Meanwhile the other danger forecast by McClellan also made itself manifest. Actual war had hardly begun, yet the treasury was nearly empty. With a daily expenditure of almost $2,000,000 and a steadily increasing public debt that threatened to reach almost fabulous proportions, the government could not look upon this apparent torpor in the Army of the

Potomac with anything but the gravest anxiety. Nor was the situation improved when the loyal people of the North, paying war taxes as freely as they had recruited regiments, clamored in the midst of their sacrifices for action. From all sides came the pressure upon the administration, and McClellan himself was now no longer spared. His hold on the confidence of the nation became considerably shaken. Criticism took the place of laudation. Men, recovering from their excess of hero-worship, began to suspect that "our chicken," in the language of Lowell's *North American Review* essay, "was no eagle, after all." Even the daily bulletin, "All quiet on the Potomac," — once a welcome message throughout the land, — became a text for newspaper satire and popular derision.

Many representatives of the people, when they reached Washington in December, echoed their constituents' demands for a more spirited prosecution of the war. This was especially so among the Radical members of the House and Senate, who, finding bitter fault with McClellan's tactics, were not less severe upon his politics. A War Democrat of the conservative type, he hoped to see the Union restored without the immediate abolition of slavery. Although his attitude, in this particular, was seemingly justified by Mr. Lincoln's Border State policy, and by the declared purpose of Congress not to interfere with the established institutions of the southern commonwealths,[32] such tenderness as he manifested for the rights of slave-owners was exceedingly offensive to the most influential of the Republican leaders. Their hostility toward McClellan became intensified, moreover, by the fact that unfriendly critics of the administration appeared to be his adherents, while even outspoken opponents of the war championed his cause. Only your true Napoleon could, by force of great military triumphs, come unharmed out of such a coil; but this unfortunate general, lingering too long in the shadow of the capitol, had become involved, as we shall see, beyond relief. Idolized at the outset by Union men of all parties, he found himself presently the storm center about which beat the fiercest currents of contending political factions.

Over McClellan, thus beset, the President held the ægis of his protection. This smart young General had, it is true, been at no pains to conceal an overweening contempt for Mr. Lincoln or his civilian advisers; and whatever victories he might win would assuredly be turned into political capital by the administration's Democratic opponents, who were already getting into a position to appropriate his laurels. That he could, moreover, be continued in command only at the risk of alienating from the government some of its own party chiefs — to say nothing of a patriotic populace, press, and platform, clamoring against a so-called Fabian policy — greatly troubled the President. Yet loyalty, in the last extreme, to the men about him was one of Lincoln's dominant traits; and to support the "Young Napoleon," early in the winter of 1861–62, was loyalty to the country, as well. For the President, frankly conceding his own ignorance of military affairs, knew of no one who was likely to wield the formidable weapon which McClellan had fashioned, more effectually than the General-in-Chief himself. To sustain that officer in public, and to defend him in private against the aspersions of his powerful critics, became at this time not the least of Lincoln's cares. When ardent friends of the administration insisted upon the necessity for immediate action, he replied that McClellan was right not to advance before his preparations were completed. The faultfinding even took the shape of protests by special committees. One of these delegations consisted of three influential Representatives, Schuyler Colfax, Reuben E. Fenton, and Galusha A. Grow, Speaker of the House. They came to point out the importance not only of appeasing popular discontent with the lagging army, but also of averting a heated discussion about its commander, which threatened daily to break out on the floor of Congress. What they had to say was hardly news to the President. Yet he received them in the jocular mood behind which so often lay hidden the anxiety that gnawed at his heart. It seemed to him, he said, as if Providence, with favoring sky and earth, beckoned the army on; but that General McClellan, who knew his business, no doubt had his reasons for disregarding these hints. "As we have got to stand by the General," continued Mr. Lincoln, "I think a good way to do it may be for Congress to take a recess for several weeks, and by the time you get together again, if McClellan is not off with the army, Providence is very likely to step in with hard roads and force us to say, 'the army can't move.' You know Dickens said of a certain man that if he would always follow his nose he would never stick fast in the mud. Well, when the rains set in, it will be impossible for even our eager and gallant soldiers to keep their noses so high that their feet will not stick in the clay mud of old Virginia."[33] To the General himself, the President used a very different tone. He sought, at every opportunity, to impress privately upon that officer how serious the situation had become, and how vital to the cause which they both held dear was the striking of a decisive blow.

Military affairs were in this unsatisfactory state at Christmas time, when McClellan took to his bed, for what proved to be a period of three weeks, with an attack of typhoid fever. As he had not conferred adequate authority upon any one to act for him meanwhile, "his absence," to quote a far from unfriendly member of the general staff, "paralyzed work at headquarters."[34] The outlook for the Army of the Potomac was consequently as gloomy as ever when Congress reassembled after the holiday recess. Members no longer restrained themselves from demanding explanations; the Joint Committee appointed to inquire into the conduct of the war[35] held daily sessions, at which one military expert after another testified to the readiness of the troops for a campaign; and protests against their continued idleness focused upon the President, from every conceivable direction, with a heat that became almost intolerable. Matters had evidently reached a crisis. Having failed in several attempts to consult with the sick man, Mr. Lincoln, on January 10, summoned two division commanders, Generals Irvin McDowell and William B. Franklin. To them the harassed chief unburdened himself. "The President," as McDowell relates, "said he was in great distress, and, as he had been to General McClellan's house, and the General did not ask to see him, and as he must talk to somebody, he had sent for General Franklin and myself, to obtain our opinion as to the possibility of soon commencing active operations with the Army of the Potomac. To use his own expression, if something was not soon done, the bottom would be out of the whole affair; and, if General McClellan did not want to use the army, he would like to 'borrow it,' provided he could see how it could be made to do something."[36] Then followed a series of conferences with Mr. Lincoln, in which, at one time or another, Secretaries Seward and Chase, Postmaster-General Blair, Assistant Secretary of War Scott,[37] Quartermaster-General Meigs, and the two officers mentioned, took part. Their advice—excepting that of Judge Blair, McClellan's stanch supporter—was in favor of moving, within a short time, as the President had suggested six weeks before, upon the enemy's position at Centreville and Manassas.[38]

Deliberations had progressed thus far when rumors of what was going on reached the General-in-Chief. His friend, Edwin M. Stanton, then about to be made Secretary of War, brought the first hint, in characteristically acrid language. "They are counting," said he, "on your death, and are already dividing among themselves your military goods and chattels."[39] No tonic on the invalid's table could have done so much to hasten his convalescence.

Mustering his returning strength, he had himself driven, on Sunday morning,[40] to the White House, where the President, receiving him kindly, invited him to attend one of the conferences, which was to be held on the following day. At the appointed time, McClellan met the cabinet officers and military men, already spoken of, in Mr. Lincoln's office. The situation was, to say the least, embarrassing, especially for the President. He wished to preserve cordial relations among these men; but he wished, still more, to carry out the program on which most of them had virtually agreed. At his request, General McDowell explained the plan under consideration, concluding what he had to say with somewhat of an apology for the peculiar position in which McClellan's critical illness and the President's orders had placed the three subordinate officers present. To this the General-in-Chief curtly replied, "You are entitled to have any opinion you please," adding, with evident resentment, that, as he was again restored to health, further investigations or explanations were unnecessary. Here Mr. Lincoln interposed to ask what was to be done and when. McClellan rejoined that "the case was so clear a blind man could see it." Yet he straightway proceeded to raise difficulties, in a way that left most, if not all, of those present less enlightened than that hypothetical person of impaired vision. At last, Mr. Chase — once McClellan's friend and sponsor, now his declared opponent [41] — repeated, with manifest impatience, the President's question. To which the General-in-Chief promptly replied that the Secretary of the Treasury had no right to interrogate him about military affairs. Turning to Mr. Lincoln, he protested, on grounds of secrecy, against developing his plans before such advisers; and declared that he would do so only in obedience to a written order, and on the President's responsibility. It was obviously high time to terminate this discussion, which appeared to be drifting into a dangerous channel. So Mr. Lincoln asked McClellan whether he had fixed upon a date, in his own mind, for commencing operations. The General answered, "Yes." "Then," said the President, "I will adjourn this meeting."[42]

In averting a disclosure of his plans to a mixed council of civilians and soldiers, McClellan conformed to time-honored military traditions. Absolute secrecy is the cardinal rule of strategy. It received pithy expression from the Great Frederick, when he said that if his night-cap knew what was in his head, he would throw it into the fire; and President Lincoln, trying to put down a civil war from a Capital infested with spies, had not been slow to recognize the truth of the principle. In fact, just a week before the meeting here described, he had, at a conference with his cabinet and the Committee on the Conduct of the War, surprised the latter gentlemen, not only by admitting that the administration was ignorant of McClellan's plans, but still more, by approving of the General's reticence. It was to a sympathetic judgment, therefore, that our officer had addressed his plea against divulging military secrets. The President, as we have seen, yielded gracefully. Restoring McClellan to the saddle, he adjourned, without date, the meeting from which so much had been expected. Yet this was done, be it said, not without a feeling that his own wishes had again been thwarted; and that the General-in-Chief, now more than ever, stood obligated to lose not a day in getting the army under way.

Here closed what may be called the first phase in the relations between President Lincoln and General McClellan. That the pretensions of this accomplished but autocratic soldier had been suffered to go month after month unchecked was owing, of course, to unique conditions. If during that period "the Chief Magistrate," as one caustic pamphleteer expressed it, "went into voluntary or involuntary eclipse" so far as directing the movements of the army was concerned, he did what any prudent leader without military training would have done. Yet so heavy were the drafts made on Lincoln's forbearance, that his almost unbounded patience had, by this time, nearly reached the vanishing point. Indeed, an incident which happened within a week after McClellan's triumphant dispersal of the President's little council affords a glimpse once more of the master whose strong hand curbed Seward, Chase, and Stanton.

Early in the winter of 1861–62, Washington had been visited by the tuneful Hutchinson family. Their concerts of ballads and patriotic songs had drawn enthusiastic audiences. After singing at one of the White House receptions, greatly to the enjoyment of Mr. Lincoln, they had applied to the Secretary of War for permission to entertain the soldiers in the camps across the Potomac. A pass was readily secured from Mr. Cameron,[43] through the good offices of Secretary Chase, between whom and the Hutchinsons existed the strong bond of anti-slavery opinions. As it happened, the singers did not journey far. Their first concert was given before two New Jersey regiments of General Franklin's division, in the spacious chapel connected with Fairfax Seminary, near Alexandria. Number after number was applauded by the soldiers, until the vocalists began John G. Whittier's hymn of liberty, "Ein Feste Burg Ist Unser Gott." They had finished the third verse, —

"What gives the wheat fields blades of steel?
What points the rebel cannon?
What sets the roaring rabble's heel
On the old star-spangled pennon?
What breaks the oath
Of the men o' the South?
What whets the knife
For the Union's life? —
Hark to the answer: *Slavery!*"

when a hiss was heard from a corner of the church. Surgeon Lewis W. Oakley had taken this method of showing his contempt for abolition doctrine. The gage was picked up by Major David Hatfield. Rising in a front pew, he angrily threatened to have any one ejected who should repeat the interruption. A brief altercation ensued, amidst cheers, hisses, and much confusion. Order was at last restored, but the song was not finished. On the following morning, General Kearney, in command at Fairfax, prohibited the next concert, for which preparations were making; and a copy of the obnoxious hymn was forwarded to Franklin's headquarters, whence the matter finally reached General McClellan. He promptly disposed of it by revoking the pass, as well as the permit to sing for the troops. Returning to Washington, the Hutchinsons laid their grievance before a sympathetic listener in the person of their friend, Secretary Chase. He carried into the next cabinet meeting a copy of the alleged "incendiary" verses; and, what was of greater moment, entered a protest against the action of McClellan in annulling a permit issued by his superior, Secretary Cameron.[44] On hearing the words read, Mr. Lincoln warmly approved of the hymn. It was, he remarked, just the kind of a song for the soldiers to hear; and, as far as canceled passes were concerned, the Hutchinsons should have the right to go among any of the troops whose commanders invited them to sing. Our melodious friends retraced their steps, forthwith, to Alexandria, where they gave two concerts — interdicted song and all — before delighted audiences of soldiers.[45]

Throughout the North, meanwhile, this interlude had created much excitement. Factional feeling ran high. Incensed as the Radicals were, they found not a little comfort in the fact that the President had brought himself, at last, directly to reverse an order of the General-in-Chief; while McClellan's admirers gloried in his recent recovery of the command, and insisted that he should not be hampered by civilian interference. Standing between these two forces, Lincoln now opposed his masterful will to both. He declined to remove McClellan, as one faction demanded, or to leave him in absolute military control, as was urged by the other. The President had, in fact, been preparing himself to take that control into his own hands. For weeks he had devoted every available moment to a study of strategy. Text-books, reports, plans, and maps, over which he pored, at times, late into the night, as well as numerous consultations with commanders in active service, had gone far toward removing the feeling of helplessness with which he originally approached military matters. Consequently, when the General-in-Chief came, near the close of January, with his project for a campaign against Richmond by way of Chesapeake Bay, the President received him in a new rôle. Disapproving of this route, which involved prolonged preparation, he determined to put forward his own plan again, not, however, as before, in the form of a suggestion, but of a positive command.

On the 27th of January, Mr. Lincoln, without consulting the General-in-Chief, or his cabinet advisers, to whom he merely read the document for their information, issued the "President's General War Order No. 1." In this he directed "that the 22d day of February, 1862, be the day for a general movement of the land and naval forces of the United States against the insurgent forces." Specifying, moreover, which troops were chiefly meant, — the list of course included the Army of the Potomac, — he announced "that the heads of departments, and especially the Secretaries of War and of the Navy, with all their subordinates, and the General-in-Chief, with all other commanders and subordinates of land and naval forces, will severally be held to their strict and full responsibilities for prompt execution of this order." [46] Having by virtue of his constitutional authority thus assumed the active direction of military operations, Mr. Lincoln, four days later, issued the "President's Special War Order No. 1." This commanded "that all the disposable force of the Army of the Potomac, after providing safely for the defence of Washington, be formed into an expedition for the immediate object of seizing and occupying a point upon the railroad southwestward of what is known as Manassas Junction, all details to be in the discretion of the Commander-in-Chief, and the expedition to move before or on the 22d day of February next."[47] McClellan protested. He asked permission to submit in writing his objections to the overland route, and his reasons for preferring to advance by way of the Chesapeake. These arguments had doubtless already been considered in the course of his recent discussions with the President, yet Mr. Lincoln gave the desired consent. He even furnished McClellan with a basis for his memorandum, in the following note:

EXECUTIVE MANSION, WASHINGTON,
February 3, 1862.

MAJOR-GENERAL McCLELLAN,

My dear Sir: — You and I have distinct and different plans for a movement of the Army of the Potomac — yours to be down the Chesapeake, up the Rappahannock to Urbana, and across land to the terminus of the railroad on the York River; mine to move directly to a point on the railroad southwest of Manassas.

If you will give me satisfactory answers to the following questions, I shall gladly yield my plan to yours.

First, Does not your plan involve a greatly larger expenditure of time and money than mine?

Second, Wherein is a victory more certain by your plan than mine?

Third, Wherein is a victory more valuable by your plan than mine?

Fourth, In fact, would it not be less valuable in this, that it would break no great line of the enemy's communications, while mine would?

Fifth, In case of disaster, would not a retreat be more difficult by your plan than mine?

Yours truly,
ABRAHAM LINCOLN.[48]

These questions were never directly answered. What might be regarded as McClellan's replies to them were embodied in an elaborate statement of his views, addressed, on the same day, not to the President, but to the Secretary of War. Opening this paper with a defence of his course in not advancing until the Army of the Potomac was fully prepared for action, the General-in-Chief proceeded to give both plans of campaign detailed consideration. He opposed the attack upon Manassas in a series of ingenious objections, which were based primarily — as transpired too late — on a gross exaggeration of the enemy's strength. He advocated, with equal earnestness, the adoption of the Chesapeake route, by way preferably of Urbana. Should that fail him, however, as a landing point, Mob Jack Bay was suggested, or — "the worst coming to the worst" — Fortress Monroe. And these considerations brought the General to a significant summing up. "It is by no means certain," he wrote, "that we can beat them at Manassas. On the other line, I regard success as certain, by all the chances of war."[49] There was nothing equivocal about such language, and the writer flattered himself that it should have carried conviction.[50] "This letter," he said later, "must have produced some effect upon the mind of the President, since the execution of his order was not required, although it was not revoked as formally as it had been issued."[51]

True, the letter had "produced some effect" on Lincoln's mind, but hardly in the way implied by McClellan's contemptuous phrase. The President's confidence in the merits of his own plan remained unshaken. For political, no less than for military reasons, an immediate attack upon the enemy before Washington, by a column which should protect the Union Capital while advancing upon Richmond, appeared wiser to him than a flank movement that, uncovering Washington for a shorter march to the Confederate Capital, would still consume, in transportation down the Chesapeake, much more time and money. Experts, reviewing McClellan's plan since the war, along purely strategical lines, have differed widely in their opinions of its soundness. The President's plan, on the other hand, as more nearly meeting the requirements of the situation, had the approval, at the time, of some able soldiers, and of well-nigh all the civilians whom he consulted. Mr. Stanton, the new Secretary of War, was especially earnest in its support; and he urged Mr. Lincoln, as has been related, to insist upon having his way. Here is where the "effect," produced on the President's mind by McClellan's views, came into play. Though the General-in-Chief had failed to prove that the Chesapeake route was the better of the two, he had committed himself, in his letter, so unreservedly against the overland plan, as to put all thought of forcing it upon him out of the question. Lincoln's abundant common sense, to say nothing of his recent military studies, saved him from the blunder of ordering a commander upon a campaign in which that officer placed no confidence. The Chief Magistrate had, it is true, taken the reins into his own hands; yet he knew with unerring precision — as we have repeatedly seen — when to tighten and when to slacken his hold. So, despite the vigorous remonstrance of the Committee on the Conduct of the War, Secretary Stanton, and many other influential men, preparations were begun for transporting the army down the Chesapeake.

The President directed, however, that the troops should not leave Washington for this distant field, until the Baltimore and Ohio Railroad had been reopened, and the enemy's batteries on the Potomac destroyed. Here arose another source of disagreement between Lincoln and McClellan. According to the General's theory, these positions would necessarily be abandoned by the Confederates, as soon as his prospective operations on the Lower Chesapeake should be developed; but that this would inevitably be the result, he failed — no less than in the case of the project itself — to convince the President or his advisers. "They had," wrote McClellan scornfully, some years later, "neither the courage nor the military insight to understand the effect of the plan." [52] Yielding, nevertheless, to Mr. Lincoln's decided opinions, he reluctantly prepared to carry out the President's wishes in these two particulars. As the railroad was interrupted near Harper's Ferry, McClellan determined to cross the Upper Potomac at that point, in force, by means of a permanent bridge to be constructed of canal-boats, cover the rebuilding of the railroad-bridge, and push on to Winchester, where he expected to fight a battle. Meanwhile, the Confederate batteries on the Lower Potomac were to be stormed by a division under General Hooker. So sanguine was McClellan of the result that he assured Mr. Lincoln, before leaving Washington, of a brilliant and successful dash. Every contingency had seemingly been provided for. "If this move fails," he said, "I will have nobody to blame but myself." [53] In fact, there is reason to believe that, all his theories to the contrary notwithstanding, the General-in-Chief thought, at the time, of turning these simple operations into what the President had wanted — a decisive overland campaign.[54]

About Washington's birthday, — the date set by Mr. Lincoln, — an advance may be said to have been in progress. A strong force, collected near Harper's Ferry, held itself ready to move. The canal-boats lay in the Chesapeake and Ohio Canal, whence they were to be floated into the Potomac. Everything looked favorable for the immediate construction of a stout bridge and the rapid passage of a powerful army into Virginia. McClellan himself hastened to the spot. A considerable portion of his troops were under orders to follow. On February 26, he despatched back to the War Department an enthusiastic message. On the 27th, all was gloom and disappointment. When the canal-boats had, that morning, reached the lift-lock through which alone they could pass into the river, they were found to be too wide by several inches.[55] With this discovery, celerity of movement — the essential factor in the affair — became impossible. The expedition, as planned, was at once abandoned. McClellan countermanded his order for an advance from the Capital, and revoked, at the same time, Hooker's instructions to attack the batteries.[56] After taking measures to cover the restoration of the railroad, the General-in-Chief returned to Washington. Another brilliant project had come to naught, in rather a ridiculous manner. As some wag, at the time, remarked, it "died of lockjaw."

The fiasco at Harper's Ferry increased the number and bitterness of McClellan's opponents. In their denunciations to the President, they accused him, all told, of every fault that may be charged against an unsuccessful general, not stopping short of even the most heinous — treason to his cause. What impression, if any, such wild talk made upon Lincoln cannot now be known. Without really doubting the General's loyalty, he probably deemed it necessary to let him know how others felt on the subject. Perhaps the President hoped, by a revelation of this sort, to sting that self-satisfied officer into doing what had become as important to his impaired reputation as to the success of the Union arms. At all events, we have McClellan's own word for an extraordinary interview between Lincoln and himself.[57] The President, according to this account, sent for his General-in-Chief, early on the morning of the 8th of March. After expressing his chagrin at the outcome of the Harper's Ferry expedition,[58] Mr. Lincoln said that he desired to talk about another — "a very ugly matter." It had been represented to him, he continued, that the movement by way of the Lower Chesapeake "was conceived with the traitorous intent of removing its defenders from Washington, and thus giving over to the enemy the Capital and the government, thus left defenceless." If it was the President's purpose to arouse McClellan, he certainly succeeded; for the General resented, with hot indignation, this imputation on his honor. Mr. Lincoln hastened to assure him "that he merely repeated what others had said, and that he did not believe a word of it," himself. McClellan replied with a suggestion, by which he hoped to set all doubts on the subject at rest. He had called, he explained, a meeting of division commanders at his headquarters, that very morning, to consider another proposed attack upon the enemy's Potomac batteries. Why not lay before them, he asked, the question of the Chesapeake route? And to this the President readily consented.

It was more than a coincidence that Mr. Lincoln on the same day emphasized, by a step in another direction, the passing of McClellan's military supremacy. For some time the advisability of dividing the Army of the Potomac into army corps had been under consideration. That so large a body of troops could not be maneuvered to advantage by brigades and divisions was generally conceded. All the experienced officers whom the President consulted advised against a campaign in any but corps formation; every modern text-book that he could lay his hands on, as well as the practice in European warfare, sustained this counsel; and leading supporters of the administration, especially the Committee on the Conduct of the War, besought him to effect such an organization before the army took the field. McClellan, himself, acknowledged the wisdom of the measure. Nevertheless, when urged by Mr. Lincoln to form army corps, he declared his intention not to do so until active service "had indicated what general officers were best fitted to exercise those most important commands." Taking the ground, correctly enough, that incompetent men in such positions "might cause irreparable damage," he determined to pick his corps commanders, later on, with the greatest possible care.[59] It did not occur to him, apparently, that any one but he would venture to make these selections — they came so clearly within his province. Had he not, moreover, while at the zenith of his popularity, served notice on the administration concerning such very matters? In a letter addressed to Secretary Cameron, as early as September 8, 1861, McClellan had written: —

"I have selected general and staff officers with distinct reference to their fitness for the important duties that may devolve upon them. Any change or disposition of such officers without consulting the commanding General may fatally impair the efficiency of this army and the success of its operations. I therefore earnestly request that in future every general officer appointed upon my recommendation shall be assigned to this army; that I shall have full control of the officers and troops in this department; and that no orders shall be given respecting my command without my being first consulted. It is evident that I cannot otherwise be responsible for the success of our arms."[60]

The theory on which this precept rested was sound. But the all-powerful General, who asserted his prerogative with such spirit in September, 1861, had, during the intervening six months, frittered away, by this and that, as we have seen, much of the prestige essential to the lofty part he desired to play. A military rôle can be sustained, in the last analysis, by military prowess alone. The McClellan who stood before Lincoln on the defensive, in that early morning interview after Harper's Ferry, was a very different man, so to say, from the McClellan to whom Lincoln had deferred after Bull Run. At all events, the President treated him differently. For that very day, as soon as their conflicting plans of campaign were submitted to the division commanders, Mr. Lincoln, anticipating an advance either way, took the matter of army corps into his own hands. Without consulting the General-in-Chief, he framed the "President's General War Order No. 2," directing McClellan forthwith to organize that part of the Army of the Potomac which was intended for active operations into four corps; and assigning them, respectively, to the ranking division commanders, Generals

McDowell, Sumner, Heintzelman, and Keyes.[61] Three of these, it has been frequently remarked, were known to favor the President's rather than McClellan's plan. That they felt out of sympathy, to this extent at least, with the General-in-Chief, and that none of the appointments were, for other reasons, of an ideal character, cannot be gainsaid. Yet it was once in McClellan's power—his own partisans agree — to order things otherwise. Had he formed the army corps when Mr. Lincoln desired them, the selection of their commanders would, most likely, have been left to his judgment. As it was, lieutenants whom he would probably not have chosen were, at the eleventh hour, imposed upon him, to the exclusion of officers who enjoyed his confidence. McClellan's first intimation of these radical changes in his own army is said to have reached him only after the order had been issued. Surprised and pained beyond measure, he realized too late what embarrassment might have been averted in this quarter by more courteous attention to the President's wishes.

Meanwhile the council of war called by the General-in-Chief had taken place. Eight of the twelve generals present, without discussion or deliberation, voted offhand in favor of McClellan's plan.[62] At a subsequent interview between them and the President, in which the Secretary of War participated, these officers were put through a searching examination; but the same majority stood by their approval of the Chesapeake route. Before so strong an endorsement Mr. Lincoln's opposition fell away, once for all. Mr. Stanton, on the other hand, stubbornly persisted in his antagonism. Like Chase, Wade, Chandler, and so many other earnest leaders, the head of the War Department was fast losing confidence in the commander upon whom they had all looked, not many months previous, as the rising hope of the Union cause. McClellan's Fabian tactics cost him much. Perhaps the heaviest single price was Stanton's regard. Totally unlike Lincoln in this respect, the grim war minister, once a man had fallen under his displeasure, could never again entirely divest himself of the resulting prejudice. It was with more than his customary vehemence, therefore, that Stanton, believing firmly in the President's plan, opposed McClellan's. He decried — to repeat somewhat from a preceding chapter — the project under which more than one hundred thousand troops were to be set afloat in wooden bottoms to seek a battle-field many miles away, while the enemy lay fortified before the Capital. Stanton's ingenious reasoning — for the question was discussed at length — failed to move Mr. Lincoln. Admitting the force of the Secretary's objections, he remained steadfast in his decision to abide by the action of the council, and instructed him to proceed with the preparations for the campaign. McClellan's plan was to have right of way, after all.

How closely Mr. Lincoln, notwithstanding this concession, adhered to some of his purposes, may be gathered from the "President's General War Order No. 3." This, like its immediate predecessor, he issued without consulting McClellan, on that same eventful 8th of March. It prohibited any change of base by the Army of the Potomac, unless such a force were stationed around Washington as would, "in the opinion of the General-in-Chief and the commanders of all the army corps," leave that city "entirely secure." It ordered "an immediate effort to capture the enemy's batteries" upon the Lower Potomac; and, until this was accomplished, "no more than two army corps" were to embark on the Chesapeake. Finally, the movement down the bay was to begin "as early as the 18th day of March," with the General-in-Chief held personally "responsible" for attention to that date.[63] The peremptory, almost harsh tones of this order should have warned McClellan that he had won a precarious victory. Still, it may be doubted whether the President's rising ire, or his anxiety for the safety of Washington, made much of an impression on the General's mind. He was, however, greatly troubled over the restrictions laid upon him in these last two mandates of the President — General Orders Nos. 2 and 3. They are not, it is true, entirely defensible from a military point of view; yet McClellan had clearly brought them upon himself by his own errors, his dilatory tactics, and, above all, his total failure to recognize Lincoln's dual responsibility to the nation for success in the field as well as in the cabinet. It has been said, with some force, that a General-in-Chief who needed to be hampered by such orders had outlived his usefulness in that exalted office. Doubtless the President was approaching this conclusion, but he did not contemplate the removal of McClellan from the command of the particular army which owed so much of its discipline and enthusiasm to the General's administrative talents. Lincoln's faith in McClellan's star was far from spent. He still believed that this commander, at the head of the Army of the Potomac, — once they were fairly launched together upon a campaign, — would justify all his forbearance.

The test came sooner than the President had expected. Within twenty-four hours after Orders 2 and 3 were put forth, on Sunday, March 9, startling news reached Washington — the Confederate batteries on the Potomac had been abandoned, and the Army of Northern Virginia was retreating southward from Manassas. Incredulous, almost stupefied, at this unlooked-for intelligence, McClellan, as soon as it could be verified, ordered the entire army to move, the following day, upon the enemy's lines. Before he started, however, occurred a tilt between him and the Secretary of War, which illustrates down to how slender a thread had worn the once cordial ties between the General-in-Chief and the government. During that Sunday evening, McClellan telegraphed to Stanton, from the front: —

"In the arrangements for the advance of to-morrow it is impossible to carry into effect the arrangements for the formation of army corps. I am obliged to take groups as I find them and to move them by divisions. I respectfully ask a suspension of the order directing it, till the present movement be over."

To this the Secretary curtly replied: —

"I think it is the duty of every officer to obey the President's orders, nor can I see any reason why you should not obey them in present instance. I must therefore decline to suspend them."

At one o'clock A. M., McClellan sent this explanation over the wire: —

"You have entirely misunderstood me, and the idea I intended to convey was simply that I could not, under the pressure of the new aspect of affairs, immediately carry out the President's orders as to the formation of army corps. It is absolutely necessary that I should at once move divisions as they stand. If you require me to suspend movements until army corps can be formed, I will do so; but I regard it as a military necessity that the divisions should move to the front at once, without waiting for the formation of army corps. If it is your order to wait until the corps can be formed, I will, of course, wait. I will comply with the President's order as soon as possible. I intended to do so to-morrow, but circumstances have changed. If you desire it, I will at once countermand all the orders I have given for an advance until the formation of army corps is completed. I have only to add that the orders I have given to-night to advance early in the morning will be dictated solely by the present position of affairs. If the leave to suspend the order be granted, there will be no unreasonable delay in the formation of army corps. I await your reply here. If you so direct that I may countermand my orders at once, please reply at once."

Stanton promptly rejoined: —

"I do not understand the President's order as restraining you from any military movement by divisions or otherwise that circumstances in your judgment may render expedient, and I certainly do not wish to delay or change any movement whatever that you have made or desire to make. I only wish to avoid giving my sanction to a suspension of a policy which the President has ordered to be pursued. But if you think that the terms of the order as it stands would operate to retard or in any way restrain movements that circumstances require to be made before the army corps are formed, I will assume the responsibility of suspending the order for that purpose, and authorize you to make any movement by divisions or otherwise, according to your own judgment, without stopping to form the army corps. My desire is that you should exercise every power that you think present circumstances require to be exercised, without delay; but I want that you and I shall not seem to be desirous of opposing an order of the President without necessity. I say, therefore, move just as you think best now, and let the other matter stand until it can be done without impeding movements."

It was nearly three o'clock in the morning when the General closed the incident with this message:—

"Your reply received. The troops are in motion. I thank you for your despatch. It relieves me much, and you will be convinced that I have not asked too much of you." [64]

Redeeming his promise, three days later, McClellan constituted the army corps in accordance with Mr. Lincoln's orders.[65]

Important history was making in the mean time. The Army of the Potomac had started at last. Advancing into Virginia with unaccustomed celerity, it gallantly stormed those abandoned works at Centreville and Manassas. The recent tenants, it is true, were safely on their way to a new haven beyond the Rappahannock. As they had taken the precaution, moreover, to destroy the bridges behind them, there was nothing left for the disgusted pursuers but to retrace their steps from the deserted camps. On all sides were unmistakable indications of how inferior, in numbers and munitions of war, had been the Confederate force to the splendid array which it had kept at bay so long.

That the dismantled barracks evidently had not held one half the men McClellan affirmed to be there, looked bad enough; but that, for lack of sufficient heavy artillery, painted logs filled a number of the embrasures in the fortifications, was infinitely worse. These "Quaker guns," as they were called, made the whole North laugh. On the under side of its merriment, however, lay a feeling of mortification and disappointment that boded no good to the fame of the "Young Napoleon." Painfully alive to the blow-holes in his armor, he poured out the bitterness of his soul to the fond wife at home. "I regret," he wrote from Fairfax Court House, "that the rascals are after me again. I had been foolish enough to hope that when I went into the field they would give me some rest, but it seems otherwise. Perhaps I should have expected it. If I can get out of this scrape, you will never catch me in the power of such a set again. The idea of persecuting a man behind his back! I suppose they are now relieved from the pressure of their fears by the retreat of the enemy, and that they will increase in virulence."[66] Who "the rascals" were may be surmised. The men who had, week after week, supported the President's plan for immediate operations against the enemy's position at Manassas now claimed that Mr. Lincoln's judgment had been vindicated by the event. They grew hot over McClellan's failure to seize so cheap a victory when it lay within his grasp, and sarcastic at the manner in which vast hosts and impregnable ramparts had melted away together. What seemed most difficult to understand was the General's ignorance of how matters had been going within the lines of an enemy stationed, for over seven months, not more than a day's march from his camp.[67] McClellan's loyalty again became a debated question, and friends of the administration once more beset the Executive with appeals for his removal.

Circumstances had certainly conspired to place the General in an awkward situation; yet he, or more precisely speaking, his facile pen, was almost equal to the emergency. In his official papers he ascribes the Confederates' "very sudden" retreat to information which they had received of his intended movement down the Chesapeake, and he points to this retirement toward Richmond as conclusive proof that his projected operations would have compelled the evacuation of Manassas. Persisting, moreover, in his delusions, or those of his secret service officers, as to the enemy's strength, he claims to have found ample corroboration of their estimates. A stack of affidavits were introduced to bear out the official report of March 8 that credited the southern army before Washington with "115,500 men, about 300 field guns, and from 26 to 30 siege guns." Upon these figures he impales, with fine scorn, "the ignorance which led some journals at that time, and persons in high office, unwittingly to trifle with the reputation of an army, and to delude the country with Quaker-gun stories of the defences and gross understatements of the numbers of the enemy."[68] Verily McClellan's pen was mightier than his sword, yet it could not slay the facts. It is now established beyond a doubt that General Joseph E. Johnston, commanding the Confederate Army of Northern Virginia, had long regarded his position at Manassas and Centreville as untenable. Anticipating attack, he commenced on the 23d of February the retrograde movement which was skilfully completed on the 9th of March. So the "very sudden" retreat which McClellan and his eulogists charged to indiscreet disclosures of what took place at the council of March 8[69] had, in fact, been going on for two weeks previous to that date. We have General Johnston's own word for it that he received no warning concerning the Chesapeake plan, and that his withdrawal was due solely to fear of some such flank movement as Lincoln is now known to have advocated. An advance along this route the Confederate leader looked upon as "the most difficult to meet." True to the rules of strategy, he assumed that McClellan would discover the weak spot, and strike there.[70] But nothing, as we have seen, could convince the Union commander of his opportunity. During the very period in which he was declaring the President's plan impracticable, chiefly on the ground that the Manassas line held a force, variously estimated at from 115,500 to 150,000 men, Johnston's official report showed just 47,306 men, present for duty, in the entire Department of Northern Virginia.[71] McClellan, at the same time, had present for duty in the Army of the Potomac officers and men amounting to 185,420.[72] Nor does the General-in-Chief emerge in any better light from the episode of the imitation guns. His sweeping denial breaks down beneath the evidence of trustworthy men who saw them in the defences, to say nothing of General Johnston's explanation of how they came to be there. The Confederate commander, referring to his officers at Centreville, writes: —

"As we had not artillery enough for their works and for the army fighting elsewhere, at the same time, rough wooden imitations of guns were made, and kept near the embrasures, in readiness for exhibition in them. To conceal the absence of carriages, the embrasures were covered with sheds made of bushes. These were the Quaker guns afterward noticed in northern papers." [73]

At every essential point in this affair McClellan stands condemned. To what precise extent was of course not revealed until long thereafter; yet enough became known without delay to justify the opinion that he had been completely outgeneraled.

When failure overtakes a commander through his own repeated neglect to carry out the desires of his superiors, he becomes a proper subject for discipline. So at last thought Lincoln. Though "slow to smite and swift to spare," he could withhold the blow no longer. For, what the President's most influential advisers had not succeeded in bringing about, speedily ensued upon McClellan's fruitless "promenade" to Manassas. This revelation of how much the General's inaction probably cost the Union cause aroused Lincoln's belated indignation. All the pent-up irritation of weeks found vent in one mighty outburst of wrath. A scene not unlike that enacted by President Washington when he received the tidings of St. Clair's disaster is said to have taken place. Lincoln's passion was hailed by Senator Chandler, who related the incident, as an omen of better days. "Old Abe," said he exultingly, "is mad, and the war will now go on."[74] Before the Executive slept on the first night that saw the retreating Confederates securely encamped behind the Rappahannock, he issued the "President's Special War Order No. 3."[75] This mandate deposed McClellan from the command-in-chief on the ostensible ground that he had "personally taken the field," and limited his authority to the Department of the Potomac. All department commanders, furthermore, including several newly appointed, were instructed to report directly to the Secretary of War.[76] Here was a serious reverse in McClellan's fortunes, yet he knew nothing about it until the Washington newspapers reached Fairfax Court House on the following day. Taken "entirely by surprise," as he tells us, the General appears to have seen no reason — and how characteristic of the man that was! — for Mr. Lincoln's order, while his partisans resented the way in which the change had been made perhaps more than the act itself. Nevertheless, McClellan kissed the chastening rod. He straightway sent the President a graceful letter, in which, with expressions of esteem and gratitude, the writer promised cheerful submission.[77]

One of McClellan's first steps thereafter was to obey Mr. Lincoln's General Order No. 3, for a council of corps commanders. Summoning the four who were with him at Fairfax Court House, as has been narrated in a previous chapter, he laid the President's requirements before them. They unanimously pronounced the Chesapeake route by way of Urbana, on the Rappahannock, unavailable, since the enemy had retreated south of the river; and agreed that the projected operations down the bay could best be carried out — the navy coöperating — on the peninsula between the York and the James rivers, with Fortress Monroe as a base. They stipulated, moreover, that the force left behind for the protection of Washington should be sufficient "to give an entire feeling of security for its safety from menace." This required between 40,000 and 55,000 men, according to the commanders' several estimates, in which McClellan apparently acquiesced.[78] Though the Peninsula plan had been described by him, not many weeks before, as a last resort, to be adopted only when the worst came to the worst, he approved of that too, and telegraphed Mr. Stanton: "The council of commanders of army corps have unanimously agreed upon a plan of operations. General McDowell will at once proceed with it to Washington and lay it before you."

The Secretary immediately replied: "Whatever plan has been agreed upon, proceed at once to execute without losing an hour for my approval." [79]

Later in the day, however, came the President's approval, in a form which still further illustrates the temper of the government. Directing McClellan again to "leave Washington entirely secure," it authorized him to choose a new base anywhere between Fortress Monroe and the Capital, so long as he moved "the army at once in pursuit of the enemy, by some route." [80] Official courtesy does not admit of much stronger language; but between the lines we read, as plainly as did a noted war correspondent: —

"Go anywhere, move anywhere you please, only let us have an end of excuses — do *something*." [81]

McClellan complied. He made an address to his soldiers in approved Napoleonic style, and marched them to Alexandria, where transports were collecting for the voyage down the Chesapeake.

Before sailing, McClellan was again made to feel how great a change had come over his standing with the President. Mr. Lincoln, while on a visit to Alexandria, mentioned to him that he was "strongly pressed" by friends of Frémont to transfer Blenker's command of about 10,000 men from the Army of the Potomac to the newly created Mountain Department. It was not his intention, he added, when the General objected, to deprive McClellan of this division. Yet the discussion touched that officer on a sensitive spot. In the first flush of his power, during the autumn of 1861, he had forbidden his superiors to detach any troops from the army under him, in language even more dictatorial than that employed to protest against their appointment of officers without his consent;[82] and the President had meekly promised, at the time, to leave his force intact. Such promises are outlawed, however, as the circumstances under which they were given alter. Thus, no doubt, thought Mr. Lincoln six months later, in the spring of 1862. For, changing his mind a few days after the interview at Alexandria, he ordered Blenker's division to join Frémont. "I did so with great pain," he wrote to McClellan, "understanding that you would wish it otherwise. If you could know the full pressure of the case, I am confident that you would justify it, even beyond a mere acknowledgment that the Commander-in-Chief may order what he pleases."[83] This act has properly enough been condemned by military writers. Still, in justice to the President, it should be said that by placating the Frémont wing of the Republican Party, he hoped to keep united the support without which the war could not have been carried on. Unfortunately, his political cares evoked no sympathy from McClellan. The General, it is true, at a later interview, acquiesced reluctantly in what he regarded as an unwarrantable exercise of the supreme authority; but this was only after Mr. Lincoln had assured him — so McClellan relates — that no other troops should be withdrawn from his command. Yet, worse remained behind.

Hardly had McClellan, with part of his army, reached

Fortress Monroe, when a cry went up that he had left Washington insecure. An anxious investigation by the War Department followed. This revealed, as was fully narrated elsewhere, less than half the number of troops prescribed by the corps commanders, on guard over the city. Lincoln's order, so oft repeated, to leave the Capital "entirely secure" had been flatly disobeyed. That McClellan, after his recent discipline at the hands of the President, should again have ventured to pit his will against Lincoln's, in a matter of such moment, seems inconceivable. The General himself, as well as his defenders, disclaim that he did so. By what might fairly be called a plea in confession and avoidance, they assert that more than the required number of men were left at Manassas, in the valley of the Shenandoah, before Washington, and elsewhere; but they fail utterly to show, as indeed they cannot, that McClellan had heeded the President's explicit instructions to leave, "in and about Washington," the force deemed necessary for its protection by the council of corps commanders. Nor does it improve the General's case to treat with contempt Lincoln's acute anxiety for the safety of the National Capital.[84] Unfortunately situated as it was near the frontier, that city, on several occasions during the war, narrowly escaped capture. Such an event would have been damaging enough to the Union cause, at any time; in the spring or summer of 1862, it might have been fatal. The fall of Washington, to touch upon but one aspect of a manifold disaster, would most likely have precipitated European intervention — a proceeding against which the whole diplomatic strength of the administration had for months been strained, as against dissolution itself. It is not surprising, therefore, that the President placed the defence of the Capital above every other strategic consideration, or that he had again and again renewed his instructions to McClellan on the subject.

But the General had other views. Assuming that the

troops left in northern Virginia were ample, all told, to guard Washington, he had deliberately determined not to detach from his main army the number of men required for garrison duty by Mr. Lincoln's orders. Whether or not this belief was well founded has nothing to do with the fact of McClellan's insubordination. Equally beside the question is his much quoted argument that the safety of the Union Capital could best be secured on the Peninsula, by an advance in force against Richmond. Whether McClellan was correct, moreover, in believing that the Confederates would surely defend the lesser, rather than seize the greater prize, may be doubted. According to military rules, it is true, the defence of Washington lay at the gates of Richmond; but unluckily, some of the southern generals, like the fencer quoted in Macaulay, did not always fight by rule. Violating the very A B C of warfare, they more than once thrust in quarte when they should have thrust in tierce, and incidentally, be it said, made "a hit, a very palpable hit." Had Lee found the Army of the Potomac operating on the Peninsula, and Washington inadequately guarded, would he not have thrown all his strength into the capture of that city? To borrow one of his favorite expressions, might he not have swapped queens?[85] Or worse still, was there any assurance that he could not have held McClellan in check long enough to take the Federal piece, and return in time to defend his own? The Confederates had recently demonstrated their skill at blocking the Union general's way, with notably inferior numbers; while his record for deliberation hardly warranted much dependence upon him, if suddenly recalled from a distant field to rescue the Capital. That it should now be imperiled, or even subjected to a chance of peril, after so many cautions, aroused the President's just indignation. There seemed but a single thing for him to do. As soon as the extent of his lieutenant's disobedience was definitely ascertained, he ordered one of the army corps, which had not yet embarked for the Peninsula, to be held back for the protection of Washington. General McDowell's corps, comprising about 36,000 men and 68 guns, was accordingly detached from the Army of the Potomac. Mr. Lincoln, at the same time, fearing lest Fortress Monroe — recently placed under McClellan's command — might also be stripped of its troops, further humiliated the General by practically withdrawing the post from his control.[86]

The news of these changes staggered McClellan. He was especially distressed over the loss of McDowell's corps, to which had been assigned the important duty of turning the Confederate positions at the lower end of the Peninsula, while the main body attacked in front. "It is the most infamous thing that history has recorded," read his private comment on the President's course, at the time; and he straightway — to quote him further — "raised an awful row." [87] Protest followed protest, until Lincoln replied: —

"Your despatches, complaining that you are not properly sustained, while they do not offend me, do pain me very much.

"Blenker's division was withdrawn from you before you left here, and you knew the pressure under which I did it, and, as I thought, acquiesced in it — certainly not without reluctance.

"After you left I ascertained that less than 20,000 unorganized men, without a single field-battery, were all you designed to be left for the defense of Washington and Manassas Junction, and part of this even was to go to General Hooker's old position; General Banks's corps, once designed for Manassas Junction, was divided and tied up on the line of Winchester and Strasburg, and could not leave it without again exposing the Upper Potomac and the Baltimore and Ohio Railroad. This presented (or would present, when McDowell and Sumner should be gone) a great temptation to the enemy to turn back from the Rappahannock and sack Washington. My explicit order that Washington should, by the judgment of all the commanders of corps, be left entirely secure, had been neglected. It was precisely this that drove me to detain McDowell.

"I do not forget that I was satisfied with your arrangement to leave Banks at Manassas Junction; but when that arrangement was broken up and nothing was substituted for it, of course I was not satisfied. I was constrained to substitute something for it myself.

"And now allow me to ask, do you really think I should permit the line from Richmond *via* Manassas Junction to this city to be entirely open, except what resistance could be presented by less than 20,000 unorganized troops? This is a question which the country will not allow me to evade."[88]

Yet McClellan would not, or could not, then or thereafter, recognize how proper was Mr. Lincoln's solicitude. Indeed, the General's military harness seems to have been equipped with blinkers of so prodigious a size that, while he saw his own ends distinctly enough, the duties and prerogatives of this mere civilian — President though he was — made but a hazy impression upon his mind. Only such purblindness can account for the man's conduct. It never, apparently, occurred to him that he was in any way at fault; no more than it did to certain military critics who, touched by the plight in which he now found himself, lost sight of his own responsibility in bringing it about, and cried out against the administration. Yet the facts confute them. Whatever may have been the errors of strategy chargeable during this luckless campaign to Lincoln, Stanton, or McClellan — for honors were easy in that respect — the loss of McDowell's corps, as well as the resultant train of mishaps, lies, beyond a doubt, at the recalcitrant General's door.

McClellan's disappointments rapidly multiplied. Not only did he find himself deprived of the flanking column that was to have turned Yorktown, but the gunboats upon which he had erroneously depended to reduce its batteries failed him also; while the Warwick River, represented on his faulty maps as off to one side, proved to be a fortified barrier reaching almost across the Peninsula. Another General — or rather a truly great one — at the head of so powerful an army, would have modified his plans to meet these changed conditions, and have pushed on. Not so McClellan. Seized with his old weakness for underrating his own strength and overrating that of the enemy, he sat down before Yorktown to besiege the place scientifically. Yet Magruder, the Confederate commander, opposed him, at first, with but 11,000 men, all told. Six thousand of these were required for the fortifications at Yorktown and elsewhere, leaving only 5,000 to defend the line of the Warwick, thirteen miles across the Peninsula. This latter obstacle could easily have been pierced by McClellan's overwhelming force, had he acted promptly. When it became apparent, therefore, that the opening skirmishes were not to be followed up forthwith by vigorous fighting, Magruder could hardly believe his good luck. He reported jubilantly: —

"Thus, with 5,000 men exclusive of the garrisons, we stopped and held in check over 100,000 of the enemy. Every preparation was made in anticipation of another attack by the enemy; the men slept in the trenches and under arms, but to my utter surprise he permitted day after day to elapse without an assault." [89]

Another leading Confederate officer wrote to Richmond, in terms of mingled contempt and astonishment: —

"No one but McClellan could have hesitated to attack." [90]

Meanwhile Mr. Lincoln, not less surprised, had telegraphed to the Union commander: —

"I think you better break the enemy's line from Yorktown to Warwick River at once." [91]

Whereupon McClellan relieved his mind privately with the scornful comment: —

"I was much tempted to reply that he had better come and do it himself."[92]

In official despatches, however, to the President and to the Secretary of War, he lamented, on the following day, that he could not attack because his diminished ranks numbered but 85,000 men, while the enemy's had been increased to "100,000 and probably more." It is now known how extravagant this figure was. No considerable additions to Magruder's small force were made for several days; and when reënforcements did come, in the course of the month, they raised the effective strength of Johnston, his successor, to just 55,633 men.[93] McClellan's failure to attack before these new troops arrived was indefensible. Had he obeyed Lincoln, the Union army would not have wasted the precious month before Yorktown, that enabled the South to concentrate its energies around Richmond; the Peninsular campaign would have furnished a vastly different story; and the "Young Napoleon" might have led a triumph in the Confederate Capital, after all.

These circumstances the downright common sense of the President must have grasped as he hastened to answer McClellan's complaints.

"There is a curious mystery," he wrote, "about the number of the troops now with you. When I telegraphed you on the 6th, saying you had over 100,000 with you, I had just obtained from the Secretary of War a statement, taken as he said from your own returns, making 108,000 then with you and *en route* to you. You now say you will have but 85,000 when all *en route* to you shall have reached you. How can this discrepancy of 23,000 be accounted for?

"As to General Wool's command [at Fortress Monroe], I understand it is doing for you precisely what a like number of your own would have to do if that command was away. I suppose the whole force which has gone forward to you is with you by this time; and if so, I think it is the precise time for you to strike a blow. By delay the enemy will relatively gain upon you — that is, he will gain faster by fortifications and reinforcements than you can by reinforcements alone.

"And once more let me tell you, it is indispensable to you that you strike a blow. I am powerless to help this. You will do me the justice to remember I always insisted that going down the bay in search of a field, instead of fighting at or near Manassas, was only shifting and not surmounting a difficulty; that we would find the same enemy and the same or equal intrenchments at either place. The country will not fail to note — is noting now — that the present hesitation to move upon an intrenched enemy is but the story of Manassas repeated.

"I beg to assure you that I have never written you or spoken to you in greater kindness of feeling than now, nor with a fuller purpose to sustain you, so far as in my most anxious judgment I consistently can; but you must act."[94]

Unfortunately, advice from this quarter was as cheap as ever in the estimation of the General commanding. His overweening professional conceit would not allow him to admit that Lincoln could be right in a military matter, or that there was any parallel between Manassas and Yorktown. So the siege continued. It went forward with a precision which would have done credit to the allies in Flanders. Yet McClellan was not so much occupied that he could not find time to keep up an almost incessant demand for more men. Yielding at last to his entreaties, the President, as has been told more at length elsewhere, sent down Franklin's division of McDowell's corps. We have seen how these reënforcements lay below Yorktown a whole fortnight, idly in the transports; and how, when preparations for a grand assault all along the line had been nearly completed, the beleaguered Confederates contrived to

"fold their tents, like the Arabs,
And as silently steal away."

Lincoln's phrase, "the story of Manassas repeated," had been verified in more ways than one. For the second time in eight weeks, McClellan led the Army of the Potomac into deserted trenches, under conditions that rendered his victory a tactical defeat; and for the second time, the President's directions to attack, had they been followed, would have averted a costly blunder.

McClellan of course blamed this inauspicious opening of the Peninsular campaign on the authorities at Washington. Nor were they less answerable, according to his Own Story, for the failures that followed. A morbid belief in the jealousy of Lincoln and his advisers had taken firm hold of him. He fancied them engaged in a conspiracy to sacrifice the Army of the Potomac rather than allow its commander to reap the political reward which might result from its success. "That they were not honest," he says in his book, "is proved by the fact that, having failed to force me to advance at a time when an advance would have been madness, they withheld the means of success when I was in contact with the enemy, and finally relieved me from command when the game was in my hands. They determined that I should not succeed, and carried out their determinations only too well and at a fearful sacrifice of blood, time, and treasure."[95] Having worked himself into this frame of mind, McClellan — we are not surprised to find — easily traversed the narrow interval between contempt for his superiors and something akin to hatred. In fact, from the beginning to the end of the Peninsular campaign, his private and at times even his official utterances reveal far more enmity toward the administration than toward the opposing foe.

To what extreme the General's embittered feelings carried him, a few extracts may perhaps sufficiently show. Writing to his wife, on the steamer which conveyed him down the Chesapeake, he exults over his escape from "that sink of iniquity," the National Capital. A few days later, after the McDowell episode, he sends her this soothing message: —

"Don't worry about the wretches; they have done nearly their worst, and can't do much more. I am sure that I will win in the end, in spite of all their rascality. History will present a sad record of these traitors who are willing to sacrifice the country and its army for personal spite and personal aims. The people will soon understand the whole matter."

During the siege of Yorktown, he lamented: —

"I am tired of public life; and even now, when I am doing the best I can for my country in the field, I know that my enemies are pursuing me more remorselessly than ever, and 'kind friends' are constantly making themselves agreeable by informing me of the pleasant predicament in which I am — the rebels on one side, and the Abolitionists and other scoundrels on the other."

A few days thereafter, the fond wife at home received this despondent note: —

"I feel that the fate of a nation depends upon me, and I feel that I have not one single friend at the seat of government."

So the General punctuated his whole luckless expedition with acrimonious faultfindings. Achilles crying, —

"My wrongs, my wrongs, my constant thought engage,"

was not more dismal. On one occasion, McClellan writes:

"My government, alas! is not giving me any aid."

On another, a midnight postscript reads: —

"Those hounds in Washington are after me again."

Then he explains: —

"I am as anxious as any human being can be to finish this war. Yet when I see such insane folly behind me, I feel that the final salvation of the country demands the utmost prudence on my part, and that I must not run the slightest risk of disaster, for if anything happened to this army, our cause would be lost. . . . But I will yet succeed, notwithstanding all they do and leave undone in Washington to prevent it. I would not have on my conscience what those men have for all the world."

Still later, the sympathetic helpmeet is assured: —

"You do not feel one bit more bitterly towards those people than I do. I do not say much about it, but I fear they have done all that cowardice and folly can do to ruin our poor country, and the blind people seem not to see it. It makes my blood boil when I think of it."

And again: —

"I am sick and weary of all this business. I am tired of serving fools. God help my country! He alone can save it."[96]

Needless to add, when our country was saved, the writer of those letters had no hand in the operation. Saviours of nations are made of different stuff.

Side by side with the General's unsoldierlike, almost childish railings to Mrs. McClellan against the government must be considered his official despatches. If less violent than his private messages, they still evince a spirit of antagonism, which at times breaks through all proper restraint. As the Duke of Wellington, when he came to publish his despatches, was righted in the good opinion of those who had misjudged him, it may be said reversely of the American commander that a similar publication on his part has caused him to fall in the estimation of many war-time admirers. To judge by a few of McClellan's military communications, he fancied himself and Lincoln to be playing some sort of a game, with men for the counters and personal glory for the stakes. It seems as if the General accused the administration of cheating over the count, and as if his incessant calls for more troops must be satisfied or there would be an end of the whole affair, with the President overwhelmed beneath a carefully fixed responsibility for the failure. McClellan's pet delusion, moreover, that the enemy outnumbered him two to one, apparently accompanied him throughout the campaign.

After repeating this belief, at some length, in a letter to Mr. Lincoln from Cumberland, he wrote: —

"I most respectfully and earnestly urge upon your excellency that the opportunity has come for striking a fatal blow at the enemies of the Constitution, and I beg that you will cause this army to be reinforced without delay by all the disposable troops of the government. I ask for every man that the War Department can send me." [97]

In rather a sharper vein, on the day after the battle of Hanover Court House, he telegraphed to the War Department: —

"It is the policy and duty of the government to send me by water all the well-drilled troops available. I am confident that Washington is in no danger. . . . It cannot be ignored that a desperate battle is before us; if any regiments of good troops remain unemployed, it will be an irreparable fault committed." [98]

Another despatch, sent at about the same time, read: —

"The enemy are even in greater force than I had supposed. I will do all that quick movements can accomplish, but you must send me all the troops you can, and leave to me full latitude as to choice of commanders." [99]

McClellan's insistence upon absolute authority in the field was theoretically correct. His disobedience, however, of the President's directions concerning the safety of Washington had seriously impaired the General's title to untrammeled command over one particular column, at least. When McDowell finally advanced overland to coöperate with him, Mr. Lincoln especially stipulated that the junior officer should retain control of all his troops, and that he should receive from the General commanding no orders which would place him out of position to cover the Capital. Nevertheless, as these reënforcements approached, McClellan telegraphed to the Secretary of War: —

"It ought to be distinctly understood that McDowell and his troops are completely under my control. I received a telegram from him requesting that McCall's division might be placed so as to join him immediately on his arrival.

"That request does not breathe the proper spirit. Whatever troops come to me must be disposed of so as to do the most good. I do not feel that, in such circumstances as those in which I am now placed, General McDowell should wish the general interests to be sacrificed for the purpose of increasing his command.

"If I cannot fully control all his troops, I want none of them, but would prefer to fight the battle with what I have, and let others be responsible for the results." [100]

This ultimatum apparently received no attention. And as McDowell was again recalled, at the eleventh hour, to the defence of Washington, the question raised by McClellan never came to an issue. Some time later, on the eve of his Seven Days' Retreat, the "Young Napoleon," still hedging against failure, telegraphed to Stanton: —

"The rebel force is stated at 200,000, including Jackson and Beauregard. I shall have to contend against vastly superior odds, if these reports be true. But this army will do all in the power of men to hold their position and repulse any attack.

"I regret my great inferiority in numbers, but feel that I am in no way responsible for it, as I have not failed to represent repeatedly the necessity of reinforcements; that this was the decisive point, and that all the available means of the government should be concentrated here. I will do all that a general can do with the splendid army I have the honor to command, and, if it is destroyed by overwhelming numbers, can at least die with it and share its fate.

"But if the result of the action, which will probably occur to-morrow or within a short time, is a disaster, the responsibility cannot be thrown on my shoulders; it must rest where it belongs." [101]

The President's reply was a trifle firmer, though not

less kind than previous messages with which he had sought to encourage this weak-kneed campaigner. Your despatch, he wrote, "suggesting the probability of your being overwhelmed by 200,000, and talking of where the responsibility will belong, pains me very much. I give you all I can, and act on the presumption that you will do the best you can with what you have; while you continue ungenerously, I think, to assume that I could give you more if I would. I have omitted and shall omit no opportunity to send you reinforcements whenever I possibly can."[102]

But such assurances were in vain. Neither fair words nor additional troops — the administration had responded from time to time with both — served to mollify McClellan's rancor. On the contrary, they seemed to act merely as water upon his mill, for he went right on grinding out more complaints.

Amidst the bloodshed and disaster of the "Seven Days" that followed, the General's truculence, as has been set forth in a previous chapter, reached its shrillest note. At midnight, after the defeat of Gaines's Mill, he despatched a report of the battle to Secretary Stanton. Judging him by this production, we should say in passing, that McClellan, whatever may have been his habitual bravery, was not then eminently endowed with 12 P. M. courage. The message closed with these extraordinary lines: —

"In addition to what I have already said, I only wish to say to the President that I think he is wrong in regarding me as ungenerous when I said that my force was too weak. I merely intimated a truth which to-day has been too plainly proved. If, at this instant, I could dispose of ten thousand (10,000) fresh men, I could gain the victory to-morrow.

"I know that a few thousand more men would have changed this battle from a defeat to a victory. As it is, the government must not and cannot hold me responsible for the result.

"I feel too earnestly to-night. I have seen too many dead and wounded comrades to feel otherwise than that the government has not sustained this army. If you do not do so now, the game is lost.

"If I save this army now, I tell you plainly that I owe no thanks to you or to any other persons in Washington.

"You have done your best to sacrifice this army." [103]

Insubordination could go no further. It may be doubted whether any general ever before sent from stricken field such a message to his government. Even after making due allowance for the terrible strain under which McClellan must have labored when he wrote the despatch, such insolence seems unpardonable. Though directed at Stanton, the stroke was manifestly meant for Lincoln as well, with an eye, perhaps, to its effect upon the onlooking public in the background.[104] How the blow was softened as it passed through the War Department telegraph office has already been told. Yet enough of the message, as we have seen, reached the General's superiors to carry home his accusation that they had failed to sustain the army, and were responsible for its defeat. Any other President would probably have made short work of the insult; but Lincoln here, as elsewhere, was incapable of turning into a personal affair what vitally concerned the welfare of the nation. His self-surrender appears to have been as complete in the one direction as was McClellan's egotism in the other. The President's anxious thoughts were fixed upon the Army of the Potomac, not upon its General or himself. For between the lines of this wild denunciation he read panic and disaster. It appeared to him that nothing but the imminent danger of losing the whole army — and such a catastrophe had lately been more than hinted at — would account for McClellan's bitter words. Overlooking them entirely, Lincoln put all his heart into this reply, which was speedily placed on the wire: —

"Save your army, at all events. Will send reinforcements as fast as we can. Of course they cannot reach you to-day, to-morrow, or next day. I have not said you were ungenerous for saying you needed reinforcements. I thought you were ungenerous in assuming that I did not send them as fast as I could. I feel any misfortune to you and your army quite as keenly as you feel it yourself. If you have had a drawn battle, or a repulse, it is the price we pay for the enemy not being in Washington. We protected Washington, and the enemy concentrated on you. Had we stripped Washington, he would have been upon us before the troops could have gotten to you. Less than a week ago you notified us that reinforcements were leaving Richmond to come in front of us. It is the nature of the case, and neither you nor the government is to blame. Please tell at once the present condition and aspect of things." [105]

Before McClellan could relieve the President's anxiety, his communications were cut, and the Army of the Potomac was again fighting its way to a safe haven at Harrison's Landing. Here the Peninsular campaign presently came to an end, one of the costliest failures of the war.

On what ground, if any, could this lack of success be charged against the administration? Was it true that Lincoln and his advisers were jealous of McClellan, and conspired to destroy him, together with his army, by withholding reënforcements? Of the General's disfavor in certain governmental quarters, there can be no doubt. Before the opening of the Peninsular campaign he had lost standing, as we have seen, with many of the strong men by whom the President was surrounded. But we have also seen how loyally Lincoln stood by the commander of his choice against all comers; how he supported him, moreover, with "good measure, pressed down, and shaken together, and running over," through the delays and disappointments of the winter. Taking sides with neither McClellanites nor anti-McClellanites, — for unhappily this had become a matter of factions, — the President viewed every question as it arose, with an eye single to the preservation of the Union. Even the appeal to Cæsar that the General's military fame would become a menace to his superior's tenure of office had failed in its purpose. When one of Lincoln's friends warned him of McClellan's reputed ambition to reach the White House, the President answered: —

"I am perfectly willing, if he will only put an end to this war."[106]

That, however, is just what the General's opponents believed him incapable of doing. Their distrust of him, need we add, was deepened by his deliberate attempt to carry off down the Chesapeake troops which, under the Chief Magistrate's orders, should have been left to guard Washington. Nevertheless, McClellan's claim that these leaders tried to compass his defeat on the Peninsula is as absurd as it is unfounded. Such treason could have been accomplished through only one of two men in the government — Lincoln or Stanton.

The Secretary of War, despite his occasional outbursts of indignation over the General's course, gave the Army of the Potomac, as far as the records show, conscientious support;[107] and the discussions on this subject that have outlived the war furnish no substantial proofs to the contrary. While recriminations were at their height, moreover, during the summer of 1862, a calm, straightforward statement made by Mr. Lincoln, at a public meeting, obviously placed the matter in its proper light.

"There has been a very widespread attempt," said he, "to have a quarrel between General McClellan and the Secretary of War. Now, I occupy a position that enables me to observe that these two gentlemen are not nearly so deep in the quarrel as some pretending to be their friends. General McClellan's attitude is such that, in the very selfishness of his nature, he cannot but wish to be successful, and I hope he will; and the Secretary of War is in precisely the same situation. If the military commanders in the field cannot be successful, not only the Secretary of

War, but myself — for the time being the master of them both — cannot but be failures. I know General McClellan wishes to be successful, and I know he does not wish it any more than the Secretary of War for him, and both of them together no more than I wish it. Sometimes we have a dispute about how many men General McClellan has had, and those who would disparage him say that he has had a very large number, and those who would disparage the Secretary of War insist that General McClellan has had a very small number. The basis for this is, there is always a wide difference, and on this occasion perhaps a wider one than usual, between the grand total on McClellan's rolls and the men actually fit for duty; and those who would disparage him talk of the grand total on paper, and those who would disparage the Secretary of War talk of those at present fit for duty. General McClellan has sometimes asked for things that the Secretary of War did not give him. General McClellan is not to blame for asking for what he wanted and needed, and the Secretary of War is not to blame for not giving when he had none to give. And I say here, as far as I know, the Secretary of War has withheld no one thing at any time in my power to give him. I have no accusation against him. I believe he is a brave and able man, and I stand here, as justice requires me to do, to take upon myself what has been charged on the Secretary of War, as withholding from him."[108]

This narrows the question down, and properly so, to how the President treated McClellan on the Peninsula.

The army of invasion, according to the original estimate of its commander, was to comprise "from 110,000 to 140,000" troops. War Department returns show that 121,500 men were transported, at the outset, to Fortress Monroe. McClellan may consequently be said to have started on his campaign with an effective force equal at least to the minimum number that he had required. Notwithstanding this, Lincoln strained every effort, from beginning to end, in his anxiety to satisfy the General's strident calls for more. When McClellan, a few days after his arrival on the Peninsula, despatched that he would hold himself "responsible for the results" of the campaign, if he could have Franklin's division, the 12,000 men constituting that splendid body were immediately forwarded. They failed, as we know, to be utilized in time; but the President was not deterred by the disappointment from meeting further demands, to the best of his ability. In fact, his coöperation later drew from the insatiable General this acknowledgment: —

"I am glad to learn that you are pressing forward reinforcements so vigorously. I shall be in perfect readiness to move forward and take Richmond the moment McCall reaches here and the ground will admit the passage of artillery." [109]

McCall's 10,000 men duly arrived. McClellan's promises, however, as in the case of Franklin, went by default. He now wanted the rest of McDowell's detained corps, from which these two divisions had been detached. That command, after starting several times to join him, was each time recalled to the defence of the Capital. It never reached McClellan, and finally participated, despite McDowell's own earnest protests, in the government's faulty tactics against Jackson in the Shenandoah valley.[110] Other reënforcements had, however, been sent to the Army of the Potomac, so that by the middle of June, over 39,000 men were, according to McClellan's own official returns, added to his original force. In brief, as may be seen at a glance over the figures, there were enough Union troops, from first to last, on the Peninsula, to take Richmond.

At every point throughout the campaign the northern forces outnumbered — and at times heavily so — their southern foes; but McClellan failed to bring his entire strength into action. He fought battle after battle with inferior numbers, while unemployed divisions stood idle within striking distance. The conclusion is inevitable.

This commander, who kept the wires hot with demands for reënforcements, and accused the administration of treason because he did not get as many as he wanted, had more men than he knew how to use. Napoleon's opinion that the Archduke Charles and he, himself, were the only men of his day who could maneuver one hundred thousand troops, would evidently not have been modified in favor of his American namesake. McClellan's errors under this head, however, were more than once redeemed by the conduct of the army, which he had so effectively disciplined. Officers and men fought their way from Williamsburg to Malvern Hill like heroes. The story of the Peninsular campaign, which, by the way, it does not lie within the scope of this work to tell, abounds in brilliant exploits. Twice, perhaps three times, the Confederate Capital seemed within the Union grasp. A Grant, a Sherman, a Thomas, or a Hooker would have marched into Richmond; but the talented McClellan, without initiative or dash in the field, retreated from his victories. Through the cloud of controversy, in which he and his friends have tried to envelop these operations, looms the rigid truth that McClellan was again outgeneraled. What lions he had to slay were not in far-away Washington. They blocked his path right on the Peninsula, in the shape successively of three able Confederate commanders — J. Bankhead Magruder, Joseph E. Johnston, and Robert E. Lee.

McClellan's attempt to shift the blame for his failure upon Stanton, Chase, and the rest was bad enough — to hint, even, that the President desired his defeat was monstrous. Any formal refutation of such a charge would almost seem insulting to the memory of the most magnanimous public man of his time. Yet this topic should not be dismissed without reference, at least, to Lincoln's earnest interest in the campaign. His yearning for success on the Peninsula was pathetic. Moving, like the central figure of some old Greek tragedy, through the shadow of successive misfortunes, he seems to have entered into every conflict, though he could not be actually seen to take part in any. And at the close of these three harrowing months, as the action reaches its climax, we find him in an agony of disappointment, second not even to that of McClellan, himself. "When the Peninsula campaign terminated suddenly at Harrison's Landing," said the President to a friend, "I was as nearly inconsolable as I could be and live."[111] Indeed, only one whose soul was bound up in the hope that McClellan might win, would have sent the General such messages, or have suffered such answers, as passed between them. A father advising, chiding, encouraging, by turns, a wilful son could not have treated this rasping officer with more uniform indulgence. We rise from a reading of their correspondence with a nicer perception of the President's nobility of character — a keener admiration than ever of his rugged strength. Strong enough to hold McClellan where he had put him, in the teeth of perhaps as powerful an opposition as has ever been massed against a commander; strong enough to ignore the signs which foreshadowed McClellan's political rivalry; and strong, above all, in the perfect self-control with which he met McClellan's unmerited reproaches, Lincoln manifested, throughout this trying period, how high he deserves to rank among the masters of men.

With the arrival of the army at Harrison's Landing, fresh perplexities beset the President. He was not ready yet to give up its commander, though that officer had hardly a friend left at court. Stirred by the fruitless sacrifices of the campaign, McClellan's opponents now redoubled their efforts to bring about his removal. In their prejudiced eyes, the embattled march to the James River, which he had described as a change of base, was a retreat, pure and simple. Whatever the movement may be called, — it partook, in fact, of the nature of both, — Lincoln recognized how skilful had been those defensive operations on the way, that finally saved the army from destruction. Hence there were no reproaches from the White

House for the unsuccessful General. When he announced, on the 2d of July, that his entire force had reached the protection of the gunboats, the President, haggard with suspense, telegraphed:—

"I am satisfied that yourself, officers, and men have done the best you could. All accounts say better fighting was never done. Ten thousand thanks for it." [112]

As if not content with this praise, which McClellan himself, by the way, termed "kind," the General entered a special plea for more, after the following fashion:—

"Never did such a change of base, involving a retrograde movement, and under incessant attacks from a most determined and vastly more numerous foe, partake so little of disorder. . . . When all the circumstances of the case are known, it will be acknowledged by all competent judges, that the movement just completed by this army is unparalleled in the annals of war. Under the most difficult circumstances, we have preserved our trains, our guns, our material, and, above all, our honor." [113]

To which Mr. Lincoln promptly responded:—

"Be assured, the heroism and skill of yourself, officers, and men, is and forever will be appreciated. If you can hold your present position, we shall hive the enemy yet." [114]

But to "hive the enemy," which had driven the Grand Army of the Potomac to cover, required, McClellan asserted, heavy reënforcements. "I need 50,000 more men," he had telegraphed the day before his arrival at Harrison's Landing, "and with them I will retrieve our fortunes." [115]

To which the President had made one of his characteristic replies. "Your despatch of Tuesday morning," it read, "induces me to hope your army is having some rest. In this hope allow me to reason with you a moment. When you ask for 50,000 men to be promptly sent you, you surely labor under some gross mistake of fact. Recently you sent papers showing your disposal of forces made last spring for the defence of Washington and advising a return to that plan. I find it included in and about Washington 75,000 men. Now, please be assured I have not men enough to fill that very plan by 15,000. All of Frémont's in the valley, all of Banks's, all of McDowell's not with you, and all in Washington, taken together, do not exceed, if they reach, 60,000. With Wool and Dix added to those mentioned, I have not, outside of your army, 75,000 men east of the mountains. Thus the idea of sending you 50,000, or any other considerable force, promptly, is simply absurd. If, in your frequent mention of responsibility, you have the impression that I blame you for not doing more than you can, please be relieved of such impression. I only beg that in like manner you will not ask impossibilities of me. If you think you are not strong enough to take Richmond just now, I do not ask you to try just now. Save the army, material and personal, and I will strengthen it for the offensive again as fast as I can. The Governors of eighteen States offer me a new levy of 300,000, which I accept." [116] There can be no doubt of Lincoln's intention, when this letter was written, to support McClellan in an early resumption of his campaign.

From every available source, meanwhile, from Hunter at Hilton Head, Burnside at New Berne, Halleck at Corinth, and certain commands around Washington, detachments were ordered to the Peninsula. Most of these, it should be said, for one reason or another, never reached McClellan. Yet had they all come, his appetite would probably still have remained unappeased. In less than three days from the time of that promise to "retrieve our fortunes" with "50,000 more men," he wrote:—

"To accomplish the great task of capturing Richmond and putting an end to this rebellion reinforcements should be sent to me rather much over than much less than 100,000 men." [117]

The difference in these figures puzzled Mr. Lincoln, as did the more startling statement, in the same despatch:—

"It is of course impossible to estimate as yet our losses, but I doubt whether there are to-day more than 50,000 men with their colors."

That the army had shrunk to anything like the extent thus indicated was inconceivable to the President. He could not hope to learn the facts, however, from McClellan's inconsistent messages; nor was he disposed, in view of the partisan feelings that had been aroused, to rely on the reports of others. There appeared to be no alternative for him but to judge of the situation at Harrison's Landing with his own eyes. So, on the 8th of July, Lincoln paid McClellan a visit.

The President stayed less than twenty-four hours, but he spent the time to advantage. A hasty inspection of the army, and conferences with its principal officers, sufficiently revealed the condition of affairs. McClellan's 50,000 men had unaccountably become 86,500.[118] The days of miracle-workers were past, so no one suggested that he had, like the King of the Myrmidons, recruited his ranks overnight from among certain insects, which plagued the camp on the banks of the James. But what troubled Lincoln more than this discrepancy between the commander's understated figures and his actual strength was the large number of soldiers, a host in itself, still missing from the ranks. "Sending men to that army," he once said, "is like shoveling fleas across a barn-yard — not half of them get there."[119] And shortly after this visit, the President, with official returns before him, thus summed up his conclusions on the subject, in a despatch to McClellan: —

"I am told that over 160,000 men have gone into your army on the Peninsula. When I was with you the other day, we made out 86,500 remaining, leaving 73,500 to be accounted for. I believe 23,500 will cover all the killed, wounded, and missing in all your battles and skirmishes, leaving 50,000 who have left otherwise. Not more than 5,000 of these have died, leaving 45,000 of your army still alive and not with it. I believe half or two thirds of them are fit for duty to-day. Have you any more perfect knowledge of this than I have? If I am right, and you had these men with you, you could go into Richmond in the next three days. How can they be got to you, and how can they be prevented from getting away in such numbers for the future?"[120]

McClellan's reply was hardly satisfactory. He felt confident, he said, that so many men had not reached him; but he admitted that there were 40,000 absentees, over 34,000 of whom were absent by authority. His explanation of how this surprising number got away on leave, during the very period in which he clamored most desperately for additional troops, was far from adequate.[121] Nor did Mr. Lincoln take much comfort in the admission, "If I could receive back the absentees and could get my sick men up, I would need but small reinforcements to enable me to take Richmond."[122] Unfortunately, "ifs" capture no citadels. So we presently find McClellan telegraphing to the President, as of old, "It appears manifestly to be our policy to concentrate here everything we can possibly spare from less important points,"[123] etc., etc. And thus his dreary nagging continued to the end of the story; but we look in vain, at about this juncture, for more of Lincoln's soothing answers. That they ceased after his return from Harrison's Landing is significant.

During this visit, brief as it was, the President had learned several things besides the real size of the army. Not the least of these was the size of McClellan's self-esteem. That officer, several weeks before, while in the midst of the Peninsular campaign, when every thought should have been fixed on the task before him, had telegraphed to Mr. Lincoln for permission to submit his "views as to the present state of military affairs throughout the whole country," requesting, at the same time, detailed information about the troops not under his orders.[124] The President had replied: —

"If it would not divert too much of your time and attention from the army under your immediate command, I would be glad to have your views as to the present state of military affairs throughout the whole country, as you say you would be glad to give them. I would rather it should be by letter than by telegraph, because of the better chance of secrecy. As to the numbers and positions of the troops not under your command in Virginia and elsewhere, even if I could do it with accuracy, which I cannot, I would rather not transmit either by telegraph or letter, because of the chances of its reaching the enemy. I would be very glad to talk with you, but you cannot leave your camp, and I cannot well leave here."[125]

The reproof was too delicately hinted. McClellan deferred the execution of his purpose, but he did not give it up. As soon as Mr. Lincoln arrived at Harrison's Landing, the General hastened on board the steamer to receive him. When they had been together in the cabin for a short time, McClellan handed the President a letter. Having read it through, Lincoln, with some such expression as "All right," put the document into his pocket, and made no reference to it during the rest of his visit.

This reticence is not to be wondered at. In that letter a defeated commander tried to impose upon his President an entire system of civil, as well as military, doctrine. Assuming, after the manner of Mr. Seward, in a no less remarkable communication, that Lincoln lacked a policy, McClellan undertook to supply him with one, "covering the whole ground of our national trouble." A large contract, to be sure, for a soldier whose strategy had just ended in a pitiable failure, and whose neglect of things political, all his life, had usually kept him from performing even the simplest duties of citizenship. Yet McClellan seems to have appreciated, at least, the rhetorical demands of the situation. His letter is a marvel. The exordium solemnly pleads the privilege of speaking freely, because the army under him might be overwhelmed, any moment, by the enemy in its front, though that enemy — let us whisper — was, at this very time, turning back to Richmond. Wherefore his conclusion, as artfully calculated to disarm criticism, also becomes a mere flourish of language. "I may be on the brink of eternity," it reads, "and as I hope for forgiveness from my Maker, I have written this letter with sincerity towards you, and from love for my country." The body of the lecture — for that in fact it is — tells the President what he must do to save the Union; while a sweeping criticism of what he has done is written large between the lines. After adjuring Lincoln never to abandon the fight, McClellan says, "Let neither military disaster, political faction, nor foreign war shake your settled purpose to enforce the equal operation of the laws of the United States upon the people of every State." Advising against the subjugation of the southern people, he urges that there "should not be at all a war upon population, but against armed forces and political organizations. Neither confiscation of property, political executions of persons, territorial organization of States, or forcible abolition of slavery should be contemplated for a moment." Then the President is admonished that "military arrests should not be tolerated, except in places where active hostilities exist; and oaths not required by enactments — constitutionally made — should be neither demanded nor received." Here follow some confused suggestions favoring compensated emancipation of slaves, in certain States, "upon grounds of military necessity," tacked to the stipulation that "military power should not be allowed to interfere with the relations of servitude." Unless these principles are made known, he adds, "the effort to obtain requisite forces will be almost hopeless." But "a declaration of radical views, especially upon slavery," warns the oracle, "will rapidly disintegrate our present armies." His final piece of advice, still strikingly reminiscent of the Seward memorandum, reads: —

"In carrying out any system of policy which you may

form, you will require a commander-in-chief of the army, — one who possesses your confidence, understands your views, and who is competent to execute your orders by directing the military forces of the nation to the accomplishment of the objects by you proposed. I do not ask that place for myself. I am willing to serve you in such position as you may assign me, and I will do so as faithfully as ever subordinate served superior."[126]

Had Julius Cæsar refused the kingly crown by mail, he would have employed, perhaps, some such phraseology.

The Harrison's Landing letter was broader in scope, to raise a parliamentary objection, than the petition on which it rested — so much broader, in fact, as to be out of order. Such an utterance from a victorious general would have been inept, from a defeated one it was impertinent. "You know," McClellan once wrote to his wife, "that I have a way of attending to most other things than my own affairs," and the avowal applies here with particular force. An adept in military lore, he must have recognized, if any one did, how improper it was for a general in the field to meddle with purely political questions. Yet he plunged into the mazes of this forbidden domain, foreign alike to his office and his experience, under the honest delusion, apparently, that Lincoln needed his guidance there. "I have written a strong, frank letter to the President," McClellan informs the lady at home. "If he acts upon it, the country will be saved."[127] But the silence with which Mr. Lincoln received his lesson kept the General guessing. "I do not know," he wrote her, after the President's departure, "to what extent he has profited by his visit; not much, I fear. I will enclose with this a copy of a letter I handed him, which I would be glad to have you preserve carefully as a very important record."[128] This anxiety about his "record," by the way, cropped out so often with McClellan as to give one the impression of a man who was building up a case. Indeed, however deeply he might have been engrossed in saving the country, he never failed to save the evidence by which he expected, some day, to prove how hard the administration had made the task for him; and of the documents so cherished the most important, beyond a question, was this Harrison's Landing letter. Under the form of advising the President, it condemned, with peculiar emphasis, his attitude toward the war; while the whole spirit of the production, as we shall see, made its author, later, when it became public property, the logical standard-bearer of those various discontented elements which fused for the purpose of defeating Lincoln's reëlection. There is no good reason, however, to doubt the sincerity of the letter. It appears to have correctly expressed McClellan's ultra-conservative views. Nor are we disposed to dispute the claim of his editor that it was composed without the aid of the politicians.[129] But how about their influence in the matter? The friendly overtures of prominent Democrats, on the one hand, and the hostility of Radical Republicans, on the other, must have given McClellan's mind a distinctly political bias. If he did not openly respond to proffers of party leadership, he felt called upon, apparently, to declare himself concerning party questions, in a form available for future reference. At all events, the writing of the famous letter when his military fortunes were on the ebb looks decidedly, whatever else may be said on the subject, like the proceeding which a certain astute politician of later distinction described in a memorable phrase, as casting an anchor to windward.

Of course the President took no public notice of the singular document which he brought home in his pocket. So far was he from heeding the General's solemn warnings — threats, some writers have called them — that, within eight days after his return, Mr. Lincoln had determined upon emancipation, and had signed the drastic Confiscation Act.[130] In one particular, however, he seemingly adopted McClellan's counsel. The four months that had elapsed since the Chief Executive and his war minister undertook to handle the armies in the field, without a military expert in supreme command, had left the President, at least, in no doubt as to the unwisdom of the step. For some weeks he had contemplated the selection of a general-in-chief, and almost immediately after the historic lesson at Harrison's Landing, he decided upon the man; but to his mentor's chagrin, the appointment read, "Henry W. Halleck," not "George B. McClellan."[131] How deep this cut may be inferred from one of the little private notes to Mrs. McClellan. "You ask me," it ran, "whether I advised the President to appoint Halleck. The letter of which I sent you a copy is all that ever passed on the subject, either directly or indirectly; not another word than is there written. We never conversed on the subject. I was never informed of his views or intentions, and even now have not been officially informed of the appointment. I only know it through the newspapers. In all these things the President and those around him have acted so as to make the matter as offensive as possible."[132] Hardly less agreeable was one of the new Chief's earliest duties. On the day after his arrival at Washington,[133] Mr. Lincoln hurried him to the camp on the Peninsula, in order that he might determine, by personal observation, what was best to be done with the Army of the Potomac.

Halleck found McClellan eager for a new campaign against Richmond, along the line of the river on which the column rested. There, according to its commander, — and later events corroborated him, — "the fate of the Union should be decided." With all the facts before us, we now realize that McClellan's plan was correct. But who could have guessed it from his faulty data? For the evil genius of miscalculation, which had pursued him from the beginning, still bedeviled his counsels. He told the General-in-Chief that the force opposed to him outnumbered the Army of the Potomac by over 100,000 men. The figures were out of all reason. This imaginary preponderance of gray-coats might perhaps be accounted for, in a way, by the vapors rising above the Chickahominy swamps. The squadrons of spectral troopers, that from time to time sweep over the Scotch moors, are no less real than were those 100,000 Confederates. As a matter of fact, the advantage lay on the northern side by some 12,800 men.[134] This Halleck, of course, did not know. He had to decide, by the light of the figures laid before him, whether such additional troops — 20,000 in all — as the President had authorized him to promise, would constitute a sufficient reënforcement. If this increase, so ran Mr. Lincoln's instructions, enabled McClellan to operate against Richmond with a strong probability of success, the Peninsular campaign was to be renewed; if not, the army was to be withdrawn, and united with General John Pope's recently formed command, in front of Washington.[135] Anxious as McClellan was to go forward, he would not say that the chances, even when improved by those 20,000 men, were in his favor. He declared himself "willing to try it," but dwelling upon the imaginary odds, on the opposing side, he pleaded for heavier reënforcements. These Halleck could not give. And what he learned from the other officers, whom he consulted at Harrison's Landing, hardly improved the outlook; for they were about evenly divided in their opinions as to whether the army should advance or retreat. Under these circumstances, it is not to be wondered at that the General-in-Chief, upon his return to Washington, added his voice to the counsels of the powerful group — soldiers, cabinet ministers, and representatives, who were urging the President to recall McClellan. That officer now lost the last vestige of his influence with Mr. Lincoln, and the President no longer hesitated to give the fateful order.

McClellan's instructions to return from the Peninsula caused him, as he said, "the greatest pain" he had "ever experienced." The bitterness of his mortification at this inglorious finish to the campaign was heightened not a little by a sincere belief that the contemplated movement would be a blunder. He protested against the retreat in a despatch which has been deservedly praised. Still, Halleck's reply, it must be said, seemed equally cogent; and what was more to the purpose, it directed his subordinate to obey orders, "with all possible promptness."[136] Whether McClellan did so or not is one of the doubtful questions which have grown out of his much debated doings. It took him somewhat over three weeks to remove the troops with their material from the James to the Potomac. "Gross mismanagement," said one contemporary critic in the Army of the Potomac. "No human power could prevent delays in such a delicate operation," said another.[137] Wide as this difference of opinion was, it still divides historians of the Peninsular campaign; but happily there is no need of rehearsing the whole stale controversy here. He would be a wise man, moreover, who could, with the information now available, determine just what degree of blame attaches to the General commanding. That he appeared culpably slow, at the time, to Halleck and the administration, is not surprising. In their feverish anxiety to reënforce Pope, against whom the enemy was massing, they doubtless expected too much of McClellan; while he, eating his heart out with disappointment, failed to respond in that spirit of single-minded obedience to which they were clearly entitled. Halleck showered him with telegraphic appeals to hasten. He invariably answered, in effect, that the movement was progressing with all reasonable despatch, but he continued his protests. "It is not possible," declared a typical message, "for any one to place this army where you wish it, ready to move, in less than a month. If Washington is in danger now, this army can scarcely arrive in time to save it. It is in much better position to do so from here than from Acquia."[138] Once, indeed, he came dangerously near to expressing these protests in action. Just a week after the order to withdraw, a letter meant for the eyes of his wife told a singular story.

"I hope to be ready to-morrow afternoon," it ran, "to move forward in the direction of Richmond. I will try to catch or thrash Longstreet, and then, if the chance offers, follow into Richmond while they are lamming away at Pope. It is in some respects a desperate step, but it is the best I can do for the nation just now; and I would rather even be defeated than retreat without an effort to relieve Washington in the only way at all possible. . . . I half apprehend that they will be too quick for me in Washington, and relieve me before I have the chance of making the dash. If so, well and good. I am satisfied that the dolts in Washington are bent on my destruction, if it is possible for them to accomplish it." A postscript to this letter added: —

"I received a very harsh and unjust telegram from Halleck this morning. . . . Under the circumstances I feel compelled to give up the idea of my intended attack upon Richmond, and must retrace my steps."[139]

The fate of eminent commanders who have disobeyed under somewhat similar circumstances may have come to the fore in McClellan's well-stocked recollections of military history; or the despatch, which had so nettled him, may have brought the General to his senses. It read: —

"The enemy is crossing the Rapidan in large force. They are fighting General Pope to-day; there must be no further delay in your movements. That which has already occurred was entirely unexpected and must be satisfactorily explained. Let not a moment's time be lost, and telegraph me daily what progress you have made in executing the order to transfer your troops."[140]

Though McClellan complied, he answered sharply enough. For, by this time, Halleck, and Pope as well, had been relegated to his black book. They were in accord with Lincoln and Stanton. That — if there had been no other reasons — was enough to render them contemptible, in his eyes. He took no pains, moreover, to hide the feeling; while his private correspondence evinces how strained relations had become between the administration and the captain of its principal army. If McClellan moved, as he claimed, "with the utmost rapidity possible," appearances certainly failed to do him justice. So far, indeed, had they gone against him, during these weeks of suspense and recrimination, that when at last he got his troops back to the Potomac, he was, as far as his superiors were concerned, the most discredited officer in the whole command.

McClellan's removal now seemed inevitable. But who should succeed him? To this question the President gave prayerful consideration, for upon its answer might hinge the fate of the Union. He looked about him, as indeed he had been looking many anxious weeks, to find some sign of the coming man. His quest was thus far, however, in vain. "A great captain," said one of the old dramatists, "is the chiefest gift of Providence to a nation." He might have added, "and the rarest." At all events, the Lord seemed to have withheld his bounty in this direction from the people of the North. Two prominent Generals, Ambrose E. Burnside, McClellan's intimate friend, and Ethan Allen Hitchcock, a talented soldier on duty at the War Department, are known to have in turn declined the command. Both of them shrank from a post which they deemed, not without reason, beyond their powers; and the field-marshal's batons still lay unrevealed in the camp-chests of the few officers who really were equal to the task. Until one of these great captains could be distinguished from among a host of epauleted heroes, Lincoln did not see his way clear to McClellan's retirement. It was when the matter presented this aspect, no doubt, that Halleck promised the General command of all the forces in Virginia, as soon as they should become united.[141] At the same time, McClellan's opponents, eager to get rid of him at any price, proclaimed Pope the rising sun of the army's hope; and urged the President to appoint their latest favorite to McClellan's place. This Mr. Lincoln would gladly have done, but the new-comer, though he had given a good account of himself in a limited western field, had still to prove his mettle on the larger theater of Virginian operations. So the President determined to test Pope before letting go of McClellan; and the manner in which he set about this delicate proceeding was peculiarly Lincolnian. McClellan should not be removed from the Army of the Potomac, but the Army of the Potomac should be removed from him. It was to be merged, part by part, into the Army of Virginia, so that Pope might fight the impending campaign before Washington, at the head of the combined forces. If the new man won, the problem of commanders would be solved; if he lost, the old chief would still be available.

This explains the anomalous situation in which McClellan found himself, at Alexandria, during the closing days of August. He had reminded Halleck, as soon as he reached the Potomac, of that promise to place all the troops under his orders; but Halleck was too busy, perhaps, to answer. Then he begged the President, as well as the General-in-Chief, to have his status at least defined. "Tell me what you wish me to do," pleaded the despatch to Lincoln, "and I will do all in my power to accomplish it. I wish to know what my orders and authority are. I ask for nothing, but will obey whatever orders you give."[142] In the President's brief answer this important question was again ignored. It received no more attention, in fact, than was vouchsafed to a request, which McClellan had previously made, that "a handsome order" issue from Washington, thanking the Army of the Potomac for its services on the Peninsula. Lincoln was obviously in no mood for tossing bouquets at McClellan. The President's sole concern with the "Young Napoleon," at this time, must have been to get his troops away from him in season to reënforce Pope, whose second Bull Run campaign now rapidly developed. Corps after corps was detached from McClellan, amidst a cross-fire of impatient telegrams, until, as he pathetically reported, every fighting man — to the very guard around his camp — had gone.[143] Then at last came the answer to those repeated requests for official light on the eclipsed commander's position. "General McClellan," proclaimed an order from the War Department, "commands that portion of the Army of the Potomac that has not been sent forward to General Pope's command."[144] This piece of seeming irony, in which, however, we discern rather the sober operation of Mr. Lincoln's plan, added not a little to McClellan's discomfiture. A spectacle for gods and men, the chief so lately of a hundred thousand veterans sat idle in his tent, stripped of all but a fleeting shadow of his splendid authority. Declining to issue a countersign for this mockery of an army, he bore himself with what dignity his trying situation admitted of, until the cannonading in a far-away battle echoed through the deserted camp. Only a soldier can fathom the depths to which that noise stirred McClellan. He telegraphed to Halleck: —

"I cannot express to you the pain and mortification I have experienced to-day in listening to the distant sound of the firing of my men. As I can be of no further use here, I respectfully ask that, if there is a probability of the conflict being renewed to-morrow, I may be permitted to go to the scene of battle with my staff, merely to be with my own men, if nothing more; they will fight none the worse for my being with them. If it is not deemed best to entrust me with the command even of my own army, I simply ask to be permitted to share their fate on the field of battle. Please reply to this to-night."[145]

On the following day the General-in-Chief responded:

"I cannot answer without seeing the President, as General Pope is in command, by his orders, of the department."[146]

McClellan's humiliation was complete. He realized, we venture to say, as nearly as any nineteenth century leader could realize, how King Saul felt on awaking to find the skirt of his robe cut off.

What especially chagrined McClellan was the destination of his troops. It must, indeed, have seemed hard that the army, which his skilful and loving care had brought to a high degree of effectiveness, should be marched away from him to swell the forces of an obnoxious rival. For in this light he regarded Pope. That officer had assumed command with a flourish of trumpets and a rattle of innuendoes, at which the whole Army of the Potomac, from Major-General McClellan down to Private John Doe, took grave offence.[147] If, therefore, any lack of enthusiasm marked their manner of supporting him, it is not surprising. Articles of War may impose obedience upon a soldier, to the last ditch; but the clause which shall compel his affection for a commander has still to be devised. That is, of course, the commander's lookout; and Pope, vigorous, gallant captain though he was, had tactlessly cut himself off from reaching the hearts of these men. They had no confidence in him from the beginning. Their opinion was probably summed up by McClellan when he wrote in one of his private letters: —

"I see that the Pope bubble is likely to be suddenly collapsed. Stonewall Jackson is after him, and the young man who wanted to teach me the art of war will, in less than a week, either be in full retreat or badly whipped." [148]

Believing that "Mr. Pope," as he sometimes called him, would inevitably be repulsed, McClellan, with a view to protecting the Capital, had not forwarded his troops from Alexandria as promptly as Halleck's urgent despatches required. Part of the delay, to be sure, was due to inadequate means of transportation, and ill-will towards Pope in not an entirely negligible quantity; but the idea of a reserve for the defence of Washington appears to have finally determined McClellan's course. After a lively interchange of messages, he had appealed from the General-in-Chief to the President. This was rank insubordination. Franklin's corps was kept marking time, halfway on the road, and Pope was actually fighting the Second Battle of Bull Run, when McClellan telegraphed to Lincoln: —

"I am clear that one of two courses should be adopted: first, to concentrate all our available forces to open communication with Pope; second, to leave Pope to get out of his scrape, and at once use all our means to make the Capital perfectly safe. No middle course will now answer."[149]

The President immediately confirmed Halleck's order,[150] and McClellan obeyed; but obedience came too late. By the time Franklin reached the scene of action, Pope, severely defeated, was in retreat.

McClellan's phrase, "leave Pope to get out of his scrape," was unfortunate. It appeared to confirm the charges of treachery in the Army of the Potomac, that were now showered upon the President. According to these charges, McClellan's apathy in withdrawing from the Peninsula had been duplicated at Alexandria; he had diverted most of his troops from Pope, while those who did reach that officer gave him half-hearted service; the rank and file were demoralized by factious sympathy for "Little Mac"; his favorite lieutenants had dishonorably failed the new commander, on the battle-field, and so forth, through the whole catalogue of disloyalty. As many of the stories came to Lincoln from Stanton, Halleck, or Pope, they lost nothing in the telling. It is not strange, therefore, that at last he too thought ill — if not indeed the worst — of McClellan's conduct. "He has acted badly towards Pope," said the President sadly, on the last day of Second Bull Run; "he really wanted him to fail."[151] So impressed, in fact, was Mr. Lincoln with these reports of disaffection, that when McClellan, at Halleck's call, presented himself in Washington, shortly after the battle, nothing would content the President but a despatch from the General to his friends in the Army of the Potomac, asking them to give Pope their cordial support. Precisely to what extent McClellan, McClellan's officers, or McClellan's troops were remiss will probably never be known. Out of their relation to this disastrous campaign grew the most stubbornly contested military quarrel left over from the war. Forty years of controversy have not brought the discussion down to the final word, but they have sufficed to work a reversal of our harshest judgments. Time, passing soothing fingers over partisan animosities, leaves us clear-eyed to see that McClellan, Porter, Griffin, and the rest were guiltless — whatever may have been their shortcomings — of the most serious charges laid at their door. Nevertheless, during the closing days of August, in the battle summer of 1862, every circumstance seemed to condemn them; and not a few of the leading men in Washington shared Pope's opinion that "the greatest criminal" of all was McClellan.

How far some members of the cabinet carried their indignation was detailed in a previous chapter. We have seen how they sought to bring about McClellan's dismissal in disgrace from the army; how fierce became the demand, in certain other quarters, for his punishment, and how signally all these efforts failed. Those who wanted to crush him had still to reckon with Lincoln. That the President would stand in their way seemed inexplicable. Why should he interpose to save a general who had flouted him, whose unsoldierly conduct had, to all appearances, sacrificed a campaign, whose failures had embarrassed the administration, and whose successes, if he achieved any, might menace its very existence, at the polls? To cashier McClellan, then, out of hand, would doubtless have placed him under a cloud from which he could hardly have emerged in time to trouble Lincoln's political peace of mind. But the President, shrewd tactician though he was, did not fight that way. In the crisis produced by the disaster at Manassas, his thoughts were neither of revenge, of discipline, nor yet of personal ambition. Towering gaunt and hollow-eyed above the little-big men who clamored around him, he saw through the fog of their intrigues and recriminations the one thing needful to be done at once. As soon as the retreating army reached the defences of Washington, it would have to be faced about to protect the Capital against the victorious Confederates. Who, Lincoln asked himself, was to rally the dispirited and, in fact, disorganized troops, — Halleck? The General-in-Chief had recently shirked lesser responsibilities; and when the news of Pope's overthrow reached headquarters, he had, in a condition bordering on collapse, summoned McClellan to his aid.[152] No, Halleck was clearly not the man. Pope? — The trumpet upon which he had sounded the advance so stridently, as he rode to the war, must have been lost in the mêlée; for he was returning without it. The despondent tone of certain official despatches, as he approached Washington,[153] to say nothing of his increased unpopularity with the army, put him as plainly out of the question. From that army, itself, the President received his answer. Most of the officers and men who had been on the Peninsula called for their old commander. They trusted, indeed loved him with a devotion such as has been lavished upon few generals. Cæsar, Turenne, Condé, Napier, Napoleon — all swayed the affections of their armies amidst inspiring victories; McClellan had won the hearts of his soldiers without great triumphs, and, remarkable to relate, he held their confidence in spite of severe reverses. When to this is added that he had, thus far, shown himself to be the most capable organizer and best defensive officer on the Union side, we see the wisdom of what followed. Mr. Lincoln, brushing aside his advisers, without even telling them his purpose, determined upon McClellan's reinstatement.

Early on the morning of September 2, the President, accompanied by Halleck, went to McClellan's house, and asked him to take command of all the returning troops, for the defence of Washington.[154] The General promptly assented. His courteous behavior during the interview made it none the less trying to Mr. Lincoln, who, we remember, had but a few days before subjected McClellan to a "sort of snubbing," as the President phrased it, with a view to his dismissal as soon as a new general could be found to take his place. It was somewhat humiliating, therefore, to call upon him now for help. At the same time, Lincoln, with unique foresight, had kept McClellan in a position from which he might be recalled to the command as easily as he had been deprived of it; while the President's bearing toward him, through all these vexations, had rarely been otherwise than cordial. So the General met his visitors fully halfway, and immediately on their departure, entered upon his new duties, with all the enthusiasm of which he was capable.

The restoration of McClellan was, as far as Lincoln's civil supporters were concerned, the most unpopular act of his administration. It aroused a storm of disapproval that would have shaken a less masterful man, but the President stood firm. The fiercest opposition, as we have seen, was in his own political family; and the turbulent cabinet meeting which followed the appointment has been fully described elsewhere. What Lincoln said to his excited ministers, therefore, need not be repeated here. He, himself, summarized it later, in these two pithy sentences: —

"There is no one in the army who can man these fortifications and lick these troops of ours into shape half as well as he can." "We must use the tools we have; if he cannot fight, himself, he excels in making others ready to fight."[155]

Such reasoning was unassailable, and McClellan's harshest ministerial critics bowed to the President's will. When that meeting adjourned, Mr. Lincoln had not only averted a cabinet crisis, but he had, at the same time, strengthened his executive authority over all its members. How different this was from his military relations, the Presi dent realized keenly. Discussing his surrender of September 2, after the event, he confided to a friend that the restoration of McClellan was the most painful duty of his official life. "There has been," he said to another, "a design, a purpose in breaking down Pope, without regard to the consequences to the country, that is atrocious. It is shocking to see and know this, but there is no remedy at present. McClellan has the army with him." Pointing out, moreover, in these private talks, how the General's incessant faultfinding had impaired the confidence of the troops in the administration, and how culpably that officer had contributed, generally speaking, to the demoralization which he was now counted upon to correct, Lincoln conceded that his course in recalling McClellan was a good deal like "curing the bite with the hair of the dog." Yet during this brief period of panic, not to say insubordination, the civil power, as the President explained, seemed under military subjection; and Commander-in-Chief though he was, he could find no way out but that of placing the factious commander again in the saddle.[156]

The rapidity with which McClellan restored the morale of his now delighted troops amply justified Lincoln's course. It was not the President's purpose, however, to entrust him with another campaign; and the command in the field was again offered to Burnside. That phenomenally modest officer declined the offer as before. Declaring himself incompetent to lead so large a force, he warmly repeated his opinion that McClellan "could command the Army of the Potomac better than any other general in it." The question was still unsettled when news came that Lee purposed crossing the Upper Potomac into Maryland. To oppose him, Lincoln ordered an immediate advance and, under the pressure of events, committed the movement — what alternative had he? — to McClellan. "Again I have been called upon to save the country," wrote the General, in his grandiose style. "The case is desperate, but with God's help I will try unselfishly to do my best, and, if He wills it, accomplish the salvation of the nation." [157] As McClellan departed for the front, however, he disclosed a change of heart in one respect, at least. "The feeling of the government towards me," reads a farewell telegram to his wife, "I am sure, is kind and trusting. I hope, with God's blessing, to justify the great confidence they now repose in me, and will bury the past in oblivion." [158] His brief sojourn on the mourners' bench had evidently been not without its chastening effect; but this submissive mood, as we shall see, wore off all too quickly.

No sooner was McClellan well into the Maryland campaign than his old quarrel with the administration broke out afresh. He won the battles of South Mountain and Antietam, to his great credit be it said, with the men who, less than three weeks before, had fled in defeat from the very army which now gave way before them; but his excessive caution held him back from vigorously following up an advantage that, in the grasp of a more intrepid general, might have led to the total overthrow of the Confederate host. When he telegraphed, therefore, to Washington that Lee had been driven back over the Potomac into Virginia, the President's joy was flecked with disappointment. For Mr. Lincoln, in the hope of a decisive campaign at last, had recently urged McClellan not to let the enemy "get off without being hurt"; [159] and his congratulatory despatch after South Mountain had closed with the entreaty, "Destroy the rebel army if possible." [160] That it was possible, even the General's military eulogists for the most part concede. In fact, the Confederates were several days later so badly shattered at Antietam, that it needed but a single well-directed blow, within the following twenty-four hours, to crush them.[161] Yet McClellan turned what should have been an overwhelming victory into almost a drawn battle. Commanding three men to Lee's two, he fatally overrated, as of old, his opponent's strength, and allowed the adroit Southerner to escape, over "a very deep and difficult ford,"[162] without further damage. Important as was McClellan's service to the Union in heading off this invasion of the Northern States, his failure to reap the full fruits of victory aroused indignant criticism throughout the country. On every hand, men counting the cost declared Antietam to have been the bloodiest day of the war; and aghast at its slaughter, they severely blamed the Federal commander because what he did fell so far short of what he might have done.

Those who desired McClellan's removal now besieged the President with all their old-time vigor. Lincoln gave them scant encouragement; yet how closely he kept his accounts with the General checked up may be gathered from a few remarks made by him to one of the political friends who urged that officer's dismissal.

"I am now," said he, "stronger with the Army of the Potomac than McClellan. The supremacy of the civil power has been restored, and the Executive is again master of the situation. The troops know that if I made a mistake in substituting Pope for McClellan, I was capable of rectifying it by again trusting him. They know, too, that neither Stanton nor I withheld anything from him at Antietam, and that it was not the administration, but their own former idol, who surrendered the just results of their terrible sacrifices and closed the great fight as a drawn battle, when had he thrown Porter's corps of fresh men and other available troops upon Lee's army, he would inevitably have driven it in disorder to the river and captured most of it before sunset."[163]

McClellan, it goes without saying, gave abundant reasons for not seizing this golden opportunity. His troops, we are told, were "overcome by fatigue," provisions, forage, and ammunition had to be distributed, certain divisions were "somewhat demoralized," reënforcements were expected, there was no "absolute assurance of success," and so on. Yet all this fails to explain why his victorious force, in much better condition than the pitiably ragged, half-starved army which it had just defeated, could not pursue where Lee's war-worn soldiers fled. As a matter of fact, fortune favored the Union arms, at this juncture, in every respect but one — that of generalship. McClellan insisted upon the necessity of reorganizing and resting the army before advancing. His demands, moreover, for fresh troops, equipments, supplies, and what not, were painfully reminiscent of the delays that had brought his previous campaign to naught. The impatience of the government began to show itself again in the despatches from headquarters, to which McClellan responded with something of his former asperity. Consoling himself, meanwhile, in familiar letters, as of old, he wrote home:

"I am tired of fighting against such disadvantages, and feel that it is now time for the country to come to my help and remove these difficulties from my path. If my countrymen will not open their eyes and assist themselves, they must pardon me if I decline longer to pursue the thankless avocation of serving them. . . . I feel that I have done all that can be asked in twice saving the country. If I continue in its service, I have at least the right to demand a guarantee that I shall not be interfered with. I know I cannot have that assurance so long as Stanton continues in the position of Secretary of War and Halleck as General-in-Chief." [164]

Yet the writer's persistent inaction after Antietam rendered interference of some sort from Washington imperative. So, at all events, thought the President, as he presented himself in McClellan's camp on October 1, a fortnight from the day of the battle, to find out for himself where the trouble lay.

During this visit, which lasted three days, the General found ample opportunity to defend his course. He flattered himself that Lincoln — affable as ever — became "fully satisfied" with what had been done. The President "more than once assured me," says McClellan, "that he was fully satisfied with my whole course from the beginning; that the only fault he could possibly find was that I was perhaps too prone to be sure that everything was ready before acting, but that my actions were all right when I started." [165] But an anecdote related by one of the presidential party throws rather a different light upon the situation. Early on the morning of their second day in camp, Lincoln took a stroll with his friend, the Hon. O. M. Hatch of Illinois. As they stood upon the summit of a near-by hill, and looked down over the city of white tents, among which the men were beginning their daily duties, the President, waving his hand toward the scene, said in a low, earnest voice: —

"Hatch, Hatch, what is all this?"

"Why, Mr. Lincoln," answered his companion, "this is the Army of the Potomac."

The President hesitated a moment, and then said in a louder tone: —

"No, Hatch, no. This is General McClellan's body-guard." [166]

How far Mr. Lincoln was from being satisfied may be still further inferred from one of his first military orders after returning to Washington. "The President directs," telegraphed Halleck on October 6, "that you cross the Potomac and give battle to the enemy, or drive him south. Your army must move now, while the roads are good." [167] On the following day, to emphasize the urgency of immediate action, the General-in-Chief wrote: —

"The country is becoming very impatient at the want of activity of your army, and we must push it on. I am satisfied that the enemy are falling back toward Richmond. We must follow them and seek to punish them. There is a decided want of legs in our troops. They have too much immobility, and we must try to remedy the defect." [168] Still McClellan did not move. It was partly to find out why, that the Confederate General, "Jeb" Stuart, crossed the Potomac, with a division of cavalry, a few days later. His reconnoissance developing into a raid across Maryland and Pennsylvania, he rode entirely around McClellan's army, and, despite Union attempts to head him off, recrossed the river unharmed. Stuart had subjected Napoleon's namesake to this humiliation once before, on the Peninsula; but the second raid was especially galling, as it took place on northern territory. Lincoln must have been smarting under the ridicule evoked by the affair, when, shortly afterward, one of a group who were chatting familiarly with him asked: —

"Mr. President, what about McClellan?"

Without looking at his questioner, Mr. Lincoln drew an imaginary circle and said deliberately: —

"When I was a boy we used to play a game, three times round and out. Stuart has been round him twice; if he goes round him once more, gentlemen, McClellan will be out."[169]

The General himself, ascribing Stuart's success to a lack of horses for the Federal cavalry, telegraphed that unless this deficiency was supplied, there would be constant danger of similar expeditions. To which Halleck curtly replied: —

"The President has read your telegram, and directs me to suggest that if the enemy had more occupation south of the river, his cavalry would not be so likely to make raids north of it."[170]

Mr. Lincoln's peremptory order to advance was a week old. Every day had seemed to furnish McClellan with fresh reasons for not obeying it. The fine autumn season was slipping by, and the Potomac still separated him from his rapidly recruiting enemy. Another effort to drive the General forward now came by special messenger, in one of the President's characteristic letters. It read: —

"You remember my speaking to you of what I called your over-cautiousness. Are you not over-cautious when you assume that you cannot do what the enemy is constantly doing? Should you not claim to be at least his equal in prowess, and act upon the claim? As I understand, you telegraphed General Halleck that you cannot subsist your army at Winchester unless the railroad from Harper's Ferry to that point be put in working order. But the enemy does now subsist his army at Winchester, at a distance nearly twice as great from railroad transportation as you would have to do without the railroad last named. . . . Again, one of the standard maxims of war, as you know, is to 'operate upon the enemy's communications as much as possible without exposing your own.' You seem to act as if this applies against you, but cannot apply in your favor. Change positions with the enemy, and think you not he would break your communication with Richmond within the next twenty-four hours? You dread his going into Pennsylvania; but if he does so in full force, he gives up his communications to you absolutely, and you have nothing to do but to follow and ruin him. If he does so with less than full force, fall upon and beat what is left behind all the easier. Exclusive of the water-line, you are now nearer Richmond than the enemy is by the route that you can and he must take. Why can you not reach there before him, unless you admit that he is more than your equal on a march? His route is the arc of a circle, while yours is the chord. The roads are as good on yours as on his. . . . If he should move northward, I would follow him closely, holding his communications. If he should prevent our seizing his communications and move toward Richmond, I would press closely to him, fight him if a favorable opportunity should present, and at least try to beat him to Richmond on the inside track. I say 'try'; if we never try, we shall never succeed. If he makes a stand at Winchester, moving neither north nor south, I would fight him there, on the idea that if we cannot beat him when he bears the wastage of coming to us, we never can when we bear the wastage of going to him. This proposition is a simple truth, and is too important to be lost sight of for a moment. In coming to us he tenders us an advantage which we should not waive. We should not so operate as to merely drive him away. As we must beat him somewhere or fail finally, we can do it, if at all, easier near to us than far away. If we cannot beat the enemy where he now is, we never can, he again being within the intrenchments of Richmond. . . . When at length running for Richmond ahead of him enables him to move this way, if he does so, turn and attack him in rear. But I think he should be engaged long before such point is reached. It is all easy if our troops march as well as the enemy, and it is unmanly to say they cannot do it. This letter is in no sense an order."[171]

McClellan answered briefly that he would advance as soon as his troops were in suitable condition. Some such result — we have reason to know — was expected by Mr. Lincoln. Before the letter left his hands, he confided a fear to Vice-President Hamlin that it would do no good, and that he would soon be compelled to retire McClellan.

And now came another soul-trying period of recrimination. The General commanding the army refused to move because the horses and supplies, which he incessantly demanded, did not arrive in sufficient quantities. The General-in-Chief replied that they were forwarded with all possible speed, that no armies in the world had been better cared for on a campaign, and that no such lack of things existed, at any time, as would justify McClellan in not obeying the President's order to advance. Lincoln himself, as the controversy grew warmer, was betrayed by the "cheerless, almost hopeless prospect" of accomplishing anything, into several caustic little messages.[172] They stung McClellan into everything but action. "If you could know," he wrote to his wife, "the mean character of the despatches I receive, you would boil over with anger. When it is possible to misunderstand, and when it is not possible; whenever there is a chance of a wretched innuendo, then it comes."[173] A less self-centered man would have read his danger in all this. McClellan had eyes only for that "ideal completeness of preparation," which he now again, as on previous occasions, strove to attain at the expense of more important military considerations. He still refused to see that Lee's army was incomparably worse off than his. It would, in all likelihood, have made no difference to him had he seen it; for McClellan was by temperament incapable of grasping the full significance of Napoleon's maxim, "The commander who allows himself to be guided by the commissaries will never stir, and all his expeditions will fail." That this expedition, at all events, would fail, seemed inevitable. The situation suggested to Lincoln one of his little stories, which he told to a friend of the General, who called at the White House.

"McClellan's tardiness," said he, "reminds me of a fellow in Illinois who had studied law, but had never tried a case. He was sued, and, not having confidence in his ability to manage his own case, employed a lawyer to manage it for him. He had only a confused idea of the meaning of law terms, but was anxious to make a display of learning, and, on the trial, constantly made suggestions to his lawyer, who paid but little attention to him. At last, fearing that his lawyer was not handling the opposing counsel very well, he lost all his patience, and springing to his feet cried out: 'Why don't you go at him with a *fi. fa.*, a *demurrer*, a *capias*, a *surrebutter*, or a *ne exeat*, or something; and not stand there like a *nudum pactum*, or a *non est*?'"[174]

Whether the parable reached McClellan, as the President doubtless intended, deponent saith not; but it is of record that "Little Mac's" inertia gave way, at last, under Lincoln's persistent goad. Suddenly, on the 26th of October, with many supplies still undistributed, reënforcements not yet up, and preparations as planned generally incomplete, the army was put in motion. A week later, on November 2, McClellan announced to the President that his entire force had crossed the river, and would forthwith advance upon the enemy.

But it was too late. Lee, with heavily recruited ranks, again faced him. Most of the Union advantages, so dearly bought at Antietam, were gone. One still remained, however, — the inside track to Richmond; and Mr. Lincoln, while trying to get McClellan started, during the closing days of October, had worried lest his dilatory tactics should sacrifice that too. The President had then, in his own mind, fixed a test whereby the General was to rise or fall. If McClellan should cross the Potomac in time to deal the Confederates a telling blow, all would be well; but if he allowed them to pass over the Blue Ridge, so as to get between Richmond and the Army of the Potomac, it would cost him his command.[175] Accordingly, when it was reported in Washington that Lee had reached Culpeper Court House, orders were issued for McClellan's removal.[176] Late on the night of November 7, during a driving snowstorm that appropriately linked the close of his military career with the close of the beautiful autumn weather which he had frittered away, the General was deposed. An officer from the War Department, arriving in camp with the still protesting Burnside, delivered this message: —

"By direction of the President of the United States, it is ordered that Major-General McClellan be relieved from the command of the Army of the Potomac, and that Major-General Burnside take the command of that army." [177]

A supplementary message from Halleck read: —

"Repair to Trenton, N. J., reporting on your arrival at that place, by telegraph, for further orders." [178]

With a subordination which surprised those who had feared a *coup d'état*, McClellan promptly turned the command over to his successor, and took an affectionate leave of the army.

The rest is soon told. In McClellan's dismissal the Democratic politicians found their opportunity. His antagonism to Lincoln's policy, his personal grievances against the government, his measure of fame as a military hero, his popularity in the army, and his attractive personality — all combined to make him the available candidate of the party. He was nominated at the Democratic National Convention, in the summer of 1864, to contest the presidency with Mr. Lincoln, whom the Republicans had again named for that office. The vital issue between them was squarely made. Lincoln stood for the preservation of the Union, by a vigorous prosecution of the war and the extinction of slavery. McClellan declared for a policy of conciliation and compromise, whereby peace might be restored to the Union, without any impairment of State rights. A spirited canvass followed. Its rancor still lingers in the memory, if not in the blood, of those who took part. At the outset, indications pointed, from many directions, to McClellan's success. Even the demand in the Democratic platform — which he disavowed as going too far — for an immediate cessation of hostilities, on the ground that the war was a failure, seemed to meet with the momentary approval of the people. They were weary of a struggle which had plunged almost every household into mourning; and the horror of Grant's terrible but apparently futile losses, during the recent campaign from the Rapidan to the James, was still uppermost in their thoughts. A heavy weight of condemnation — popular discontent readily finds a scapegoat — rested on the administration. So wide-spread, indeed, did this feeling become, that toward the end of the summer Lincoln's prospects for reëlection were gloomy in the extreme. Some of his own party leaders intriguing against him had, as we have seen, placed General John C. Frémont in nomination; while those who remained loyal to him entered upon the canvass with grave misgivings. The President, himself, sensed the omens of defeat.

But a seasoned campaigner like Lincoln could not, to use his own expression, be easily "stampeded." All the political sagacity, and tact in the management of men, that characterized his previous contests were brought to bear, with signal potency, upon this, the crowning conflict of his career. As President he maintained, it should be said, a dignified attitude toward the canvass; yet opportunities for making himself felt, at the critical junctures, were not lacking. Frémont's withdrawal was soon secured, influential Republican malcontents were brought one after the other into line, local partisan differences in divers places yielded to compromise, and steadily closing ranks gave promise at last of a solid party vote. With the opportune victories, meanwhile, of Farragut in Mobile Bay, Sherman at Atlanta, and Sheridan in the Shenandoah valley, the tide of popular favor set strong in Lincoln's direction. His ability to make a successful end of the war was no longer doubted by the people. They became convinced, moreover, that Lincoln's election would lead to peace, union, and the abolition of slavery; but that McClellan's election would as surely involve a surrender of some, if not all, the principles for which they had poured out their blood and their treasure. Nations do not deal in syllogisms, but give them time, and they will arrive in their own way at essentially sound conclusions. When the North registered its decision at the polls, on November 8, Lincoln was elected by an overwhelming vote. A popular majority of almost half a million, and States enough to cast 212 electoral votes, out of a possible 233, gave him one of the notable triumphs in our history.[179] McClellan received the 21 electoral votes of New Jersey, Delaware, and Kentucky, two of which, it should be said, were originally Slave States. With this meagre consolation stake the Democratic candidate, his military commission resigned, passed into the limbo, already well tenanted, of ungratified presidential ambitions.

Amidst the rejoicing over Lincoln's success, Secretary Seward, addressing a public meeting, said:—

"The election has placed our President beyond the pale

of human envy or human harm, as he is above the pale of human ambition. Henceforth all men will come to see him as we have seen him — a true, loyal, patient, patriotic, and benevolent man. Having no longer any motive to malign or injure him, detraction will cease, and Abraham Lincoln will take his place with Washington, and Franklin, and Jefferson, and Adams, and Jackson — among the benefactors of the country and of the human race."[180]

This noble utterance offered a felicitous close to an unusually fierce campaign, but it erred, alas, in one particular. Lincoln was not beyond the pale of human harm. In less than six months from the day of that triumph, the man before whom leaders, great and small, had gone down in unbroken succession, went down himself before the only thing that ever wholly mastered him — an assassin's bullet.

A LIST OF THE BOOKS CITED,

WITH THE CORRESPONDING ABBREVIATIONS USED IN THE NOTES

ADAMS: The Address of Charles Francis Adams, of Massachusetts, on the life, character, and services of William H. Seward. Delivered by invitation of the Legislature of the State of New York, in Albany, April 18, 1873. New York: D. Appleton & Co. 1873.

ADAMS'S DANA: Richard Henry Dana. A biography by Charles Francis Adams. Two volumes. Boston and New York: Houghton, Mifflin & Co. 1890.

ALLAN: The Army of Northern Virginia in 1862. By William Allan, A. M., LL. D. With an introduction by John C. Ropes. Boston and New York: Houghton, Mifflin & Co. 1892.

AMERICAN CONFLICT: The American Conflict. A History of the Great Rebellion in the United States of America, 1860–65. Its causes, incidents, and results. By Horace Greeley. Two volumes. Hartford: O. D. Case & Co. 1864 and 1867.

ARNOLD: The Life of Abraham Lincoln. By Isaac N. Arnold. Seventh edition. Chicago: A. C. McClurg & Co. 1896.

BAKER: The Works of William H. Seward, edited by George E. Baker. Four volumes. New York: Redfield. 1861.

BANCROFT: The Life of William H. Seward. By Frederic Bancroft. Two volumes. New York and London: Harper & Bros. 1900.

BARRETT: Life of Abraham Lincoln. Presenting his early history, political career, and speeches in and out of Congress. By Joseph H. Barrett. Cincinnati: Moore, Wilstach & Baldwin. 1865.

BARTLETT: The Life and Public Services of Hon. Abraham Lincoln. To which is added a biographical sketch of Hon. Hannibal Hamlin. By D. W. Bartlett. New York: H. Dayton. 1860.

BATES: The Battle of Chancellorsville. By Samuel P. Bates. Meadville, Pa.: Edward T. Bates. 1882.

BATTLES AND LEADERS: Battles and Leaders of the Civil War. Being for the most part contributions by Union and Confederate Officers. Edited by Robert Underwood Johnson and Clarence Clough Buel, of the editorial staff of the *Century Magazine*. Four volumes. New York: The Century Co. 1887.

BLACK: Essays and Speeches of Jeremiah S. Black. With a biographical sketch. By Chauncy F. Black. New York: D. Appleton & Co. 1885.

BLAINE: Twenty Years of Congress, from Lincoln to Garfield. With a Review of the Events which led to the Political Revolution of 1860. By James G. Blaine. Two volumes. Norwich, Conn.: The Henry Bill Publishing Co. 1884.

BOUTWELL: Reminiscences of Sixty Years in Public Affairs. By George S. Boutwell. Two volumes. New York: McClure, Phillips & Co. 1902.

BROCKETT: The Life and Times of Abraham Lincoln, Sixteenth President of the United States. Including his speeches, messages, inaugurals, and proclamations. By L. P. Brockett, M. D. Philadelphia: Bradley & Co. 1865.

BROOKS: Abraham Lincoln and the Downfall of American Slavery. By Noah Brooks. New York: G. P. Putnam's Sons. 1896.

BROWN'S DOUGLAS: Stephen Arnold Douglas. By William Garrott Brown. Boston and New York: Houghton, Mifflin & Co. 1902.

BROWNE: The Every-day Life of Abraham Lincoln. Lincoln's life and character portrayed by those who knew him. Prepared and arranged by Francis P. Browne. St. Louis: William G. Hills. 1896.

BUCHANAN: Mr. Buchanan's Administration on the Eve of the Rebellion. New York: D. Appleton & Co. 1866.

BUTLER: Autobiography and Personal Reminiscences of Major-General Benjamin F. Butler. By Benjamin F. Butler. Boston: A. M. Thayer & Co. 1892.

BYERS: Iowa in War Times. By S. H. M. Byers. Des Moines: W. D. Condit & Co. 1888.

CAMPBELL: Reminiscences and Documents relating to the Civil War, during the Year 1865. By John A. Campbell. Baltimore: John Murphy & Co. 1887.

CARPENTER: The Inner Life of Abraham Lincoln. Six months at the White House. By F. B. Carpenter. New York: Hurd & Houghton. 1867.

CHANDLER: Zachariah Chandler. An outline sketch of his life and public services. By *The Detroit Post and Tribune.* With an introductory letter from James G. Blaine, of Maine. Detroit: The Post and Tribune Co. 1880.

CHASE PAPERS: Annual Report of the American Historical Association for the year 1902. Volume II. Diary and Correspondence of Salmon P. Chase. Washington: Government Printing Office. 1903.

CHITTENDEN: Recollections of President Lincoln and his Administration. By L. E. Chittenden, his Register of the Treasury. New York: Harper & Bros. 1891.

Chittenden's Reminiscences: Personal Reminiscences, 1840–90, including some not hitherto published of Lincoln and the War. By L. E. Chittenden. New York: Richmond, Croscup & Co. 1893.

Coffin: Abraham Lincoln. By Charles Carleton Coffin. New York: Harper & Bros. 1893.

Coleman: The Life of John J. Crittenden. With selections from his correspondence and speeches. Edited by his daughter, Mrs. Chapman Coleman. Two volumes. Philadelphia: J. B. Lippincott & Co. 1871.

Committee on the War: Report of the Joint Committee on the Conduct of the War. Nine volumes. Washington: Government Printing Office. 1863–66.

Comte de Paris: History of the Civil War in America. By the Comte de Paris. Translated, with the approval of the author, by Louis F. Tasistro. Edited by Henry Coppée, LL. D. Four volumes. Philadelphia: Jos. H. Coates & Co. 1876.

Condon: Life of Major-General James Shields, Hero of Three Wars and Senator from Three States. By Hon. William H. Condon. Chicago: Press of the Blakely Printing Co. 1900.

Conway: Autobiography, Memories, and Experiences of Moncure Daniel Conway. Two volumes. Boston and New York: Houghton, Mifflin & Co. 1904.

Cox: Union — Disunion — Reunion. Three Decades of Federal Legislation, 1855–85. Personal and historical memories of events preceding, during, and since the American Civil War. By Samuel S. Cox. Providence, R. I.: J. A. & R. A. Reid. 1885.

Crawford: The History of the Fall of Fort Sumter. The Genesis of the Civil War. By Samuel W. Crawford, the surgeon stationed at Fort Sumter, later Brevet Major-General U. S. A. New York: S. F. McLean & Co. 1898.

Curtis: Life of James Buchanan, Fifteenth President of the United States. By George Ticknor Curtis. Two volumes. New York: Harper & Bros. 1883.

Curtis's Lincoln: The True Abraham Lincoln. By William Eleroy Curtis. Philadelphia and London: J. B. Lippincott Co. 1904.

Curtis's McClellan: Life, Character, and Public Services of General George B. McClellan. An Address delivered December 4, 1886, at the Academy of Music in Philadelphia, at the request of the McClellan Memorial Association of Philadelphia. By George Ticknor Curtis. Boston: Cupples, Upham & Co. 1887.

Cutts: A brief treatise upon Constitutional and Party Questions, and the History of Political Parties, as I received it orally from the late Senator Stephen A. Douglas, of Illinois. By J. Madison Cutts, Brevet Lieutenant-Colonel U. S. A. New York: D. Appleton & Co. 1866.

CYCLOPEDIA: The American Annual Cyclopedia and Register of important events. [1861 to 1865 inclusive.] Five volumes. New York: D. Appleton & Co.

DANA: Recollections of the Civil War. With the Leaders at Washington and in the Field in the Sixties. By Charles A. Dana, Assistant Secretary of War from 1863 to 1865. New York: D. Appleton & Co. 1898.

DAVIDSON: A Complete History of Illinois from 1673 to 1873. By Alexander Davidson and Bernard Stuvé. Springfield: Illinois Journal Co. 1874.

DAVIS: The Rise and Fall of the Confederate Government. By Jefferson Davis. Two volumes. New York: D. Appleton & Co. 1881.

DEBATES: Political Debates between Abraham Lincoln and Stephen A. Douglas, in the Celebrated Campaign of 1858 in Illinois. Including the preceding speeches of each at Chicago, Springfield, etc. Also the Two Great Speeches of Abraham Lincoln in Ohio in 1859. Cleveland: O. S. Hubbell & Co. 1895.

DE JOINVILLE: The Army of the Potomac. Its organization, its commander, and its campaign. By the Prince de Joinville. Translated from the French. With notes. By William Henry Hurlbert. New York: Anson D. F. Randolph. 1862.

DIPLOMATIC HISTORY: The Diplomatic History of the War for the Union. Being the fifth volume of the Works of William H. Seward. Edited by George E. Baker. Boston: Houghton, Mifflin & Co. 1884.

DIX: Memoirs of John Adams Dix. Compiled by his son, Morgan Dix. Two volumes. New York: Harper & Bros. 1883.

DOUBLEDAY: Reminiscences of Forts Sumter and Moultrie in 1860–61. By Abner Doubleday, Brevet Major-General U. S. A. New York: Harper & Bros. 1876.

DRAPER: History of the American Civil War. By John William Draper, M. D., LL. D. Containing also the causes of the War, and the events preparatory to it, up to the close of President Buchanan's administration. Three volumes. New York: Harper & Bros. 1867–70.

FIELD: Memories of Many Men and Some Women. By Maunsell B. Field. New York: Harper & Bros. 1874.

FLINT: Life of Stephen A. Douglas. To which are added his Speeches and Reports. By H. M. Flint. Philadelphia: The Keystone Publishing Co.

FLOWER: Edwin McMasters Stanton, the Autocrat of Rebellion, Emancipation, and Reconstruction. By Frank Abial Flower. Akron, Ohio: The Saalfield Publishing Co. 1905.

FORNEY: Anecdotes of Public Men. By John W. Forney. Two volumes. New York: Harper & Bros. 1873 and 1881.

FOSTER: A Century of American Diplomacy. Being a brief review of the foreign relations of the United States, 1776–1876. By John W. Foster. Boston and New York: Houghton, Mifflin & Co. 1900.

FRÉMONT: Memoirs of My Life. By John Charles Frémont. Including in the Narrative Five Journeys of Western Exploration, during the years 1842, 1843–44, 1845–46–47, 1848–49, 1853–54. Together with a sketch of the life of Senator Benton, in connection with western expansion. By Jessie Benton Frémont. Vol. I. Chicago and New York: Belford, Clarke & Co. 1887.

FRENCH: Abraham Lincoln, the Liberator. A biographical sketch. By Charles Wallace French. New York: Funk & Wagnalls. 1891.

GILMORE: Personal Recollections of Abraham Lincoln and the Civil War. By James R. Gilmore (Edmund Kirke). Boston: L. C. Page & Co. 1898.

GOBRIGHT: Recollections of Men and Things at Washington, during the third of a Century. By L. A. Gobright. Philadelphia: Claxton, Remson & Haffelfinger. 1869.

GORHAM: Life and Public Services of Edwin M. Stanton. By George C. Gorham. Two volumes. Boston and New York: Houghton, Mifflin & Co. 1899.

GRANT: Personal Memoirs of U. S. Grant. Two volumes in one. New York: Charles L. Webster & Co. 1894.

GRAY: Letters of Asa Gray. Edited by Jane Loring Gray. Two volumes. Boston and New York: Houghton, Mifflin & Co. 1893.

GREELEY: Greeley on Lincoln. With Mr. Greeley's Letters to Charles A. Dana and a Lady Friend. To which are added Reminiscences of Horace Greeley. Edited by Joel Benton. New York: The Baker & Taylor Co. 1893.

GREG: History of the United States from the Foundation of Virginia to the Reconstruction of the Union. By Percy Greg. Two volumes. London: W. H. Allen & Co. 1887.

GRINNELL: Men and Events of Forty Years. Autobiographical Reminiscences of an active career from 1850 to 1890. By the late Josiah Busnell Grinnell. With introduction by Professor Henry W. Parker, D. D. Boston: D. Lothrop Co. 1891.

GUROWSKI: Diary from March 4, 1861, to November 12, 1862. By Adam Gurowski. Volume I. Boston: Lee & Shepard. 1862. Diary, from November 18, 1862, to October 18, 1863. By Adam Gurowski. Volume II. New York: Carleton. 1864. Diary, 1863–64–65. By Adam Gurowski. Volume III. Washington: W. H. & O. H. Morrison. 1866.

HAMILTON: Reminiscences of James A. Hamilton; or, Men and Events, at Home and Abroad, during three quarters of a century. New York: Charles Scribner & Co. 1869.

HAMILTON'S WORKS: The Works of Alexander Hamilton. Comprising his Correspondence, and his Political and Official Writings, exclusive of the Federalist, Civil and Military. Edited by John C. Hamilton. Seven volumes. New York: Charles S. Francis & Co. 1851.

HAMLIN: The Life and Times of Hannibal Hamlin. By his grandson, Charles Eugene Hamlin. Cambridge: Riverside Press. 1899.

HAPGOOD: Abraham Lincoln, the Man of the People. By Norman Hapgood. New York: The Macmillan Co. 1899.

HART: Salmon Portland Chase. By Albert Bushnell Hart. Boston and New York: Houghton, Mifflin & Co. 1899.

HERNDON: Abraham Lincoln. The True Story of a Great Life. By William H. Herndon and Jesse W. Weik. With an introduction by Horace White. Two volumes. New York: D. Appleton & Co. 1896.

HILLARD: Life and Campaigns of George B. McClellan, Major-General U. S. Army. By G. S. Hillard. Philadelphia: J. B. Lippincott & Co. 1864.

HOLLAND: The Life of Abraham Lincoln. By J. G. Holland. Springfield, Mass.: Gurdon Bill. 1866.

HOWELLS: Lives and Speeches of Abraham Lincoln and Hannibal Hamlin. By W. D. Howells and John L. Hayes. Columbus, O.: Follett, Foster & Co. 1860.

HUME: The Abolitionists. Together with personal memories of the struggle for human rights, 1830-64. By John F. Hume. New York and London: G. P. Putnam's Sons. 1905.

HUTCHINSONS: Story of the Hutchinsons (tribe of Jesse). By John Wallace Hutchinson. Compiled and edited by Charles E. Mann. With an introduction by Frederick Douglass. Boston: Lee & Shepard. 1896.

IRELAN: History of the Life, Administration, and Times of Abraham Lincoln, Sixteenth President of the United States. War of the Rebellion and Downfall of Human Slavery. By John Herbert Irelan, M. D. Two volumes. Chicago: Fairbanks & Palmer Publishing Co. 1888.

JOHNSTON: Narrative of Military Operations, directed, during the late war between the States. By Joseph E. Johnston, General C. S. A. New York: D. Appleton & Co. 1874.

JONES: Lincoln, Stanton, and Grant. Historical sketches. By Major Evan Rowland Jones. London: Frederick Warne & Co. 1875.

JULIAN: Political Recollections, 1840–72. By George W. Julian. Chicago: Jansen, McClurg & Co. 1884.

KECKLEY: Behind the Scenes. By Elizabeth Keckley. Formerly a slave, more recently modiste, and friend to Mrs. Abraham Lincoln. Or, Thirty Years a Slave, and Four Years in the White House. New York: G. W. Carleton & Co. 1868.

KELLEY: Lincoln and Stanton. A study of the war administration of 1861 and 1862, with special consideration of some recent statements of General George B. McClellan. By William D. Kelley, M. C. New York and London: G. P. Putnam's Sons. 1885.

KING: Turning on the Light. A dispassionate survey of President Buchanan's administration, from 1860 to its close. By Horatio King, ex-Postmaster-General of the United States. Philadelphia: J. B. Lippincott Co. 1895.

LAMON: The Life of Abraham Lincoln; from his Birth to his Inauguration as President. By Ward H. Lamon. Boston: James R. Osgood & Co. 1872.

LAMON'S RECOLLECTIONS: Recollections of Abraham Lincoln, 1847–65. By Ward Hill Lamon. Edited by Dorothy Lamon. Chicago: A. C. McClurg & Co. 1895.

LELAND: Abraham Lincoln and the Abolition of Slavery in the United States. By Charles Godfrey Leland. New York: Merrill & Baker. 1879.

LINCOLN AND DOUGLAS: Abraham Lincoln. A Paper Read before The Royal Historical Society, London, June 16, 1881. By Hon. Isaac N. Arnold, F. R. H. S. Stephen A. Douglas: An Eulogy Delivered before the Chicago University, July 3, 1861. By Hon. James W. Sheahan. Chicago: Fergus Printing Co. 1881.

LINCOLN'S TIME: Washington in Lincoln's Time. By Noah Brooks. New York: The Century Co. 1895.

LOTHROP: William Henry Seward. By Thornton Kirkland Lothrop. Boston and New York: Houghton, Mifflin & Co. 1897.

MCCLELLAN: McClellan's Own Story. The war for the Union; the soldiers who fought it, the civilians who directed it, and his relations to it and to them. By George B. McClellan, late Major-General commanding the Armies. New York: Charles L. Webster & Co. 1887.

MCCLELLAN'S LAST SERVICE: McClellan's Last Service to the Republic, together with a tribute to his memory. By George Ticknor Curtis. New York: D. Appleton & Co. 1886.

MCCLURE: Abraham Lincoln and Men of War-Times. Some personal recollections of War and Politics during the Lincoln administration. With introduction by Dr. A. C. Lambdin. By A. K. McClure, LL. D. Second edition. Philadelphia: The Times Publishing Co. 1892.

MCCLURE'S STORIES: Abraham Lincoln's Stories and Speeches. Edited by J. B. McClure, A. M. Chicago: Rhodes & McClure Publishing Co. 1899.

MCCONNELL: Western Characters or Types of Border Life in the Western States. By J. L. McConnell. New York: Redfield. 1853.

MCKEE: The National Conventions and Platforms of all Political

Parties. 1789–1904. Convention, Popular and Electoral Vote. Also the Political Complexion of both Houses of Congress at each biennial period. By Thomas Hudson McKee. Fifth edition, revised and enlarged. Baltimore: The Friedenwald Co. 1904.

McPherson: The Political History of the United States of America during the great Rebellion. By Edward McPherson of Gettysburg, Pennsylvania, Clerk of the House of Representatives of the United States. Second edition. Washington: Philip & Solomons. 1865.

Merriam: The Life and Times of Samuel Bowles. By George S. Merriam. Two volumes. New York: The Century Co. 1885.

Moore: The Rebellion Record. A diary of American events, with documents, narratives, illustrative incidents, poetry, etc. Edited by Frank Moore. With an introductory address, on the causes of the struggle and the great issues before the country, by Edward Everett. Twelve volumes. New York: D. Van Nostrand. 1867 and 1868.

Morse: Abraham Lincoln. By John T. Morse, Jr. Two volumes. Boston and New York: Houghton, Mifflin & Co. 1896.

Naval History: The Naval History of the Civil War. By Admiral David D. Porter, U. S. Navy. New York: The Sherman Publishing Co. 1886.

Nicolay: A Short Life of Abraham Lincoln. Condensed from Nicolay & Hay's Abraham Lincoln. By John G. Nicolay. New York: The Century Co. 1904.

Nicolay & Hay: Abraham Lincoln, A History. By John G. Nicolay and John Hay. Ten volumes. New York: The Century Co. 1890.

Nicolay's Outbreak: The Outbreak of Rebellion. By John G. Nicolay, private secretary to President Lincoln. New York: Charles Scribner's Sons. 1894.

Oberholtzer: Abraham Lincoln. By Ellis Paxson Oberholtzer, Ph. D. Philadelphia: George W. Jacobs & Co. 1904.

Oldroyd: The Lincoln Memorial. Album-Immortelles. Original Life Pictures, with autographs, from the hands and hearts of eminent Americans and Europeans, contemporaries of the great martyr to liberty, Abraham Lincoln. Together with extracts from his speeches, letters, and sayings. Collected and edited by Osborn H. Oldroyd. With an introduction by Matthew Simpson, D. D., LL. D., and a sketch of the patriot's life by Hon. Isaac N. Arnold. Chicago: Gem Publishing House. 1883.

Onstot: Pioneers of Menard and Mason Counties. Made up of personal reminiscences of an early life in Menard County, which we gathered in a Salem life from 1830 to 1840, and a Petersburg life from 1840 to 1850, including personal reminiscences of

Abraham Lincoln and Peter Cartright. By T. G. Onstot. Forest City, Illinois: T. G. Onstot. 1902.

PETERSEN: Military Review of the Campaign in Virginia and Maryland, under Generals John C. Frémont, N. P. Banks, Irvin McDowell, Franz Sigel, John Pope, James S. Wadsworth, Henry W. Halleck, and George B. McClellan. In 1862. By Frederick A. Petersen. New York: Sinclair Tousey. 1862.

PHILLIPS: Speeches, Lectures, and Letters. By Wendell Phillips. Boston: James Redpath. 1863.

PIATT: Memories of the Men who saved the Union. By Donn Piatt. New York and Chicago: Belford, Clarke & Co. 1887.

PIATT'S THOMAS: General George H. Thomas. A critical biography by Donn Piatt, with concluding chapters by Henry V. Boynton. Cincinnati: Robert Clarke & Co. 1893.

PIERCE: Memoir and Letters of Charles Sumner. By Edward L. Pierce. 1811–74. Four volumes. Boston: Roberts Bros. 1893.

POLLARD: Life of Jefferson Davis. With a secret history of the Southern Confederacy. Gathered "behind the Scenes in Richmond." By Edward A. Pollard. Philadelphia: National Publishing Co. 1869.

POORE: Perley's Reminiscences of Sixty Years in the National Metropolis. By Ben: Perley Poore. Two volumes. Philadelphia: Hubbard Bros. 1886.

PORTER: Campaigning with Grant. By General Horace Porter, LL. D. New York: The Century Co. 1897.

RAYMOND: The Life and Public Services of Abraham Lincoln, Sixteenth President of the United States, together with his State Papers. By Henry J. Raymond. To which are added anecdotes and personal reminiscences of President Lincoln. By Frank B. Carpenter. New York: Derby & Miller. 1865.

RECORDS: The War of the Rebellion. A Compilation of the Official Records of the Union and Confederate Armies. 130 volumes. Washington: Government Printing Office. 1880–1901.

REID: Ohio in the War. Her Statesmen, her Generals, and Soldiers. By Whitelaw Reid. Two volumes. Cincinnati: Moore, Wilstach & Baldwin. 1868.

REYNOLDS: Reynolds' History of Illinois. My Own Times. Embracing also the History of my Life. By John Reynolds, late Governor of Illinois. Chicago: Chicago Historical Society. 1879.

RHODES: History of the United States from The Compromise of 1850. By James Ford Rhodes. Five volumes. New York: Harper & Bros. 1893–99. The Macmillan Co. 1904.

RICE: Reminiscences of Abraham Lincoln. By distinguished men of his time. Collected and edited by Allen Thorndike Rice. New York: The North American Review. 1888.

RICHARDSON: A Compilation of the Messages and Papers of the Presidents. 1789–1897. By James D. Richardson. Ten volumes. Washington: Government Printing Office. 1899.

RIDDLE: Recollections of War Times. Reminiscences of men and events in Washington. 1860–65. By Albert Gallatin Riddle. New York: G. P. Putnam's Sons. 1895.

ROPES: The Story of the Civil War. A concise account of the war in the United States of America between 1861 and 1865. By John Codman Ropes. Two volumes. New York: G. P. Putnam's Sons. 1894, 1898.

RUSSELL: My Diary North and South. By William Howard Russell. Boston: T. O. H. P. Burnham. 1863.

SALTER: The Life of James W. Grimes, Governor of Iowa, 1854–58; a Senator of the United States, 1859–69. By William Salter. New York: D. Appleton & Co. 1876.

SAVAGE: The Life and Public Services of Andrew Johnson, Seventeenth President of the United States. Including his State Papers, Speeches, and Addresses. By John Savage. New York: Derby & Miller. 1866.

SCHOFIELD: Forty-Six Years in the Army. By Lieutenant-General John M. Schofield. New York: The Century Co. 1897.

SCHOULER: History of the United States of America, under the Constitution. By James Schouler. Six volumes. Revised edition. New York: Dodd, Mead & Co. 1880–99.

SCHUCKERS: The Life and Public Services of Salmon Portland Chase. By J. W. Schuckers. To which is added the eulogy on Mr. Chase, delivered by William M. Evarts, before the Alumni of Dartmouth College, June 24, 1874. New York: D. Appleton & Co. 1874.

SEWARD I: Seward at Washington, as Senator and Secretary of State. A memoir of his life, with selections from his letters. 1846–61. By Frederick W. Seward. New York: Derby & Miller. 1891.

SEWARD II: Seward at Washington, as Senator and Secretary of State. A memoir of his life, with selections from his letters. 1861–72. By Frederick W. Seward. New York: Derby & Miller. 1891.

SEWARD'S AUTOBIOGRAPHY: Autobiography of William H. Seward, from 1801 to 1834. With a memoir of his life, and selections from his letters from 1831 to 1846. By Frederick W. Seward. New York: D. Appleton & Co. 1877.

SHEAHAN: The Life of Stephen A. Douglas. By James W. Sheahan. New York: Harper & Bros. 1860.

SHERMAN: John Sherman's Recollections of Forty Years in the House, Senate, and Cabinet. An Autobiography. Two volumes. Chicago: The Werner Co. 1895.

SPEED: Reminiscences of Abraham Lincoln and Notes of a Visit to California. Two Lectures by Joshua F. Speed. With a sketch of his Life. Louisville: John P. Morton & Co. 1884.

STANTON: Random Recollections. By Henry B. Stanton. New York: Harper & Bros. 1887.

STANWOOD: A History of the Presidency. By Edward Stanwood, Litt. D. Boston and New York: Houghton, Mifflin & Co. 1898.

STEPHENS: A Constitutional View of the late War between the States: its causes, character, conduct, and results presented in a series of colloquies at Liberty Hall. By Alexander H. Stephens. Two volumes in one. Philadelphia: National Publishing Co. 1868–70.

STODDARD: Abraham Lincoln. The True Story of a Great Life. By William O. Stoddard, one of President Lincoln's Private Secretaries during the War of the Rebellion. New York: Fords, Howard & Hulbert. 1896.

STODDARD'S WHITE HOUSE: Inside the White House in War Times. By William O. Stoddard. One of the President's private secretaries. New York: Charles L. Webster & Co. 1890.

STOVALL: Robert Toombs. Statesman, Speaker, Soldier, Sage. By Pleasant A. Stovall. New York: Cassell Publishing Co. 1892.

STOWE: Men of Our Times, or Leading Patriots of the Day. Being a narrative of the lives and deeds of Statesmen, Generals, and Orators. By Harriet Beecher Stowe. Hartford: Hartford Publishing Co. 1868.

SWINTON: Campaigns of the Army of the Potomac. A critical history of operations in Virginia, Maryland, and Pennsylvania, from the Commencement to the close of the War. 1861–65. By William Swinton. Revision and Reissue. New York: Charles Scribner's Sons. 1882.

TARBELL: The Life of Abraham Lincoln. Drawn from original Sources and containing many speeches, letters, and telegrams hitherto unpublished. Two volumes. By Ida M. Tarbell. New York: The Doubleday & McClure Co. 1900.

TARBELL'S EARLY LIFE: The Early Life of Abraham Lincoln. Containing many unpublished documents and unpublished reminiscences of Lincoln's early friends. By Ida M. Tarbell, assisted by J. McCan Davis. New York: S. S. McClure. 1896.

THAYER: From Pioneer Home to the White House. Life of Abraham Lincoln. By William M. Thayer. With eulogy by Hon. George Bancroft. Boston: James H. Earle. 1882.

VILLARD: Memoirs of Henry Villard, Journalist and Financier. 1835–1900. Two volumes. Boston and New York: Houghton, Mifflin & Co. 1904.

WARD: Abraham Lincoln. Tributes from his associates. Reminiscences of soldiers, statesmen, and citizens. With introduction by The Rev. William Hayes Ward, D. D. New York: Thomas Y. Crowell & Co. 1895.

WARDEN: An Account of the Private Life and Public Services of Salmon Portland Chase. By Robert B. Warden. Cincinnati: Wilstach, Baldwin & Co. 1874.

WARRINGTON: "Warrington" Pen-Portraits. A Collection of Personal and Political Reminiscences from 1848 to 1876, from the writings of William S. Robinson. Edited and published by Mrs. W. S. Robinson. Boston: 1877.

WEED: Autobiography of Thurlow Weed. Edited by his daughter, Harriet A. Weed. [Volume I.] Memoir of Thurlow Weed. By his grandson, Thurlow Weed Barnes. [Volume II.] Boston: Houghton, Mifflin & Co. 1884.

WEISS: Life and Correspondence of Theodore Parker, Minister of the Twenty-eighth Congregational Society, Boston. By John Weiss. Two volumes. New York: D. Appleton & Co. 1864.

WELLES: Lincoln and Seward. Remarks upon the memorial address of Charles Francis Adams, on the Late William H. Seward, with incidents and comments illustrative of the measures and policy of the administration of Abraham Lincoln. And views as to the relative positions of the late President and Secretary of State. By Gideon Welles, ex-Secretary of the Navy. New York: Sheldon Co. 1874.

WHITNEY: Life on the Circuit with Lincoln. With sketches of Generals Grant, Sherman, and McClellan, Judge Davis, Leonard Swett, and other contemporaries. By Henry C. Whitney. Boston: Estes & Lauriat. 1892.

WILSON: History of the Rise and Fall of the Slave Power in America. By Henry Wilson. Three volumes. Boston: James R. Osgood & Co. 1872–77.

WINTHROP: A Memoir of Robert C. Winthrop. Prepared for the Massachusetts Historical Society by Robert C. Winthrop, Jr. Boston: Little, Brown & Co. 1897.

WORKS: Abraham Lincoln. Complete Works. Comprising his speeches, letters, state papers, and miscellaneous writings. Edited by John G. Nicolay and John Hay. Two volumes. New York: The Century Co. 1894.

NOTES

NOTES TO CHAPTER I

1. Abraham Lincoln was born February 12, 1809, on the Big South Fork of Nolin Creek in Hardin, now La Rue County, Kentucky. Four years later, his family moved to Knob Creek, not far away, where they remained until they left the State in the autumn of 1816.
2. Samuel Haycraft, in Herndon i, 14.
3. Whitney, 11.
4. Near Little Pigeon Creek in what is now Spencer County.
5. Lincoln's autobiographical letter to Jesse W. Fell, secretary of the Illinois State Central Committee, December 20, 1859. Arnold, 14; Works i, 596; Facsimile in Lamon, 539, and in Lamon's Recollections, 9–12.
6. Lincoln's short autobiography in the third person, written at the request of a friend to be used in the preparation of a biography for the canvass of 1860. Works i, 639.
7. Lamon, 36, 69; Herndon i, 32, 39–40, 52; Stoddard, 36; Brooks, 31; Nicolay & Hay i, 35; Tarbell i, 29–30; Tarbell's Early Life, 46–48.
8. "Abraham now thinks that the aggregate of all his schooling did not amount to one year." — Lincoln's Autobiography in 1860. Works i, 639.
9. Herndon i, 32.
10. For references to this superiority in spelling and writing, see Tarbell's Early Life, 83, 84, 90; Tarbell i, 41–42; Stoddard, 34; Nicolay & Hay i, 42; Holland, 30; Arnold, 20; Herndon i, 35, 38; Lamon, 34–35; Thayer, 118.
11. "He said to me that he had got hold of and read through every book he ever heard of in that country, for a circuit of about fifty miles." — Swett's Reminiscences, in Rice, 459.
12. Mrs. Allen Gentry, *née* Roby. See Lamon, 34, 35, 70, 71; Herndon i, 35–36.
13. David Turnham, in Thayer, 119.
14. Nathaniel Grigsby, in Lamon, 71.
15. Lamon, 40.
16. Herndon i, 48–49; Lamon, 67; Morse i, 13.
17. "I induced my husband to permit Abe to read and study at

home as well as at school. At first he was not easily reconciled to it, but finally he too seemed willing to encourage him to a certain extent." — Mrs. Thomas Lincoln, September 8, 1865, in Herndon i, 33. This lady, Sarah Bush Johnston, had married Thomas Lincoln about a year after the death of Abraham's mother. The boy was in his eleventh year when the second wedding took place.

18. Lamon, 67.
19. Herndon i, 39; see also Lamon, 36.
20. "Away back in my childhood, the earliest days of my being able to read, I got hold of a small book, such a one as few of the younger members have ever seen — Weems's Life of Washington." — Lincoln's address to the Senate of New Jersey, February 21, 1861. Works i, 688.
21. Lamon, 68; Arnold, 25; Tarbell's Early Life, 62; Nicolay & Hay i, 43.
22. "The Lincolns through which the President's genealogy is traced were, for six generations, with a single exception, pioneers in the settlement of new countries. 1st, Samuel, from England, an early settler at Hingham, Massachusetts;

    "2d, Mordecai, of Scituate, lived and died near where he was born;

    "3d, Mordecai, settled in Pennsylvania, thirty years previous to the organization of Berks County;

    "4th, John, went into the wilds of Virginia;

    "5th, Abraham, went to Kentucky with Daniel Boone when the country was inhabited by savages and wild beasts;

    "6th, Thomas, who went with his son Abraham, the future President, into the sparsely settled portion of Indiana." — Samuel Shackford, in *New England Historical and Genealogical Register*, vol. xli, p. 156.
23. Works i, 639.
24. Leonard Swett claims to have been told by Abraham Lincoln himself, that Thomas Lincoln had recourse to this mode of raising money in order to meet unpaid notes bearing his endorsement. The explanation hardly accounts for all of the boy's drudgery. Moreover, his father, according to Colonel Chapman, a relative by marriage, "habitually treated him with great barbarity"; and cousin Dennis Hanks, who insists that the elder Lincoln loved his son, admits that he knocked him off the fence merely for questioning a passing traveler or answering his inquiries about the roads. See Rice, 458; Lamon, 40, 69, 70, 77; Browne, 53.
25. For one brief period, he chafed so under his burden that he begged a friendly neighbor to help him cast it off by getting him a place on one of the Ohio River boats. The man pointed out to him that his time legally belonged to his father until he became

of age, and that he was under a moral obligation, as well, not to leave his parents without their consent. Whereupon he returned to his work. See Herndon i, 53.

26. "He is usually above the medium height, and rather spare. He stoops a little too; for he has done a deal of hard work, and expects to do more; but you see at once, that unless his lungs are weak, his strength is by no means broken, and you are quite sure that many a stately tree is destined to be humbled by his sinewy arm." — The Pioneer, in McConnell, 138.

27. Mrs. Crawford, in Lamon, 51.

28. William Wood, in Herndon i, 53; Lamon, 52, 68, 69.

29. Browne, 53.

30. Lamon, 52.

31. May not this, in Weems's Washington, also have had its influence? — "His delight was in that of the manliest sort, which, by stringing the limbs and swelling the muscles, promotes the kindliest flow of blood and spirits. At jumping with a long pole, or heaving heavy weights, for his years he hardly had an equal."

32. The town of central Illinois in which, during the summer of 1831, Lincoln began life on his own account.

33. Herndon i, 116; Lamon, 154. The latter states that the feat was performed often, and that the weight varied between a thousand and twelve hundred pounds.

34. Brockett, 62–63; Herndon i, 116–117. For a fanciful account, see Thayer, 233–234. Major Whitney, the author of Life on the Circuit with Lincoln, informed the writer that Greene gave him a somewhat different version of the affair. According to this story, which is somewhat borne out by an account in Onstot (84), Greene was given to habits of betting and petty gambling, which Lincoln sought to correct. After much persuasion, Greene promised to reform as soon as he had made good his losses. Whereupon Lincoln, to put an end to the vice at once, suggested that his friend might win back the exact amount by laying the wager described in the text.

35. This was so, in a considerable degree, to the day of his death. Says Charles A. Dana, speaking of the President: —

"I remember that the last time I went to see him at the White House — the afternoon before he was killed — I found him in a side room with coat off and sleeves rolled up, washing his hands. He had finished his work for the day, and was going away. I noticed then the thinness of his arms, and how well developed, strong, and active his muscles seemed to be. In fact, there was nothing flabby or feeble about Mr. Lincoln physically. He was a very quick man in his movements when he chose to be, and he had immense physical endurance. Night after night he would work late and hard without being wilted by it, and he always seemed as ready for the next day's work as though he had done nothing the day before." — Dana, 172–173.

36. *New England Historical and Genealogical Register* xix, 360; Holland, 20–21; Nicolay & Hay i, 4; Barrett, 11; Works i, 117, 596, 638.
37. Lamon, 8, 16; Herndon i, 8.
38. Nicolay & Hay i, 21; McClure's Stories, 56; Lamon, 7; Herndon i, 7; Browne, 41; Arnold, 16.
39. Swett's Reminiscences, in Rice, 463.
40. Dennis Hanks, in Browne, 53.
41. Interview with sculptor Thomas D. Jones, in December, 1860, quoted in *Century Magazine*, n. s. xx, 933.
42. The Chronicles were published in Herndon i, 50–55, edition of 1889, and were omitted from some later editions.
43. Lamon, 63–66.
44. Ferrying and paddling about on the Ohio, canoeing on the Sangamon, two flat-boat voyages down the Ohio and the Mississippi to New Orleans, a flat-boat voyage as pilot down the Sangamon, a steamboat voyage as assistant in getting the stranded Talisman up the Sangamon, comprised, according to the records, his activities on the water.
45. In April, 1828.
46. For various versions of the episode see: Holland, 35–36; Coffin, 43; Lamon, 71–72; Herndon i, 54; Browne, 75–77; Thayer, 158–168; Nicolay & Hay i, 44; Works i, 640; Stoddard, 52–56; Swett's Reminiscences, in Rice, 462; McClure's Stories, 33–34.
47. Stoddard, 64; Lamon, 83–84; Herndon i, 67; Browne, 101–102; Coffin, 60; Thayer, 202–203.
48. The reports of this affair vary, but in unimportant particulars. Compare Arnold, 32; Stoddard, 67–69; Herndon i, 72–75; Coffin, 64–67; Browne, 98–99; Holland, 45; Tarbell's Early Life, 120–122; Lamon, 90–94; Nicolay & Hay i, 79–81; French, 42; Morse, i, 18–19; Brooks, 51–52; McClure's Stories, 57–58; Chittenden's Reminiscences, 352–354; Irelan xvi, 86–88; Thayer, 220–224; Tarbell i, 63–64.
49. Lamon, 94–95; Thayer, 225–226.
50. Lamon, 151–152.
51. A. Y. Ellis, in Lamon, 152.
52. The original account of this incident is to be found in Holland, 44. For modifications see: Coffin, 63–64; Browne, 99–100; Nicolay & Hay i, 83; Tarbell's Early Life, 122–123; French, 42–43; Tarbell i, 64–65; Thayer, 209–210; McClure's Stories, 29; Onstot, 85–87.
53. On a certain occasion, Lincoln acted as one of the seconds while

two neighbors settled a quarrel growing out of a lawsuit, with their fists. When the fight was over, the other second, a very small person, remarked, "Well, Abe, my man has whipped yours, and I can whip you." To which Lincoln soberly replied that he was willing to fight, provided the challenger would chalk the outline of his figure upon the big man's more ample proportions, and every blow struck outside of that mark should be counted foul. This sally, like the repartee of the famous Curran, under somewhat similar circumstances, wound up the whole affair in good humor.

54. Chittenden's Reminiscences, 316.
55. Thayer, 56–57. See also Pierce iv, 235; McClure's Stories, 181.
56. Brockett, 696; McClure's Stories, 249; Ward, 122–123. In the last, General Viele says:—

"On board ship, I have never seen a man who could perform this feat. Any man who will attempt to do it will see how difficult it is."

57. Tarbell's Early Life, 102; Tarbell i, 50–51.
58. "In 1864, five six-footers, accompanied by two representatives, called on the President and were introduced to him. These six-footers seemed to astonish the Chief Magistrate, who, after carefully surveying the tall specimens, exclaimed, 'Are they all from your State?' 'All,' was the spontaneous response. 'Why, it seems to me,' said the President, glancing at the short representatives, 'that your State always sends her *little* men to Congress.'" — Gobright, 329.
59. Lincoln as a representative from Sangamon County, Douglas as a candidate for the office of State's Attorney, for the first judicial district.
60. Lamon, 185; Herndon i, 154; Morse i, 43; Nicolay & Hay i, 124.
61. Works i, 111; Herndon i, 268.
62. Coffin, 480. See also Browne, 680; Lamon's Recollections, 128; Grant, 590–592; Porter, 385.
63. The list of Lincoln's comments on small men would be incomplete without his reference to Colonel Ellsworth as "the greatest little man I ever met"; and his description of General Sheridan as "a little chap with round head, red face, legs longer than his body, and not enough neck to hang him by."
64. Kelley's Reminiscences, in Rice, 259; Bartlett, 140–145; Irelan xvi, 346–350.
65. Sherman i, 231.
66. C. Van Santvoord, in *Century Magazine*, n. s. iii, 613.
67. Poore ii, 63; Rice, 223; Diary of a Public Man, *North American Review* cxxix, 266–267.
68. Mr. Sumner's height in his prime was six feet and three inches.
69. "A wager was made one day in Springfield, between some

friends of Mr. Lincoln and of O. M. Hatch, late Secretary of the State of Illinois (also a tall, slender man), as to their relative height. Mr. Hatch was first placed against the wall, so a mark could be made over his head, Mr. Lincoln remarking, at the time, 'Now, Hatch, stand fair.' When the mark was duly made, Mr. Lincoln was placed beside it, and at first Mr. Hatch's friends declared that they had won the wager. 'Wait,' said Mr. Lincoln, 'the mark is not yet made for me.' Then he began to stretch himself out like India rubber, and went nearly two inches above Mr. Hatch's mark, carrying off the stakes amidst the shouts and laughter of the bystanders." — Leonard W. Volk, in *Century Magazine*, n. s. iii, 462. For other measuring scenes see: Browne, 352, 355, 360, 387; Curtis's Lincoln, 28–29.

NOTES TO CHAPTER II

1. According to Lamon, Lincoln had been decided upon as captain the previous autumn, at a militia muster in Clary's Grove.
2. Tarbell's Early Life, 137–138; Holland, 49; Brooks, 58; Stoddard, 74; Arnold, 34; Morse i, 35–36; French, 45–46; Thayer, 231–232; Tarbell i, 75–76; Nicolay & Hay i, 89–90; Works i, 597, 641. Lamon (78 and 101, 102) questions, though not consistently, the story that Lincoln worked for Kirkpatrick. Leonard Swett, in Rice, 464–465, gives a version that differs from the commonly accepted one; but his evidently faulty memory impairs the value of what might otherwise be an important contribution to Lincoln literature.
3. Ben: Perley Poore, in Rice, 218–219; Coffin, 68–69; Herndon i, 84; Tarbell's Early Life, 138; Browne, 107; French, 47; Tarbell i, 76–77.
4. Another volunteer captain, who had been a railroad conductor, improved upon this during a later war. While drilling a squad, that was marching by flank, he turned to talk to a friend, for a moment. Upon looking again at his men, he saw that they were in the act of marching into a fence. Something had to be done to halt them, and that at once; so he shouted: "Down brakes! Down brakes!" This command was probably as effectual as that of the English militia officer who, wishing to have his company fall back that it might dress with the line, gave the order: "Advance three paces backwards! March!"
5. Lamon, 102–103; Herndon i, 86; Stoddard, 75.
6. Herndon i, 86–87; Lamon, 103–104; Stoddard, 76.
7. Ben: Perley Poore, in Rice, 219.
8. Lamon, 109–112; Browne, 112–113; Herndon i, 87–88; Thayer,

239–240; Nicolay & Hay i, 94; Letter of the Hon. Joseph Gillespie, in Lincoln and Douglas, 194 a–194 b.

9. Lamon, 108–109; Tarbell's Early Life, 141; Browne, 107–109; Stoddard, 77–78; Arnold, 34–35; Brooks, 59; Herndon i, 87; Coffin, 69; Tarbell i, 77; Thayer, 236–238; French, 46–47. This episode vividly recalls Andrew Jackson's encounter with mutineers during the Creek War.

10. Stoddard, 79; Lamon, 111; Thayer, 240.

11. Among these, besides Lincoln, were Zachary Taylor, Winfield Scott, Albert Sidney Johnston, and Robert Anderson.

12. Captain Lincoln was enrolled with his company in the Fourth Illinois Mounted Volunteers, April 21, 1832. Mustered out of service May 27, he at once enlisted as a private in Captain Elijah Iles's Independent Spy Company. Mustered out again June 16, he reënlisted in the company June 20, when it was reorganized under Captain Jacob M. Early. Upon the disbandment of the company, July 10, he received his final discharge.

13. Arnold, 36.

14. The first State Convention, in Illinois, was held by the Democrats, December 7, 1835.

15. For the address in full, see Lamon, 129; Works i, 4.

16. Reynolds, 185.

17. There are slight differences in the reports of this vote. Herndon i, 96, says that 208 (probably a misprint for 280) votes were cast, and that Lincoln received all but 3. Lamon, 134, gives his vote as 277 out of a total of 280. Nicolay & Hay i, 109, quote the same figures from the *Sangamo Journal* of August 11, 1832. Mr. Lincoln, himself, in the autobiography of 1860, gives the vote as "277 for and 7 against him." Miss Tarbell (Early Life, 158, and Tarbell i, 91) bases upon an examination of the official returns in the county clerk's office at Springfield, the statement that, of 290 votes cast for representatives, Lincoln received 277.

18. Mark the further parallel with Washington, who was also a surveyor, when a young man.

19. Offutt's business having gone to ruin in the spring of 1832, Lincoln, on his return from the war, opened a store in partnership with William F. Berry. It soon "winked out." In the spring of 1833 he was appointed postmaster of New Salem, and a few months later he became Calhoun's assistant.

20. A. Y. Ellis, in Lamon, 127; Herndon i, 94.

21. Herndon i, 117–118; Lamon, 156; Thayer, 261–262.

22. Lincoln is generally credited with the first place. Nicolay & Hay i, 122, Morse i, 42, and Brooks, 71, report the vote for the four successful candidates to have been: Lincoln, 1376; Dawson, 1370; Carpenter, 1170; and Stuart, 1164. Mr. Lincoln, himself,

after an interval of twenty-six years, stated that he "was then elected to the legislature by the highest vote cast for any candidate." He probably confused this election in his memory with that of 1836. For, Herndon (i, 118) and Tarbell (Early Life, 196) quote the official returns in Springfield, as *revised* shortly after election, to be: Dawson, 1390; Lincoln, 1376; Carpenter, 1170; and Stuart, 1164.

23. Lamon, 125; Herndon i, 94–95; Stoddard, 85; Morse i, 39; Brooks, 65; Coffin, 72; Tarbell's Early Life, 156; Nicolay & Hay i, 107–108.

24. James Gourley, in Lamon, 187.

25. The news of Franklin's discoveries, more than eighty years before, and of the subsequent use of the lightning-rod, had evidently not yet become current in Illinois. Lincoln's ignorance of the subject, however, was short-lived after he had seen Forquer's rod. The sight of it led him, as he once told Speed, "to the study of the properties of electricity and the utility of the rod as a conductor."

26. The reply to Forquer has been compared to Pitt's famous philippic against Horace Walpole, beginning, according to the Johnsonian version, with "The atrocious crime of being a young man, which the honorable gentleman has with such spirit and decency charged upon me." The Englishman was five years older, at the time of its delivery, than Lincoln was when he spoke ; yet for crushing, biting invective, the few words of the backwoodsman easily excel the collegian's elegant periods.

27. Arnold, 47–49; Lamon, 188–189; Morse i 51–52; French, 60–62; Stoddard, 104–105; Brooks, 74–75; Oberholtzer, 67–68; Coffin, 88–89; Tarbell i, 128–130; Herndon i, 161–163; Joshua F. Speed, in Oldroyd, 143–145. There are unimportant variations in the conclusion of the speech as quoted from Speed by Herndon, and as contributed by Speed to the Memorial.

28. Raymond, 27; Browne, 140; Herndon i, 159–160; Works i, 7–8. There is a slight difference between the version published by Herndon and that published in the Works.

29. A speech delivered by Lincoln, at Springfield, some time during December, 1839, in the course of a formal political debate, is the only one of this canvass that has been preserved entire.

30. Arnold, 49–50; Lamon, 189–190; Herndon i, 185–186; Coffin, 98–99; Brooks, 75–76; French, 59–60. Arnold and Lamon place this incident in 1836; but Herndon, who bases his statement on the manuscript of Lincoln's associate, Ninian W. Edwards, assigns it to 1840.

31. Herndon i, 186–188; Lamon, 230–231; Nicolay & Hay i, 171–172; Coffin, 99–101; Arnold, 67–68; Brooks, 88; Oberholtzer,

66–67. Possibly Mr. Herndon had this scene in mind when he said to Thomas Hicks, the painter, some time in the summer of 1860: —

"Lincoln never had any personal fear, and he has the courage of a lion. In the old political struggles in this State, I have seen him go upon the platform when a dozen revolvers were drawn on him; but before he had spoken twenty words they would go back into the pockets of their owners. And such were the methods of his eloquence that, likely as not, these men would be the first to shake hands with him when he came among them after the meeting." — Rice, 604.

32. U. F. Linder, in Browne, 175–176; Holland, 96.

33. This recalls Rosalind's play on words: "You 'll be rotton ere you be half ripe, and that 's the right virtue of the medlar." — As You Like It iii, 2.

34. Lamon, 230; Nicolay & Hay i, 172; Browne, 176–177.

35. The "Long Nine" comprised: Representatives Ninian W. Edwards, Robert Lang Wilson, Daniel Stone, William F. Elkin, John Dawson, Andrew McCormick, and Abraham Lincoln; Senators Archer G. Herndon, and Job Fletcher, Sr. They averaged over six feet in height, and over two hundred pounds in weight.

36. Robert L. Wilson, in Herndon i, 168, and in Lamon, 200.

37. In the *Sangamo Journal* of January 28, 1837.

38. Browne, 147–148; Whitney, 33.

39. Herndon i, 188–189; Lamon, 231.

40. Tarbell i, 155–157.

41. The Lost Townships articles, with the correspondence that resulted therefrom, are to be found complete in Herndon i, 219–245, and in Lamon, 253–269.

42. This attitude recalls that of Alexander Hamilton. On the eve of his fatal duel with Aaron Burr, he wrote: —

"To those who, with me, abhorring the practice of dueling, may think that I ought on no account to have added to the number of bad examples, I answer that my *relative* situation, as well in public as private, enforcing all the considerations which constitute what men of the world denominate honor, imposed on me (as I thought) a peculiar necessity not to decline the call."

Henry Clay, who fought several duels, said in somewhat the same strain: —

"The man with a high sense of honor and nice sensibility, when the question is whether he shall fight or have the finger of scorn pointed at him, is unable to resist; and few, very few, are found willing to adopt such an alternative."

43. Said to be Bloody Island, which owed its gruesome name to the fact that many duels had been fought there.

44. Edward Levis, in Tarbell i, 189–190.
45. William Butler, who, with Dr. Merryman, represented Lincoln in the Shields affair.
46. Works i, 71; Lamon, 252; Herndon i, 245.
47. Herndon i, 246.
48. Whitney, 36.
49. *McClure's Magazine* vi, 528.
50. Herndon i, 217.
51. A garbled though friendly version, published during the canvass in a Chicago newspaper and probably elsewhere, was reprinted in Bartlett's Campaign Life of Lincoln; but it appears to have attracted little or no attention.
52. Carpenter, 304–305.
53. See: Holland, 88–89; Arnold, 70; Whitney, 35; Browne, 185; French, 88–89; Lamon, 269; Stoddard, 116; Carpenter, 303; Irelan xvii, 656–658, 661–662; Leland, 55.
54. Carpenter, 302–303.
55. Irelan xvii, 660–661.
56. Davidson, 625–626.
57. Herndon i, 246; Brooks, 93; Holland, 89; Arnold, 71; Nicolay, 68; Curtis's Lincoln, 42–43; Nicolay & Hay i, chap. xii. For an account of the episode from the other point of view, see Condon, 44–50.
58. One other slight quarrel that occurred, previous to this, exhibited Lincoln at its conclusion in somewhat of the mood that later became characteristic of him. While at Lawrenceville, Ill., in October, 1840, he had an altercation with one W. G. Anderson. The nature of the dispute is not known. The only facts concerning it are to be found in the letters exchanged at the time. Anderson, in one of those stiffly formal notes that usually figured in "affairs of honor," threw no light upon the cause of the quarrel, but styled Lincoln "the aggressor" and demanded an explanation. Lincoln's reply reads rather like an apology to himself than to his correspondent. He wrote:—

"In the difficulty between us of which you speak, you say you think I was the aggressor. I do not think I was. You say my 'words imported insult.' I meant them as a fair set-off to your own statements, and not otherwise; and in that light alone I now wish you to understand them. You ask for my present 'feelings on the subject.' I entertain no unkind feeling to you, and none of any sort upon the subject, except a sincere regret that I permitted myself to get into any such altercation." For both letters, see *Century Magazine*, n. s. xv, 477.
59. Nicolay & Hay i, 212; Brooks, 94.

NOTES TO CHAPTER III

1. Lamon, 232–236; Herndon i, 182–183; Browne, 173–174; Nicolay & Hay i, 172–177.
2. For the speech in full, see Works i, 21. Douglas frequently spelled his name, in the early days, with the double "s."
3. Lincoln was a candidate on the Whig electoral ticket.
4. Lamon, 236; Browne, 174–175.
5. Judge Gillespie, in Herndon i, 189–190; Lamon, 237.
6. Herndon i, 192–215; Lamon, 238–243; Irelan xvii, 647–654; Keckley, 228–230. The marriage took place November 4, 1842.
7. He was, as usual, a candidate on the Whig electoral ticket.
8. Lamon, 340–341; Herndon ii, 30–31; Irelan xvi, 172–173.
9. In a speech delivered at Springfield, Ill., on October 23, 1849, and published in the *State Register* of November 8.
10. "I passed the Kansas-Nebraska Act myself. I had the authority and power of a dictator, throughout the whole controversy, in both houses." — Douglas to Cutts, in Cutts, 122; Brown's Douglas, 90.
11. "The author of the bill was regarded with execration; his middle name was Arnold, and this suggested a comparison to Benedict Arnold. The term which is used in every Christian land as a synonym of traitor was likewise applied to him, and one hundred and three ladies of an Ohio village sent him thirty pieces of silver. He could travel, as he afterwards said, "from Boston to Chicago by the light of his own effigies." — Rhodes i, 496.
12. For Douglas's own entertaining account of the affair, see Cutts, 97–101.
13. Nicolay & Hay i, 378–379.
14. Nicolay & Hay i, 374–380; Herndon ii, 36–38; Arnold, 117–118; Lamon, 348–350; Brooks, 136–140; Holland, 135–139; Stoddard, 141–142 ; Browne, 246–248.
15. Weldon's Reminiscences, in Rice, 199.
16. Works i, 180.
17. Arnold, 118–119; Herndon ii, 42; Lamon, 358; Brooks, 141. See also W. M. Dickson, in *Harper's Magazine* lxix, 64.
18. Whitney, 29. See also Bartlett, 67–69.
19. Lincoln, doubtless considering himself thus absolved from his part of the agreement, spoke in Urbana, shortly thereafter.
20. "It is true that, owing to the popularity of their candidate for State Treasurer, the Democrats carried the State ticket, and Douglas made the most of it ; but the Anti-Nebraska people elected five out of nine Congressmen, and their majority in the State on the Congressional vote was more than seventeen thousand. They also controlled the legislature." — Rhodes ii, 62.

21. He had been elected to this legislature contrary to his wishes, and he had resigned that he might be eligible to the senatorship.
22. The first ballot, according to Sheahan (275), stood: Lincoln, 45; Shields, 41; Trumbull, 5; Koerner, 2; Ficklin, 1; Denning, 1; Ogden, 1; Kellogg, 1; Edwards, 1; and Matteson, 1.
23. "I regret my defeat moderately, but I am not nervous about it. I could have headed off every combination and been elected, had it not been for Matteson's double game — and his defeat now gives me more pleasure than my own gives me pain. On the whole, it is perhaps as well for our general cause that Trumbull is elected. The Nebraska men confess that they hate it worse than anything that could have happened. It is a great consolation to see them worse whipped than I am. I tell them it is their own fault — that they had abundant opportunity to choose between him and me, which they declined, and instead forced it on me to decide between him and Matteson." — Lincoln to Congressman Elihu B. Washburne, February 9, 1855.
24. The Dred Scott decision, the Kansas constitution, and the Utah rebellion were the questions debated.
25. In the presidential election of 1856, the popular votes of Frémont and Fillmore combined amounted to 2,215,798. Buchanan, though elected, had but 1,838,169, plus the eight electoral votes of South Carolina cast by its legislature. Illinois gave him 105,348; and the two other candidates, 133,633.
26. William A. Richardson, Douglas's political lieutenant in Illinois, who had introduced the Kansas-Nebraska Bill in the House, had been Douglas's nominee for the governorship of the State, the previous autumn. His defeat, by Colonel William H. Bissell, the Republican candidate, is the execution referred to.
27. Barrett, 139; Howells, 179; Works i, 231.
28. Their attitude is thus explained by one of them: —

"Desirous of breaking the iron rule of the Democratic Party, so long wielded, and with such terrible effect, by the Slave Power, they not unnaturally felt that no voice and no arm could be more potent in producing such a result than the voice and arm of Mr. Douglas, if triumphantly returned to his place in the Senate by the aid of Republican support." — Wilson ii, 568.

Henry Villard, who reported the ensuing debates as special correspondent for the New York *Staats-Zeitung*, says in this connection: —

"I believed, with many prominent leaders of the Republican Party, that, with regard to separating more effectively the anti-slavery Northern from the pro-slavery Southern wing of the Democracy, it would have been better if the reëlection of Douglas had not been opposed." — Villard i, 94.

29. Theodore Parker, with a keen insight into the situation, wrote to William H. Herndon from Boston, under date of August 28, 1858:

"I never recommended the Republicans to adopt Douglas into their family. I said in a speech last January, 'he is a mad dog'; just now he is barking at the wolf which has torn our sheep. But he himself is more dangerous than the wolf. I think I should not let him into the fold." — Weiss ii, 240.

30. "Douglas had three or four very distinguished men, of the most extreme anti-slavery views of any men in the Republican Party, expressing their desire for his reëlection to the Senate last year. That would, of itself, have seemed to be a little wonderful, but that wonder is heightened, when we see that Wise of Virginia, a man exactly opposed to them, a man who believes in the divine right of slavery, was also expressing his desire that Douglas should be reëlected; that another man that may be said to be kindred to Wise, Mr. Breckinridge, the Vice-President, and of your own State, was also agreeing with the anti-slavery men in the North, that Douglas ought to be reëlected. Still, to heighten the wonder, a senator from Kentucky, whom I have always loved with an affection as tender and endearing as I have ever loved any man, who was opposed to the anti-slavery men for reasons which seemed sufficient to him, and equally opposed to Wise and Breckinridge, was writing letters into Illinois to secure the reëlection of Douglas. Now, that all these conflicting elements should be brought, while at dagger's points with one another, to support him, is a feat that is worthy for you to note and consider. It is quite probable that each of these classes of men thought, by the reëlection of Douglas, their peculiar views would gain something; it is probable that the anti-slavery men thought their views would gain something; that Wise and Breckinridge thought so too, as regards their opinions; that Mr. Crittenden thought that his views would gain something, although he was opposed to both these other men. It is probable that each and all of them thought that they were using Douglas; and it is yet an unsolved problem whether he was not using them all." — Lincoln, addressing himself to Kentuckians, in the Cincinnati speech, September 17, 1859. Works i, 568–569.

31. Herndon ii, 60.

32. The nomination of a candidate for the United States Senate by a State convention was without precedent, as the election was to be in the hands, not of the people, but of the legislature then about to be chosen.

33. Debates, 1–5; Works i, 240–245; Barrett, 145–152; Holland, 161–167; Raymond, 52–58; Arnold, 132–138; Irelan xvi, 203–211; Lamon, 399–405; Sheahan, 401–405.

34. Debates, 5–13; Flint, 105–114; Sheahan, 406–415.

35. For the Chicago, Bloomington, and Springfield speeches in full, see Debates, 5–64; for the Lincoln speeches only, see Works i, 247–273.
36. Ottawa, August 21; Freeport, August 27; Jonesboro, September 15; Charleston, September 18; Galesburg, October 7; Quincy, October 13, and Alton, October 15.
37. For the correspondence in reference to the debate, see Irelan xvi, 242–247; Bartlett, 74–79; Debates, 64–66; Works i, 273–277.
38. In 1856. See: Holland, 155–156; Arnold, 144; Lamon, 408–409; Browne, 283–284.
39. Debates, 55; Works i, 261. See also Browne, 291.
40. W. M. Dickson, in *Harper's Magazine* lxix, 64. This complaint is singularly like that, of classic memory, put by Plutarch in the mouth of Thucydides. "When I have thrown him," said he, speaking of Pericles, "and given him a fair fall, by persisting that he had no fall, he gets the better of me, and makes the bystanders, in spite of their own eyes, believe him."
41. Alley's Reminiscences, in Rice, 575.
42. W. M. Dickson, in *Harper's Magazine* lxix, 64; Browne, 282.
43. Forney ii, 179.
44. This was essentially true, notwithstanding that at the first Republican National Convention, two years before, Lincoln had, greatly to his own surprise, received 110 votes — out of 551 — for the vice-presidential nomination.
45. Tarbell i, 307. See also Whitney, 456–457.
46. Browne, 282. See also what Douglas said after the debate to Senator Wilson, in Wilson ii, 577.
47. "My father was an ardent personal and political friend of Douglas, and in his circle it was looked upon as presumptuous and ridiculous for Abe Lincoln to compete with 'the Little Giant' for the Senate of the United States." — Fry's Reminiscences, in Rice, 387.
48. For Judge Beckwith's report of the interview, see Tarbell i, 308–309. Versions less complete are to be found in Arnold, 146–147; Browne, 284; Brooks, 175–176; Coffin, 168.
49. Slightly condensed. Debates, 296; Works i, 461.
50. See Horace White, in Herndon ii, 102–103.
51. Debates, 105; Works i, 281.
52. Debates, 118; Works i, 292.
53. Debates, 286–287; Works i, 453.
54. Debates, 297–298; Works i, 462.
55. Arnold, 145. See also Horace White, in Herndon ii, 101–102.
56. Debates, 136; Works i, 308.
57. This corresponded with Lincoln's own prognosis of Douglas's course, expressed four weeks before, in a letter to Henry Asbury. It read, in part: —

"You shall have hard work to get him directly to the point whether a territorial legislature has or has not the power to exclude slavery. But if you succeed in bringing him to it — though he will be compelled to say it possesses no such power — he will instantly take ground that slavery cannot actually exist in the Territories unless the people desire it, and so give it protection by territorial legislation. If this offends the South, he will let it offend them, as at all events, he means to hold on to his chances in Illinois." — Works i, 277.

58. Variations in the accounts of these deliberations and their seeming *ex post facto* character have led cautious writers to regard the story with suspicion. The essential facts are, however, probably, as here set forth. See: Arnold, 151; Horace White in Herndon ii, 109–110; Nicolay & Hay ii, 160; Schurz, 51–52; Wilson ii, 576; Irelan xvi, 254; Lamon, 415–416; Holland, 188–189; Swett's Eulogy, in Whitney, 562; Morse i, 144; Blaine i, 148; Coffin, 168; Brockett, 106; Brooks, 172–173; Raymond, 66; Bartlett, 81; Tarbell i, 316–318.

59. It is interesting to note that the only parallel instance in which he is known to have asked advice had a similar history. This was at the beginning of the canvass, when, before delivering his house-divided-against-itself speech, he submitted it to a council of friends, who all, with one exception, urged him to omit the first paragraph. Cogent from the politicians' point of view as the objections to it were, they failed to move Lincoln. He rejected their views, and made the address exactly as it had been written.

60. To one with whom he discussed his course, some weeks thereafter, Lincoln said: "You can't overturn a pyramid, but you can undermine it; that's what I have been trying to do." — Locke's Reminiscences, in Rice, 443. How effectually Lincoln accomplished his purpose may be inferred from this incident recorded by Mr. Hume in his recently published work, The Abolitionists: —

"On a boat that carried a portion of the audience, including the writer, from Alton to St. Louis, after the debate was over, was a prominent Missouri Democrat, afterwards a Confederate leader, who expressed himself very freely. He declared that he would rather trust the institutions of the South to the hands of a conservative and honest man like 'Old Abe,' than to those of 'a political jumping-jack like Douglas.' The most of the other southern men and slaveholders present seemed to concur in his views." — Hume, 98.

61. Coleman ii, 162–166; Whitney, 383–386; Works i, 519–520; Bartlett, 83–84, 99–100; Nicolay & Hay ii, 142.

62. Nicolay & Hay ii, 146; Savage, 161.

63. Isaac N. Arnold, in Carpenter, 237; Arnold, 146.

64. Greeley, 33; Arnold, more conservative, says $50,000.

65. See Lincoln to Judd, Works i, 520–521; also Arnold, 154; Carpenter, 237.
66. Lamon's Recollections, 22.
67. Whitney, in Herndon ii, 81. For a version that varies from this in a few particulars, and for other facts of a similar nature, see Whitney, 463–465. See also Villard i, 96–97.
68. Lincoln to Judd, Works i, 594.
69. Horace White, in Herndon ii, 127; Lamon, 419; Brooks, 181; Morse i, 149; Browne, 307; Holland, 194.
70. Works i, 529.
71. Lincoln to Galloway, Works i, 537.
72. Debates, 144; Works i, 315.
73. According to McKee, Lincoln received 1,866,352 votes; Douglas, 1,375,157; Breckinridge, 847,514; and Bell, 587,830. According to Stanwood, Lincoln received 1,866,452; Douglas, 1,376,957; Breckinridge, 849,781; and Bell, 588,879. These figures contain no apportionment of the fusion vote in five States. One analysis thereof, based on the estimated strength of the several contributing parties, makes Lincoln's total 1,857,610 and Douglas's 1,291,574, giving Lincoln 566,036 votes more than Douglas. For details, see The American Conflict i, 328, by Horace Greeley, whose skill in the handling of election returns is generally conceded.
74. Rice, 225–226; Herndon ii, 205–206; Poore ii, 69–70; Arnold, 189–190; Browne, 403–404. "If I can't be President," whispered Douglas, smiling, to a relative of the Lincolns, "I at least can hold his hat." — Tarbell ii, 5.

NOTES TO CHAPTER IV

1. William H. Seward, Abraham Lincoln, Simon Cameron, Salmon P. Chase, Edward Bates, William L. Dayton, John McLean, Jacob Collamer, Benjamin F. Wade, Charles Sumner, John C. Frémont, and John M. Reed.
2. These were, to use their common titles: Free-soilers, Whigs, Know-Nothings, Anti-Slavery Democrats, and Abolitionists.
3. Some of Seward's admirers, in fact, never became entirely reconciled to the action of the Convention. Almost thirteen years thereafter, Charles Francis Adams, in an address before the New York legislature, said: —

"The veteran champion of the reforming policy was set aside in favor of a gentleman as little known by anything he had ever done as the most sanguine friend of such a selection could desire. The fact is beyond contradiction that no person, ever before nominated with any reasonable probability of success, had had so little of public service to show for his reward. Placing myself in the attitude of Mr. Seward, at the moment when the news of so strange a decision would reach his ears, I think I might, like Jaques, in the play, have moralized for an instant on man's ingratitude, and been warned by the example of Aristides, or even the worse fate of Barneveld and the two De Witts, not to press further in a career in which the strong were to be ostracized, because of their strength, and the weak were to be pushed into places of danger, on account of their nothingness." — Adams, 23. Four years later, in 1877, Richard Grant White wrote: —

"Mr. Seward saw the crown of his life petulantly snatched from him and given to — no matter whom, if not to him — but to one who had done nothing to merit it, and who was so unknown to the majority of his countrymen that his identity had to be explained to them." — *North American Review* cxxiv, 226.

4. Baker iv, 683.
5. Seward i, 454; Baker iv, 79–80.
6. Seward i, 454.
7. Oldroyd, 474. Speaking of this interview, Fell said, "There we sat down, and in the calm twilight of the evening, had substantially the following conversation." See also Weed, 606; Browne, 366.
8. In a conversation with Joseph Medill, during the spring of 1855, at the office of the Chicago *Tribune*. See Philadelphia *Saturday Evening Post*, August 5, 1899.
9. Lincoln to Seward, December 8, 1860, in Works i, 657.
10. It should be noted, however, that in so doing Lincoln followed the example set by a number of his predecessors, who had thus honored prominent rivals for the presidential nomination, or for the office itself. President Madison had appointed his competitor, Monroe; and President John Quincy Adams had appointed Clay. President Harrison had offered the State Department to that same leader, and upon his declination, to Webster. President Polk had appointed Buchanan, President Pierce had appointed Marcy, and President Buchanan had appointed Cass.
11. Works i, 657; Nicolay & Hay iii, 349.
12. There appears to have been a doubt in Weed's mind as to whether Indiana was represented, in the tentative list, by Caleb B. Smith or Colonel Henry S. Lane, both ex-Whigs.
13. Weed, 610.
14. Morse i, 379.
15. "About two o'clock on Wednesday morning sufficient information had come in to leave no doubt of his election. He then retired, but hardly to sleep. Although fatigued and exhausted, he got but little rest. Oppressed with the overwhelming responsibility that was upon him, which in the excitement of the campaign he had not

fully realized, he felt the necessity of relief and assistance to sustain him in the not distant future. . . . He did not again sleep until he had constructed the framework of his cabinet. It was essentially the same as that with which four months later he commenced his administration." — Lincoln's own account of the matter to his Secretary of the Navy, in Welles, 37–38. See also Welles, 34; Carpenter, 223; Rhodes iii, 319–320; Nicolay & Hay iii, 345–347, 372.

16. Nicolay and Hay iii, 370; Lothrop, 247.
17. Lamon's Recollections, 49–51. See also The Diary of a Public Man, *North American Review* cxxix, 271–273.
18. Nicolay and Hay iii, 370; Lothrop, 248.
19. Works ii, 7–8; Nicolay and Hay iii, 371.
20. "After the supper, when the [inauguration] ball had become more like a dance, I handed Mrs. Lincoln her bouquet and ventured to congratulate the President upon his improved health. He responded so cordially that I was emboldened to ask whether he had any special news that I might send to Mr. Bennett, the editor of the *New York Herald*. 'Yes,' he replied, looking at me significantly, 'you may tell him that Thurlow Weed has found out that Seward was not nominated at Chicago.' This was very old news, another 'Lincoln joke,' and I smiled and took my leave. But on my way to the telegraph office the joke assumed most serious proportions. It meant, on the authority of the President himself, that Weed's secret intrigues to become the power behind the cabinet had been exposed and defeated; that Chase was to remain Secretary of the Treasury and master of the situation; that the sceptre of political power had passed forever from New York and the South to the great West, and that Lincoln was to be President in fact as well as in name. So tremendous was the importance of this 'joke' that it crowded out for a day the description that I had previously telegraphed of the costumes at the curious ball which ended the first inauguration of President Lincoln." — Stephen Fiske, in the *Ladies' Home Journal* xiv, 4.
21. Seward i, 487, 491, 497, 518.
22. It has been especially noted that the address was read by Judge David Davis, in Springfield; by Orville H. Browning, in Indianapolis; and by Francis Preston Blair, Sr., in Washington.
23. For the first inaugural address in full, see Holland, 279; Irelan xvi, 421; Raymond, 162; McPherson, 105; Barrett, 203; Brockett, 237; Works ii, 1; Richardson vi, 5; Nicolay & Hay iii, 327–344. In the last-named volume will also be found Mr. Seward's suggestions.
24. Seward i, 512; Nicolay & Hay iii, 320.
25. "The Godlike Daniel" was especially hard upon poor Harri-

son's classical allusions. Returning home in the evening after his arduous session with the blue pencil, Mr. Webster looked so worried and fatigued that a friend asked him whether anything amiss had happened. "You would think that something had happened," he answered, "if you knew what I have done. I have killed seventeen Roman proconsuls."

26. Samuel Bowles to H. L. Dawes, in Merriam i, 318.
27. Black, 156.
28. Welles, 49–50.
29. Mrs. Lincoln to William H. Herndon, in Herndon ii, 223.
30. This is missing from the files. For references to it, see: Records i, 191, 196, 197, 200; Works ii, 9, 15; Nicolay & Hay iii, 376–377; Crawford, 353, 355, 363; Buchanan, 211–214.
31. Records, series i, vol. i, 202.
32. Nicolay & Hay iii, 378; Lincoln to Scott, in Works ii, 9.
33. Secretary Chase is sometimes said to have joined Mr. Blair, at the outset, in advocating a relief expedition; but there is no conclusive evidence that he did so, and there is ground for a contrary belief. See Welles, 56; Crawford, 364–367; Warden, 371; Rhodes iii, 343; Cox, 63; McClure, 52; Hart, 209–210. Mr. Chase, it should be added, however, at an early date expressed the opinion that the President's oath of office "seemed to bind him to support Major Anderson." — Chase to Wirt, March 10, 1861, in Warden, 373; in Schuckers, 422. On March 16, 1861, he declared for provisioning Sumter. See also Chase to Black in Crawford, 367.
34. Tarbell ii, 16.
35. Message of July 4, 1861. Works ii, 56; Richardson vi, 21.
36. Speech of January 12, 1861. Baker iv, 666.
37. Commissioners Forsyth and Crawford to the Confederate Secretary of State. See Crawford, 322.
38. On the 10th of April, Seward wrote to Charles Francis Adams, our Minister to Great Britain: —

"Firmness on the part of the government in maintaining and preserving the public institutions and property, and in executing the laws where authority can be exercised without waging war, combined with such measures of justice, moderation, and forbearance as will disarm reasoning opposition, will be sufficient to secure the public safety until returning reflection, concurring with the fearful experience of social evils, the inevitable fruits of faction, shall bring the recusant members cheerfully back into the family, which, after all, must prove their best and happiest, as it undeniably is their most natural home. The constitution of the United States provides for that return by authorizing Congress, on application to be made by a certain majority of the States, to assemble a National Convention, in which the organic law can, if it be needful, be revised so as to remove all real obstacles to a reunion, so suitable to the habits of the people and so eminently conducive to the common safety and welfare." — Diplomatic History, 205.

39. "The impression undoubtedly left upon my mind was that the new administration would not resort to coercion. This was still further strengthened by the voluntary pledge of honor of Mr. Seward, in the presence of Mr. Taylor of Washington, and Messrs. Rives and Somers, that there should be no collision. 'Nay,' said he to me, 'if this whole matter is not satisfactorily settled within sixty days after I am seated in the saddle, and hold the reins firmly in my hand, I will give you my head for a football.' These were the identical words used, as I put them on paper in less than two hours after they were uttered." — C. S. Morehead to John J. Crittenden, in Coleman ii, 338.

40. At the suggestion of O. H. Browning. The clause cut out ran: —

"All the power at my disposal will be used to reclaim the public property and places which have fallen." See Nicolay & Hay iii, 333. Notwithstanding the omission, keen students of the inaugural address had no difficulty in still reading the suppressed part between the lines. On March 5, L. Q. Washington wrote from the Capital to the Confederate Secretary of War: —

"I was present last evening at a consultation of southern gentlemen, at which Messrs. Crawford, Garnett, Pryor, De Jarnette of Virginia, and Wigfall of Texas, were present. We all put the same construction on the inaugural, which we carefully went over together. We agreed that it was Lincoln's purpose at once to attempt the collection of the revenue, to reënforce and hold Fort Sumter and Pickens, and to retake the other places. He is a man of will and firmness." — Records, series i, vol. i, 263.

41. Works ii, 56; Morse i, 244–245; Crawford, 346–347; Lothrop, 253; Nicolay & Hay iii, 379, 381–382; Buchanan, 171.

42. Works ii, 11–22, where all the answers are published in full.

43. John Forsyth of Alabama; Martin J. Crawford of Georgia; and A. B. Roman of Louisiana.

44. He was accompanied on several occasions by his associate, Justice Nelson. The other go-betweens were Gwin of California and Hunter of Virginia.

45. "About this time, my wife, who was in Washington, was very much surprised at receiving a call from the President. He came quietly to request her to show him my letters from Fort Sumter, so that he might form a better opinion as to the condition of affairs there, more particularly in regard to our resources." — General Doubleday. Doubleday, 130.

46. The opinions are to be found in Nicolay & Hay iii, 430–432.

47. Records, series i, vol. i, 226–227.

48. "I was at the White House one evening," says Assistant Secretary of the Treasury George Harrington, "and found there, with the President, Mr. Welles, Mr. Fox, and Mr. Montgomery Blair, and ere they separated it was determined to relieve and provision Fort Sumter. I went to Mr. Seward and informed him of the fact, which, though, as he said, 'difficult to believe,' he subsequently found to be true." See Crawford, 368.

49. The student who desires to follow the episode of the Confederate Commissioners, through all its devious windings, will find some of the clues, at least, in the following works: Crawford, 314–345; Rhodes iii, 328–340; Welles, 56; Ropes i, 80–81; Morse i, 238–240, 245; Lothrop, 258–275; American Conflict i, 430–436, 632; McPherson, 108–112; Nicolay's Outbreak, 54–57; Blaine i, 292–294; Irelan xvi, 491–503; Seward i, 530–531, 537–538; Cox, 146–148; Moore i, Doc. 42–44, 426–428; Nicolay & Hay iii, 396–414; Records, series i, vol. li, part ii, supplement, p. 8; series i, vol. liii, supplement, pp. 161–164; Stephens ii, 345–355, 735–746; Greg ii, 216–222; Davis i, 263–281, 675–685; Stovall, 222–226; Bancroft ii, 93–132.

50. It should be borne in mind that there is no warrant for the recent fashion of calling cabinet officers "the President's constitutional advisers." They are merely heads of departments, whom he consults, or not, as seems best to him. When he does ask their opinions, he casts the deciding vote, however they may stand; because in him, alone, rests the authority and the responsibility, not only for his own course, but for their executive acts, as well.

51. The standard of Spain had just been raised in Santo Domingo; and France had poorly disguised the hostility toward the Union which culminated later in her efforts to force European intervention upon the North. Great Britain, France, and Spain, in the interests of their subjects who had suffered from the revolutions in Mexico, were contemplating the invasion which later placed Maximilian upon a throne in that country. Russia had been invited to join her continental neighbors in their policy of American interference. She had refused to do so, but her attitude, friendly to the northern cause throughout the war, was not yet understood, at this time, in the State Department.

52. Seward i, 535; Works ii, 29–30; Nicolay & Hay iii, 445–447.

53. Seward's method on this occasion differed widely from that of an eminent predecessor in the State Department. When Secretary Van Buren wished to engineer a difficult scheme, he would, as Senator Poindexter relates, hint at it in President Jackson's presence. The General would say, "Eh!" and "the wizard" would adroitly change the subject. Soon Van Buren would allude to it again, whereupon Jackson would ask, "How 's that?" And again would

come an evasive answer. By this time the President had been set thinking, so that when next the subject was broached, he would advocate the Secretary's plan, himself. Then Van Buren would exclaim, "What a grand, a glorious idea! No man in the land would have thought of it but yourself."

54. Secretary Seward's attack of Jingoism, though violent, was not of long duration. His theory that a foreign war would cement the Union had been foreshadowed by his speech, at the dinner of the New England Society in New York, on December 22, 1860. Though the idea was not, at the time, supported by other popular leaders, the people had thus, in a way, been prepared for its formal presentation. After the administration entered office, newspaper articles and the speeches of public men abounded in suggestions of hostilities against violaters of the Monroe Doctrine. As late as January, 1865, we find Francis Preston Blair, Sr., seeking at Richmond to unite the North and the South in a Mexican crusade, and the Confederate Vice-President, Alexander H. Stephens, making a similar proposition, a few weeks later, to President Lincoln, at the Fortress Monroe conference.

55. By a singular coincidence Mr. Seward had made the same reply four days before to Dr. Russell, the correspondent of the London *Times*. Russell, 40.

56. Works ii, 30; Nicolay & Hay iii, 448–449. See also Conway i, 350–351.

57. Mr. Lincoln's method of maintaining his authority over his first cabinet officer was in striking contrast to that of the Confederate President, a few months later, under almost parallel conditions. R. M. T. Hunter, the southern Secretary of State, like his northern prototype, had been a first choice for the presidency. He, too, took office under his successful competitor, and, like Mr. Seward, volunteered unwelcome counsel. But there the similarity ceased, for his chief, instead of retaining this valuable minister and bending him to his will, so grossly insulted the offender as to render his continuance in the administration impossible. "There had been a disgraceful quarrel in the cabinet," says the biographer of Mr. Davis, "and when Mr. Hunter had offered some advice about the conduct of the war, Mr. Davis had said with a flushed and almost insolent manner: 'Mr. Hunter, you are Secretary of State, and when information is wanted of that particular department, it will be time for you to speak.' The spirited Virginian next day sent in his resignation." See Pollard, 150–151.

58. Seward i, 590.

59. Mr. Seward's manner of monopolizing the President's attention is illustrated in an anecdote told by General Egbert L. Viele, who visited Mr. Lincoln to lay a certain document before him. "As I

entered the room," relates the General, "Secretary Seward came in with some important despatches, and took his seat alongside the President, just as I had handed him the paper I wanted him to look at. Secretary Seward, with an air of impatience, took it out of the President's hand and handed it back to me, saying, 'Some other time — I have important business with the President.' Mr. Lincoln said, 'Not so fast, Seward,' taking back the document from him, 'I want to hear what Viele has to say about this matter.'" — Ward, 121.

60. By a remarkable coincidence, Mr. Seward, as a friend and disciple of Mr. Adams's father, had twenty-five years before performed a similar duty over John Quincy Adams. Not only had the earlier oration been delivered in the same city, and during the same month of the year, as the later one, but also at the invitation of the New York legislature. Nor did the parallel end there, for Mr. Seward had claimed, in 1848, that his hero, as Secretary of State under President Monroe, "swayed the government"; and the son of The Old Man Eloquent, in 1873, made the almost identical plea, as we have seen, on behalf of his father's eulogist.

61. Mr. Chase was still alive when the address was delivered; but he died within three weeks thereafter, and before a joint statement, contemplated by the three ministers, could be prepared.

62. Welles, 9, 79. To ascribe the control of Presidents to certain of their cabinet officers is not a novelty in American history. Hamilton was said to have ruled Washington; John Quincy Adams, Monroe; and Van Buren, Jackson.

63. Seward i, 528; Lothrop, 361.

64. Seward i, 511.

65. The letter as completed by Mr. Seward and sent to Mr. Adams is published in the Diplomatic History, 241–245. The draft as submitted to Mr. Lincoln and his corrections are to be found in Nicolay & Hay iv, 270–275; Works ii, 48–51. The introduction to Rice's Reminiscences contains the corrected despatch and an autograph facsimile of it, as it left the President's hands. See also Foster, 360–363.

66. Pierce iv, 121; Welles, 161.

67. "He parted with his temper now and then, when friends pressed him to perform impossibilities, as, for example, on the occasion of a visit from leading New York Republicans of his type, who complained that their followers were not receiving a due share of federal patronage. It was reported and believed that he broke into a rage, exclaiming, in substance, 'Why come to me about this? Go to the White House! I, who by every right ought to have been chosen President! What am I now? Nothing but Abe Lincoln's little —— clerk!'" — Stanton, 222–223.

68. Alexander H. Stephens, Vice-President of the Confederate States; R. M. T. Hunter, Confederate Senator and Confederate Ex-Secretary of State; John A. Campbell, Ex-Justice of the United States Supreme Court and Confederate Assistant Secretary of War.
69. Brockett, 575; Raymond, 657; McPherson, 568; Nicolay & Hay x, 115; Works ii, 633, 644–645; Stephens ii, 798; Richardson vi, 264.
70. Records, series i, vol. xlvi, part ii, 342–343; Stephens ii, 800; Raymond, 659; Works ii, 635, 646–647; Nicolay & Hay x, 116–117; Richardson vi, 266–267; McPherson, 568.
71. Gilmore, 50; Herndon ii, 222; Pierce iv, 195 note. See also Hamlin, 495.
72. On the 4th of June, 1861, R. H. Dana wrote to C. F. Adams, then in England:—

"Sumner has spent ten days at Washington, and comes back as full of denunciations of Mr. Seward as ever. He gave me some anxiety, as I listened to him, lest he was in a heated state of brain. He cannot talk five minutes without bringing in Mr. Seward, and always in bitter terms of denunciation. I mention this to you because I have reason to believe that his correspondence with England (which is large, and in influential quarters) and his conversations with the foreign diplomats at Washington are in the same style. His mission is to expose and denounce Mr. Seward, and into that mission he puts all his usual intellectual and moral energy." — Adams's Dana ii, 258–259.
73. Hamilton, 530; Warden, 467–468; Chase Papers, 72–73.
74. Seward ii, 196–197, 225; Bancroft ii, 403–406; Diplomatic History, 514. But see also Welles, 80–85.
75. "In due time, gentlemen of the jury, when I shall have paid the debt of nature, my remains will rest here in your midst, with those of my kindred and neighbors. It is very possible they may be unhonored, neglected, spurned! But, perhaps, years hence, when the passion and excitement which now agitate this community shall have passed away, some wandering stranger, some lone exile, some Indian, some negro, may erect over them an humble stone, and thereon this epitaph, '*He was faithful.*'" — Defence of the negro, Freeman, tried for murder, in 1846. — Seward's Autobiography, 822.

NOTES TO CHAPTER V

1. Chase was one of the founders of the Cincinnati Lyceum, before which he, himself, delivered four lectures. Two of these had the honor of appearing in the *North American Review*. He also compiled and published, in three volumes, the Statutes of Ohio, an admirable piece of work, that won for him praise from high quarters.

2. "The writer hereof was a witness to one incident that showed something of the loss that Mr. Chase sustained in a business way because of his principles. While a law student in a country village he was sent down to Cincinnati to secure certain testimony in the form of affidavits. During his visit he called at Mr. Chase's law office, introduced himself, and was very pleasantly received. He noticed that there was a notary public in the office. Among other instructions he had been directed to get the affidavit of a leading business man in Cincinnati, a railroad president. The document was prepared and signed, but there was no one at hand before whom it could be sworn to. The writer remarked that he knew where there was a notary in a nearby office. We proceeded to Mr. Chase's chambers, and were about to enter, when my companion noticed the name on the door. He fell back as if he had been struck in the face. 'The —— Abolitionist!' he exclaimed, 'I would n't enter his place for a hundred dollars!' We went elsewhere for our business, and on the way my companion expressed himself about Mr. Chase. 'What a pity it is,' he said, 'that that young man is ruining himself. He is a bright man,' he went on, 'and I employed him professionally until he went daft on the subject of freeing the niggers whom the Lord made for the purpose of serving the white people.'" — Hume, 63.

3. Lincoln to Galloway, July 28, 1859, and March 24, 1860, in Works i, 538, 632; Schuckers, 201; Hart, 187–188; Rhodes ii, 338; Nicolay & Hay i, 368–369.

4. *Ante*, pp. 126–127: This view, so far as it related to Chase, was slightly modified, however, as Lincoln's chances for the nomination improved. See the letter to Galloway of July 28, 1859, Works i, 538.

5. "After the second ballot, I whispered to Cartter, of Ohio: 'If you can throw the Ohio delegation for Lincoln, Chase can have anything he wants.' 'H-how d-d' ye know?' stuttered Cartter. 'I know, and you know I would n't promise if I did n't know.' So Cartter got up and announced eighteen or nineteen votes of Ohio for Lincoln. Giddings challenged the vote, but on the poll it was found that Cartter had n't 'nigged' more than one or two votes. That settled the nomination of Lincoln." — Interview with Joseph Medill in Philadelphia *Saturday Evening Post*, August 5, 1899.

6. Schuckers, 201; Nicolay & Hay iii, 359. But see Warden, 364–365.

7. Hart, 203.

8. Said to have been based on a paper prepared by Joshua R. Giddings.

9. Lincoln's entire estate, at the time, consisted of his home with its contents, in Springfield; a lot which had been presented to him, in the town of Lincoln; and 160 acres of wild land in Iowa granted

by Congress for military services during the Black Hawk War. Herndon i, 91–92; Lamon's Recollections, 20; Whitney, 26; Lamon, 472; Arnold, 83.

10. This neglect of financial problems was not unlike that of Prince Bismarck in his early days. "Formerly," said he, "I never concerned myself seriously with economic questions, and should not have known what to say had any one asked me as to the state of Swedish iron. I should, in fact, have felt like Rothschild, when once applied to by a business man for his opinion on the same subject. 'Meyer,' said Rothschild, turning in some embarrassment to one of his clerks, 'Meyer, what is my opinion about Swedish iron?'"
11. Lamon's Recollections, 215–217.
12. House Report No. 140, 38th Congress, 1st Session.
13. Piatt's Thomas, 442.
14. Schuckers, 424.
15. To Edwin D. Mansfield of Morrow, Ohio, in Schuckers, 439.
16. To Enoch T. Carson of Cincinnati, in Schuckers, 451–452.
17. Chase Papers, 74; Warden, 469.
18. To William M. Dickson, in Schuckers, 443.
19. To Murat Halstead, in Warden, 549; Schuckers, 393.
20. To O. Follett, in Warden, 491–492.
21. Warden, 593.
22. Nicolay & Hay vi, 255; Warden, 484–485.
23. Hart, 293.
24. Warden, 562.
25. Schuckers, 280.
26. To E. D. Mansfield, in Warden, 565.
27. To A. S. Latty, in Warden, 454.
28. Warden, 385–386.
29. Hart, 262–263.
30. Schuckers, 376–378.
31. Schuckers, 378–379. See also Boutwell i, 308.
32. Chase Papers, 76; Warden, 470.
33. Warden, 564.
34. Major-General David Hunter, in Warden, 505; Chase Papers, 105.
35. Browne, 494–495.
36. Piatt, 117–118; Chase Papers, 87; Schuckers, 453; Warden, 481.
37. Hart, 125.
38. Chase Papers, 83; Warden, 475.
39. Seward ii, 147.
40. Nicolay & Hay vi, 265.
41. Seward ii, 147; Bancroft ii, 367.
42. Nicolay & Hay vi, 266.
43. Senator Trumbull.

44. Nicolay & Hay vi, 268.
45. Seward ii, 148. See also Nicolay & Hay vi, 271; Rhodes iv, 206; Morse ii, 180.
46. For the correspondence on this subject, in part or entire, see Warden, 508–510; Schuckers, 489–491; Nicolay & Hay vi, 268–270; Works ii, 282; Seward ii, 148; Diplomatic History, 15; Morse ii, 179.
47. It may be of interest to compare the purport of this letter with that of the one addressed by Washington's Secretary of the Treasury to the President, while the quarrel between Hamilton and Secretary of State Jefferson was at its height. "If your endeavors [toward 'terminating the differences which exist'] should prove unsuccessful," wrote Chase's great predecessor, "I do not hesitate to say, that in my opinion the period is not remote, when the public good will require *substitutes* for the *differing members* of your administration. The continuance of a division there must destroy the energy of government, which will be little enough with the strictest union. On my part there will be a most cheerful acquiescence in such a result." — Hamilton's Works iv, 303–304.
48. Warden, 524; Schuckers, 492; Works ii, 313.
49. Warden, 524–525; Schuckers, 492.
50. The appointment went to J. G. Bolles of Hartford.
51. Warden, 525.
52. Works ii, 334–335.
53. Warden, 528; Schuckers, 493.
54. Lincoln's Time, 120.
55. To Dr. A. G. Henry, Smith's inveterate enemy, Mr. Lincoln wrote: —

"Governor Chase's feelings were hurt by my action in his absence. Smith is removed, but Governor Chase wishes to name his successor, and asks a day or two to make the designation." — Tarbell ii, 364.
56. Field, 303.
57. Committee on Public Expenditures, House Report No. 111, 38th Congress, 1st Session; and House Report No. 25, 38th Congress, 2d Session.
58. Field, 305; Schuckers, 495–496; Warden, 556.
59. See Lincoln's letter to Chase, February 12, 1864, Works ii, 481; Schuckers, 498–499.
60. Field, 304.
61. Chase's conduct in this particular recalls the less scrupulous, though not more eager, intrigues of William H. Crawford, Monroe's Secretary of the Treasury. Dissimilar as were these two ambitious finance ministers in character and attainments, the student of curious parallels will find several striking points of resemblance in their careers. Says Schouler, of Crawford (iii, 17): —

"No sooner, in fact, were his relations to the incoming administration settled than he began to persuade himself that he had made a personal sacrifice, and only remained in the cabinet for prudential and public reasons; and to his friends he showed, thus early, that he was in neither a grateful nor a docile frame of mind. . . . Embarrassments arose, through the persistent efforts of Crawford's friends in Congress; embarrassments traceable to the instigation of Crawford himself, who staked his chances, first upon the probable errors of the new administration and his ambitious associates, and next, upon securing a following in Congress strong enough to carry the next caucus nomination for himself."

The coincidence between Crawford and Chase, it may be added, extended beyond the Secretaries themselves to their treatment by the Presidents whom they sought respectively to supplant; for both Monroe and Lincoln manifested remarkable forbearance toward their cabinet rivals.

62. Schuckers, 494.
63. Brooks, 385.
64. Brooks, 385; Browne, 661. See also Works ii, 532.
65. Julian, 243.
66. For the circular, see: Schuckers, 499–500; Nicolay & Hay viii, 319–320; Cyclopedia (1864), 783–784.
67. Warden, 574; Schuckers, 501.
68. Works ii, 489–490; Riddle, 273; Schuckers, 501–502; Warden, 575.
69. Arnold, 194.
70. Arnold, 194.
71. Schuckers, 488.
72. How this was viewed by some of the public men who were friendly to Mr. Lincoln may be inferred from a conversation, reported by General Butler as having taken place, in the spring of 1864, between Simon Cameron and himself:—

"Is Mr. Chase making any headway in his candidature?" I asked.

"Yes, some; and he is using the whole power of the Treasury to help himself."

"Well," said I, "that is the right thing for him to do."

"Do you think so?" said he.

"Yes. Why ought not he to do that if Lincoln lets him?"

"How can Lincoln help letting him?"

"By tipping him out. If I were Lincoln I should say to the Secretary of the Treasury, 'You know I am a candidate for reelection, as I suppose it is proper for me to be. Now, every one of my equals has a right to be a candidate against me, and every citizen of the United States is my equal who is not my subordinate. Now, if you desire to be a candidate I will give you the present opportunity to be one by making you my equal and not my subordinate, and I will do that in any way which will be the most pleasant to you, but things cannot go on as they are.' You see I think it is Lincoln's fault and not Chase's that he is using the Treasury against Lincoln."

"Right again," said Cameron. "I will tell Mr. Lincoln every word you have said." — Butler, 635. See also Rice, 155–160.

At about the same time, David Davis, one of Lincoln's intimates, wrote to Thurlow Weed, from Washington: —

"There was a meeting of Chase's friends in the city last night. They resolved not to support Lincoln, etc., etc.; the greater part present were Treasury office-holders. How long can these things last?" — Weed ii, 445.

73. Hay's Diary, October 16, 1863, in Nicolay & Hay viii, 316–317.

74. Carpenter, 129–130. The incident probably happened in Indiana rather than in Kentucky, but Mr. Carpenter's account of it is quoted without change.

75. McClure, 122–123.

76. A striking exception was furnished by the Missouri Assembly, which tabled a resolution in favor of renominating Mr. Lincoln, by a vote of 45 to 37. Cyclopedia (1864), 783; Nicolay & Hay ix, 56. The grievances of the Missouri Radicals, or "Charcoals" as they were called, are stated at length, in Hume, chaps. xx and xxi.

77. Chase to James C. Hall, March 5, 1864.

78. J. M. Winchell, in *Galaxy* xvi, 38.

79. *Congressional Globe*, 38th Congress, 1st Session, part ii, 1828–32.

80. Riddle, 275. Even if Mr. Lincoln had previously known of the speech, he was bound in honor to restore General Blair's commission. On November 2, 1863, the President had written to Montgomery Blair: —

"Some days ago I understood you to say that your brother, General Frank Blair, desires to be guided by my wishes as to whether he will occupy his seat in Congress or remain in the field. My wish, then, is compounded of what I believe will be best for the country and best for him, and it is that he will come here, put his military commission in my hands, take his seat, go into caucus with our friends, abide the nominations, help elect the nominees, and thus aid to organize a House of Representatives which will really support the government in the war. If the result shall be the election of himself as Speaker, let him serve in that position, if not, let him retake his commission and return to the army." — Works ii, 433–434. For Lincoln's letter directing Blair's reinstatement, see *Ibid.*, 515. For all the documents, see Raymond, 473–475.

81. The Blair episode in the history of the relations between Lincoln and Chase furnishes a further parallel with what happened forty years before, in the course of the rivalry between Monroe and his Secretary of the Treasury. Senator Ninian Edwards of Illinois, after assailing Crawford in a series of anonymous newspaper articles, was appointed by President Monroe to the Mexican mission. While on the way to his post, Edwards sent back a letter to the Capital avowing himself to be the author of the attacks. This affair was exceedingly painful to Monroe. It gave a severe wrench, as in Lincoln's case afterward, to the already greatly strained relations between the President and his rival subordinate.
82. Gray to Darwin, in Gray ii, 523.
83. McClure, 124.
84. Schuckers, 507; Warden, 611; Works ii, 538–539.
85. Schuckers, 507–508; Warden, 613; Works ii, 539.
86. Warden, 613; Schuckers, 508.
87. Schuckers, 509; Warden, 614; Works ii, 540.
88. Chittenden, 378–379.
89. For a detailed account of this by one of the participants, see Conness's Reminiscences, in Rice, 561–565.
90. This was not unlike the cry wrung from President Washington while smarting under the blows of partisan contentions. "I would rather," he exclaimed, "go to my farm, take my spade in my hand, and work for my bread than remain where I am."
91. Warden, 619.
92. Chase's Diary, June 30, 1864. — Warden, 618; Schuckers, 509–510.
93. Chase's Diary, July 4, 1864. — Warden, 623.
94. Sumner to Cobden, September 18, 1864. — Pierce iv, 200. There was more than a passing resemblance between Chase and Necker. The French Director of the Finances, like the American Secretary, evinced his genius by filling, under difficult conditions, an empty treasury. Necker, no less than Chase, enjoyed the confidence of the people, and both financiers set a sufficiently high valuation on their services. Reaching out, in somewhat the same manner, after enlarged powers, they made much trouble for their respective rulers. The ambitions of Necker were stimulated, moreover, by his brilliant daughter, Madame de Staël; while Chase's aspirations were the constant care of the beautiful and accomplished Kate Chase Sprague. Both statesmen, deeming themselves to be indispensable, resigned with the expectation of strengthening their respective positions. Both, to their keen disappointment, were taken at their word, and were allowed, amid general protests, to lay down their portfolios. Necker was later recalled by the impotent Louis, and Chase — but here the parallel ceases.

95. In the preceding spring, Mr. Lincoln had promised Charles Sumner to make this appointment, upon the demise of Chief Justice Taney, then daily expected. Before that death took place, however, came the rupture which led to Chase's resignation from the cabinet. Consequently, when the vacancy on the Supreme Court bench occurred, some of the President's friends earnestly opposed the ex-Secretary's selection. Discussing the situation, at the time, with two admirers of that gentleman, — Judge E. R. Hoar and Richard H. Dana, — Lincoln said: —

"Mr. Chase is a very able man. He is a very ambitious man, and I think on the subject of the presidency, a little insane. He has not always behaved very well lately, and people say to me, — 'Now is the time to *crush him out*.' Well, I'm not in favor of crushing anybody out. If there is anything that a man can do and do it well, I say, let him do it. Give him a chance." See Rhodes v, 45–46.

NOTES TO CHAPTER VI

1. Early in his career, Mr. Stanton had attended conventions, and had made some political speeches. He had also held minor offices, in the line of his profession, such as that of Reporter for the Ohio Supreme Court, County Prosecuting Attorney, and City Solicitor in Steubenville.
2. For various versions of this incident see: Tarbell i, 260–266; Herndon ii, 22–25; Browne, 266–269; Arnold, 89–90; Lamon, 332; Nicolay & Hay v, 133–134; Gorham i, 44–45; Flower, 62–65; Stoddard, 316; Hapgood, 121, 254; Piatt, 56; Rhodes ii, 312; Morse i, 326; Chittenden, 185; French, 126–128; Lamon's Recollections, 231–232; Coffin, 162; W. M. Dickson, in *Harper's Magazine* lxix, 62–66.
3. This opinion was not perceptibly modified by the fact that Secretary Cameron, from the time he entered the War Department, and General McClellan, on assuming command of the army, had both made it a practice to consult Mr. Stanton as to legal matters; while Generals Scott and Dix had also employed him in a similar way.
4. Dix ii, 19.
5. Some of these letters were printed in the *North American Review* (1879), cxxix, 473–483; and perhaps all that have been published appeared during 1883, in Curtis ii, 528–559.
6. Poore's Reminiscences, in Rice, 223; The Diary of a Public Man, *North American Review* cxxix, 261–262.
7. McClellan, 152.
8. Gorham (i, 79) quotes good authority for this statement, but

Flower (80) asserts that Stanton, while friendly to Breckinridge, hoped for the election of the other Democratic candidate, Stephen A. Douglas.

9. Piatt, 57–58.
10. Letter to the Rev. Heman Dyer, one of Stanton's instructors at Kenyon College. See Gorham i, 430; Flower, 157–161; *Congressional Record*, June 8, 1886, pp. 5417–5418.
11. Nicolay & Hay v, 137.
12. Holland, 357; Stoddard, 317; Stowe, 370; Jones, 95–96; H. L. Dawes, in *Atlantic Monthly* lxxiii, 163.
13. "I well remember," said General Vincent, "an order given at one time which the Secretary deemed based upon misconception. I was instructed to take the case to the President and invite his consideration to its prominent points. On reaching the Executive Mansion I found the President in the reception-room surrounded by a large number of persons. He immediately recognized me, stepped forward, and conducted me into the most retired corner of the room. After I had stated the object of my visit, he said, 'Stanton is careful and may be right. I was very busy when I examined the case, but I will take the papers, reëxamine, and by four o'clock this afternoon send them by messenger to your office.' Before the hour indicated the papers were in my hands. The President had revoked his order and affirmed the decision of the Secretary." — Address by Assistant Adjutant-General Thomas M. Vincent, before Burnside Post No. 8, April 25, 1889.
14. Carpenter, 245–246.
15. Gobright, 333.
16. For another of these anecdotes, see Flower, 346–347.
17. J. P. Usher's Reminiscences, in Rice, 100. Stanton's manner of exercising this veto privilege is nicely illustrated in a little incident recalled by his confidential clerk, Major A. E. H. Johnson. Colonel Payton, he relates, was recruiting his regiment in Philadelphia. Finding that the quota could not be completed in the time allowed, he asked for an extension of thirty days. A recommendation to that effect, signed by Governor Curtin and other prominent Pennsylvanians, was forwarded to the President, who endorsed on the document, "Allow Colonel Payton the additional time required, unless there be reason to the contrary, unknown to me." Under these words Mr. Stanton wrote, "There is good and valid reason for not extending the time, and the Secretary of War refuses to do it."
18. Former Vice-President William A. Wheeler, in the Malone (N. Y.) *Palladium*, May 7, 1885.
19. Julian, 211–212; Rice, 56–57; Stanton, 232; Coffin, 369; Browne, 483–484. See also Boutwell ii, 90.
20. Flower, 369–370.

21. The riot took place on March 28, 1864.
22. For versions of the affair, see Herndon ii, 227–230; and an interview with Dennis Hanks, in the New York *Tribune*, February 3, 1889.
23. McClure, 162–166.
24. Lincoln to Banks, December 2, 1864.—Works ii, 602–603.
25. Lincoln to Stanton, March 18, 1864.—Works ii, 499; Nicolay & Hay v, 144.
26. Nicolay & Hay v, 144.
27. Rice, 379–384.
28. The question was on the reconsideration of the motion to investigate.—*Congressional Globe*, 38th Congress, 2d Session, part i, 319.
29. Flower, 348–349.
30. Markland's Reminiscences, in Rice, 328–329.
31. Grant, 639. The anecdote had received currency as early as December 30, 1869, a few days after Mr. Stanton's death, when it had been related by the Rev. Dr. Thompson, in the course of the memorial meeting, at the Union League Club of New York.
32. John A. Campbell, former Associate Justice of the United States Supreme Court. He had remained in Richmond, when the other members of the southern government had fled, for the purpose of acting as mediator.
33. Lincoln to Weitzel, April 6, 1865. For the letter in full, see Works ii, 669; Records, series i, vol. xlvi, part iii, 612.
34. Lincoln to Weitzel, April 12, 1865.—Works ii, 676; Records, series i, vol. xlvi, part iii, 725.
35. In justice to General Grant's truthfulness as a historian, we should mention the conditions under which his Memoirs were written. The concluding chapters—one of them contains the incident about the Virginia legislature—had to be penned between the agonies of a mortal disease. His memory was naturally impaired, and verification by reference to official documents was perforce left to others. The wonder is not that there are errors in the book, but that they are not more numerous.
36. See Mr. Stanton's own statement of the affair, in his testimony given before the Judiciary Committee of the House of Representatives, in the investigation of the charges against President Johnson. Reports of Committees, 40th Congress, 1st Session, p. 400; General Weitzel's testimony before the Committee on the War, 1865, vol. i, 521–522; Records, series i, vol. xlvi, part iii, 612, 655, 656, 657, 723, 725, 735; Campbell, 38–44; Nicolay & Hay x, 220–228; Flower, 269–272; Gideon Welles, in *Galaxy* xiii, 524. Admiral Porter's account of the matter (Naval History, 799–800), though he was on the scene at Richmond, is obviously inaccurate.

37. Lincoln to Huidekoper, September 1, 1864. — Works ii, 570–571.
38. Fry's Reminiscences, in Rice, 396–399; Nicolay & Hay v, 145–147; House Executive Document No. 80, 38th Congress, 2d Session.
39. Lincoln to Grant, September 22, 1864. — Works ii, 579.

On March 17, 1865, Mr. Lincoln wrote a letter that apparently alluded to this matter. It read: —

COL. R. M. HOUGH AND OTHERS, CHICAGO, Ill.

Yours received. The best I can do with it is to refer it to the War Department. The Rock Island case referred to, was my individual enterprise, and it caused so much difficulty in so many ways that I promised to never undertake another. A. LINCOLN.

40. Fenton's Reminiscences, in Rice, 71–73.
41. Major William G. Moore, in a letter to the author; Charles F. Benjamin, in *Century Magazine* xxxiii, 758–759.
42. According to an anecdote told by Flower (347–348), Stanton finally obtained a promise from Lincoln that the President would not interfere in capital cases without consulting the Secretary of War. A young soldier, so runs the story, whose mother was one of Thaddeus Stevens's constituents, had been sentenced to be shot for sleeping at his post on the picket line. The mother, in the morning of the day fixed for the execution, applied to Mr. Stevens for help to save her son, and the Congressman at once took the case to Mr. Lincoln.

"I am sorry, but I can't help you," said Lincoln. "Mr. Stanton says I am destroying discipline in the army, and I have promised him I will grant no more reprieves without first consulting him."

"There is no time to consult anybody," rejoined Stevens, looking at the clock. "There is not an hour to spare."

"It is too bad, but I must keep my promise to sign no more reprieves," said Lincoln, "without first referring them to Mr. Stanton."

Picking up a telegraph blank, Stevens wrote a reprieve and, handing it to Lincoln, inquired whether the form was correct. The President said that it was, whereupon Stevens signed "A. Lincoln" to the message, and despatched a messenger on the run to the telegraph office, whence it was sent to the officer in command of the post at which the young man was to be shot. Within a few minutes Stanton hurried into the Executive Chamber, exclaiming: —

"I see, Mr. President, you have signed another reprieve contrary to your agreement not to do so without first consulting the War Department."

"No," responded Lincoln, "I have signed no reprieve. I have kept my word."

"But I just now saw one going over the wires," persisted Stanton, by whose orders all telegraphic messages were recorded at the War Department, "and your name is signed to it."

"But I did not write it," replied Lincoln.

"Did not write it! Who did write it?"

"Your friend, Thad Stevens."

Stanton took his hat and left without another word; but the trick was never repeated.

43. H. L. Dawes, in *Atlantic Monthly* lxxiii, 165–166.

44. Coffey's Reminiscences, in Rice, 242–244.

45. Andrew's Reminiscences, in Rice, 516–518. Secretary Stanton was not generally so intolerant as might be inferred from the foregoing narrative. Mr. Charles F. Benjamin, who served as a clerk in the War Department, says: —

"Doubtless Mr. Stanton knew fairly well the extent to which quiet partisanship for McClellan pervaded his entire department; but politics under him was as free as religion, so long as fidelity and industry accompanied it. The chief of his military staff, Colonel Hardie, came to him fresh from cordial and confidential service on the staff of the deposed General McClellan." — *Century Magazine*, n. s. xi, 763.

46. In *North American Review* clxiii, 672–675.

47. Lincoln to Stanton, August 12, 1862. — Works ii, 222.

48. Lincoln to Stanton, March 1, 1864. — Works ii, 490–491.

49. Speed, 26–27.

50. To appreciate the full significance of this episode, it must be borne in mind that Mr. Stanton, with good reason, was especially nervous about paymaster appointments. When Secretary Usher asked the Secretary of War to make a young friend paymaster, Mr. Stanton inquired, "How old is he?" "About twenty-one, I believe," answered the Secretary of the Interior; he is of good family and excellent character." "Usher," was the reply, "I would not appoint the Angel Gabriel a paymaster, if he was only twenty-one."

51. William A. Wheeler, in the Malone (N. Y.) *Palladium*, May 7, 1885. In his article Mr. Wheeler referred to this affair as having happened during the latter half of 1861. But Mr. Stanton did not enter upon his duties in the War Department until January 20, 1862. Hence, either he was not the officer encountered by Mr. Wheeler, or that gentleman was in error as to the time. When the inconsistency was called to his attention by Ward Hill Lamon, one of Lincoln's friends and biographers, the venerable author of the article ascribed his "gross blunder," as he termed it, to the lapse of time and his enfeebled condition. "The mistake," he wrote, "must be one of *time*, for the actors in the transaction are too vividly impressed upon my memory ever to be forgotten until that

faculty is wholly dethroned." It should be added that this explanation is worthy of credit, as Major Sabin, according to the Official Army Register, was commissioned on July 29, 1862, when Secretary Stanton had been in office over six months.

52. Grinnell, 172–173; Byers, 473–474.

53. General Orders No. 138, September 23, 1862. — Records, series i, vol. xvi, part ii, 539.

54. Thomas to Halleck, September 29, 1862.— Records, series i, vol xvi, part ii, 555.

55. Piatt's Thomas, 198.

56. Piatt, 81; Piatt's Thomas, 198–199. Mr. Stanton's disappointment was again revealed, almost a year later, in a despatch which he sent to Assistant Secretary of War Dana, at the front with the Army of the Cumberland. This read, in part: —

"The merit of General Thomas and the debt of gratitude the nation owes to his valor and skill are fully appreciated here, and I wish you to tell him so. It was not my fault that he was not in chief command months ago." — September 30, 1863. — Records, series i, vol. xxx, part iii, 946.

57. The proposed orders relieved from duty with the Army of the Potomac: Major-General William Buel Franklin, Major-General William Farrar Smith, Brigadier-General Samuel D. Sturgis, Brigadier-General Edward Ferrero, and Assistant Adjutant-General (Lieutenant-Colonel) J. H. Taylor; they dismissed from the service: Major-General Joseph Hooker, Brigadier-General W. T. H. Brooks, Brigadier-General John Newton, and Brigadier-General John Cochrane.

58. In command of the Centre Grand Division, Army of the Potomac.

59. The nickname originated in the Associated Press reports of the battle of Malvern Hill. It displeased General Hooker, who frequently protested against its use. "People will think I am a highwayman or a bandit," he said on one occasion. "It always sounds to me," he said at another time, "as if it meant 'Fighting Fool.' It has really done me much injury in making the public believe I am a furious, headstrong fool, bent on making furious dashes at the enemy. I never have fought without good purpose, and with fair chances of success."

60. These charges were indignantly, but not conclusively answered by General Hooker, three months later, when General Orders No. 8 had found their way into the newspapers.

61. Extracts from the Journal of Henry J. Raymond, in *Scribner's Magazine* (1879), xix, 705.

62. The relations of Secretaries Stanton and Chase to this affair are set forth, more at length, in Battles and Leaders iii, 239–243, by Charles F. Benjamin, whose confidential positions at the head-

quarters of the Army of the Potomac and in the War Department afforded him exceptional facilities for observation.

63. "General Fry, who was greatly in the confidence of the President, told me that Mr. Lincoln had said to him that he had chosen Hooker partly out of deference to public opinion and partly out of personal belief that he was worth trying on his merits. Fry and Meigs were among the staff officers that the President consulted on the matter. Both admitted the value of popular opinion, and neither sought to deny that the true Hooker, the original Hooker, was a man of power and promise. The President took the chances. The way in which Hooker went to pieces, in the midst of the great promise of the Chancellorsville campaign, justified all those who had been reluctant to advise his elevation."— Letter of Charles F. Benjamin to the author.

64. The McClellan plan was favored by Generals Keyes, Franklin, Fitz-John Porter, W. F. Smith, McCall, Blenker, Andrew Porter, and Naglee of Hooker's division; the President's plan, by Generals McDowell, Sumner, Heintzelman, and Barnard. This was the council once referred to by Stanton when he said, "We saw ten generals afraid to fight."

65. McClellan to Stanton, February 3, 1862. — Records, series i, vol. v, 45.

66. Kelley, 33–34. The conversation, from which this is an extract, is obviously not reported literally by the author. His intimate acquaintance with Secretary Stanton, however, and certain corroborative conditions justify us in accepting it as furnishing at least the tenor of the interview. See also Flower, 138–139.

67. Julian, 210.

68. Extract from President's General War Order No. 3, March 8, 1862.— Records, series i, vol. xi, part iii, 57–58; and vol. v, 50.

69. General Sumner voted that a total of 40,000 men would suffice. Generals McDowell, Keyes, and Heintzelman stated that there should be 25,000 men "in front of the Virginia line," with the forts on the right bank of the Potomac fully garrisoned and those on the left bank occupied. — Records, series i, vol. v, 56; vol. xi, part iii, 58; Committee on the War, part i, 12. With the forts so defended, the entire force, according to Generals Thomas and Hitchcock, should have been 55,000 men. — Records, series i, vol. xi, part iii, 61; Committee on the War, part i, 16. According to General McClellan, himself, the "necessary garrison" was 35,000 men. — Records, series i, vol. v, 9.

70. Records, series i, vol. v, 56; vol. xi, part iii, 59; Committee on the War, part i, 13.

71. Records, series i, vol. xi, part iii, 60–61; Committee on the War, part i, 14–15.

72. Records, series i, vol. xi, part iii, 61–62; Committee on the War, part i, 15–17.
73. McClellan, 308.
74. Records, series i, vol. xi, part iii, 86.
75. See Assistant Secretary Tucker's report, Records, series i, vol. v, 46; and McClellan's report, Records, series i, vol. xi, part iii, 97.
76. There were about 1100 Confederates under Magruder in and about Yorktown when McClellan arrived. Most of his errors in overrating the enemy were due, it should be said, to the gross miscalculations of his Secret Service officers, which the General in command, however, might have corrected by the means at his disposal.
77. Nicolay & Hay v, 366.
78. April 11, 1862.—Records, series i, vol. xi, part iii, 90.
79. The complete despatch is to be found in Records, series i, vol. xi, part i, 61; and in McClellan, 425. When Major-General E. A. Hitchcock, of the War Department, testified before the Joint Committee on the Conduct of the War, in January, 1863 (see Committee on the War, part i, 340), he furnished, among other documents, a copy of the telegram in its mutilated form. Some months later, McClellan, making his official report, after he had been relieved of his command, quoted the message in full as he had sent it. The variation in the despatches led to the charge that Mr. Stanton had suppressed the two closing sentences. On the other hand, Gorham, in defence of his hero (Gorham i, 454), assumes them to have been in McClellan's retained draft, and to have been omitted from the despatch which he sent. This was mere assumption, and the onus of having tampered with the message lay upon the great War Secretary until recently, when the facts were brought to light through the industry of Frank Abial Flower, who tells the story in chapter xxx of his Life of Stanton.
80. Pope, in Battles and Leaders ii, 457.
81. For the complete text of this letter, see Gorham ii, 38–39.
82. Tarbell ii, 130; Gorham ii, 40, where is also to be found an autograph facsimile.
83. Welles, 193.
84. This recalls a similar episode in the history of John Adams's cabinet, when Secretary Timothy Pickering, with whom Stanton had some points of resemblance, drafted a remonstrance to the President against the appointment of Knox to the senior major-generalship of the army. Pickering's protest was suppressed by his colleague, Wolcott, as Stanton's was, sixty-four years later, by the diplomatic Welles. But there the similarity ceased, for Adams yielded the point, and Lincoln did not.
85. Welles (194) says, "The President never knew of this paper";

but Tarbell (ii, 130) quotes Major Johnson, Stanton's confidential clerk, as authority for the assertion that Mr. Lincoln had cognizance of both protests. See also Flower, 177.

86. Nicolay & Hay vi, 23.
87. Pope to Halleck, September 2, 1862. — Records, series i, vol. xii, part iii, 797.
88. Secretary Stanton later had the signature changed. As published in the Records (series i, vol. xii, part iii, 807), it reads, "By command of Major-General Halleck." See also Gorham ii, 44–45; McClellan, 546; Battles and Leaders ii, 551.
89. Welles, 194–196.
90. Warden, 459.
91. Blair, in McClellan, 545.
92. The sixth paragraph in the platform read: —

"Resolved, That we deem it essential to the general welfare that harmony should prevail in the national councils, and we regard as worthy of public confidence and official trust those only who cordially endorse the principles proclaimed in these resolutions, and which should characterize the administration of the government."

93. Halleck to Stanton, July 13, 1864. — Records, series i, vol. xxxvii, part ii, 261.
94. Lincoln to Stanton, July 14, 1864. — Works ii, 548.
95. Works ii, 548.
96. When Mr. Lincoln, ten weeks later, did accept Mr. Blair's long proffered resignation, his action was due to influences operating outside the cabinet.
97. Carpenter, 246. On a letter written by G. Montague Hicks, found among Mr. Lincoln's papers, was the following endorsement: —

"This note, as Colonel Hicks did verbally yesterday, attempts to excite me against the Secretary of War, and therein is offensive to me. My 'order,' as he is pleased to call it, is plainly no order at all. — A. Lincoln, May 22, 1862." — Works ii, 157.

98. Rhodes v, 181–182.
99. Gorham ii, 470; Chittenden, 192. According to Flower (405), the President said: —

'If Mr. Stanton can find a man he himself will trust as Secretary of War, I 'll do it."

100. Charles F. Benjamin, in *Century Magazine* xxxiii, 760.
101. Stanton to Chase, November 19, 1864. — Schuckers, 512–513.
102. Carpenter, 265–266. See also Lamon's Recollections, 234–235; Stowe, 375–376; Irelan xvii, 588–589; McClure, 172; Henry Wilson, in *Atlantic Monthly* xxv, 243.
103. Stanton to Ashley, September 14, 1866. — Flower, 310–312.

104. "General Eckert, who then had charge of the telegraph department of the War Office, was coming in continually with telegrams containing election returns. Mr. Stanton would read them and the President would look at them and comment upon them. Presently there came a lull in the returns, and Mr. Lincoln called me up to a place by his side. 'Dana,' said he, 'have you ever read any of the writings of Petroleum V. Nasby?' 'No, sir,' I said, 'I have only looked at some of them, and they seemed to me quite funny.' 'Well,' said he, 'let me read you a specimen'; and, pulling out a thin yellow-covered pamphlet from his breast pocket, he began to read aloud. Mr. Stanton viewed this proceeding with great impatience, as I could see, but Mr. Lincoln paid no attention to that. He would read a page or a story, pause to con a new election telegram, and then open the book again and go ahead with a new passage. Finally Mr. Chase came in and presently Mr. Whitelaw Reid, and then the reading was interrupted. Mr. Stanton went to the door and beckoned me into the next room. I shall never forget the fire of his indignation at what seemed to him to be mere nonsense." — Dana, in Rice, 372.

105. Stanton to Lincoln, April 3, 1865. — Records, series i, vol. xlvi, part iii, 509.

106. Lincoln to Stanton, April 3, 1865. — Records, series i, vol. xlvi, part iii, 509.

107. Chittenden, 186.

NOTES TO CHAPTER VII

1. At Savannah, Ga., on the 21st of January, 1813.
2. He was also nominated by anti-slavery seceders from the National Convention of the American Party.
3. Records, series i, vol. iii, 390.
4. "Several commands in the East were suggested to me, but I preferred the West, which I knew; and I held the opinion that the possession of the immediate valley of the Mississippi River would control the result of the war. Who held the Mississippi would hold the country by the heart." — Frémont, in Battles and Leaders i, 278.
5. Frémont i, 602.
6. Whitney, 361; Nicolay & Hay iv, 422; Works ii, 81.
7. Records, series i, vol. iii, 467; Moore iii, documents, p. 33; McPherson, 246; Barrett, 278; Cyclopedia (1861), 491.
8. Lincoln to Browning, September 22, 1861. — Whitney, 360; Works ii, 81; Nicolay & Hay iv, 421–423.
9. This act provided, as its title indicates, for the seizure of such

property and slaves, only, as were employed in hostile service against the government. See Moore ii, documents, pp. 475–476.

10. Records, series i, vol. iii, 469–470; McPherson, 246; Nicolay & Hay iv, 418; Works ii, 77.

11. McPherson, 245–246; Records, series i, vol. iii, 693.

12. Records, series i, vol. iii, 477; McPherson, 247; Committee on the War, part iii, 152.

13. Colonel T. T. Taylor, in command at Springfield, Mo. For Frémont's letter to him, see McPherson, 247.

14. "In the night I decided upon the proclamation and the form of it. — I wrote it the next morning and printed it the same day. I did it without consultation or advice with any one." — Frémont to Lincoln, September 8, 1861. Notice, however, the apparent inconsistency between the foregoing and this other statement, made in the same letter: "I acted with full deliberation, and upon the certain conviction that it was a measure right and necessary, and I think so still."

15. From the diary of John Hay, in Nicolay & Hay iv, 415.

16. Congressman Grinnell of Iowa, who called on the President at this time with sundry complaints, records that as he opened the budget of his grievances, Mr. Lincoln said: —

"Don't mention them. I meet insults, standing between two fires, and the constant blazes of anger. Why, not an hour ago, a woman, a lady of high blood, came here, opening her case with mild expostulation, but left in anger, flaunting her handkerchief before my face, and saying, 'Sir, the general will try titles with you. He is a man and I am his wife.' I will tell you before you guess. It was Jessie, the daughter of 'Old Bullion,' and how her eye flashed! Young man, forget your annoyances. They are only as flea-bites to mine." — Grinnell, 174.

The President must have received his visitors late that September night, or the Congressman was in error concerning the time of this interview.

17. Frémont to Lincoln, September 8, 1861. — McPherson, 246–247; Committee on the War, part iii, 151–152; Records, series i, vol. iii, 477–478.

18. Lincoln to Frémont, September 11, 1861. — McPherson, 247; Irelan xvii, 97; Barrett, 280; Works ii, 78–79; Moore iii, documents, p. 126; Records, series i, vol. iii, 485–486, and series ii, vol. i, 768.

19. Phillips, 457.

20. Hoadly to Chase, September 19, 1861. — Rhodes iii, 474. See also a letter of the previous day from Hoadly to Chase, in Chase Papers, 503–505.

21. Frémont reached St. Louis July 25. The battle of Wilson's Creek was fought on August 10, 1861.

22. Schofield, 39-41. Lyon's acknowledgment of the missing despatch is to be found in Records, series i, vol. iii, 57; and in Committee on the War, part iii, 36, 106.
23. September 20, 1861.
24. Between the Blairs and the Bentons existed a devoted friendship, in which Frémont had naturally been included. One of his sons was named, on August 1, 1855, Francis Preston Frémont.
25. Nicolay & Hay iv, 415.
26. This letter was published in the Cincinnati *Enquirer*, and was quoted in the New York *Tribune* of October 7, 1861.
27. Lincoln to Hunter, September 9, 1861. — Works ii, 78; Nicolay & Hay iv, 413.
28. The correspondence between Lincoln and Mrs. Frémont was republished, from the Cincinnati *Enquirer*, in the New York *Tribune* of October 7, 1861. For Lincoln's letter, see also Works ii, 79; Nicolay & Hay iv, 414.
29. Frémont to Assistant Adjutant-General Townsend, September 15, 1861. — Committee on the War, part iii, 136. The charges and specifications were published in the New York *Tribune* of October 7, 1861.
30. Blair's charges and specifications, dated September 26, 1861, were published at the time in the Cincinnati *Enquirer*, and were reprinted in the New York *Tribune* of October 9, 1861. See also Nicolay & Hay iv, 430.
31. Cameron to Lincoln, October 14, 1861. — Nicolay & Hay iv, 430.
32. Records, series i, vol. iii, 540-549; Committee on the War, part iii, 7-16. Before leaving St. Louis, the Secretary of War had given Frémont orders whereby he hoped to remedy some of the abuses in the department. (Records, series i, vol. iii, 532-533.) These orders were not wholly obeyed.
33. Congressman Elihu B. Washburne of Illinois, who with William S. Holman, Henry L. Dawes, and W. G. Steele had spent two weeks in St. Louis taking testimony for the House Committee on Government Contracts, wrote to Secretary Chase, before the news of Frémont's removal had reached Missouri: —

"I was on the point of writing you from St. Louis several times, but the situation of things there was so terrible and the frauds so shocking, I did not know where to begin or where to end; and then again it appeared that everything communicated by our best men there in regard to Frémont and the condition of matters in the City and State was utterly disregarded. Our committee labored for two weeks, and our disclosures will astound the world and disgrace us as a nation. Such robbery, fraud, extravagance, peculation, as have been developed in Frémont's department can hardly be conceived of. There has been an organized system of pillage, right under the eye of Frémont. Governor Chase, what does the administration mean by permitting this state of things to exist in the Western Department? It cannot be ignorant of what the situation of matters is. I fear things have run on so far there is no remedy, and that all has gone. Frémont has really set up an authority over the government, and bids defiance to its commands. McKinstry, who directs and controls him, is not only a robber but a traitor. The government, in failing to strike at Frémont and his horde of pirates, acknowledges itself a failure. The credit of the government is ruined." — October 31, 1861. — Chase Papers, 506–508.

For a contrary view of the situation, defending Frémont, see a letter written about a fortnight later by Grimes to Fessenden, in Salter, 155–156; also B. Rush Plumley to Chase, October 9, 1861, in Chase Papers, 505–506. See also a brief defence of Frémont in Hume, 184–185.

34. A statement of this transaction had previously been laid before the administration in Colonel Blair's charges.
35. Records, series i, vol. iii, 553.
36. Lincoln to Curtis, October 24, 1861. — Works ii, 86; Nicolay & Hay iv, 433; Records, series i, vol. iii, 553.
37. Frémont's farewell address to his army, on November 2, 1861, is a model performance. It is published in Moore iii, documents, p. 270; Cyclopedia (1861), 493.
38. Warrington, 271.
39. Grimes to his wife, November 13, 1861. — Salter, 154.
40. Smith to Chase, November 7, 1861. — Chase Papers, 508–509.
41. Carpenter, 221–222.
42. President's War Order No. 3, March 11, 1862. — Records, series i, vol. x, part ii, 28–29.
43. Before Frémont entered upon his new duties, he received from the War Department this significant caution: —

"In consequence of embarrassments having been thrown upon the officers of the government in the settlement of accounts growing out of contracts irregularly made in some parts of the country for army supplies, transportation, &c., it becomes necessary to call the attention of commanders to this subject, and to direct that no contract whatever will be made by your authority except in conformity with the Regulations for the Army and through the proper officers of the several departments of the Army. The necessities of the country and the credit of the service demand strict regularity and rigid economy." — Thomas to Frémont, March 22, 1862. — Records, series i, vol. xii, part iii, 8.

44. Frémont's Report in Records, series i, vol. xii, part i, 11–12.
45. Warrington, 270.

46. Frémont's Report.
47. June 26, 1862. — Records, series i, vol. xii, part iii, 435; Works ii, 188.
48. Frémont to Stanton, June 27, 1862. — Records, series i, vol. xii, part iii, 437–438.
49. Great soldiers have, in all ages, echoed Young Clifford's maxim, —

"He that is truly dedicate to war,
Hath no self-love."

And the two most eminent English-speaking generals of the nineteenth century have left on record their contempt for this species of military egotism. When an officer in Wellington's army complained that he had been appointed to a command beneath his merits, the Iron Duke said: —

"In the course of my military career, I have gone from the command of a brigade to that of my regiment, and from the command of an army to that of a brigade or a division, as I was ordered, and without any feeling of mortification."

Our own Grant, commenting on an act of insubordination similar to that of Frémont, remarked: —

"The worst excuse a soldier can make for declining service is that he once ranked the commander he is ordered to report to."

50. "It may not be out of place here to mention that the authority to appoint a general of lower rank to command over officers outranking him — an authority interfering materially with the universally established military rules, calculated, when exercised, in nine cases out of ten, to cause mischief and ill-will, to destroy harmony and cordial coöperation, and thereby to undermine elements essential for the success of any army — that this authority was given to the President by an Act of Congress, originating with, and carried principally by the votes of the friends of General Frémont, with the intention, it was said, to see General McClellan — who would not allow anybody to interfere with his official business — superseded by General Frémont, whom he outranked. As if Nemesis had willed it, the first [?] instance in which the President thought himself justified to exercise this dangerous authority, he had to exercise it against General Frémont." — Petersen, 29.
51. Stanton to Frémont, June 27, 1862. — Records, series i, vol. xii, part iii, 438.
52. Hay's Diary, in Nicolay & Hay iv, 415.
53. Four weeks before, Mr. Julian had severely arraigned the administration from his place in Congress. "The Government," he said, "cannot escape history, but it can atone, in some degree, for the great wrong it has done the country and General Frémont, by restoring him, without further delay, to active service, with a command befitting his rank and merits. Every consideration of

justice and patriotism pleads for this. He has been the victim of the most cruel injustice, and the most unmerited and mortifying humiliation." — February 18, 1863. — *Congressional Globe*, 37th Congress, 3d Session, part ii, 1068.

54. Julian, 229–230; Rice, 55.
55. James Taussig to Emil Preetorius and others. — Brockett, 505–507.
56. Lincoln to Sumner, June 1, 1863. — Nicolay & Hay vi, 456–457; Works ii, 342–343.
57. Moncure D. Conway's London letter of July 20, 1864, in the Boston *Commonwealth* of August 12, 1864. See also Conway i, 376–381; Winthrop, 240.
58. It called itself the National Union Convention.
59. Frémont to Snethen and others, June 4, 1864. — McPherson, 413–414; Cyclopedia (1864), 787. On the same day General Frémont resigned from the army.
60. The fullest report of this incident is to be found in Carpenter, 220–221. According to this writer, the conversation took place after Frémont had withdrawn from the canvass, and was suggested by Colonel Deming's examination of the handsome bible that had been presented to the President a few weeks before, by the negroes of Baltimore. According to Nicolay & Hay (ix. 40–41), the Cave of Adullam reference was made by Mr. Lincoln the morning after Frémont's nomination. It may be added that this witticism was applied with brilliant effect, two years later, in the British Parliament, by John Bright, to the Liberals who seceded from their party during the struggle over the Reform Bill.
61. General Cochrane withdrew at the same time.
62. Frémont to Stearns, September 21, 1864. See also Frémont to Snethen, September 17, 1864. — McPherson, 426–427. One crumb of comfort Frémont carried with him into his retirement. A few days thereafter, his enemy, Montgomery Blair, left the cabinet. All attacks upon the Postmaster-General had failed to set the President against him, but he had made so many enemies among the Radicals and others that his withdrawal had been inferentially suggested by the National Convention, as well as urged by Frémont's followers. To unite the party, this unpopular minister was willing to retire, so Lincoln finally asked for his resignation. The request was made with so much kindness, however, that the President held the loyal support of the Blair family, to the end. See Chandler, 273–277. It should be added that directly after the second inauguration, Mr. Lincoln offered Montgomery Blair his choice between the Austrian and the Spanish missions, but that the offer was courteously yet firmly declined.

NOTES TO CHAPTER VIII

1. This department had been constructed out of Ohio, Indiana, and Illinois, on May 3, 1861, with McClellan in command. Its confines were extended, on May 9, 1861, so as to include portions of western Virginia and western Pennsylvania. On June 6, 1861, the State of Missouri was added.
2. For some of these documents, see Cyclopedia (1861), 744–748; and Hillard, 88–103.
3. McClellan was in his thirty-fifth year.
4. General Orders No. 47, July 25, 1861. The division comprised the Department of Washington and the Department of Northeastern Virginia. — Records, series i, vol. ii, p. 763. See also General Orders No. 1, July 27, 1861. — *Ibid.*, 766.
5. He was born in Philadelphia, December 3, 1826, and was graduated from West Point during 1846, with general standing number two in a class of fifty-nine.
6. The work on cavalry service was adapted from the Russian to the needs of the United States Army. It appeared as an appendix to The Armies of Europe, and was published later in amplified form as a handbook of instruction. The manual of bayonet exercise was adapted from the French of Gomard.
7. He had in 1855 been appointed Captain in the First Regiment of Cavalry, United States Army.
8. April 23, 1861.
9. "On the 14th of May, while the Governor was in Cincinnati, on a hasty trip to look after the requirements of the southern border, a dispatch was handed him from Mr. Chase: 'We have today had McClellan appointed a Major-General in the regular army.' He was in a room with McClellan, Marcy, and others, and he immediately handed over the dispatch to the one whom it most concerned. Governor Dennison has since described the utter amazement that overspread the face of the young officer, and the difficulty with which he could be persuaded that so overpowering an honor had really been conferred upon him. His father-in-law and chief-of-staff, Major Marcy, was equally incredulous; and the next day the Governor had even to produce the dispatch again, before Mrs. McClellan could satisfy herself that her husband had been so suddenly raised so high. They all seemed to imagine that it must be some inexplicable mistake, and that the Washington authorities could really intend nothing of the kind." — Reid i, 33–34.
10. McClellan, 162.
11. *Ibid.*, 82.

12. McClellan, 83.

13. *Ibid.*, 91. Several months later, McClellan, describing an evening meeting with the President, wrote:—

"As I parted from him on Seward's steps, he said that it had been suggested to him that it was no more safe for me than for him to walk out at night without some attendant. I told him that I felt no fear; that no one would take the trouble to interfere with me. On which he deigned to remark that they would probably give more for my scalp at Richmond than for his."—McClellan, 176.

14. *Ibid.*, 176.

15. For this and the four following extracts, see McClellan, 84–87.

16. For this and the six following extracts, see McClellan, 167, 168, 169, 175, 176.

17. Gurowski i, 123.

18. Stoddard's White House, 115.

19. Nicolay & Hay iv, 468. See also Kelley, 7; Brooks, 327; Russell, 552; Comte de Paris i, 574; Warden, 399; Whitney, 307–308; King, 241–242; Draper ii, 373.

20. Nicolay & Hay iv, 469.

21. Scott to the Secretary of War, August 9 and August 12, 1861.—Records, series i, vol. xi, part iii, 4–6. See also Scott to Cameron, October 31, 1861.—Records, series iii, vol. i, 611–612.

22. General Orders No. 94.—Records, series i, vol. v, 639.

23. McClellan's Memorandum of August 2, 1861.—McClellan, 101.

24. McClellan to Lincoln, December 10, 1861.—Swinton, 70–71; Records, series i, vol. xi, part iii, 6–7.

25. McClellan's own answers to Lincoln's questions show that there were 104,000 troops ready to move. See, for the Federal figures, Records, series i, vol. xi, part iii, 6; and McClellan, 79. For the Confederate figures, see Records, series i, vol. v, 974, and Johnston, 83.

26. McClellan to Cameron, in the latter part of October, 1861.—Records, series i, vol. v, 9.

27. *Ibid.*, 9–10.

28. McClellan, 162.

29. Swinton, 97.

30. Records, series i, vol. v, 6.

31. "We are endeavoring to see if there is any way in God's world to get rid of the Capital besieged, while Europe is looking down upon us as almost a conquered people."—Senator Wade, December 26, 1861.—Committee on the War, part i, 140.

32. Resolution adopted in the House, July 22, 1861, and in the Senate, July 26, 1861.—Cyclopedia (1861), 241, 244.

33. Reuben E. Fenton, in Rice, 74–75.

34. Comte de Paris, in Battles and Leaders ii, 120.
35. This Committee organized, December 20, 1861, with the following members: Senators Wade, Chandler, and Johnson; Representatives Gooch, Covode, Julian, and Odell.
36. McDowell's narrative in Raymond, 772–778.
37. Secretary Cameron did not attend, as he was about to resign.
38. General Franklin, who was somewhat in McClellan's confidence, had at first suggested a campaign against Richmond, by way of the York River. Upon careful investigation, however, he agreed that action, within a few weeks, was feasible only by the overland route. But Judge Blair, warmly opposing the plan of direct attack in any event, insisted throughout that decisive results were to be secured solely by the Lower Chesapeake, with a base on the York River, or at Fortress Monroe.
39. McClellan, 155.
40. January 12, 1862.
41. Chase may be said at this time to have represented the anti-slavery element, in the cabinet. On January 5, 1862, he wrote to T. C. Day: —

"I agree with you, that the administration has put too many enemies in places of great power and influence, and has acted most unwisely in so doing. No part of this responsibility, however, is mine, unless the appointment of McClellan be an exception. I really thought he was the very man for the time. I was mistaken, and make no more rash dependencies." — Warden, 397.

42. For complete accounts of this affair from both points of view, see McDowell's narrative, in Raymond, 772–778; and McClellan, 156–159.
43. Dated January 14, 1862.
44. Cameron himself could not make the protest, as he had resigned from the cabinet a few days before.
45. Hutchinsons i, 391.
46. Records, series i, vol. v, 41; Works ii, 119. In a confidential letter to a friend, Secretary Stanton, several months later, made this comment: —

"It is not necessary, or perhaps proper, to state all the causes that led to that order, but it is enough to know that the government was on the verge of bankruptcy, and at the rate of expenditure, the armies must move, or the government perish." — Stanton to Dyer, May 18, 1862. — Gorham i, 427; Flower, 157.

47. Records, series i, vol. v, 41; Works ii, 119.
48. Accompanying the note were a few tactical suggestions that evinced how closely the President was studying the situation. See Records, series i, vol. v, 41–42, and 713; Works ii, 120–121.
49. Records, series i, vol. v, 42–45.

50. Archibald Forbes said of this letter: —

"McClellan's reply was voluminous, plausible, and full of ingenious special pleading. Could McClellan have fought as well as he wrote, he would have taken rank among the great commanders." — *North American Review,* clv, 66.

51. Records, series i, vol. v, 45.

52. McClellan, 194.

53. Kelley, 22.

54. See Comte de Paris i, 610–611; Schuckers, 446.

55. It was characteristic of McClellan to telegraph Stanton, not that the boats which he, himself, had caused to be collected were too wide, but that the lift-lock was too narrow. See McClellan to Stanton, February 27, 1862. — Records, series i, vol. v, 728.

56. Lincoln's private secretary has left the following account of how the news was received: —

"'What does this mean?' asked the President, in amazement.

"'It means,' said the Secretary of War, 'that it is a damned fizzle. It means that he does n't intend to do anything.'

"The President's indignation was intense; and when, a little later, General Marcy, McClellan's father-in-law and chief-of-staff, came in, Lincoln's criticism of the affair was in sharper language than was his usual habit.

"'Why, in the name of common sense,' said he, excitedly, 'could n't the General have known whether canal-boats would go through that lock before he spent a million dollars getting them there? I am almost despairing at these results. Everything seems to fail. The impression is daily gaining ground that the General does not intend to do anything. By a failure like this we lose all the prestige gained by the capture of Fort Donelson.'" —Nicolay, 294.

57. McClellan, 195–196.

58. According to McClellan, the President was especially displeased because he had received no explanation of this affair. "While at Harper's Ferry," writes the General, "I learned that the President was dissatisfied with my action, and on reaching Washington I laid a full explanation before the Secretary [of War], with which he expressed himself entirely satisfied, and told me that the President was already so, and that it was unnecessary for me to communicate with him on the subject. . . . The President sent for me [on the 8th of March]. I then learned that he had received no explanation of the Harper's Ferry affair, and that the Secretary was not authorized to make the statement already referred to; but after my repetition of it, the President became fully satisfied with my course." — McClellan, in Battles and Leaders ii, 165–166. See also McClellan, 195.

59. McClellan, 222; Battles and Leaders ii, 166; Records, series i, vol. v, 13, 50.
60. Records, series i, vol. v, 589.
61. The order also provided for a fifth corps, to be commanded by Major-General N. P. Banks, and placed the forces that were to be left for the defence of Washington under Brigadier-General James S. Wadsworth, as Military Governor of the District of Columbia.
62. It was approved of by Generals Naglee, W. F. Smith, Blenker, McCall, Franklin, Fitz-John Porter, Andrew Porter, and Keyes; opposed were Generals Barnard, Heintzelman, McDowell, and Sumner. Keyes voted in the affirmative, with the proviso "that no change should be made until the rebels were driven from their batteries on the Potomac."
63. Works ii, 131; Records, series i, vol. v, 50.
64. Records, series i, vol. v, 739–741; McClellan, 223–224.
65. The incident of the army corps did not close here. After McClellan reached the Peninsula, he still balked. A correspondence between him and the government resulted in the formation of two additional corps under his favorites, Fitz-John Porter and William B. Franklin, respectively. See Records, series i, vol. xi, part iii, 153–154, 155, 327–328, 333.
66. March 11, 1862. — McClellan, 179.
67. One of these civilian critics, Secretary Chase, had, as long before this as February 17, somehow arrived at a perfect comprehension of the situation. "The time has now come," he wrote to Bishop McIlvaine, "for dealing decisively with the army in front of us, weakened by sickness, desertions, and withdrawals of troops, until a victory over it is deprived of more than half its honor." — Warden, 416. See Johnston, 91–106.
68. Records, series i, vol. v, 52–53, 742, 763–764.
69. The Comte de Paris, who was on McClellan's staff at the time, more than hinted at this opinion, in his history (i, 613); but he modified it, some years thereafter, in his contribution to Battles and Leaders ii, 121. See also De Joinville, 27; Hillard, 157; McClellan's testimony before the Committee on the War, part i, 426.
70. Johnston, 102.
71. Records, series i, vol. v, 1086.
72. *Ibid.*, 732.
73. Johnston, 78. That this was no very recent device either, may be inferred from a letter of Beauregard to Johnston, dated Centreville, December 9, 1861. It reads, in part: "To prevent spies and others from communicating to 'George' our arrangements, I think it would be advisable to keep in reserve, at some safe place, our 'wooden guns,' to be put in position only when required. I have

so instructed Longstreet for the armament of his batteries." — Records, series i, vol. v, 990.

74. Julian's Reminiscences, in Rice, 53.

75. It had been laid, during the evening (of March 11), before Secretaries Stanton, Seward, and Chase, whom the President summoned for the purpose. They heartily approved. — See Nicolay & Hay v, 178–179.

76. Works ii, 137; Flower, 140–141.

77. It appears from this letter that Lincoln, considerate as ever, must have softened the blow with kindly words for McClellan, spoken to his friend, Governor Dennison. The concluding paragraph reads: —

"I believe I said to you some weeks since, in connection with some Western matters, that no feeling of self-interest or ambition should ever prevent me from devoting myself to your service. I am glad to have the opportunity to prove it, and you will find that, under present circumstances, I shall work just as cheerfully as before, and that no consideration of self will in any manner interfere with the discharge of my public duties. Again thanking you for the official and personal kindness you have so often evinced towards me, I am, most sincerely your friend,

GEO. B. MCCLELLAN."

McClellan, 225–226.

78. A note appended to the memorandum read: "N. B. — That with the forts on the right bank of the Potomac fully garrisoned and those on the left bank occupied, a covering force in front of the Virginia line of 25,000 men would suffice. (Keyes, Heintzelman, and McDowell.) A total of 40,000 men for the defense of the city would suffice. (Sumner.)" — Committee on the War, part i, 312; Records, series i, vol. v, 55–56; series i, vol. xi, part iii, 58.

79. Committee on the War, part i, 311–312.

80. Records, series i, vol. v, 56; Committee on the War, part i, 313.

81. Reid i, 289.

82. "I will not consent to one other man being detached from this army for that [General Thomas W. Sherman's] expedition. I need far more than I now have to save this country, and cannot spare any disciplined regiment. Instead of diminishing this army, true policy would dictate its immediate increase to a large extent. It is the task of the Army of the Potomac to decide the question at issue. No outside expedition can effect the result. I hope that I will not again be asked to detach anybody." — McClellan to Assistant Secretary of War Scott, October 17, 1861. — Records, series i, vol. vi, 179.

83. Works ii, 140–141; McClellan, 164–165; Records, series i, vol. v, 58. The reasons for the order are set forth in Lincoln's

rather sharp letter of June 16, 1862, to Frémont. — Works ii, 182–183.

84. When he came to write his Own Story, McClellan conceded (McClellan, 97) that "in view of its exposed position and immense political importance, it was impossible to allow Washington to be endangered."

85. "It is said that the rebels would willingly exchange Richmond for Washington." — General Wool to Secretary Stanton, July 21, 1862. — Records, series i, vol. xi, part iii, 331.

86. Records, series i, vol. xi, part iii, 38, 39, 65.

87. McClellan to his wife, April 6 and 8, 1862. — McClellan, 307, 308.

88. Lincoln to McClellan, April 9, 1862. — Works ii, 142.

89. Magruder to Adjutant and Inspector-General Cooper, May 3, 1862. — Records, series i, vol. xi, part i, 406 ; Flower, 148–149.

90. General Joseph E. Johnston to General Robert E. Lee, April 22, 1862. — Records, series i, vol. xi, part iii, 456.

91. Lincoln to McClellan, April 6, 1862. — Works ii, 142.

92. McClellan to his wife, April 8, 1862. — McClellan, 308. Elsewhere in the book he relates an anecdote which probably inspired this impudent idea. "When in front of Sebastopol in 1855," writes McClellan, "I asked General Martimprey, chief-of-staff of the French army in the Crimea, how he found that the cable worked which connected the Crimean with the European lines of telegraph. He said that it worked admirably *from* the Crimea to Paris, but very badly in the opposite direction ; and by way of explanation related the following anecdote. He said that immediately after the failure of the assault of June, 1855, the Emperor telegraphed Pélissier to renew the assault immediately. Pélissier replied that it was impossible without certain preliminary preparations which required several weeks. The Emperor repeated the peremptory order to attack at once. Pélissier repeated his reply. After one or two more interchanges of similar messages Pélissier telegraphed : 'I will not renew the attack until ready. If you wish it done, come and do it yourself.' That ended the matter."

93. Records, series i, vol. xi, part iii, 484 ; Allan, 11–12, note.

94. Lincoln to McClellan, April 9, 1862. — Works ii, 143.

95. McClellan, 150.

96. These quotations are from McClellan, 306, 310, 316–317, 356, 359, 407, 449, 453.

97. McClellan to Lincoln, May 14, 1862. — McClellan, 344; Records, series i, vol. xi, part i, 27.

98. McClellan to Stanton, May 28, 1862. — McClellan, 372 ; Records, series i, vol xi, part i, 35.

99. McClellan to Stanton. — McClellan, 373 ; Records, series i, vol. xi, part i, 36.

100. McClellan to Stanton, June 14, 1862. — McClellan, 389 ; Records, series i, vol. xi, part i, 48. McCall's division, belonging to McDowell's corps, had just arrived in advance of the main body. The request to which McClellan took exception was obviously in accordance with the President's orders. For previous correspondence on this subject, see Records, series i, vol. xi, part i, 27, 28, 29, 30; *Ibid.*, part iii, 184; McClellan, 349, 351; Works ii, 153–154, 156, 158.

101. McClellan to Stanton, June 25, 1862. — Records, series i, vol. xi, part i, 51; McClellan, 392.

102. Lincoln to McClellan, June 26, 1862. — Works ii, 186–187.

103. McClellan to Stanton, June 28, 1862. — McClellan, 425; Records, series i, vol. xi, part i, 61.

104. It may be profitable to contrast McClellan's accusation of June 28, 1862, with this paragraph from his report of August 4, 1863:

"I cannot omit the expression of my thanks to the President for the constant evidence given me of his sincere personal regard, and his desire to sustain the military plans which my judgment led me to urge for adoption and execution. I cannot attribute his failure to adopt some of those plans, and to give that support to others which was necessary to their success, to any want of confidence in me, and it only remains for me to regret that other counsels came between the constitutional Commander-in-Chief and the General whom he had placed at the head of his armies, counsels which resulted in the failure of great campaigns."

105. Lincoln to McClellan, June 28, 1862. — Works ii, 190; Records, series i, vol. xi, part iii, 269.

106. Herndon ii, 254–255.

107. See also Flower, 147.

108. Works ii, 219–220.

109. McClellan to Stanton, June 7, 1862. — Records, series i, vol. xi, part i, 46; McClellan, 387.

110. McClellan's oft-repeated assertion that in trying to effect a junction with McDowell he was compelled fatally to disarrange his plans, is not borne out by the record. In fact, this claim was clearly an afterthought. He had, in the first place, adopted his route without regard to McDowell; and later, when it was found that the junction would not take place, there were ample opportunities for a change of plan, had McClellan desired to make one.

111. Carpenter, 219.

112. Lincoln to McClellan, July 3, 1862. — Works ii, 198; Records, series i, vol. xi, part iii, 291.

113. McClellan to Lincoln, July 4, 1862. — McClellan, 484–485; Records, series i, vol. xi, part i, 71–72.

114. Lincoln to McClellan, July 5, 1862. — Works ii, 200; Records, series i, vol. xi, part i, 72.

115. McClellan to Thomas, July 1, 1862. — Records, series i, vol. xi, part iii, 281.

116. Lincoln to McClellan, July 2, 1862. — Works ii, 196–197; Records, series i, vol. xi, part iii, 286.

117. McClellan to Stanton, July 3, 1862. — Records, series i, vol. xi, part iii, 291–292. General R. B. Marcy, McClellan's chief-of-staff, who carried the letter, telegraphed back to his commander: —

"I have seen the President and Secretary of War. Ten thousand men from Hunter, 10,000 from Burnside, and 11,000 from here have been ordered to reënforce you as soon as possible. Halleck has been urged by the President to send you at once 10,000 men from Corinth. The President and Secretary speak very kindly of you and find no fault." — *Ibid.*, 294.

118. See Memorandum of Questions and Answers in Interviews between the President and General McClellan and other Officers during a Visit to the Army of the Potomac at Harrison's Landing, Virginia. — Works ii, 201.

119. Whitney, 183; also Mary A. Livermore, in Bates, 22.

120. Lincoln to McClellan, July 13, 1862. — Works ii, 206; Records, series i, vol. xi, part iii, 319.

121. The President's questions bore fruit in McClellan's despatch of July 27, 1862, to Adjutant-General Thomas. "I respectfully apply," it began, "for permission to send an officer from each regiment to the place where it was raised, with authority to bring on every officer and man he can find fit for duty, whether on leave of absence or not, no matter from what source the leave may be granted." — Records, series i, vol. xi, part iii, 338.

122. McClellan to Lincoln, July 15, 1862. — Records, series i, vol. xi, part iii, 321–322.

123. McClellan to Lincoln, July 17, 1862. — McClellan, 490; Records, series i, vol. xi, part i, 75.

124. McClellan to Lincoln, June 20, 1862. — Records, series i, vol. xi, part i, 48.

125. Lincoln to McClellan, June 21, 1862. — Work sii, 185; Records, series i, vol. xi, part i, 48.

126. For an authenticated copy of the letter, see Nicolay & Hay v, 447–449. It is also to be found in McPherson, 385–386; McClellan, 487–489; Records, series i, vol. xi, part i, 73–74.

127. McClellan, 444–445.

128. *Ibid.*, 446.

129. W. C. Prime, in McClellan, 489–490.

130. Gilmore, 75–76; Nicolay & Hay vi, 121–126.

131. Order of July 11, 1862. — Records, series i, vol. xi, part iii, 314.
132. McClellan, 456.
133. Halleck did not reach Washington until July 23.
134. McClellan's morning report of July 20, 1862, showed present for duty, exclusive of Dix's corps at Fortress Monroe, 91,694. Lee's return for the same day, excluding the Department of North Carolina, was 78,891. — Records, series i, vol. xi, part iii, 329, 645. Most of McClellan's officers shared his delusion as to the strength of the enemy. See Halleck's Memorandum and Keys's letter. *Ibid.*, 338, 339. But Meigs, at Headquarters in Washington, came much nearer the mark. — *Ibid.*, 340–341.
135. By the President's order of June 26, 1862, the forces under Generals Frémont, Banks, McDowell, and Sturgis were consolidated into the Army of Virginia, with General Pope at its head.
136. The entire correspondence is published in Records, series i, vol. xi, part i, 81–84.
137. The first was General Victor Le Duc, whose private diary is quoted in American Conflict ii, 171; the second was the Comte de Paris ii, 249.
138. McClellan to Halleck, August 12, 1862. — Records, series i, vol. xi, part i, 87–88.
139. August 10, 1862. — McClellan, 465–466. See also Pleasanton to Marcy, August 11, 1862. — Flower, 173.
140. Halleck to McClellan, August 10, 1862. — Records, series i, vol. xi, part i, 86.
141. Halleck to McClellan, August 7, 1862. — Records, series i, vol. xi, part iii, 359–360; McClellan to Burnside, August 20, 1862. — Records, series i, vol. xii, part iii, 605; McClellan, 466, 468, 482, 508.
142. August 29, 1862. Records, series i, vol. xi, part i, 98; Committee on the War, part i, 463–464; McClellan, 515.
143. "I have no sharpshooters except the guard around my camp. I have sent off every man but those, and will now send them with the train, as you direct. I will also send my only remaining squadron of cavalry with General Sumner. I can do no more. You now have every man of the Army of the Potomac who is within my reach." — McClellan to Halleck, August 30, 1862. — Committee on the War, part i, 468; McClellan, 520; Records, series i, vol. xi, part i, 101.
144. Records, series i, vol. xi, part i, 103; McClellan, 520. The portion that had not been sent forward comprised McClellan's staff, less than one hundred orderlies, invalids, etc., about his camp, and part of a corps left near Fortress Monroe.
145. Records, series i, vol. xi, part i, 102; McClellan, 522–524.

146. Records, series i, vol. xi, part i, 102.

147. Pope's most objectionable utterance was the Address to the Army, dated July 14, 1862. In this he said: —

"I have come to you from the West, where we have always seen the backs of our enemies, — from an army whose business it has been to seek the adversary, and to beat him when he was found; whose policy has been attack and not defence. In but one instance has the enemy been able to place our western armies in defensive attitude. I presume that I have been called here to pursue the same system, and to lead you against the enemy. It is my purpose to do so, and that speedily. I am sure you long for an opportunity to win the distinction you are capable of achieving. That opportunity I shall endeavor to give you. Meantime I desire you to dismiss from your minds certain phrases, which I am sorry to find so much in vogue amongst you. I hear constantly of 'taking strong positions and holding them,' of 'lines of retreat,' and of 'bases of supplies.' Let us discard such ideas. The strongest position a soldier should desire to occupy is one from which he can most easily advance against the enemy. Let us study the probable lines of retreat of our opponents, and leave our own to take care of themselves."

148. McClellan to his wife, July 22, 1862. — McClellan, 454.

149. Records, series i, vol. xi, part i, 98. — This despatch was sent on the afternoon of August 29. The battle occurred on August 29 and 30; that of the first day is sometimes called the Battle of Groveton.

150. Lincoln's reply read: —

"Yours of to-day just received. I think your first alternative, to wit, 'to concentrate all our available forces to open communication with Pope,' is the right one; but I wish not to control. That I now leave to General Halleck, aided by your counsels." — Records, series i, vol. xi, part i, 98.

151. Nicolay & Hay vi, 23.

152. In the evening of August 31, Halleck telegraphed to McClellan: —

"I beg of you to assist me in this crisis with your ability and experience. I am utterly tired out." — Records, series i, vol. xi, part i, 103.

153. Pope to Halleck, August 31, 1862. — Committee on the War, part i, 470; Pope to Halleck, September 2, 1862. — Records, series i, vol. xii, part iii, 797.

154. Halleck himself did not know Lincoln's purpose in the matter until he heard it announced to McClellan. See Halleck to Pope, October 10, 1862. — Records, series i, vol. xii, part iii, 820.

155. Nicolay & Hay vi, 23.

156. For these conversations, see Welles, 197–198; and Kelley, 73–75.

157. McClellan to his wife, September 5, 1862. — McClellan, 567.

158. McClellan to his wife, September 7, 1862. — *Ibid.*, 567.

159. Lincoln to McClellan, September 12, 1862. — Records, series i, vol. xix, part ii, 270; Works ii, 233.

160. Lincoln to McClellan, September 15, 1862. Works ii, 236.

161. "It was heart-rending to see how Lee's army had been slashed by the day's fighting. Nearly one fourth of the troops who went into the battle were killed or wounded. We were so badly crushed that at the close of the day ten thousand fresh troops could have come in and taken Lee's army and everything it had." — General Longstreet, in Battles and Leaders ii, 670. By noon of the following day, McClellan had more than twice that number of fresh troops, and troops that had not taken part, to any considerable extent, in the battle.

162. McClellan's own language. — Records, series i, vol. xix, part i, 70.

163. Kelley, 75.

164. McClellan to his wife, September 20, 1862. — McClellan, 613–614. For other private letters of the same tenor, see those dated September 21, September 22, and September 25. — *Ibid.*, 614–615.

165. McClellan, 627.

166. Browne, 529–530. See also Nicolay & Hay vi, 175.

167. Records, series i, vol. xix, part i, 72.

168. Records, series i, vol. xix, part ii, 395.

169. Battles and Leaders ii, 544.

170. Halleck to McClellan, October 14, 1862. — Records, series i, vol. xix, part ii, 421.

171. Lincoln to McClellan, October 13, 1862. — Records, series i, vol. xix, part i, 13–14; Works ii, 245–247.

172. See four telegrams in Works ii, 250–251.

173. McClellan, 658.

174. For slightly different versions on different occasions, see Brooks, 336–337; Arnold, 297; Holland, 371; Browne, 528.

175. Nicolay & Hay vi, 188.

176. Francis P. Blair, Sr., McClellan's friend, tried to dissuade the President from taking this step. "Lincoln listened with attention," relates Montgomery Blair, "to all my father had to say, but was not communicative himself. But at the end of the conference he rose up and stretched his long arms almost to the ceiling above him, saying, 'I said I would remove him if he let Lee's army get away from him, and I must do so. He has got the 'slows,' Mr. Blair.'" — Montgomery Blair to George T. Curtis, January 21, 1880. — McClellan's Last Service, 96.

177. Records, series i, vol. xix, part ii, 545.

178. "He arrived at Trenton at four o'clock in the morning of the 12th. Why was he sent there? He was not then a citizen of New Jersey; he had no connection with the city of Trenton; there was no military duty for him to perform there; there was not a Federal soldier in the place. He was sent there to disgrace him." — Curtis's McClellan, 88.

179. Lincoln's popular majority, as recorded, was 494,567. But the soldier vote of Kansas, Minnesota, and Vermont, that arrived too late to be counted, together with certain votes which were rejected on technical grounds, would have given him a majority of over half a million. His electoral vote should have been 213, as one of the three Nevada electors died before the Electoral College met.

180. Browne, 673. See also Seward ii, 250.

INDEX

INDEX

Lincoln and Douglas